Imaginary Friends

❖ STUDIES IN AMERICAN THOUGHT ❖
AND CULTURE

Series Editor

Paul S. Boyer

Margaret Fuller: Transatlantic Crossings in a Revolutionary Age
Edited by Charles Capper and Cristina Giorcelli

Emerson's Liberalism
Neal Dolan

Observing America: The Commentary of British Visitors to the United States,
1890–1950
Robert P. Frankel

Picturing Indians: Photographic Encounters and Tourist Fantasies in
H. H. Bennett's Wisconsin Dells
Steven D. Hoelscher

Cosmopolitanism and Solidarity: Studies in Ethnoracial, Religious, and
Professional Affiliation in the United States
David A. Hollinger

Seaway to the Future: American Social Visions and the Construction
of the Panama Canal
Alexander Missal

Imaginary Friends: Representing Quakers in American Culture, 1650–1950
James Emmett Ryan

The Presidents We Imagine: Two Centuries of White House Fictions
on the Page, on the Stage, Onscreen, and Online
Jeff Smith

Unsafe for Democracy: World War I and the U.S. Justice Department's
Covert Campaign to Suppress Dissent
William H. Thomas Jr.

Imaginary Friends

Representing Quakers in American Culture,
1650–1950

James Emmett Ryan

THE UNIVERSITY OF WISCONSIN PRESS

Publication of this volume has been made possible,
in part, through support from
the ENGLISH DEPARTMENT
at Auburn University.

The University of Wisconsin Press
1930 Monroe Street, 3rd Floor
Madison, Wisconsin 53711-2059

www.wisc.edu/wisconsinpress/

3 Henrietta Street
London WC2E 8LU, England

1   3   5   4   2

Printed in the United States of America

Library of Congress Cataloging-in-Publication Data
Ryan, James Emmett.
Imaginary friends : representing Quakers in American culture, 1650–1950 /
James Emmett Ryan.
p.   cm.—(Studies in American thought and culture)
Includes bibliographical references and index.
ISBN 978-0-299-23174-3 (pbk.: alk. paper)
ISBN 978-0-299-23173-6 (e-book)
1. Quakers—United States.   2. Quakers—United States—History.
I. Title.   II Series.
BX7635.R93   2009
289.6'73—dc22
2008039541

For
Renée

❖

Contents

Illustrations   ix
Acknowledgments   xi

Introduction: National Identity, Representation,
and Genre   3

1   Quaker Religion in Colonial New England   27

2   Political Theory and Quaker Community
    in the Early Republic   63

3   Chronicles of Friendship: Quaker Historiography
    in the Early Republic   92

4   Quaker Biography in Transatlantic Context   128

5   Representing Quakers in American Fiction   158

6   Staging Quakerism: Theater and Cinema   187

    Epilogue   223

    Notes   227
    Works Cited   255
    Index   273

Illustrations

Mary Dyer being led to the gallows	39
Quaker planters in Barbados	43
Robert Barclay, *An Apology for the True Christian Divinity*	56
Quaker educator Anthony Benezet teaching African American students	72
The Quaker Giant Robert Hales and the Quaker Giantess on display at Barnum's Museum	153
"The Little Shaking Quakers"	205
"I Like Your Apron and Your Bonnet and Your Little Quaker Gown"	205
"There's a Quaker Down in Quaker Town"	209
"All the Quakers Are Shoulder Shakers (Down in Quaker Town)"	209

Acknowledgments

This project was enabled in part through research leave and publication support granted by the English Department and the College of Liberal Arts at Auburn University. Numerous colleagues and graduate students at Auburn University read or discussed sections of the manuscript with me while providing valuable advice, intellectual stimulation, administrative guidance, moral support, and friendship. For their important contributions to my work, I thank Craig Bertolet, Lindy Biggs, Paula Backscheider, Lou Freitas Caton, George Crandell, Tim Dykstal, Bert Hitchcock, Margaret Kouidis, Joy Leighton, Deborah W. Manson, Jennifer Reid Beauman, and Hilary Wyss. Library dean Bonnie Mac-Ewen, humanities reference librarian Nancy Noe, and the outstanding reference staff at Ralph B. Draughon Library at Auburn University were instrumental in locating necessary materials for my research over the past several years. Emily Maffett and Leslie Allison contributed materially to this project through their diligent work as my undergraduate research assistants at Auburn University.

Since my years of graduate study at the University of North Carolina–Chapel Hill, Philip Gura has continued to supply the scholarly example, patient mentoring, and lasting friendship that have helped to inspire and inform my work. Also at the University of North Carolina, Laurie Maffly-Kipp and Thomas A. Tweed greatly improved my understanding of American religious historiography and set their own high standard of excellence; Robert Cantwell's writing and teaching illustrated for me the kinds of goals worth achieving in American Studies. At Duke University, Thomas J. Ferraro spurred me to think about religion and American literature in ways that continue to shape my research. As fortune would have it, my years in Chapel Hill were shared with an extremely talented cohort of young scholars, among them Leslie Frost, Laura Gribbin, Susan M. Ryan, Mark Simpson-Vos, David

Syracuse, Karen Weyler, Michael Everton, and Laura Mielke. I thank them for their years of intellectual exchange and camaraderie. As a residential fellow at the 2002 Pew Charitable Trusts/Calvin College Seminar in Christian Scholarship, I learned much from the participants, but especially from seminar director Roger Lundin.

At the University of Wisconsin Press, Paul S. Boyer was unstintingly generous with warm encouragement and sage advice during the years that this project was being developed, Gwen Walker helped in many practical ways during the production of the book, and Mary Sutherland provided expert copyediting while helping me to see many opportunities for improving its prose. I am grateful for the expertise and intelligence they provided on behalf of my work.

Early versions of my work on Quakers in American culture benefited from spirited commentary by participants in the Southern American Studies Association Meeting (2003), the American Studies Association Annual Meeting (2004), the conference on Religion and the Culture of Print in America, held at University of Wisconsin (2004), and the Conference of Quaker Historians and Archivists at the Woodbrooke Quaker Study Center in Birmingham, England (2008). Substantial parts of chapter 5 have appeared previously in *Studies in American Fiction* (2003) and the recently published essay collection *Religion and the Culture of Print in Modern America* (University of Wisconsin Press, 2008); I am grateful to the editors of these publications for permission to reprint.

Many of the documents cited utilize variant or nonstandard spellings of English words. Unless otherwise noted, these original spellings have been retained.

Imaginary Friends

Introduction

National Identity, Representation, and Genre

Representations of Quakers in the American cultural archive are the main object of my attention in this study, and it is through analysis of these representations that variant rhetorics of American values, some of them quite different from the forms of discourse that historically have dominated the public sphere, can be discerned and assessed.[1] Depictions of Quakers—believers in the "Inner Light" of divine presence in the individual person who from their beginnings in seventeenth-century England were deemed to be members of a "peculiar" religious sect—circulate not just through churches but around larger social discourses that play out over more than three centuries of American national development. Religious belief and practice, political arrangements, social justice, racial categorization, women's rights, and warfare—all are issues about which Quakers have advanced radical views during American history. These radical views have frequently put Friends out of step with the broader national culture. At the same time, however, Quaker religious principles, sometimes but not always articulated within the public sphere of print culture and mass media, have frequently provided the basis for testing more popular ways of understanding American religious practice and social responsibility.

Within American culture, Christian religious practices—whether understood as a benign or a malignant aspect of national belonging—have exerted a perennial and unmistakable force, even if literary history has seldom taken full account of religion's place in the national unconscious. Since the colonial period, American cultural history has frequently been bound up with the ethical dimensions of national identity: the American people's evolving sense of justice, morality, and—perhaps less recognized by literary historians—religion.[2] For instance, Alexis de Tocqueville, author of the enduringly influential *Democracy in America* (1835, 1840), perceptively observed the sometimes-ironic development of American identity during the early national period. Tocqueville describes America as a cultural paradox: egalitarian in principle yet deeply marred by the slave trade and the immoral economies allowed by slavery; secular in governance and yet perpetually awash in a sea of religious faith and revivals; devoted to the idea of national sovereignty while pushing relentlessly at the national borders in order to satisfy proto-imperial ambitions. Alert to the role of religion in shaping culture, Tocqueville observes about the young nation's religion, morality, and law, that "in America it is religion which leads to enlightenment and the observance of divine laws which leads men to liberty."[3] Thus, religion in some form is the necessary precondition for the movement in America toward both intellectual progress and political freedom. In this formulation, moreover, religion lays the foundation for the moral structures essential to the identities that constitute national citizenship. For the dominant classes in early America and even for the middle class, religiosity and morals would quickly suffuse an emerging sense of American national identity.

It is arguable that this sense of a distinctive American national destiny or national identity persists even into more recent years. In charting the legacy of Puritan forms of colonial religion, Sacvan Bercovitch has critiqued this American national claim to morality in acerbic terms, arguing that, "To be 'middle class' in the United States was to have a moral outlook, rather than a certain income; it displayed itself less in certain manners and mannerisms than in a set of virtues that opened into a program for self perfection."[4] Put another way by cultural historian Constance Rourke, who has registered the construction of national values—or what she described as "the national character"—by evaluating the moral discourse of the nation's mythic figures and its most articulate literary voices: "Character had always been the great American subject—character enwrapped in legend, from the Yankee of the fables and the fabulous Crockett to the novels of Henry James."[5]

How, then, would American culture register and calibrate its claims to morality as colonial outposts gave way to substantial provinces and, eventually, a newly independent and increasingly powerful nation, which by the early twenty-first century could be said to have evolved entirely from colonial outpost to global empire? How would Americans of successive generations articulate the limits and parameters of the virtue and benevolence to which they laid claim first with the covenant theology of Calvinist Puritanism and later with constitutionally grounded laws and Revolutionary principles of representative government? Any comprehensive answer to these questions would necessarily be extremely complex and would involve close scrutiny of several centuries of legal and judicial proceedings, to say nothing of a vast archive of American legal and judicial commentary produced since its colonization began in earnest with the settlement of Massachusetts by English Puritans in the seventeenth century. Examination of such archives, however, lies beyond the scope of this project, which argues on the most basic level that American moral discourse has been strongly, and perhaps overwhelmingly, produced in relation to discourses within and about Christian religion and that the representation of Quakers has been an important aspect of these discourses. This is not to suggest, however, in any oversimplified way that American life and morality, either during the colonial or early national periods, have been generically "Christian" or "Protestant." Instead, the nation has utilized its long and vexed conversation about Christian religion as a technique for negotiating a host of competing pressures: domestic life, market capitalism, urban development, labor (including slavery), gender, and political activities.

Although the focus in this book is on the representations associated with a relatively small group of religious adherents, it is essential to keep in mind the complex and ongoing conversation about American religion and its relation to national culture. As religious historians like R. Laurence Moore have insisted, the extent to which the United States has been shaped by Christian principles or even by mainstream Protestant denominations should not be overstated. Moore argues that the story of American religious development alongside citizenship and national identity cannot be reduced in this way and that a large number of Protestant denominations "do not flow smoothly from the theological development that is traced always out of Puritan New England."[6] National religious culture, Moore continues, was not and is not created merely by powerful insiders such as those in the Protestant mainstream but is instead produced in a dialectic between a plethora of religious groups. Moore again: "Those who play the role of outsiders can wield enormous public influence that the alleged insiders are powerless to block. They can also determine in crucial ways the outlook and behavior of the insiders."[7] The contest between the values of American religious groups provides the larger historical context in the following chapters.

While bearing in mind the long-standing American tendency to insist upon religious principles as core elements in the national conversation about morality and national belonging in America, this book tracks certain aspects of this persistent national religious morality by focusing on the ways that one small but very important religious denomination—the Religious Society of Friends (Quakers)—has articulated its own distinctive religious vision in American culture. My argument diverges from traditional (and rightly contested) claims, that something like "the American character" has been formed out of the stuff of the Calvinist/Puritan religious heritage or the legacy of a violent frontier existence. Instead, my examination of Quakers in American culture asks about the extent to which Quaker life and religion have served as counterpoints or foils to more commonly held religious and political values. Quaker theology as articulated in the seventeenth century was harshly attacked by the Puritans who came to dominate in New England. Meanwhile, back in England, Friends who held that each member of the faithful could experience the "Inner Light" of divine presence were mocked for their beliefs and persecuted severely for countermanding the Church of England's religious authority. As the decades and centuries went by, Quakers receded into relative obscurity in the United States but became highly visible during the protracted debates over the abolition of slavery, an institution that Quakers came to oppose long before other American religious denominations. The role of women in Quaker ministry, which led to the recognition of charismatic, articulate women as recorded ministers, was part of the general egalitarian posture of Quaker theology, but the expansive role of women in Quaker meetings also portended the leadership of Quaker women in the woman suffrage debates of the nineteenth and early twentieth century. Finally, the Quaker Peace Testimony, which since 1660 has forbidden Friends from participating in any form of violence against other human beings, has been extremely controversial in the larger society, for whom certain wars have been viewed as either "necessary" or "just." Although it would be incorrect to presume that Quaker pacifism has always been complete and uniform, especially since the Civil War,[8] most Quakers have opposed *all* the wars that the larger American culture has deemed essential, from the wars against Native Americans that began in the seventeenth century to the Revolutionary War (when they were accused of being Tory sympathizers because of their reluctance to take arms) to the world wars of the twentieth century.

During more than three centuries of religious activity, Friends have added to their distinctive theology a set of antimodern and antimaterialist principles. These principles have led many Quakers to wear plain clothing, prohibit music and dance, speak in archaic and distinctive language, eschew alcohol and many of the temptations of consumerism, and prohibit marriages outside their community of faith. Quaker church membership numbers have always been relatively small compared to other church groups (exact numbers of Quakers are difficult to determine, but estimates around 120,000 current members are typical[9]), and yet their influence on American moral discourse has been persistent and substantial. Even more tellingly, the Religious Society of Friends, whose first radical missionaries were perceived to be a grave threat to religious and civic authority in seventeenth-century colonial New England, soon came to be perceived not so much as a threat to civic authority but as a quietly constructive challenge to the nation's moral structures.

Within the American Quaker movement today there exist several variant strains of worship and practice: (1) evangelical Quakers, whose mission includes spreading the Quaker message through evangelism and whose meetings focus on the Bible as the unerring word of God and usually include music, sermons, and a designated minister; (2) conservative Quakers, many of whom retain traditional habits of plain dress and Quaker speech patterns; (3) unprogrammed Quakers, many of whom de-emphasize the Christian legacy of Quaker theology and whose meetings are held silently and without sermons, music, or designated pastors; and (4) programmed Quakers (many of whom are members of evangelical Quaker meetings), who also utilize sermons, music, and/or a designated pastor. These American Quaker variants stem from divisions that had emerged before the early twentieth century and which divided Quakers at that time under the following rubrics: (1) "Hicksites," a liberal wing named for Quaker reformer Elias Hicks concentrated in the eastern United States and emphasizing social reform; (2) "Gurneyites," the more progressive and evangelical Quakers, who followed Joseph John Gurney, retained pastors, and were Bible centered; (3) "Wilburites," the traditionalists who were more devoted to individual spiritual inspiration, who followed John Wilbur, were mostly from rural areas, and retained the traditional Quaker speech and dress; and (4) "Orthodox," the Philadelphia Yearly Meeting, a Christocentric group. As with many other religious groups in America, Quaker meetings share many beliefs in common but also exhibit important differences. Individual Quaker congregations can be described along a continuum of "liberal" to "conservative" depending on their views of such matters as biblical interpretation, commitment to social issues, evangelism, and clerical authority.[10]

Like most religious movements that have a long history and extensive geographical reach, the Society of Friends has been a complex and multifaceted group whose theology has retained important principles but has also been refined and adjusted by its adherents over many generations. Despite the evolution and differentiation of their religious practices, Quakers have served a remarkably consistent role as influential religious outsiders in American cultural discourse. Since the first American Quakers began practicing their faith in New England, Friends have been an object of continuing fascination by non-Quakers, especially during those historical moments when Quaker beliefs have come into conflict with the nation's moral, political, and social agendas. This persistent fascination with Quaker lives and Quaker values therefore offers an example of sustained "outsider" group religious influence on the national culture that is unmatched within American history. The "Imaginary Friends" of my title are for the most part the Quakers of national fascination rather than the actual Friends of three centuries of religious practice. As such, their representation and appropriation (by non-Quakers and Quakers alike) must be understood as shedding only a partial light on the lived religion of members of the Religious Society of Friends.

The English Puritans who dominated colonial New England contributed greatly to the moral climate that prevailed in that part of America for several centuries, even as the orthodox Calvinist churches steadily lost their grip on a rapidly expanding population. Indeed, the Puritans created much of the intellectual and theological context in which the European settlers of New England would begin to set out their distinctive Christian model of governance, and in fact the impulses behind the seventeenth-century origins of the Quaker movement were closely related to Puritanism itself. As Lawrence Templin has argued, historians of early American religion should "begin with the simple fact that early Quakerism was simultaneously an extension of fundamental Puritan ideas and a revolt against the Puritan tendency to solidify ideas into authoritarian theology."[11] In his landmark study of the religious scene in colonial New England, Vernon Louis Parrington noted the New Testament basis for the radical new Quaker ethos and concluded that "The Quaker was a mystic, sprung from the New Testament, who denied the Scriptural validity of a Hebraized Calvinism and a hireling priesthood, and accepted the Holy Spirit as the sole guide to his feet."[12] Generations of religious historians have recognized that, although its Calvinist principles were not adhered to in every particular, Puritanism nevertheless infused civic and family life in seventeenth-century New England with profound consequences for subsequent generations of Puritans and their religious adversaries.

The theological history of America, and especially the history of theology in New England, has attracted the attention of talented scholars for nearly the past century, and for all of their many disagreements, they generally concur about the importance of Puritanism's emphasis on maintaining a coherent moral and civic identity grounded in English religious traditions. This moral identity was forged in a colonial crucible that placed Puritan communities in conflict with numerous forces and challenges, among them Native Americans hostile to English encroachments on tribal lands, tensions between religious and civic governance, and most troubling of all, competing religious discourses such as those promulgated by a variety of radical dissenting Protestant groups that appeared alongside the Puritan orthodox in New England during the Great Migration of 1620–50. In his classic account of Anglo-American Puritan radicalism, Philip F. Gura describes the English religious sects of the early colonial period as "separatists, familists, Seekers, Anabaptists, Ranters, Adamites, and Quakers, all implicitly aligned against the established church system because of their insistence that an individual's personal religious experience supersede the demands of ecclesiastical tradition and civil law. In many cases, theirs were the same Protestant principles [colonial Massachusetts governor John] Winthrop and others earlier had defended in England yet, under pressure to settle a wilderness and codify their ecclesiology, soon enough condemned as seditious or heretical."[13]

Gura's broader argument about the important influence of these groups of radical Puritan dissenters on the orthodox Puritanism of the New England colonies is a highly persuasive one. The New England Congregationalists responded perennially to the challenge of the radical sects, and as both Gura and Sacvan Bercovitch suggest, the encounter between orthodoxy and radicalism in New England led eventually to discourses about America's sense of self-importance and exceptional status in the world based on the notion of divine Providence for a chosen people.[14] As Gura summarizes this phenomenon, he makes an observation that goes to the heart of my own analysis of Quakers in American culture, which is that although orthodox Puritans understood themselves as agents of serious—even radical—religious change and reform, their guiding principles were in fact deeply conservative and openly hostile to religious dissent of other varieties. In particular, the Separatist Puritan orthodox authorities in America did indeed set themselves in defiance of the established Church of England, which it accused of numerous heresies and popish corruptions, but it also managed to resist the attraction of even more progressive ideas that were being made available in the doctrines of its radical opponents like the Quakers and other radical dissenting sects. As Gura concludes, "the New Englanders' ideological self-image was shaped less by any set of ecclesiastical principles than by an unyielding effort to neutralize the influence of those who argued for a much more radical reorganization of the society."[15]

Of the marginalized religious groups that were present during the founding of the Massachusetts Bay Colony in the mid-seventeenth century, however, none has served a more important role in the ongoing conversation about American morals and social habits than the Quakers.[16] At the core of my argument in this study is the proposition that there has been disproportionate and persistent influence by Quakers on American culture and that this influence has been registered in complex, ambivalent, and sometimes ironic ways. Anglo-American Quakers began as dissenters from the seventeenth-century Anglican Church, although their aims during the early years were similar to those of other new religious movements such as the Baptists and Seekers. But Quakers also brought significant innovation to the practice of Christian religion. Most notably, by means of their radical new notion of an Inner Light of divine presence made available to each member of the faithful, Quakers were attempting to work their way toward a goal that many religions share: the soul's approach to divinity. In a recently published and influential general theory of religion, Thomas A. Tweed universalizes religious goals in more precise sociological terms: "The religious want to negotiate the limits of embodied existence, confronting suffering and intensifying joy—and traversing the stages of life. And the religious seek ways to imagine and realize the zenith of human flourishing, however that is conceived. They draw on tropes, artifacts, and rituals to produce teleographies, representations of the ultimate horizon and the means of crossing it."[17] Like other religious seekers, and more so than many, early Quakers attempted to "negotiate the limits of bodily existence," but they did so in ways that were disturbing to the orthodox Christians of the day.

Quakers in England and America have sometimes been referred to by outsiders as a "peculiar people," and this alleged peculiarity can be registered and assessed in a number of ways. Perhaps most alarming to non-Quakers in the seventeenth century was the fundamental anti-authoritarian stance that Quakers took in both their religious practice and their social habits, such as their refusal of the customary removal of men's hats before figures of social authority such as magistrates. In addition, because Quaker founder and evangelist George Fox and the other early Quakers were convinced that each individual person could have a profound experience of God through an Inner Light, their anti-nomian religious posture was by definition one articulated by the individual person, who could interpret for herself or himself any inspiration that was felt from the Divine. This radical antinomian view led quickly to its logical extension in the form of democratized preaching and the elimination of a paid ministry. Any person who felt the call to preach in Quaker meetings could do so, without being required to submit to any special theological training or ecclesiastical credentialing; ministers were not ordained but instead were "recorded" by consensus in the minutes for the meeting.

The form of Quaker meetings, which by the early eighteenth century had taken the subdued form of a silent meeting punctuated only by extemporaneous preaching, had been conducted during the first few decades of the movement as a kind of populist religious theater that functioned to vanquish long-standing rules of liturgical decorum and centralized authority that had prevailed in English Protestant churches. Traditionally patriarchal in their organization, seventeenth-century Christian services led by male ministers and structured with care for the niceties of liturgy and decorum gave way in Quaker meetings to a potentially anarchic scene characterized by an unbounded narrative fraught with theological polyphony and gender trouble. As Milan Kundera once described the narrative politics of the novel itself, the core politics of Quaker meetings and the Inner Light frequently led to "the fascinating imaginative realm where no one owns the truth and everyone has the right to be understood," with the important and potentially overwhelming difference that being understood as a Quaker in weekly meetings meant being accepted as a conduit for the word of God itself.[18] After the tumultuous few decades after the movement's founding in 1648 by a self-educated evangelist named George Fox, it is true that for a variety of reasons Quaker meetings rarely gave way to anarchic performances or true polyvocality of the sort that Kundera imagines for fictional narratives. Although they were never ordained or paid in the conventional way of Christian ministry, talented evangelists among the Quakers were recorded as such by their meetings, and they assumed positions of leadership and control.

Other traits estranged early Quakers from their contemporaries, although esteem for Friends by non-Quakers has remained remarkably high for centuries, especially after the first turbulent half century (1650–1700) of their existence. Certain Quaker peculiarities were visible or audible even to those not belonging to the Quaker community. For instance, Quaker abstinence from alcohol, an early aspect of religious discipline for Friends, has long provided for them the reputation of being a remarkably self-contained and sober group. The earliest Quakers were not so abstemious in their personal habits as were later Friends; in fact, some early Quakers owned taverns and inns where alcohol was served, but eventually strictures against alcohol consumption became a notable aspect of Quaker social identity and discipline. These very attributes are associated with the high esteem and trust accorded to Friends in business and other pursuits, but teetotalling Quakers since at least the eighteenth century have also been used as ridiculous comic types in a variety of genres: theater, fiction, song, and film.

Because Quakers preached the availability of the Inner Light to each human, they tended toward egalitarian social arrangements that were seen as radical at the time. The spiritual equality of men and women, which George Fox had advocated from the very beginning of the Quaker movement, thereby became a radically new proposition for an Anglo-American religious world heavily structured according to patriarchal traditions and principles. Long before other Christian denominations provided official roles for women as ministers, Quaker women in the seventeenth century were already establishing themselves as evangelists and preachers. Most radical of all Quaker theological innovations was the Peace Testimony, which had strictly prohibited all forms of violence against other human beings. Writing to King Charles II in

1660 in response to his request that Quakers serve in the British Army, George Fox and several other Quaker signers made clear their aversion to armed conflict: "We utterly deny all outward wars and strife and fightings with outward weapons, for any end or under any pretence whatsoever. And this is our testimony to the whole world. The spirit of Christ, by which we are guided, is not changeable, so as once to command us from a thing as evil and again to move unto it; and we do certainly know, and so testify to the world, that the spirit of Christ, which leads us into all Truth, will never move us to fight any war against any man with outward weapons, neither for the kingdom of Christ, nor for the kingdoms of this world."[19] Conscientious objection is a central tenet of the Religious Society of Friends that spans more than 350 years and innumerable modern wars.

Over time, Quaker discipline tightened the forms of behavior deemed acceptable for Friends, and as behavior and other habits came to be regularized, Friends withdrew from their demonstrative spiritual expressiveness while adopting customs that made them easy for others to identify. From the early eighteenth century until the early twentieth century, Quakers at various times were distinguished but also criticized or ridiculed for idiosyncrasies such as their preferences for plainly decorated domestic spaces, austere clothing, and avoidance of music and alcohol. Although never so stringently antimodern as certain other long-established American religious groups like the Amish and Mennonites, Quakers have formed traditions of avoiding worldly dress and worldly behaviors. This religiously inflected austerity has in turn created the impression among non-Quakers that Quakers are not only pious but humorless and generally resistant to most of the world's pleasures. Audible signs of Quaker belief have typically come in the form of the characteristic "thee" and "thou" of Quaker personal address.[20] In addition, Quakers have traditionally used such expressions as "first-month" and "first-day" in place of pagan-derived proper names such as "January" and "Sunday." Legal proceedings in the United States that require the taking of oaths have, after many years of discrimination, been revised for Quakers who for religious reasons "affirm" but do not "swear" to truthful testimony in court. These sectarian shibboleths, especially the use of "thee" and "thou," served to identify Quakers from the early eighteenth century through the early twentieth century, when many Quakers began to relax their linguistic discipline and their rules about conforming to plain styles of dress.[21]

Relations between Quaker men and women have placed them in the vanguard of American religions working toward a progressive politics for women's rights. Women, such as the early Quaker convert Margaret Fell, were instrumental in establishing the Religious Society of Friends in England, and Quaker theology was produced with an eye toward women's participation and preaching. Gender politics also lay close to the center of early Quaker teachings and has continued to be a major distinguishing characteristic of Quaker practice. The democratization of the ministerial function in Quaker meetings was one way in which women were acknowledged as have certain expressive—even oracular— powers, since a considerable number of Quaker women distinguished themselves as preachers and were recorded as such in their meetings. Although their marriages were limited to unions with other Quakers (by the late seventeenth century, the Quaker discipline mandated endogamy; marriages outside the faith were not permitted and frequently resulted in Friends being "read out of meeting"), by the eighteenth century Quaker men and women were meeting separately, a practice that led to a number of influential women preachers. The long-standing Quaker commitment to human equality could in certain respects be said to have grown from the ethos of the earliest years of the English Quaker movement, when an affluent judge's wife named Margaret Fell (1614–1702) became a follower of George Fox and, later, one of his first ministers. This egalitarian impulse struck deep roots early on within the Quaker tradition and eventuated later in somewhat different form with the founding of the Underground Railroad by Quakers during the nineteenth century; the Society of Friends thereby extended its empowerment of women as full church participants to its proposition that African American slaves also be accorded full human rights.

The degree to which Quakers were tentatively committed to gender equity, especially during the seventeenth and eighteenth centuries, stands in sharp contrast to the traditional patriarchal structuring of Anglo-American society, with its exclusively male ministry exerting nearly total power over official religious life. Although Quakers frequently did not go much farther than the "separate but equal" mode that has become familiar from the politics of American racial discrimination, women were in fact able to function with a good deal of autonomy in their meetings for business and worship. Until the late nineteenth century, for instance, the Men's Meeting and Women's Meeting were conducted separately, and each separate meeting had its own officers, kept its own minutes, and issued its own certificates of removal for breaches of Quaker discipline. Frequently, women's charisma and talent led to positions of leadership within the Quaker movement. To take one prominent example, Elizabeth Ashbridge (1713–55), an Anglo-Irish immigrant to Pennsylvania who arrived as an indentured servant, converted to the Quaker faith and became a prominent preacher among Pennsylvania Friends; her posthumous spiritual autobiography, *Some Account of the Fore Part of the Life of Elizabeth Ashbridge* (1774), served for many years as an exemplary account of women Friends' spiritual life.[22] Describing the feminist dimension of the American Quaker experience is not the primary aim of this study, but it is nonetheless instructive to map the divergence between Quakers and American culture as a whole in terms of rights accorded to women. With its slow and incomplete advances in women's rights, and the early turn to gender equity, members of the Society of Friends, who over the centuries have frequently been mocked or ridiculed for the stern rules about sexual morality and marriage within the faith, nevertheless became the first of the American Christian denominations to authorize women to preach.

❖

In considering representations of Quaker life and religion in the American national imaginary, this study works chronologically to examine evidence from more than three centuries of American culture (ca. 1650–1950) but also divides its attention among a variety of genres. This approach has been necessary in order to understand the place of discourses concerning American Quakers as these discourses evolved and modulated over substantial periods of time. Not only did Anglo-American discourses about Quaker life evolve, but these discourses changed in terms of intensity and visibility depending on social and political circumstances. Religious debates, the existence of slavery, the ongoing conversation about women's rights, and the interrelated issues of warfare and imperialism all served to shape and condition circumstances under which Quaker social and religious values were described and fashioned into elements of the national moral culture. Shifts in religious intensity and social visibility are crucial elements in the broader argument that the study aims to make about the abiding consequences of a radically asymmetrical religious encounter: that a relatively small American religious group not only had (and has) the ability to shape the larger culture in important ways and, as a consequence had (and has) the ability to structure the nation's moral identity to an unexpected degree. This is not to say that Americans during the years in question flocked to the Society of Friends in large numbers; it would be more accurate to say somewhat the opposite. Quaker life has been fascinating to Americans for many years, but not so attractive as to be the kind of religious group that large numbers of Americans actually wish to join. The moral influence of Quaker life—that is, the influence of Quaker life both real and imagined—took shape without significant numbers of conversions to the Society of Friends. As a consequence, while the nation grew quickly in population during the past several centuries, Quakers have moved ever closer to numerical insignificance.

The chronological ordering of my study opens in the middle decades of the seventeenth century and continues to the middle of the twentieth century, and is arranged by chapter into discussions of a variety of literary genres in which representations of English and American Quakers appeared. Taking a long and broad view of American cultural and literary history forces the discussion of Quakers in American culture away from the constraints of narrow examination of single authors and/or exclusively canonical figures. Prominent writers form a part of the discussion; to name a few examples, James Fenimore Cooper, Herman Melville, Harriet Beecher Stowe, Walt Whitman, Rebecca Harding Davis, and Theodore Dreiser all found Quaker religion interesting enough to make it a substantial part of their literary projects. Nevertheless, much of the work here inclines to what recent scholarship has preferred to name as "print culture studies." The turn to print culture provides a number of advantages to scholars interested in the broader patterns extant in the history of American media, of which printed materials form a substantial part, especially before 1950 and the dawn of the television era. Literary historian Trish Loughran summarizes these advantages under two headings: "As a method, print culture would seem to do at least two things for its users: first, it takes a materialist turn towards the study of actual textual artifacts, and second, in doing so, it allows us to turn away from iconic authors and texts to focus instead on a more unstable and differential field of objects. It is . . . a fairly democratizing approach, allowing us to address a world of circulating things that defy the confines of a hierarchized canon of Great Books and Great Men."[23] Many of the "circulating things" with which this book is primarily concerned are pamphlets, books, and periodicals; these works, in turn, are divided into literary genres by chapters.

Analysis of literary genres in these chapters proceeds according to the relative importance of those genres for a particular period. Chapter 1 examines the first half century of discourse related to Quaker religion (1650–1700) and focuses mainly on the somewhat recondite theological debates that circulated soon after the appearance of the first Quakers in England and America during the 1650s. These were the years when Quakers were understood by their adversaries on both sides of the Atlantic to be dangerously radical, so much so that Friends were even compared to the dreaded Roman Catholics in their potential to disrupt the Church of England, which required membership of all English subjects at that time. Oddly enough, Pennsylvania founder William Penn was repeatedly accused while in England of secretly being a Roman Catholic sympathizer and possibly even a Jesuit. During this period Quakers had not yet arrived at clear consensus about their own doctrines, nor had they yet published the formal accounts of Quaker discipline that would serve as the increasingly regularized catechisms for eighteenth- and nineteenth-century Friends. They nevertheless were perceived by orthodox church authorities in both Anglican England and Puritan New England to be participants in a dangerous and abhorrent perversion of established Christian religion. Quakers were undoubtedly seen as a threat, but a precise definition of what it might mean theologically to be a "Quaker" would not solidify until Robert Barclay's Quaker catechism, *An Apology for the True Christian Divinity* (1676), came into wide Anglo-American circulation in the late seventeenth century.

After the first half century of their existence in England and America, Quakers remained a small minority religious group with a devoted following that had turned away from some of its more flamboyant early demonstrations of zeal, enthusiasm, and overt rebellion against established religious authority. American colonial outposts provided an important respite for Quakers harried in England by a variety of persecutors. By the late seventeenth century, on the American side of the Atlantic, the leadership of the Quaker William Penn—leveraged in part by his deft participation in the religious print marketplace—had established Pennsylvania and the Delaware Valley area as places with strong support for Quaker religion and social habits.[24] As Quakers became more securely established in America, however, their early confrontational and enthusiastic style of worship waned; at the same time, new religious denominations began to exercise overt evangelical influence in the colonies far beyond that of the Quakers. Demographic

circumstances in the fast-growing American colonies by the early eighteenth century had provided the conditions necessary (ample population, religious tolerance, vast and accessible lands) for the growth and
popularity of numerous Christian evangelical groups like Methodists,
Baptists, and many others. As the colonies grew rapidly more populous
and diverse, Quakers certainly did not disappear, but in many respects
they withdrew to the cultural margins from the main stage of the ongoing religious conversation while perpetuating small communities of a
pious and strictly disciplined faithful.

By the later years of the eighteenth century, when the most pressing
concerns in the American colonies hinged not on religious disputes but
on the complex political decisions that were leading the colonies toward
the decisive military conflicts of the Revolution, representations of
Quaker life and morals took on a newly political cast. Chapter 2 sets out
the political conversation about Quaker values from two basic perspectives. First, the discussion of eighteenth-century political discourses gives
voice to some prominent and influential Quaker activists from the period, especially the pioneering American abolitionists Anthony Benezet
(1713–84) and John Woolman (1720–72). Alongside a brief review of their
political writings is set a discussion of a prominent non-Quaker: the
French adventurer and social analyst Hector St. John de Crèvecoeur, the
author of *Letters from an American Farmer* (1782), an idiosyncratic book
blending fiction, travelogue, and social commentary, which created an
international sensation during the immediate post-Revolutionary period. Less commonly noted about Crèvecoeur's famous analysis of the
American colonial scene is his lengthy treatment of Quaker life, specifically the long-established community of Quakers then thriving on
Nantucket Island in Massachusetts. Quakers fascinated Crèvecoeur and
other politically minded European thinkers of his generation because of
the possibilities for a new set of political arrangements that might be
built on a foundation of Quaker principles. As the eighteenth-century
American public sphere continued to mature with the help of a thriving
marketplace of print, serious writers began to treat Friends not merely
as interlopers on the national scene or as a tiny and inconsequential religious sect but as dynamic moral interlocutors. The evidence of these
contributions by Quakers can be measured in a number of ways but perhaps never as clearly as in the American print archive of the eighteenth
and nineteenth centuries. Having settled into patterns of religious discipline that for the most part turned away from theological conflict with
other churches, those Quakers who were pursuing a coherent religious

movement come into sharper focus during the post-Revolutionary period, even as observers outside the Society of Friends were speculating about how Quaker life might be adapted and appropriated for a new politics.

One sign of Quakers having established themselves as vital participants in the construction of American national identity is the emergence of comprehensive histories of the movement. Just as the New England historians of earlier generations, such as William Bradford and Cotton Mather, had written with sympathy and nuance the story of early Puritans in the American colonies,[25] Quaker historians eventually created their own copious documentation of the Religious Society of Friends, including their English origins, early persecutions at the hands of the established Church, and eventual settlement into generally peaceful Quaker communities in the American colonies. Thanks especially to a pair of ambitious histories of the Society of Friends that received considerable attention in Europe and America, the genealogy of the Quaker movement was documented, and the patterns of its origins, growth, and development could be seen more clearly. Turning from political to historical representations of Quakers, chapter 3 examines William Sewel's *The History of the Rise, Increase, and Progress, of the Christian People Called Quakers* (1717, first English edition 1722), written by a Dutch convert to Quakerism. During the eighteenth century, Sewel's history—a substantially researched edition in two volumes—served for nearly a century as the standard account of the early years of the Anglo-American Quaker movement. Sewel's historical method was not without its flaws, especially in his lack of source documentation and attribution of evidence, to say nothing of his clear bias against all enemies of the Quaker movement, but he included in his history a chronologically organized anthology of writings by early Quakers sufficient to dramatize their struggle in England against the orthodox English churchmen. Although he focuses primarily on the first half century of Quaker activities in England, Sewel also remains alert to developments on the Quaker scene in New England, charting to some extent the establishment of Quaker outposts there and vigorously criticizing the civic authorities of Massachusetts Bay Colony, whom he judged to have been inexcusably harsh in their treatment of the intrepid Quaker missionaries who dared to set foot on American soil.

Nearly a century later, the great English abolitionist Thomas Clarkson,[26] who along with the more famous antislavery statesman William Wilberforce had been instrumental in agitating against the English slave trade during the late eighteenth and early nineteenth century, published his scrupulously researched three-volume *A Portraiture of Quakerism. Taken from a View of the Education and Discipline, Social Manners, Civil and Political Economy, Religious Principles and Character of the Society of Friends.* In addition, Clarkson's research comprised a major revision and updating of Sewel's earlier historical work and it soon became the standard history of the Quakers for the nineteenth century. Clarkson's history, although written by a non-Quaker, provided for intellectuals of his generation a deeply respectful overview of the Quaker tradition from the vantage point of an admiring outsider, albeit one who never joined the Society of Friends.

Placing the histories of the Quakers by Sewel and Clarkson into a comparative framework, chapter 3 aims at two related objectives. First, the new religious group, formed by radical Protestant dissenters who found themselves named as "Quakers," did not produce substantial histories of their activities during the first half century of their existence. Histories of the Quakers (and biographies of Quaker leaders like William Penn) began to proliferate beginning in the eighteenth century. This chapter makes no attempt to provide a comprehensive survey of all extant histories, but the appearance of Sewel's history in the early eighteenth century indeed provided a baseline representation of Quaker life. During a period of fast-paced American colonial and early national development, when comprehensive histories of American religion had yet to be written, these two works provided American readers the most authoritative accounts of Quaker religion.[27] Together they serve as flawed but foundational staples of American religious history in much the way as did Cotton Mather's classic account of American Puritan beginnings in *Magnalia Christi Americana* (1702).

The second aim of chapter 3, which surveys these standard histories of the Society of Friends, is to lay the groundwork for later discussions of Quaker representations in biography and fiction of the nineteenth century. The publication of these ambitious historical works by William Sewel and Thomas Clarkson, especially the more rigorous scholarship of the latter, provides a relatively clear look not only at the details of Quaker theology but also the actual workings of English (and to some extent American) Quaker communities and religious meetings. They stand as reasonably accurate documentary evidence against which to compare the imaginings of biographers and novelists at work in the American print marketplace as it burgeoned from the late eighteenth through the early twentieth century. Nevertheless, and although a certain amount of accurate documentary information about Quaker life was readily available to American readers of the nineteenth century, biographies of Quakers and fictional representations of Quakers produced at that time were sometimes oddly at variance from the lives of Friends themselves. Chapters 4 and 5 examine Quaker representations in nineteenth- and early twentieth-century biography and fiction, and we turn to some of the reasons—political, social, religious—that Quakers became a disproportionately resonant presence in American print culture, while recognizing that American readers who encountered Quakers in their reading were often encountering them through the distorting lenses of stereotype, simplification, or ridicule.

The transatlantic perspectives offered by the first comprehensive histories of the Quaker movement, which were written by Europeans but found audiences on both sides of the Atlantic, are similar in certain respects to the subsequent view of Friends provided by Quaker biographers during the nineteenth century. As debates over slavery intensified during the antebellum period and as Quakers emerged from a century (1700–1800) of religious quietism and marginality on the national political scene, readers in the United States grew increasingly fascinated by the phenomenon of a religious movement that appeared to have been the earliest among all denominations to begin repudiating slavery.[28] That this fascination with progressive Quaker politics was both intense and enduring can be measured in a variety of ways: chapter 4 takes focuses on the genre of nineteenth-century popular biography as one important index of the place of Quakers in the national imaginary. In the nineteenth century—as Quaker abolitionists like Anna E. Dickinson and Lucretia Mott grew to prominence on the antislavery lecture circuit—American readers were increasingly presented with vivid biographies of Friends to supplement the careful Quaker histories already provided by William Sewel, Thomas Clarkson, and others. In the eighteenth century, the great lexicographer Samuel Johnson famously opined on the subject of biography in his memorable comment that "Nothing can please many, or please long, but just representations of general nature." For American readers of Quaker biographies, however, the biographical representations were indeed popular for a time, but it would be difficult to describe these depictions as lives resembling the bulk of the American citizenry. Instead, like the depictions of Quakers in numerous novels published during the same period, Friends in these biographies are typically idealized and admired as virtuous individuals, who are nevertheless eerily aloof from ordinary human experiences and concerns. Although many Quaker biographies and autobiographies were published during the nineteenth century, this chapter focuses on four selected examples in order to suggest the general themes and modes of representation of Friends that were typical on the nineteenth century American literary scene. These examples drawn from the genre of biography are meant to be a fair sampling of the kinds of Quaker life-writing American readers would have had available during the antebellum period, when Quaker men and women had begun gaining prominence for their outspoken views on slavery.

Taken together as examples of Quaker life presented to the nineteenth-century reading public, these religiously inflected biographies, like the works in other genres discussed in this study, are best understood as a contested terrain of social and spiritual meanings. As didactic works that present the lives of Quakers for the edification of the average American reader, these biographies show a number of social dimensions by which to measure the contribution of nineteenth-century Friends: William Penn, the colonial governor; Thomas Battey, an earnest schoolteacher among the Plains Indians; Sarah Greer, the lapsed and disillusioned Quaker girl; and John Greenleaf Whittier, the preeminent Quaker poet of his generation.

Despite the efforts of numerous talented authors, none of the writings examined within these literary genres comes close to expressing the social totality or the religious complexities Quaker life, and this remains the case whether the writer in question is herself a Quaker or not. The inevitable limitations of each genre—theology, political theory, history, biography—lead to representations of the Society of Friends that are of necessity partial or incomplete, and the attitudes expressed toward Quakers in these writings are various. Reading them sequentially thus provides documentation of their impact on American life that oscillates between the hostile and the sympathetic, the accurate and the distorted, the religiously sophisticated and the satirically dismissive. In spite of these substantial and sometimes confusing differences between the various texts, all of the genres examined are similar in one respect: all of these writings—despite their inevitable biases—claim at the very least to show Quaker lives and religious values in the most accurate way possible. By the nineteenth century, long after careful histories of the Religious Society of Friends had appeared as tools for understanding the particulars of Quaker religion, American literary culture would find new uses for these religious outsiders. Chapters 5 and 6 change course by examining two literary genres, fiction and drama, in which far more license is customarily taken with representations of character and social setting.

Although the uses to which Friends are put in American fiction are varied, there is a consistent tendency in these narratives—many of which, following the custom of the nineteenth century, are morally didactic in nature—to use Quakerism as an unattainable moral limit for "ordinary" citizens. Whereas in early modern England and New England theological differences and resistance to church and civic authority made debates over religious practice the central controversies that played out in pamphlet wars, nineteenth-century American writers began to emphasize the antimodern and moralistic tendencies of Friends: plain speech and dress, aversion to alcohol, insular communities, resistance to consumerism, and increasingly firm opposition to slavery. In the many nineteenth-century novels that describe conflicts between Quaker and Puritan in colonial New England, for instance, Quakers are usually remembered and imagined to exemplify the qualities of bravery, piety, and personal virtue in comparison with the punitively rigid authoritarianism ascribed to Puritans, even as many of these books tend implicitly to celebrate the virtues of the American Puritan legacy. Still, the idea of Quaker faith and the persistent emblem of the virtuous Quaker retained a firm hold on the American literary imagination, written faintly but semipermanently onto the palimpsest of the nation's moral discourse.

For more than a century, many American novelists found it useful to deploy either mild and virtuous Quakers (such as the good men and women of Stowe's "Quaker Settlement" in *Uncle Tom's Cabin*) or memorably brutal Quakers (such as Herman Melville's whale-hunting Captain Ahab in *Moby-Dick* [1851]), or Robert Montgomery Bird's brutal Indian-killing Nathan Slaughter in his popular *Nick of the Woods* (1837). From early nineteenth-century writers like James Fenimore Cooper, whose Leatherstocking Tales became the first real best sellers of the nineteenth century and who was himself from a Quaker background and included a number of Quakers in those novels, to Theodore Dreiser, whose final novel, *The Bulwark* (1946), is a depressive tale focusing on a Quaker patriarch battling within his own family against the corrosive immorality of modern times, serious American writers persisted in looking to Quaker values as a fascinating alternative to secular materialism and the drive toward modernity. My survey of three centuries of debate over the role of Quakers in American society concludes with an examination in chapter 6 of theatrical and cinematic representations of Quakers from the late eighteenth century to approximately 1950. The overwhelming dominance of print as a mass medium during the nineteenth century, which by the antebellum period had made it the primary form of national acculturation, expanded unabated until the rise of cinema in the early years of the twentieth century, when visual mass media began its rapid ascent to preeminence in depicting American society for ever-larger audiences. The shift to print culture dominance for the United States had been a momentous one, as orality and local identity gave way to print and the imagined community of the American nation-state.[29] In considering the formation of national character in the late nineteenth century, however, one must look beyond the world of print culture for indications of the ways and means by which Americans were learning to understand themselves socially, politically, and morally. The transformation from an obscure seventeenth-century colonial outpost identified mainly by print culture to a more complex twentieth-century media nation that included important new forms of communication like the cinema was accompanied by continuing popular interest in stage drama. In keeping with the theme of mass media and its ability to shape perceptions about religion and morality (among many other things), I have included a sampling of both plays and films that illuminate the paradoxical role of Quakers in the national imagination over an extended time frame.

Anglo-American dramatic works that included prominent Quaker characters date from at least the early eighteenth century, when English comedies like Charles Shadwell's *The Fair Quaker of Deal; or, the Humours of the Navy* (1715), Susanna Centlivre's *A Bold Stroke for a Wife* (1718), and Richard Wilkinson's *The Quaker's Wedding: A Comedy* (1723) initiated the tendency of dramatists in England and America to mock Friends for their perceived clannishness, prudery, and pious hypocrisy. When late-eighteenth-century Philadelphia finally relaxed its prohibitions against the performance of stage plays, the city also enjoyed dramatic lampooning of Friends, despite its status as the leading American Quaker city. After the repeal of a series of eighteenth-century laws prohibiting plays of any kind, after the American Revolution, dramatists like John Murdock began featuring Quakers prominently in their works, such as his popular farce *The Triumphs of Love* (1795), which is also the first American play to broach the subject of abolitionism. As Quakers grew into newly public positions in the national discourse over slavery during the antebellum period, and distinguished writers began to include Friends as fictional characters and American types (see chapter 5), Quakers continued to make occasional appearances in plays

The perceived "theatricality" of Quakers in American life can be attributed both to specific religious views that placed them at a considerable distance from the norm and also to habits of speech, dress, and moralistic demeanor that lent their characters a large measure of peculiarity instantly recognizable as at variance from the larger culture. For example, the ease with which Quaker appearance and Quaker morality could be adapted for theatrical purposes is on view in Theodore Dreiser's *Sister Carrie* (1900), one of the most important American novels of the early twentieth century. Carrie Meeber, Dreiser's supremely adaptable protagonist, finds her greatest success not merely as an actress but as a performer of her signature role as a beautiful and coquettish young Quakeress on the New York stage. In placing the rural ingénue Sister Carrie in the role of naïve Quakeress, Dreiser was mimicking popular dramas of the period that found Quakers to be ideal types for depicting morality under siege by the temptations and excesses of modern life in America. Quaker strictures concerning marriage within the sect were a consistent topic in these plays, which provide a useful index to evolving views women's sexual prerogatives during the early twentieth century.

Quaker stage theatricality eventually gave way to Quaker cinematic theatricality. Friends as stock characters in dramatic performances remained a staple of popular entertainment throughout the from the silent film era through Hollywood's "golden era" from about 1930 to 1950. The silent era appears to have used Quakers consistently in its plotting. Although the films themselves have not survived, *A Quaker Mother* (1911, Vitagraph Company of America), *The Quakeress* (1913), *Bred in the Bone* (1915), *The Dancing Girl* (1915), *The Quack Quakers* (1916), and *Beauty's Worth* (1922) mirrored developments on the popular stage by featuring Friends as important characters. This chapter also examines representations of American Quakers in a range of films from the first half of the twentieth century, including *Down to the Sea in Ships* (1922), *The Courageous Mr. Penn* (1942), and *Angel and the Bad Man* (1947, with John Wayne). The chapter ends with a brief examination of the Academy Award–winning *High Noon* (1952, with Gary Cooper and Grace Kelly), in which Quaker pacifism is attacked as hindering the necessary, violent enforcement of law.[30]

There are enormous differences between the lived religious experience of Quakers and the many and often contradictory representations
that have been offered by those who have written about Quakers. The
same could be said about members of other religious groups in America
who have made their way into the literary and cinematic annals of the
nation. It should go without saying that lived religion cannot be understood fully by any but those who experience that religious life personally,
and this is true whether one is referring to Friends or to members of
others American religious denominations: Roman Catholicism, Bud-
dhism, Hindu, Islam, and a host of others. The ambition of this study
has not been to write the full history of Quakers in America; instead,
my aim has been to understand the ways that a relatively small religious
denomination has managed to remain an object of enduring interest
and moral influence in American culture, even as its stated principles of
egalitarian worship, pacifism, sobriety, plain living, and engagement
with Inner Light stand beyond the reach of the many. The evidence
for a sustained encounter between a marginal religious group and the
larger national culture is available in the documentary archive of the
past three centuries. This is not to say that Americans have been talking
incessantly about Quaker identity or Quaker values. The pulse of American history has, however, had the effect of creating key moments in
the past when the encounter with Quaker otherness has set off sparks
of fresh discourse leading to ever more complex estrangement from the
larger national project: Puritan colonization in Massachusetts, a Revolutionary War in which Quakers refused to take up weapons, a Quaker-led
antebellum conversation about slavery, and Quaker nonparticipation in
the great military conflicts of the past century and a half. Ultimately,
Quakers have not been placed into the national conversation as merely
one more option for yet another church that one might join. Instead,
with their frequently aloof, sometimes awkward, always variegated, but
steadily persistent commitments to peace, justice, and an authentic experience of God's Inner Light, Quakers have stood as an ongoing query
about the rightness of American morals and the parameters of national
belonging.

1

Quaker Religion in Colonial New England

This Court, being desirous to try all means, with as much lenity as may
consist with our Safety, to prevent the Instructions of the Quakers, who
besides their absurd and Blasphemous Doctrines, do like Rogues and
Vagabonds come in upon us, and have not been Restrained by the Law
already provided; Have Ordered, that every such Vagabond Quaker,
found within any part of this jurisdiction, shall be Apprehended. . . .
And being by the said Magistrate . . . adjudged to be a *Wandering Quaker,*
viz. One that hath not any Dwelling, or orderly allowance as an inhab-
itant of this jurisdiction; and not giving civil Respect, by the usual gestures thereof or by any other way or means manifesting himself to be a
Quaker shall . . . Be stripped naked from the Middle upwards, and tied
to a Carts tayle, and Whipped through the Town.

Several Laws and Orders of the General Court [Massachusetts], 1663

Descended from a populist spiritual tradition that emerged in the
1640s and organized by Protestant visionaries from the lower to
middling classes in Northern England, Quakers in seventeenth-century
New England were among the most radically subversive religious dissenters in colonial America.[1] As participants in the broad and complex
Protestant religious upheaval occurring in England at that time, Quakers resembled many of the religious dissenters of the era in their urge to
split with the Church of England and to create a form of Christian

practice based in vernacular study of scripture, congregational organization of churches, and abhorrence of the ecclesiastical politics and
misdeeds made notorious by the Roman Catholic Church. In addition,
like the Puritans themselves, early English Quakers grew quickly from a
small group of charismatic lay preachers—led by the self-educated mystic and prophet George Fox—into a religious movement of approximately 60,000 persons.[2] They were considered to be radicals and pariahs
for their departure from religious principles of the Anglican orthodoxy
(especially their refusals to swear oaths and to pay tithes), and they became even more intensely the object of discrimination and retribution
in colonial America, where they defied the still-nascent and fragile Puritan community in a number of ways.[3]

Soon after the movement had begun in mid-seventeenth century
England, Quaker theology supplemented and balanced the Protestant
emphasis on scriptural revelation with a new focus on the direct experience of an "Inner Light" of divinity available to each individual believer.
It was their belief in this indwelling of divinity in each person that has
led Quakers to reject traditional services, sacraments, and paid clergy in
favor of worship meetings at which any person moved by the Inner Light
is permitted to preach and testify. The turn toward an inner light of revelation had architectural consequences, too, as the Quakers joined other
nonconformist religious groups in their eschewal of consecrated spaces
and elaborated forms of church architecture. Plain, utilitarian Quaker
meetinghouses expressed clearly their aversion to the superstitious aura
of decorated church buildings, which were associated with materialist
excesses and mystifications of Roman Catholicism. Keith Thomas has
summarized this tendency toward architectural plainness as part of the
central impulse of the radical nonconformist sects of the day, who fostered the belief that "It was wrong to worship in consecrated surroundings: a barn, stable or pigsty would do as well."[4] Indeed, George Fox
claimed to have spent many hours during the early years of his itinerant
Quaker evangelism meditating in a worship space that consisted only of
a hollow tree.

Congregational in its arrangements,[5] the early Society of Friends
readily produced testimonies against violence and bearing arms while
affirming personal lives of simplicity and human equality, and eventually including gender equality. Even more powerfully, early Quakers
sponsored the performance of numerous miraculous cures. Quaker
founder George Fox was himself credited with having accomplished

more than 150 such cures, as attested in his posthumously collected *Book of Miracles.*[6] What is most important for understanding the disruptiveness of their presence in New England during the American colonial period, however, is that Quakers as a spiritual and social force represented an almost incomprehensible defiance of familial, civic, and religious authority. Before the late eighteenth century, when the French Revolution and the American Revolution began to turn back the tide of religious and aristocratic authoritarianism, the Society of Friends functioned as an incubator of perhaps the most significant egalitarian and liberal religious ideas ever to be promoted in Europe or America. As Sacvan Bercovitch has concluded, these new ideas grew out of a religious sect with a strong "antiauthoritarian bent" that made the early Quakers "the most individualistic of Puritans."[7]

Examples abound of the Quaker repudiation of Church of England orthodoxy, and these differences ranged widely across normative manners, educational practices, domestic habits, and theological principles. In a summary of the turmoil wrought by early Quakers, the historian Julie Sievers writes that "The earliest Friends had been 'strange' not because they furnished ample houses with 'plain' furniture and refused to swear oaths, but because they had been poor and unlettered, vagrants and itinerants, preaching the gospel of the Inner Light often on foreign shores under dangerous and unpredictable circumstances, imprisoned in Cromwell's jails, hanged in Boston's commons. Their refusal to recognize social ranks and their disruptive intrusions into Congregational churches had made them a threat to the established political order."[8] Whereas even radical dissenting Christian groups like the Puritans insisted on the stabilizing and traditionalizing presence of a paid minister for each church congregation, Quakers believed that no paid minister was needed in order to enhance, educate, or control the workings of the Inner Light of divine presence and its subsequent revelation to the individual and the meeting of Friends to whom this revelation was presented. Whether the experience of the Inner Light took the private form of an inwardly felt spirituality or the public form of outwardly directed speech, emotion, or physical expression (such as quaking, shaking, or weeping), early Quakers believed that each individual person was entitled to her or his free connection to God, without mediation, revision, or authentication by authorities such as church elders or designated ministers. Quakerism thus led inexorably to one form of the Protestant antinomian religious position—a theology in which human moral law (typically enforced by clergy, elders, or magistrates) creates no clear obligation and has no binding power over the individual. For these antinomians, faith alone is the key to salvation through an unmediated relationship with the divine.[9]

Quaker difference from Protestant orthodoxy and congregational tradition also registered itself in the form of anti-authoritarian shibboleths, as with their use of the informal second-person pronouns "thee" and "thou." The historian Carla Gardina Pestana provides what is perhaps the best and most lucid explanation of the subversive radicalism beneath what might seem a mere quirk of grammar or anachronism of speech:

> The [Quakers] arrived in Massachusetts with a number of peculiar mannerisms that were well calculated to defy secular authority, the second social institution erected by the Puritans to safeguard their holy commonwealth. For instance, the Quakers insisted upon using "thee" and "thou" instead of the more formal "you." "Thee" and "thou" were reserved in the dialect still spoken in the north of England for social inferiors and intimates, whereas "you" was used when speaking to a superior or a stranger. The use of the intimate address symbolized the equality of all people in Christ; the Puritans, depending as they did on social and spiritual hierarchies to order the world, rejected these gestures of equality.[10]

As with their refusal to show due deference to authority by means of spoken language, so too did early Quakers insist upon the defiant symbolism of refusing to doff their hats, thus avoiding what Pestana calls "the ritual of hat honor," in the presence of the upper classes and other persons with superior civic or social authority. Pestana also correctly deduces that many historians have inappropriately "projected the characteristics of the later Society of Friends onto the early Quakers" and have underestimated the extent to which these radical exponents of the Inner Light were perceived as an unambiguous danger, so that "seen through the eyes of a mid-seventeenth century saint" the Quakers "represented an awesome threat to all that was godly in this world."[11] In language as well as appearance, early Quakers represented a disturbing assault on class-based power during an age when hierarchy and order were routinely expressed and enforced through these customs and others, such as compulsory church attendance, or bowing and scraping before one's "betters." The power of the Elizabethan sumptuary laws that had been passed in the second half of the sixteenth century in order to place severe restrictions on the kinds of clothing permissible for commoners and aristocrats alike, had begun to wane by the mid-seventeenth century, but clothing remained a vital signifier of class difference and—then as now—a source of intense interest by those wishing to rise in importance and status. It was no coincidence, then, when Quakers themselves—in a characteristic turn to the spiritual rather than the worldly—adopted a distinctive code of plain dress that set them apart from the prevailing urge, familiar still in today's world of fashion, to wear clothing similar to that of one's superiors.

Quaker women and men expressed their religious enthusiasm not only through new theological views—most importantly the concept of an Inner Light—but through social actions that, in historical perspective, seem calculated to undermine those fledgling colonies founded on the basis of church authority. At the same time, given their earliest activities in the settlements of New England, it is not difficult to see how Quakers in colonial America would become not only the stuff of national legend but also the object of severe reprisals, discrimination, and abuse by the larger communities they inhabited. The historian Sydney Ahlstrom summarizes the threat the Quakers represented: "They insisted that Truth in both individuals and society could only by hampered by excessive external coercion. They rejected intolerance, university-educated ministerial authority, and most forms of civil and international force. They were a clear threat to the English social order." Perhaps the most eloquent testimony to the stark contrast between orthodox and Quaker principles may be found in Vernon Louis Parrington's classic 1927 history of American intellectual life.[12] Parrington not only explains the contrast between the orthodox and Quaker views of religion but also expresses his sincere admiration for the Society of Friends at a time in the early decades of the twentieth century when the Quakers themselves had become, in terms of membership and religious influence alike, almost entirely marginal in American culture:

> [T]he early Quakers had found that primitive gospel in the byways of Carolinian England, and had brought it to the new world. There they had borne testimony in their daily lives to the excellence of Christian fellowship, and there they had suffered the reproaches and the blows of bigoted conformists. Their faith had been tried in the fires of persecution, and the Society of Friends had justified its use of that most excellent of sectarian names. In the sincerity of their equalitarian fellowship the Quakers were the friends of humanity, of the poor and the outcast

of the world. Their religion was of the week-day as well as the Sabbath. With its mystical doctrine of the inner light—of the Holy Spirit that speaks directly to the soul without the intermediation of priest or church—it unconsciously spread the doctrine of democracy in an autocratic world. . . . [The] sharp hostility it aroused in theocratic New England, sprang from the realization that the ideals of the Quaker fellowship were dangerous to the ideals of a priestly theocracy. The autocratic rulers of Massachusetts Bay could see little good in the democracy of Friends.[13]

The presence of Quakers in seventeenth-century England and New England also presented an opportunity for orthodox Puritans to give voice to their own anxieties about what constituted acceptable Christian identity and practice as opposed to illicit or blasphemous forms of religious piety. Put another way by historian Leo Damrosch, "The early Quaker movement, before it consolidated and conventionalized itself, involuntarily played the role of scapegoat for the ascendant Puritans. In effect, the Puritans affirmed their sense of righteousness by throwing Quakers in jail. This process was much assisted, in turn, by the willingness of many Quakers to persist in forms of behavior that were virtually guaranteed to elicit punishment."[14] So it was that Anglo-American Quakers, from almost the very beginning of the movement in the middle seventeenth century, became notable in the popular imagination—a popular imagination fueled by an incendiary print culture devoted to religious controversy—not merely for their radical religious ideas and seemingly peculiar social habits but also for their legendary willingness to be jailed or punished for their beliefs.

The traditional date of Quaker beginnings is 1652, when George Fox converted a number of his followers at the comfortable home of Judge Thomas Fell and his wife, Margaret (Fox's future wife) at Swarthmoor Hall in Lancashire, which is today recognized as the first Quaker meeting house.[15] But even before he established himself as a public figure and the central agent in inaugurating a movement that would eventually be named the Religious Society of Friends, Fox had already run afoul of the English authorities. He had from his youth been an iconoclast: one whose austere principles had caused him to refuse the consumption of alcohol and toasting of "healths" in a time and place when the consumption of large amounts of alcohol was a central fact of sociability in the public and private spheres. Clearly a charismatic and forceful evangelist, Fox appears not to have been entirely literate, since his posthumous journal was dictated to others and only later corrected for publication by well-educated Quakers including Thomas Ellwood and William Penn (1644–1718), the founder of Pennsylvania.[16] Other radicalisms also set him apart from his contemporaries, who were surprised and even offended by his refusal to offer alms to the poor and his unusual interest in the correct interpretation of his own religious dreams and the dreams of his fellow Quakers. In 1649 he had his first major confrontation with the intertwined religious and legal system in England, when—in a gesture toward what would become the crucial Quaker doctrine of the Inner Light—he was briefly jailed for blasphemy: specifically for preaching the primacy of Holy Spirit over Scripture. As his notoriety grew, he was on at least one occasion beaten and stoned by a mob in Nottinghamshire and then imprisoned once again in 1651. Sensing a serious threat to established order at the hands of these upstart religious radicals, the English press quickly responded, and soon it was seething with publications meant to disclose the degree to which they feared the spiritual terrorism of the Quakers. The tumultuous arrival of Fox and his followers onto the religious stage during these years made abundantly clear that the fiery and disruptive onslaught of the London Fire of 1647, which had thrown the city into turmoil, would be followed by a different version of social turmoil with the appearance of a fiery religious dissent by members of the early Quaker movement.[17]

The popular English and American press of the seventeenth century provides much evidence of the tensions caused by Quakers.[18] By 1655, barely a decade after George Fox, James Nayler, and the first generation of English Quakers had begun to make their controversial views known to their adversaries in the Anglican and Puritan communities through their itinerant ministries, the savage pamphlet wars were well under way. "It is evident," worried one seventeenth-century English pamphleteer about the upstart religion of the Friends, "in some instances that they are Anti-Magisterical, as well as Anti-Ministerial; yea that these Quakers use inchanted [*sic*] Bracelets, Potions, Sorcery and Witchcraft to intoxicate their Novices and draw them to their party." Other publications from the period were similarly apprehensive and inflammatory in their rhetoric about Quakerism. For example: *The Quaker's Terrible Vision, or the Devil's Progress to the City of London* (1655) and *The Quaker's Dream, or the Devil's Pilgrimage in England: Being an Infallible Relation of Their Several Meetings, Shreekings, Shakings, Quakings, Roarings, Yellings, Howlings, Tremblings, with a Narration of . . . The Strange and Wonderful Satanical Apparitions and the Appearing of the Devil unto Them in the Likeness of a Black Boar, a Dog with Flaming Eyes, and a Black Man without a Head, causing the Dogs to Bark, the Swine to Cry, and the Cattel to Run, etc* (1655). Private accounts of the Quaker faithful during the early years of the movement in England were similarly impressed, even dismayed, by the danger and disorderliness of these enthusiasts. The English diarist John Evelyn, visiting a group of Quakers in the Ipswich jail in 1656, found them to be "A new Phanatic sect of dangerous Principles, the[y] shew no respect to any man, magistrate, or other & seeme a melancholy proud sort of people."[19]

In England first, and soon after in the American colonies, Quakers—heedless of the objections to their faith that boiled over in the rough-and-tumble popular press—publicized their antagonism toward orthodox religion with theatrical abandon: itinerant preaching by women, noisy interruption of orthodox and Puritan church services, unclothed reveries and naked walks through the New England villages, public self-mortification with sackcloth and ashes. Many of these displays of extreme piety occurred after the most severe persecutions on the part of the Massachusetts Puritan community. Carla Pestana summarizes the demonstrative quality of early Quaker piety:

> Boston meeting . . . was interrupted repeatedly for two decades [after 1657]. Bottles were broken on the floor of the Boston meetinghouse in 1658 to illustrate the fate in store for the congregations. Quakers in New England did not adopt the more dramatic forms of witnessing, common in England by 1656, until after the most severe period of persecution had ended in 1661. On occasion, for two decades thereafter, meetings were disrupted by women who were either naked or clad in sackcloth and smeared in ashes. The former practice, referred to as "going naked for a sign," was meant to symbolize the nakedness of the unconvinced. . . . Their faith was universalistic and highly emotional, the direct converse of the Puritan's elitism and rationalism.[20]

The quaking fervency of the early New England Friends had its roots in the pioneering Quakers in England, who were described by one early historian of the movement as being given to spiritual histrionics and perfectly willing to be described as "Quakers" filled with the spirit of God: "These Men are called *Quakers* in the English Language. Which Name was given 'em by their mocking Enemies as a note of Ignominy and Contempt, for that when they are about contemplating Sacred things, that same very moment that the Spirit overtakes 'em, through the commotion of their Minds, and agitation of their Bodies, they presently fall a-trembling, throwing themselves on the ground, oft-times froathing at the mouth, and scrieching with a horrible noise. And though they seem to resent this Reproachful Title, yet they are not so averse either to the Name or to the Thing it self, but that they'll acknowledge that both do in some measure quadrate to them."[21] As may be seen from these descriptions of their provocative behavior, Quaker rebellion against orthodoxy constituted a direct if asymmetrical challenge to the strict modes of civil and religious authority that Puritanism (and Roman Catholicism) held dear. Immediately upon their appearance in America, this sect "seen through the eyes of a mid-seventeenth-century saint" like the fiery minister John Norton, who was commissioned by the Bay Colony's General Court to write and publish his virulently anti-Quaker tract, *The Heart of New England Rent* (1659), "represented an awesome threat to all that was godly in this world."[22] The Quaker religious community—who in later generations would earn a reputation for sobriety, restraint, thrift, and silence—were frequently disruptive and charismatic activists on the hotly contested religious stage of early England and America.[23]

The first Quaker missionaries to the American colonies arrived several decades after the establishment of the Puritan community in Massachusetts, and their presence in New England—and to a lesser degree in the Middle Atlantic colonies—was immediately perceived as a potential threat to religious and social order. Those early Quakers who made the transatlantic voyage were no doubt a hardy lot to have made the still-arduous voyage by sea, as evidenced by some of the accounts left by seventeenth-century missionary Friends. On his way to America in 1659, just a few years after the exiled Quaker Mary Dyer's return from Rhode Island to Massachusetts, the twenty-two-year-old Quaker John Taylor wrote vividly of the danger and hardships of setting out by ship for the long journey to America: "altho' we had a long Passage, and much contrary Winds, being Ten Weeks before we arrived at our desired Haven in *New England:* And being short of Victuals and Drink, some of the Seamen got Rats and Eat them; and when it rained, we took up the Rain-water off the Deck to Drink; yet in all these our Exercises and Troubles, the Lord our God was with us."[24] Making matters considerably worse for earnest missionaries like John Taylor was a long-standing enmity between Quakers and established religious authorities, which had been raging in England ever since the charismatic nineteen-year-old George Fox had begun to preach against the state-controlled English Church in 1643.

Shock waves from the Quaker attack on established orthodoxies were not long in arriving, even on distant shores across the Atlantic, where the Massachusetts Bay Colony began to confront and then to legislate against its own immigrant cohort of Quaker ministers. Under enormous practical stress because of colonial privation, Native American attacks, and the nuisance of other radical Puritan dissenters, in 1658 Massachusetts quickly passed harsh legislation intended to purge the Bay Colony of Quakers. The decree of the General Court in October of that year gives a strong impression of the anxiety that Quakers had managed to create in the colony, as well as the merciless punishment (imprisonment, speedy trial, followed by banishment upon pain of death) intended for those foolhardy enough to be identified as members of the Quaker sect:

> Whereas there is a pernicious sect (commonly called Quakers) lately risen, who by word and writing have published and maintained many dangerous and horrid tenets, and do take upon them to change and alter the received laudable customs of our nation, in giving civil respect to equals, or reverence to superiors, whose actions tend to undermine the civil government, and also to destroy the order of the churches, by denying all established forms of worship, allowed and approved by all orthodox professors of the Truth, and instead thereof, and in opposition thereunto, frequently meeting themselves, insinuating themselves into the minds of the simple, or such as are least affected to the order and government of church and commonwealth, herby divers of our inhabitants have been infected, and . . . have not been deterred from their impetuous attempts to undermine our peace, and hazard our ruin.[25]

In this early American law the primary objection to Quaker practice can be discerned: an antinomian unwillingness to bow before authority and traditional modes of worship and respect. As such, the Quaker/Puritan disputes in early New England register not only theological differences but also a radical and deeply threatening new way of thinking about personal autonomy and individual control over religious life. The extent to which Quakers were perceived as radical and dangerous is indicated by the emergence of laws such as this legal statement of the Boston General Court, which specifies that such punishments shall be carried out expeditiously and that "the cursed sect of the Quakers" could be "apprehended without warrant, where no magistrate is at hand, by any constable, commissioner, or select man." Cleansing Massachusetts of the Quaker menace thus came to be a civic duty for all of those

Puritans who still desired to defend the "orthodox received opinions of the godly."[26]

In reacting to the threat posed by the new modes of religious thinking favored by the Quakers, the orthodox authorities in New England immediately saw that at the core of Quaker radicalism lay a profound restlessness under the yoke of traditional arrangements of social and political power. In making the case about the danger of the Quaker threat to established authority, anti-Quaker pamphleteers frequently pointed not only to the Quaker theology itself (which was largely uncodified in the mid-seventeenth century) but also to perceived similarities between the religious mischief of the Quakers and the more familiar corruptions of the Roman Church. Degeneracy and heresy from either side, Quaker or Catholic, according to such a point of view, deserved to be vanquished by the violently retributive justice of orthodox power. "How potent a temptation," wrote the formidable Anglo-American Puritan divine John Norton in his famous attack on Quakers in 1659, "the opening of an opportunity to the irregenerate and hungry multitude, of changing places with their Superiors, and possessing themselves with their power, honor and estates, is." Using an authoritarian rhetoric grounded on the need for both state security and compulsory religious belief, Norton explains his desire to strike fear and obedience into the hearts of those who would presume to arrogate power to themselves against the law of orthodoxy:

> That magistrates may and ought to put forth their coercive power in matters of Religion is so clear a Scripture Truth, and so mighty a Principle (as it hath been asserted by Mr. Cobbet and other in their Books published) that I am confident that Religion will never stand long where it is forsaken; and if coercive power, then corporal punishment in meet cases. For my own part, my own spirit doth (with yours) incline to gentleness and tenderness, as much as may be with public safety; but when I consider of it, I cannot see but that the terror of the Sword of Magistracy is to be used against such a plotted, Jesuitical, mischievous Design, as this of Quakerism is.[27]

The sort of freethinking in religion that Quakerism represented to a man like John Norton, an ardent opponent of any form of antinomianism since his emigration from England in 1635, was also anathema to most other church leaders in New England, although some were less bigoted in their expressions of disapproval. For the first several decades of Quaker activity in New England, then, Quakers were not merely outside of the mainstream of religious activity; they (along with a few other small, radical Puritan sects) came to stand for a potentially grave threat to the essential civic fabric woven from sturdy threads of legal order and prescriptive religious piety.[28]

Viewed from a longer historical perspective, early Quakers were, in fact, significant activists in the vanguard of Western democracy. They were also championing their religious freedoms more than a century too early to have made meaningful inroads against the arrangements of social and religious power that the Puritans had imported to New England. Consequently, American Quakers became subject to all manner of harsh condemnation during the seventeenth century. For example, banishments at first and, eventually, executions were prescribed for infamous Boston Quakers like Mary Dyer, William Robinson, and Marmaduke Stephenson, all of whom were hanged during an early Massachusetts crackdown on Quakers in 1659 and 1660.[29] Mary Dyer was especially relentless in her pursuit of religious freedom for Quakers in Massachusetts. Having narrowly avoided execution alongside Robinson and Stephenson, who were hanged in 1659—Dyer's arms and legs had been bound, her faced covered, and the noose placed around her neck when a cry went up that she had been granted an official reprieve—she was banished to Rhode Island. This shocking turn of events, we now know, had been calculated by the Massachusetts General Court, who had already determined that Mary Dyer would be sentenced to banishment, but only after having observed the execution of her Quaker comrades.[30] William Sewel, an important eighteenth-century chronicler of the Quaker movement, analyzed the Dyer's gallows reprieve as an instance of anxiety among magistrates who had sensed in the gathered mob an authentic sympathy for the Quaker martyrs and for the formidable Mary Dyer: "The magistrates now perceiving that the putting William Robinson and Marmaduke Stevenson to death, caused great discontent among the people, resolved to send away Mary Dyar [*sic*], thereby to calm their minds a little. And so she was put on horseback, and by four horse-men conveyed fifteen miles toward Rhode-Island, where she was left with a horse and a man, to be conveyed the rest of the way; which she soon sent back, and so repaired home. By the stile of her letters, and her undaunted carriage, it appears that she had indeed some extraordinary qualities; I find also, that she was of a comely and grave countenance, of a good family and estate, and a mother of several children."[31] Only upon Mary Dyer's defiant return to Massachusetts

Mary Dyer being led to the gallows. Unknown artist. Nineteenth century, public domain.

the next year, after lengthy sojourns first in Rhode Island and then on Long Island, would colonial Governor John Endicott—with the staunch support of the Reverend John Norton—finally carry out her death sentence. On 1 June 1660 she was taken to the Boston Common and hanged. Dyer was followed to the gallows on 14 March 1661 by another Quaker, the eloquent preacher William Leddra, who also was hanged for blasphemy just before the arrival of a decree against executions by Charles II, thereby achieving the unfortunate distinction of being the last Quaker to be executed in New England.[32]

Thanks in part to his reading of a Quaker martyr tract written by George Bishop that recounted the trial and execution of Mary Dyer, Charles II finally ordered the Massachusetts Bay Colony to put an end to Quaker executions in 1661. Nevertheless, violent persecutions continued as residents of the Bay Colony attempted to cleanse their settlements of the Quaker menace. Adding to the difficulties for colonial Friends, the lackadaisical authority of Charles II's government (Perry Miller characterized the administration of Charles II as "inefficient, dilatory, absentminded, inconsistent, and in general stupid"[33]) allowed the Quaker persecutions to continue for at least five years after the protective order. Having already anticipated the role of persecution in the formation of

Quaker identity, a prescient George Fox had directed English Friends to keep careful records of their sufferings, which in turn led to a substantial hagiographical literature written by Friends in subsequent decades.[34] In 1717 William Sewel, a Dutch Quaker and historian whose parents were among the first generation of convinced Quakers, summarized the slow progress of royal toleration for Quakers. By the 1660s, Sewel states, Friends and their sympathizers in the popular press had taken it upon themselves to record many accounts of violence and discrimination against Quakers. Although Quakers for the most part seem to have stoically endured their persecutions—"they did not think it unlawful, to give notice of the grievous oppression [suffered by Quakers], to those in authority, lest they might have excused themselves as ignorant of these violent proceedings. Therefore it was not omitted to publish in public print, many . . . crying instances . . . and to present them to king and parliament, with humble addresses to that purpose." Still, according to accounts by a variety of observers, including Sewel, true religious toleration for Friends was slow in coming in England or America. A succession of monarchs, though, finally provided relief over the course of several decades, "King Charles II [1660–85] it seems was not to be the man that should take off this yoke of oppression: this work was reserved for others. His brother James [1685–88] that succeeded him, made a beginning thereof, with what intention heaven knows; and William III [1689–1702], that excellent prince, brought it to perfection as far as it was in his power."[35]

As in England, slow progress in legislating religious toleration also meant fierce and violent opposition to the early American Quakers. Just a few years after the Quaker arrival in New England, as Cristine Levenduski recently observed, "the Massachusetts General Court immediately instituted in 1661 the Cart and Whip Act, which directed that Quakers be tied to the back of a cart and whipped as the cart slowly moved through the town. When the cart reached the next town, that town would assume the whipping duties until the Quakers had been 'whipped out' of the colony." Short of execution, continuing punitive measures against Quakers included indentured servitude, beatings, banishments, imprisonments, brandings, fines, and ghastly measures such as that proposed for Quakers not intimidated by branding, ear-cropping, whipping, imprisonment, and servitude. Following the example of the punishment meted out in England for the troublesome Quaker evangelist James Nayler, the American colonial authorities ruled that "for every Quaker, he or she, that shall a fourth time herein again offend, they shall have their tongues bored through with a hot iron."[36] Of Quaker fortitude in resisting such violent persecutions, the Quaker poet John Greenleaf Whittier would memorialize these victims centuries later as those "Whose fervor jail nor pillory could tame / Proud of the cropped ears meant to be their shame."[37]

John Rouse and John Copeland, writing to the king in 1661 on behalf of their fellow Massachusetts Quakers who were still being persecuted, in spite of Charles II's orders, catalogued a detailed list of grisly punishments enacted against those who aided or abetted in any way the Quaker movement. Although imprisonments were common for Quakers who appeared to pose a threat to the community welfare, public reprisals were the order of the day:

> *Two* beaten with *Pitched Ropes,* the blows amounting to an *Hundred and Thirty nine,* by which one of them was brought near unto Death, much of his Body being beaten *like unto a Jelly,* and one of their Doctors, a Member of their Church, who saw him, said *It would be a Miracle if ever he recovered, he expecting the Flesh should rot off the Bones,* who afterwards was *banished upon pain of Death.* There are many Witnesses of this there.[38]

Rouse and Copeland had been no strangers to the sorts of punishments that their letter of complaint described. Years before their appeal, they stood defiant in the face of arrest and a sentence of banishment from the Bay Colony. Escorted to the border by deputies of the magistrate, the two men in company with another Quaker named Christopher Holder responded by immediately returning to Massachusetts. When they were discovered by authorities in Dedham, they were arrested once more and taken to Boston, where they were punished by having their ears removed on 7 September 1658.[39]

Quakers continued for decades to be imprisoned in England for their religious views, until relief in the form of religious tolerance legislation was finally enacted in 1689, but the damage to the movement had already been done. Between 1660 and 1680 more than ten thousand Quakers, George Fox among them, were given long jail sentences, suggesting something of the vigor with which Friends were prosecuted during those years. Leo Damrosch concludes that during these decades, "the first generation of [Quaker] leaders was largely wiped out."[40] In the process of having its leadership harassed and incarcerated, however, the Quakers did succeed in creating a somewhat sympathetic impression of their faith among some elements of the public. However peculiar and dangerous they may have appeared during the first half century of their religious activities, by the eighteenth century English and American Quakers were gradually accepted as legitimate, even admirable, members of their communities. Officially, religious acceptance for Quakers began with the Toleration Act (1689), which finally made religious nonconformity legal, albeit with some restrictions and limits, including oaths of loyalty to the crown, a declaration against transubstantiation (aimed at papists), and registration of meetinghouses. In practice, though, the Quaker stipulation against the taking of oaths—to say nothing of their commitment to nonviolence—created severe impediments to the legal and political dimensions of their citizenship well into the nineteenth century.

So distressed were New England colonial authorities about the potential subversiveness and power of early Quaker theology that when Ann Austin and Mary Fisher, the first two Quaker preachers to set sail from England to America, arrived in Boston Harbor in July 1656, they were arrested while still on board *The Swallow*, which had recently sailed to Boston from Barbados, which at that time had a significant Quaker community.[41] This episode of detention (and eventually physical examination of the Quaker by Puritan midwives, in order to determine whether the missionaries might also be witches or agents of the devil[42]), discloses a number of concerns related to the conflict between opposed groups of Protestant radicals. The arrest of Austin and Fisher, which occurred at a crucial moment in the settlement of the Massachusetts Bay Colony, is an overdetermined historical event and one that sheds light on the fraught confluence of rising literacy, political struggle, and shifting gender relations. Anxiety about the influence of Quakerism on the established religious order in Massachusetts apparently stemmed from multiple causes. Because of the very high rates of literacy among dissenting Protestants, the circulation of controversial religious literature and ideas (such as those promulgated by Ann Austin and Mary Fisher) was a legitimate concern that grew more worrisome with each passing year, as the transmission of printed materials into the colonies grew more efficient. Adding to the difficulties for those among the orthodox who would object to the Quaker presence in America, Quaker missionaries would manage to visit all of the existing American colonies on the Atlantic seaboard, and would also make visits to West Indian settlements like Barbados, within a few years of their first arrival in Massachusetts.

Quaker planters in Barbados. Source: Carel Allard, Orbis Habitabilis Oppidaet Vestitus (Amsterdam [1680?]), number 88. Copper plate engraving, titled "Engelse Quakers en Tabak Planters aende Barbados" [English Quakers and Tobacco Planters in Barbados], shows European woman and man, slaves carrying goods on heads, houses and shipping in background. The Library of Congress tentatively dates its copy of Allard at 1698 and the British Library at 1680. There are colored copies of the print dating from a later period. During the mid- to late-seventeenth century, Barbados had a relatively large Quaker community that included many slaveholders; before the island's "sugar revolution" in the mid-seventeenth century, tobacco was an important cash crop.

By 1660, Quaker missionaries had produced converts in all American colonies with the possible exception of Connecticut.[43]

In seventeenth-century New England, the importation of religious tracts and pamphlets was a particular concern because of the nature of colonial governance and the resulting centralization of political authority. First, in the Massachusetts Bay Colony, religious pamphlets promoting heretical views thus constituted not only an irritating blasphemous gesture but also a treasonous act, given a colonial social order tightly cross-stitched with a dense fabric of mutually constitutive civil and religious laws. Second, from its inception, the Religious Society of Friends permitted and encouraged the ministry of women specifically and women's rights more generally. Moreover, as Carol F. Karlsen suggests in her analysis of colonial witchcraft, there initially were concerns that some Quaker women practiced witchcraft, which helps to explain the stark scene on shipboard as Ann Austin and Mary Fisher were being detained by the Massachusetts Puritan authorities:

> Acting Governor Richard Bellingham ordered both Austin and Fisher stripped naked on board ship and their bodies examined for signs of Devil worship. Their possessions were searched for books containing "corrupt, heretical, and blasphemous Doctrines." Apparently the incriminating evidence was found, for the literature they brought with them was burned and the women incarcerated in the Boston jail. So dangerous were these two women to Puritan society that the windows of their cells were boarded up and a fine of £5 was levied on anyone who tried to speak with them. After five weeks of confinement, they were thrown out of the colony without a trial.[44]

When the women were discovered to have smuggled a trove of more than one hundred books in their baggage, not only were the books confiscated and destroyed but the books were "by an order of the council, burnt in the marketplace by the hangman."[45] Furthermore, when the women were stripped naked and jailed in Boston by order of the deputy-governor, "their pens, ink, and paper were taken from them, and they [were] not suffered to have any candle-light in the night-season."[46] This coercive scene of persecution shows two important dimensions of Quaker culture in America: (1) its dissemination at the hands of women activists, and (2) its capable use of print culture to advance its distinctive theology and moral views. In the centuries that followed the forcible deportation of the Austin and Fisher, women would remain central figures in the advancement and representation of Quakerism in America. So too would the burgeoning world of print culture serve as a theater in which Quakers would apply themselves as religious activists while at the same time becoming staple figures in the representation of American religious life. It is striking to observe, though, the ways in which Quaker women, especially, who in the seventeenth century had been called "monstrous," "diabolical," and "a contagion" by Puritan clergy like John Norton and Cotton Mather would, many generations later, eventually become idealized by many of the descendants of the Puritan faithful and not just by Quakers themselves.[47]

Eventually, tolerance for Quakers did arrive in colonial Massachusetts, as it would in the rest of New England, but the early colonial years were ones in which Quakers were regularly abused and rejected by the established authorities. As the historian Jonathan Chu has shown, the perceived and actual disruptiveness of American Quakers in the seventeenth century led to a host of confrontations with the colonial magistrates: "Connecticut banished all the Quakers found in its jurisdiction. New Haven not only banished them, it also branded one, Humphrey Norton, with an 'H' to denote his heresy. New Plymouth was also disturbed by the increasing number of disorderly incidents in Sandwich, Duxbury, Marshfield, and Scituate caused by Quakers en route to Boston from Rhode Island."[48] Connecticut law was clearly written to punish dissenting sects like the Quakers and anyone who made bold to sympathize with them. In 1702, for example, fifty years after the first Quaker arrivals in New England, the Connecticut Acts and Laws still specified that "no Persons in this Colony shall give any unnecessary Entertainment unto any Quaker, Ranter, Adamite, or other notorious Heretick, upon penalty of *Five Pounds* for every such persons Entertainment, to be paid by him that so Entertains them: and *Five Pounds per* Week shall be paid by each Town, that shall suffer their Entertainment as aforesaid."[49]

Harsh as all of this persecution may sound, however, it seems fair to say that the intolerance directed by the New England orthodox churches and magistrates toward Quakers was not unique in the American colonies. In her *Summary History of New-England* (1799), Hannah Adams learned from her researches into colonial archives that, far from distinguishing themselves from other colonial settlers for their intolerance, New Englanders resembled their counterparts elsewhere in America. Although highly critical of the New England authorities who treated Quakers with such brutality, Adams wrote that "Several acts of the Virginia assembly of 1659, 1662, and 1663, had made it penal in the parents to refuse to have their children baptized; had prohibited the unlawful assembling of Quakers; had made it penal for any master of a vessel to bring a Quaker into the state; had ordered those already there, and such as should come thereafter, to be imprisoned till they should abjure the country; provided a milder punishment for their first and second return, but death for the third; had inhibited all persons from suffering their meetings in or near their houses, entertaining them individually, or disposing of books which supported their tenets." Probably it was luck—but certainly not conditions of religious toleration—concludes Adams, that prevented Quakers from suffering capital punishment in rugged outposts like the seventeenth-century Virginia colony.[50]

Before Quaker faith could be practiced openly in the other New England colonies, Rhode Island had begun grudgingly to permit

Quakerism. In 1657, at the behest of then-governor Benedict Arnold, freedom of religious expression was mandated for all persons, thus allowing Rhode Island to become an important sanctuary for the Religious Society of Friends.[51] Although Rhode Island at the time did not belong to the Union, the Commissioners of the United Colonies made an unsuccessful attempt in early 1657—before Arnold's proclamation of toleration for Quakers was published—to persuade Rhode Island to banish Quakers from their jurisdictions. By the time George Fox finally made a tour of the American colonies in 1672, he discovered that Newport, Rhode Island, had already become an important Quaker community, along with outposts of the Quaker faithful not only in the territory that would become eastern Pennsylvania but also in places like Maine, the Carolinas, Virginia, and Maryland. Perry Miller has noted the capacity of Rhode Island's colonial leadership to see the ironies of attempting to persecute a group who had "proved, when tolerated, to be hostile only against persecutors." Miller cites the Rhode Island authorities as explaining that "Surely we find that they delight to be persecuted by civill powers, and when they are soe, they are like to gain more adherents by the conseyte of their patient sufferings than by consent to their pernicious sayings."[52] Although Boston itself continued for years its illegal attacks on and punishments of Quakers, Plymouth Colony in Massachusetts also received Quaker migrants and converts; Quaker meetings and eventually their meetinghouses were established by 1660 in the coastal Cape Cod villages of Sandwich (a community south of Plymouth facing north onto Cape Cod Bay) and Falmouth (easily accessible by sailing east across Buzzard's Bay from Quaker Rhode Island).

In scenarios that would be replayed many times during early American history, Quaker principles formed a crucial nexus in debates concerning military allegiance, violent acts, and national allegiance. As in England during the early years of the Quaker movement, vitriolic debates over Quaker theology and its relation to the colonial project ensued through pamphlet wars in the thriving bookstalls of the late eighteenth-century American colonies. One of the major issues in these debates was the pacifist role of Quakers in conflicts between colonists and Native Americans. For instance, the anonymous pamphleteer "Philopatrius," writing from Philadelphia in 1764, assailed the Quaker attempts at protecting Natives for being at best hypocrisy and at worst a defense of their avarice or alleged sexual promiscuity:

That the Quakers have been partial, and shewn more real Affection for Enemy Savages than for their fellow Subjects, of certain Denominations, is so well known in this Province, and has on the present Occasion [of the Paxton Boys controversy, the frontier Scots-Irish who slew dozens of Moravian Indians] been so fully demonstrated to the World, that I should deem it Loss of Time to say any more on so recent and glaring a Fact: Whether the Affection which some Principals of that Sect have shewn to Indians, and the great Care they are now taking of them can possible be owing to the Charms of their Squaws, to any particular Advantages that may arise from their Trade, or perhaps rather from the Use they have made of them to asperse the Proprietaries and oppose their Interests, may be considered as a vain Question, which I will not undertake to determine.[53]

During the Paxton Boys controversy, there were other Philadelphians who defended the Quaker position of sympathy toward Native Americans, as with the pamphlet response by "Philanthropos" later in 1764. Much of the sympathy expressed by Philanthropos was rooted in his understanding of nonviolent Christian principles generally, but also in his perception of Friends as a historically persecuted sect whose sufferings had frequently come at the cruel hands of unworthy men. "I have never been told by any moderate Man," writes Philanthropos:

> that the Quakers have ever been a troublesome restless People under any Government, although I believe they have suffered the most of any religious Society now in the World, and that for Conscience sake only; how zealously steady were they at the Time that King Charles the First and Oliver [Cromwell], when in the Height of all the Quarrel; Did the Quakers ever riot, Mutiny, or plot against the Government. No but bore every Revolution with Meekness and Fortitude; in the Times of their Persecutions, when their Meetings were broken up by Officers, themselves thrown into nasty Dungeons, others suffered a Confiscation of their whole Estate, some died in Prison: in short every way afflicted that Malice could think of, and the chief Instigators of this were Men as like [Philopatrius], as a Cock is like a Dunghill Fowle.[54]

The curious doubling—or paradox—of Quaker identity is thus evident from this exchange of pamphlets associated with the protection of Native Americans. Whereas Philopatrius singles out Quakers as greedy, treacherous, and possibly licentious sympathizers with the enemy, Philanthropos defends Quaker pacifism and sympathy with Natives as fundamentally in keeping with shared Christian principles. As the Paxton

Boys controversy and the ensuing pamphlet exchanges reveal, paradox followed the evolution of Quaker religion in America, with irony not far behind. Looking through the ashes of the burned Millersburg, Pennsylvania, cabin where the first six Natives had been massacred, colonists discovered a bag containing the Susquehannock Natives' 1701 treaty signed by the Quaker governor William Penn, in which he had promised that the colonists and the Indians "shall forever hereafter be as one Head & One Heart, & live in true Friendship & Amity as one People."

Although Pennsylvania Quakers did not formally renounce office holding in Pennsylvania until 1756, when the colony's declaration of war against the Delaware and Shawnee Natives forced them to into a decision confirming the nonviolent principles that would compel them to resign from the Pennsylvania Assembly, there had long been signs that they would eventually do so, and for several reasons. Since the earliest years of the movement, Quakers had been ostracized and punished for their refusal to take oaths in court and for their unwillingness to bear the deadly arms thought necessary for warfare and criminal justice. This unwillingness to swear oaths in turn prevented Quakers from serving on juries or accepting elected offices, which would have entailed oaths about duty and loyalty.[55] Thus, lacking the ability to provide sworn testimony in court thus had always made awkward and rare any Quaker presence in government, and their devotion to pacifism made it impossible for them to serve in the military.[56] For early Quakers, civic life frequently was sacrificed because of religious commitments. As Thomas Budd, a seventeenth-century Philadelphia Quaker, wrote in a testimony published in 1692, the religious choice made by Quakers was one not merely for Christianity, but for Christian perfection, so that "If thou wilt be perfect leave the Worldly Government, and follow Christ, in order to attain the desired Perfection." At the same time, Quakers like Budd were unable to conceive of a civil authority in which physical force and punishments were absent. While insisting that Quakers could play no active part in "worldly" or carnal governance, he does insist that those Christians not called to the perfectionism of the Quaker life must be the ones to carry out warfare and corporal punishments because "for our part we do see it very clearly and plainly, that the use of the Sword, or of some carnal or bodily Weapons, is so necessary to the Worldly Magistrate to punish such as deserve it, as the executive part of his Office cannot in an ordinary way (and without Miracles) be done without it." In short, despite his Quaker beliefs, Budd was unable to conceive of civil order that did not include the use of arms to enforce the law, or the punishment of serious crimes without resort to corporal punishment. On the one hand, he argues that Quakers must avoid participation not only in wars but in physical punishments, "All rational men will judge, that a pair of Stocks, Whipping Post, and Gallows, are carnal Weapons, as really as Sword or Gun, and so is a Constable's Staff, when used, as hath been by some, to beat and knock down the Bodies of some obstinate Persons, etc." But on the other hand, Budd also acknowledged that civil governance is authorized by divine providence and therefore must be maintained according to Christian principles, albeit by non-Quakers: "To prevent all occasion or mistakes or offence, we do solemnly declare our persuasion, that we really believe and are persuaded, that Magistracy and Worldly Government in as Ordinance of God, and every Magistrate, lawfully called to his Office, is the Minister of God, a Revenger to execute Wrath upon him that doth evil, and that he beareth not the Sword in vain, the which Sword is the Sword of Justice, that ought to be drawn to punish Offenders with corporal Punishment, greater or smaller, according to the Offence." With such apparently contradictory testimony, it is not difficult to understand the frustration felt by non-Quaker authorities when faced with this group of radical dissenting Christians who appeared to desire Christian perfection in their lives while remaining unwilling to take up the arms against enemies of the state or—even more incredibly—to carry out the requisite harsh punishments on the bodies of criminals.[57]

As Quaker rebelliousness against the strictures of civil and ecclesiastical authority in New England went into decline during the 1660s, Quakers began to develop stable and prosperous communities of their own in places like Rhode Island, Cape Cod, and especially eastern Pennsylvania and the Delaware River Valley region. Despite the difficult colonial beginnings for Friends, whose persecution endured for the second half of the seventeenth century, their growing reputation for honesty and truthfulness led soon to prosperity in the commercial arena in both England and America. Although he had himself suffered persecution during his early years as an evangelist, George Fox lived long enough to see Quakers thrive in business. Because, reflected Fox,

> Friends could not put off their hats to people, nor say you to a particular, but thee and thou; and could not bow, nor use the world's salutations nor fashions nor customs . . . the people would not trade with them nor trust them. And for a time people that were tradesmen could hardly get money enough to buy bread, but afterwards when people

came to see Friends' honesty and truthfulness and "yea" and "nay" at a word in their dealing, and their lives and conversations did preach and reach to the witness of God in all people, and they knew and saw that they would not cozen and cheat them for conscience sake towards God:—and that at last they might send any child and be as well used as themselves at any of their shops, so then the things altered so that all the inquiry was where was a draper or shopkeeper or tailor or shoemaker or any other tradesman that was a Quaker: then that was all the cry, insomuch that Friends had double the trade beyond any of their neighbors: and if there was any trading they had it, insomuch that the cry was of all the professors and others, if we let these people alone they will take the trade of the nation out of our hands.[58]

The American Quaker success in commercial enterprises reflected a similar development in England. Even by the early 1650s, according to Larzer Ziff, "The Quaker movement began so rapid a growth in England that by the end of the century Gracechurch Street [Quaker] Meeting in London was made up of the richest traders in the city: Barclays, Gurneys, Hanburys, Osboods, Hoares, Dimsdales, and Christys."[59] Eastern Pennsylvania, with its superb farmland and its bustling major port of Philadelphia, rapidly became a destination of choice for the increasingly prosperous English Quakers immigrating to the American colonies. By the early 1680s William Penn had finally laid claim to part of the newly named Pennsylvania in the mid-Atlantic colonies after Charles II of England settled a £16,000 debt to Penn's late father by providing a large tract of colonial land to William himself. With unprecedented religious tolerance promised in the new colony of Pennsylvania, Quaker migration to Pennsylvania and other areas of the Middle Atlantic region began in earnest, with thousands of English Quakers following Penn to the New World after his arrival in what would later become the Commonwealth of Pennsylvania. Thomas D. Hamm has observed that increased migration to America led eventually to increasing prosperity among Quakers, as well as better-organized (and sometimes lessradical) Quaker church bureaucracies: "Migration [of English Friends to Pennsylvania] began in 1681, and by the end of 1683 more than three thousand Friends had arrived. They quickly replicated the system of monthly, quarterly meetings that George Fox had established earlier. . . . The first sessions of Philadelphia Yearly Meeting were held in the fall of 1681."[60] As the seventeenth century drew to a close, however, Quakers

had relinquished most of their evangelical enthusiasm for converting
others to their faith, and would seldom proselytize until the schism of
1827, when the followers of Elias Hicks (1748–1830) parted ways with
the more evangelically oriented branch of American Quakerism.[61]

The nineteenth-century marketplace of print would document
amply what can be understood as the late phase of Quaker controversialism, which occurred in the late seventeenth and early eighteenth
century (see chapter 5 for a discussion of Quakers in American fiction).
Still operating at the margins of American religious discourse, Quaker
civic moralism would see its legitimacy in the public sphere grow as increasing numbers of American citizens grew sympathetic with the Un-
ionist and abolitionist causes. This late phase of controversialism, however, followed many decades during which religious writings vigorously
promoting or disparaging their Quaker views had been a steady seller in
the marketplace of English—and later American—print culture. Enthusiasm for printed works dealing with Quakerism was especially fervent
during the first half century of the movement (1650–1700), as may be
seen from Edwin B. Bronner's observations in his introduction to an
anthology of early Quaker publications. Bronner estimates that in addition to a rich assortment of Quaker manuscripts and letters extant from
that period, Friends also published at least 3,750 books, while a corresponding number of anti-Quaker tracts also appeared in response.[62] In
a somewhat more conservative but still impressive estimate of Quaker
activity in publishing, Elbert Russell observes that although there were
some arrests of English Quakers for circulating religious printed materials, the efforts made by Oliver Cromwell on behalf of religious toleration led to a tremendous outpouring of Quaker writing in the years during and just after the Commonwealth period, and he concludes that "In
the seven decades after 1653 there were 440 Quaker writers, who published 2,678 separate publications, varying from a single page tract to fo-
lios of nearly a thousand pages." Recent analysis by the print historian
Kate Peters indicates that about one hundred identifiably "Quaker"
writers had published 291 works in England by as early as 1656, and that
of these writers, the most prolific appear to have been residents of Yorkshire and Westmorland, two areas visited by the Quaker evangelist
George Fox in 1652.[63]

This intense religious controversy, which thrived in the public sphere
of theological discourse in Anglo-American print culture from 1650 to

at least 1800, diminished substantially as Quakers underwent a number of changes internal and external to their religious organization as a society. First, Quakers by the early decades of the eighteenth century entered what has frequently been described as a substantially more quietistic period, during which their religious expression was marked far less by exuberance and enthusiasm and far more by the central religious experience of the silent meeting for worship. As Phyllis Mack has argued in her analysis of eighteenth-century Quaker women, "By the 1730s, Quakerism had evolved from a movement of radical visionaries into a community of respectable citizens. Although the first Friends continued to be revered as heroes within the movement, the new generation of leaders no longer countenanced the traumatic physical and emotional violence of the early, ecstatic, quaking Friends, who preached naked and in sackcloth and whose words evoked the convulsive, apocalyptic language of ancient Hebrew prophets."[64] In her study of Elizabeth Ashbridge, a charismatic Quaker preacher of the early eighteenth century, Julie Sievers arrives at a similar conclusion by noting the exceptional nature of Ashbridge's return to primitive Quaker enthusiasm. Most Quakers by this time had become oriented toward order rather than toward inspiration: "as the Society of Friends became an increasingly well-ordered institution, divine madness could come to be seen as a threat, rather than as a necessary component of piety. Friends . . . attempt[ed] to define their differences from other reforming Protestants. Their internal reform movement, begun in the late 1750s, often focused upon increasing group solidarity within the Quaker community by regularizing and disciplining outward behavior. Instead of a socially disruptive spirituality, reformers sough to produce a socially predictable morality."[65]

An anonymous British essay review, which surveyed a number of key Quaker historical texts for an 1891 issue of the *Edinburgh Review*, assessed the eighteenth-century Quaker transformation away from enthusiasm in similar terms, noting approvingly the shift by Friends from disruptive sect to serene religious outsiders with even the once-fervent George Fox serving as a notable example of the quickly evolving Quaker restraint: "The sectarian wild-oat sowing, which is so pronounced in the case of the [early] Friends, subsides into a calm placid serenity, unexampled in the evolution of any other body of English Christians. The vehemently fermenting spirit, with its natural products of froth and scum, is gradually transformed into a potent liquor, becoming continually clearer and stronger as it reaches its mellow maturity. Passing from the first years of

George Fox's activity, with its unseemly violence and eccentricity, its perpetual outrages on the religious belief and social usages of his fellow Englishmen, to the later years of his life, is like passing from a savage desert into a cultivated religion." In addition, as the reviewer more succinctly described the situation, the new "cultivated" religiosity of the Quakers decimated their numbers through the "minute scrupulosity" of their discipline, and their membership in the eighteenth century was quickly hollowed out by what he calls "the peevish stepmotherly severity of Quaker discipline."[66] After the very earliest years of Quaker settlement in America, most New England and Pennsylvania Quakers had already begun to repudiate the most radical expressive practices of splinter sects such as the "singing Quakers" or "Ranters," and this conservative and traditionalizing trend of restrained worship continued into the nineteenth century.[67]

One should be cautious, though, in presuming that intensity of belief and piety among Quakers had uniformly evaporated during these years, as the example of pious Quakers like Jane Hoskens (1694–ca. 1760) can attest. After emigrating from England to Philadelphia at the age of nineteen, Hoskens worked as an indentured servant, specifically as a teacher for prosperous Quaker families in Philadelphia. Later, having converted to the Quaker faith, she became an enthusiastic and influential Quaker preacher, who by the time she was thirty had already traveled widely in America. She continued for many years to preach the Quaker message in New York, Massachusetts, Jersey, Maryland, Virginia, North Carolina, Delaware, and Rhode Island, with additional itinerant missions to Barbados, Ireland, and England. She is also notable for having written a popular memoir, *The Life and Spiritual Sufferings of the Faithful Servant of Christ Jane Hoskens, a Public Preacher Among the People Called Quakers* (1771), the first autobiography to be published in America by a Quaker woman. Although Hoskens describes the Quaker meetings she attended as being generally silent rather than effusive or rapturous, she also indicates that her own favored practice was to attend meetings on a daily basis rather than only on First Day (Sunday). Daily meetings—a sure sign of fervency of religious practice—were apparently available to her not only in Pennsylvania but also in many of the colonies and countries that she visited.[68] Nevertheless, and despite the example of enthusiastic Quakers like Hoskens, these were also the years when Quakerism began its unmistakable decline in popularity as a religion. Within the Quaker fold, stricter versions of the Quaker discipline, which were enacted steadily during the late eighteenth century, reshaped the Quaker faith not only by forbidding its members to hold slaves but also by strengthening the rules concerning marriage outside the faith. Consequently, between 1750 and 1850 large numbers of Quaker youth were abandoning the Society of Friends voluntarily or being "read out of meeting" for having transgressed the strict principle of intradenominational marriage.

As Quakers diminished the level of their threatening behavior toward other denominations, the American branch of orthodox Puritanism itself underwent its well-documented transformation into the generally milder Calvinistic form of Congregationalism. It was joined on the American religious scene by a welter of powerful religious movements from the Protestant tradition (Methodist, Baptist, Anglican, etc.) and even, after the waves of Irish immigration during the antebellum period, an increasingly formidable Roman Catholic population concentrated especially in the larger American cities. In short, after several fraught decades of severe conflict with the dominant Puritan authority in New England, and with the dominant Anglican majority in England itself, circumstances altered so that theological antagonisms, which had seemed so pressing during the rambunctious decades following the Quaker invasion of America in the mid-seventeenth century, eventually gave way to other concerns. As a consequence, Quaker theology and practice declined sharply as a subject for religious debate in an increasingly complex culture of print in the late eighteenth and early nineteenth century.

These major changes in the relationship between the Religious Society of Friends and its many theological adversaries, along with the transformation and regularization of the Quaker discipline itself, brought the once-fierce religious debates concerning Quakerism to a close in the Anglo-American marketplace of print, so that by the earlier decades of the eighteenth century, Quakers had receded in importance as subjects for theological debate in the specialist and popular press. Their religious principles—once they had been codified into a regularized discipline— still seemed peculiar to many American and English Christians but came to be understood as less theologically dangerous and much less of a perceived threat to the civic order. Many basic doctrinal issues were worked out to the satisfaction of Quakers themselves during the very earliest years of the movement. The participation of women as Quaker ministers was already firmly in place thanks to the publication and acceptance of teachings by Margaret Fell in her *Womens Speaking Justified* (1666), which argued on the basis of scriptural evidence for the value of women's preaching in meeting.[69]

By the late seventeenth century, mere decades after the boisterous and disruptive (and unsystematic) Quaker enthusiasm of the early English and American Quakers, Quaker discipline had in fact become quite regularized, as its guiding theological principles were codified and generally accepted in the form provided by such key theologians as William Penn, George Keith (1638–1716), and especially Robert Barclay (1648–90), author of *An Apology for the True Christian Divinity* (1676). In particular, Barclay "refuted Calvinist doctrines of predestination and scriptural authority, and argued for universal salvation and the authority of direct revelation."[70] Originally published in Latin, Barclay's *Apology* was translated into English by its author and subsequently became the first widely studied Quaker theological treatise, with its theology systematized into fifteen specific propositions about Quaker doctrine. After several tumultuous decades, Barclay's writings finally made it possible for Quakers to be associated with a specific theological program, even as the debates about Quaker theology had begun to die out in the public sphere.

The late seventeenth century also marked the beginning of Quaker meetings held in silence, with no recourse to either singing or music, and frequently with no preaching at all to break the silent worship period. The Quaker historian Ralph K. Beebe singles out this era for helping to solidify the quietist religious style that has come to characterize most Friends meetings ever since. Beebe points to the publication of Hugh Turford's *The Grounds of Holy Life* (1702) as an early signal of what would become a renovated and regularized but far less exuberant mode of Quaker worship. Inverting the enthusiastic approach of Mary Dyer and other Friends of a half century before, Turford insisted that "We must retire from outward objects, and silence all the desires and wandering imaginations of the mind; that in this profound silence of the whole soul, we may hearken to the ineffable voice of the Divine Teacher. We must listen with an attentive ear; for it is a still small voice. . . . But how seldom it is that the soul itself keeps itself silent enough for God to speak." Taking to heart teachings like those of Turford, Quakers entered a period in which it was not uncommon for their meetings to be conducted in complete silence, with one itinerant minister recording "22 consecutive meetings with only a single break in silence."[71]

AN
APOLOGY
FOR THE
True Christian Divinity,

As the same is Held Forth, and Preached, by the
People, called in Scorn,

QUAKERS:
BEING

A Full Explanation and Vindication of their *Principles*
and *Doctrines*, by many Arguments, deduced from
Scripture and *Right Reason*, and the Testimonies of
Famous Authors, both Ancient and Modern:
With a full Answer to the strongest Objections
usually made against them.

Presented to the KING.

Written in *Latin* and *English*,
By ROBERT BARCLAY,
And since Translated into *High Dutch, Low Dutch,*
and *French*, for the Information of Strangers.

The Fifth Edition in English.

Acts 24. 14.—*After the way, which they call Heresie, so worship I the God of my
Fathers; believing all things, which are written in the Law and the Prophets.*
Titus 2. v. 11. *For the Grace of God, that bringeth Salvation, hath appeared
to all Men.* Verf. 12. *Teaching us, that denying Ungodliness and worldly
Lusts, we should live Soberly, Righteously, and Godly in this present World.*
Verf. 13. *Looking for that blessed Hope, and glorious Appearing of the great
God, and our Saviour Jesus Christ.* Verf. 14. *Who gave himself for us,
that he might redeem us from all Iniquity, and purifie unto himself a peculiar People, Zealous of good Works.*
1 Thess. 5. 21. *Prove all things, hold fast that which is good.*

LONDON, Printed and Sold by T. Sowle, in
White-Hart-Court in *Gracious-Street,* 1703.

Robert Barclay, *An Apology for the True Christian Divinity* 1676 (1703). An
early and widely distributed Quaker catechism.

Even as Quakers began to resemble such groups as their old adversaries the Congregationalists in terms of higher socioeconomic status and declining religious fervor, the relative strength and volubility of women in the Quaker community continued to mark a radical difference between Quaker communities and their counterparts in the American Protestant mainstream, whose church governance and preaching continued to be dominated by male clergymen. Christine Heyrmann points to the anxiety created in a 1706 meeting in Newbury, Massachusetts, when the Quakeress Lydia Norton "having a very strong Manly Voice extended it very loud but to no purpose, for the People were as loud as she, calling for a Dram and sporting themselves in their Folly." And, as with the consternation over Quaker gender-bending and putative sexual misconduct in the mid-seventeenth century, accusations continued at times to be directed at Quaker women's defiance of sexual conventions, so that, as Heyrmann has argued, "the assertiveness of female preachers and the greater equality accorded all women within the Quaker community was tinged in the orthodox imagination with a suggestion of sexual libertinism."[72] Nor did Quaker men escape charges of sexual profligacy and misbehavior. As late as the Pennsylvania Indian massacres of 1763–64 at the hands of the Paxton Boys, the frontier Scots-Irish who slew dozens of Moravian Indians, Quakers were accused by some of protecting those same Indians against vigilante attack in order to satisfy their avarice and lust. As one critic wrote sardonically at the time, "Whether the Affection which some Principals of that Sect have shewn to Indians, and the great Care they are now taking of them can possibly be owing to the Charms of their Squaws, to any particular Advantages that may arise from their Trade, or perhaps rather from the Use they have made of them to asperse the Proprietaries and oppose their Interests, may be considered as a vain Question, which I will not undertake to determine."[73] Still, and despite this undercurrent of real anxiety about Friends from outside the sect, the unmistakable and more general trend of Quakerism of the late seventeenth and early eighteenth century was an implacable retreat from the countercultural radicalism that it stood for during the years of its early missionaries in New England.[74]

Thus, by the late nineteenth century, the history of American Quakerism had been beset with at least two competing narratives, two competing mythical frameworks: subversiveness and quietism. Quaker theology and religious practice had long been understood to be antithetical to the Puritan ethos that would come to dominate New England life for many generations. Richard Hallowell takes great pains to demonstrate that long-repeated tales of colonial Quakers as "wild and crazy freaks" whose women would commonly "parade the streets and . . . enter the churches unattired" were apocryphal tales intended to justify Puritan discrimination against them. Instead, he argues, "The records furnish instances of two women who were literally stripped of their clothing by the authorities; and many other instances of women who were stripped from the waist upwards and exposed to public gaze," but these outrageous scenes apparently were instigated not by Quakers but by their persecutors, who then went on to create a distorted legal record of their actions.[75]

The social historian Barry Levy has described in detail how the outrage against purported Quaker lewdness and, especially, women's misbehavior, had for decades been a favorite subject in the late seventeenth- and early eighteenth-century English press, where Grub Street hacks churned out sensational accusations in works like *The Quaker's Dream* (1655), which used Quaker claims about free grace to argue that in fact Friends were attempting to liberate themselves from all social restraint and propriety. Featuring a lurid frontispiece illustrating six naked and wildly dancing Quakeresses, *The Quaker's Dream* warned Christians against the dangers of a religious faith that allowed women such unbridled spiritual (and sexual) license. Other profligate behaviors like bestiality, incest, and adultery were durable themes in the popular press, which provided its readers with semi-pornographic, anti-Quaker titles like *The Quaker Wedding* (London, 1671), *The Secret Sinners* (London, 1675), *The Quaker's Wanton Wife* (1690), and *The Quaker's Art of Courtship* (London, 1710). Ironically, as Levy argues, the complaints about Quaker licentiousness and sexual misbehavior appeared precisely at the moment when Quakers were creating radical new family arrangements and religious forms of community surveillance that would produce remarkable levels of companionate domesticity among Quaker couples while extending unprecedented amounts of nurturance and attentiveness to Quaker children. These aspects of Quaker community life would, during the years of the French and American Revolutions, become a point of real interest by Enlightenment thinkers like Voltaire and Crèvecoeur, who saw Quaker way of life as a prototype for new, egalitarian social arrangements. Nevertheless, during the earlier period Quaker family life was consistently the focus of attacks, both from those who accused Quakers—such as "the gallivanting male Quaker hypocrite"—of a range of hypersexual behaviors, to those who argued that "the Quaker male was trapped by his religion into a marriage too spiritualized for conjugal sexual exercise. He usually used Quakerly language to seduce a forbidden woman, though less forbidden than his own wife." Eventually, though, the eighteenth and nineteenth centuries were inarguably witness to Quakers as social activists and abolitionists whose quietism, decorum, and probity provided evidence to non-Quakers of their moral rectitude. Quakers became models of Christian virtue in America, but only *after* their early religious enthusiasms were overwhelmed by colonial-era Puritan authority and persecution.[76]

In due course, Quaker virtues would be recognized by American writers with the talent and influence to publish widely their enthusiasm for the spiritualized domestic and moral world of the American Quaker, and in particular the sphere occupied by Quaker women. Specifically, "New England women would . . . use literary and economic talents developed in a society with a more variegated social role for women to create the fiction to nationalize, sadly or not, the Quakers' more constrained and focused female role."[77] Still, and as Hallowell points out, the world of colonial Quakers is difficult to delineate with any real accuracy or precision because of the dominance of Puritan-inflected historiography that too frequently justified Puritan prejudice on the basis of the perceived social threat represented by other religious radicals, especially the Quakers. From the earliest colonial moment in New England, Quakers entered the narratives of Puritan history in imaginative forms that were calculated to place them at the margins of power. Nineteenth-century historian George Bancroft and others, writes Hallowell, were complicit in a distorted view—indeed a largely imaginary narrative—of colonial Quakerism. As Hallowell argued in 1883, during a period when Quakers had become a favorite staple of American local color fiction, American historians were still exaggerating the actual extent to which colonial Quakers had embodied a socioreligious threat to Puritan power in the ways typically described by historians: interruption of church services and testimony (often by women) against religious authority (always the authority of men):

> The modern Quaker has a right to appeal from the fiction to the truth
> of history in the vindication of his ancestors. There are scholars in the
> old Bay State who are never backward when the Puritan fathers are to
> be defended. . . . Let anyone of them examine all the records carefully,
> with an eye for the truth, and publish the evidence upon which the

verdict of these popular writers is supposed to rest. It will be found to be astonishingly meager.[78]

The deep irony of seeing this proliferation of Quakers represented in distorted versions of American history and simultaneously in American fiction is, of course, related to the general reluctance of Quakers to either produce (as writers) or consume (as readers) very much history or fiction themselves, As Caroline Crew shrewdly observed in 1913, in an early study of the Quaker in American fiction, "there is something of the perverseness of fate in the fact that a people who have been taught to look upon the reading of fiction as baneful should themselves come to play a considerable role in imaginative literature." (Crew's insight about the Quaker role in American imaginative literature is supported by my analysis of fictional representations in chap. 5).[79]

Such distortions are perhaps understandable in light of the pressure to absorb a dark history of Puritan punishments and persecutions against the early Quaker enthusiasts, many of whom were women. The story of Lydia Wardwell serves as one useful illustration of the dynamic of Puritan persecution during the era of colonial settlement in Massachusetts. When she married Eliakim Wardwell in 1659, Lydia joined the household of a prickly and rebellious man who would soon raise the ire of local authorities by avoiding the payment of his tithes and persistently refusing church attendance. After she and her husband had converted to Quakerism, Lydia was singled out for public punishment in 1663. She had already observed her husband's confinement to the stocks for missing church services, the floggings of several of her friends, and the authorized raiding of her home in order to extract the church tithe by force. Although Lydia Wardwell appears to have been one early Quaker who actually disrobed before answering her Ipswich court summons, her punishment is perhaps even more shocking than her nudity, even taking into account the seventeenth-century custom of humiliating public punishments. Not only did Wardwell have to pay substantial court costs (financial considerations being always so closely intertwined with "religious" differences for the still-fledgling Massachusetts colony); George Bishop's *New England Judged* (1661) reports that after receiving her sentence, Wardwell "was tied to the fence post of the tavern . . . stripped from her waist upwards, with her naked breasts to the splinters of the posts and then sorely lashed with twenty or thirty cruel stripes." There is no need to rehearse unto tedium the many accounts of persecuted

Quakers in early America; but the human costs of religious intolerance were grave and, because of their traumatic nature, probably life-changing for the individuals set upon with abuse and torture.[80]

Unquestionably, early Quakers in America were perceived as a fanatical and potentially subversive group on the margins of even the more radical interpretations of what it might mean to be a Protestant Christian. Still, the turmoil would soon subside and be subdued into quietism, as most current historians of the Quaker movement would agree. Within fifty years of their notorious arrival in Boston Harbor in 1656, Quakers would come to be understood less as a theological danger than as members of a community that existed quietly, albeit mostly apart from their fellow American colonists. One critic, the former Quaker John Hancock, abandoned his Irish Quaker ministry because he was convinced there was something absurd about the Society of Friends continuing to identify itself primarily through its practices in avoiding titles of honor, hewing to plain attire, living separately from non-Quakers, and naming months and days of the week in their numerical order ("first day" for Monday, "first month" for January). The earliest Quakers were admirable Christians, wrote Hancock in 1801, but "many of their successors were stiff in these outward matters, while they neglected more essential things; these things ought they to have done, and not left the others undone; and a scrupulous attention to the smaller matters while the greater are neglected, is hurtful to the persons who act so, and becomes truly ridiculous in the view of others, who are desirous to examine into things closely and not superficially." During later generations of the nineteenth century, however, the Quaker movement—always and increasingly a relatively small fraction of Christians living in America—would continue to stimulate the imaginations of the larger citizenry.[81]

It was abundantly obvious to the Puritans (and Anglicans)—such as William Sewel and Thomas Clarkson—who produced the first and most influential religious histories of the colonial and early national period, that whatever attention was paid to American Quakers after about 1700 had much less to do with their theological peculiarity and demonstrative piety than their social restraint, archaic language, moral rectitude, willfully drab attire, and sincere (but steadfastly nonviolent) political and social radicalism. If the early Quaker (and especially the Quakeress) *individual* teemed with enthusiasm, self-expression, personal testimony, and boundless contempt for the rule of legitimate social and religious authority, the eighteenth- and nineteenth-century Quaker *community* came to stand in the minds of many political theorists as an exemplary form of egalitarian social arrangement. While the colonial Quaker was reputed to live too exuberantly through her body, the nineteenth- and twentieth-century Quaker figured in the popular and historical imaginary as a profoundly and even peculiarly benevolent figure, and yet a paradoxical figure that remained insufficiently embodied, or perhaps inadequately assimilated into an impending Gilded Age that would embrace relentless nationalism, consumerism, ostentation, and religious fluidity.

2

Political Theory and
Quaker Community in
the Early Republic

The love of peace, which we sincerely feel and profess, has begun to
produce an opinion in Europe that our government is entirely in
Quaker principles, & will turn the left cheek when the right has been
smitten. This opinion must be corrected when just occasion arises, or
we shall become the plunder of all nations.

Thomas Jefferson (1806)

Get the writings of John Woolman by heart; and love the early Quakers.

Charles Lamb, "A Quaker's Meeting" (1820)

In examining the lives of eighteenth-century British Quakers, the
historian Phyllis Mack has observed that the most vital tension in
the lives of Friends during the period was arranged around an opposition between the increasingly powerful modern values spawned by
the Enlightenment and the strongly mystical (and thus essentially antimodern) historical legacy of Quakerism. "Eighteenth-century Quakers
felt themselves to be both denizens of the Enlightenment and seekers of
the supernatural. They were in the vanguard of movements we view as

modern, including the industrial revolution; the crusade for the abolition of slavery; reforms in education, prisons, and mental health; and feminism; they were also in the vanguard of the religious revival that began in the early eighteenth century and continued in the nineteenth-century missionary movement."[1] Mack's view of English Quakers is largely in agreement with the more concise summary, advanced by Daniel Richter, of American Quaker ambivalence during the years of the early republic: "Quakers were an especially anxious lot, trapped as they were between competing ideals of simplicity and success, separatism and benevolence."[2] By the middle decades of the eighteenth century, Quakers were still the object of a certain amount of ridicule, much of it directed at the substantial role of women as preachers at Friends' meetings. In fact, it was in response to his friend James Boswell's description of hearing a woman preach at a Quaker meeting that Samuel Johnson, in 1763, uttered his famous remark about women in the pulpit: "Sir, a woman' preaching is like a dog's walking on its hinder legs. It is not done well; but you are surprised to find it done at all."[3] Seen in the larger transatlantic context, ambivalence and scorn of the sort voiced by Johnson is in some ways not surprising. The growing social and cultural separation between Quakers themselves and the objects of their missionary work and other benevolent projects were drastically altering the visibility and cultural force of Quakers and their religious activities. No longer the grimy, itinerant, and rambunctious outsiders of the early phase of Anglo-American Quaker enthusiasm, Quakers in the British Atlantic by the late eighteenth century certainly remained pious, but they had also abandoned much of their earlier tendency toward religious enthusiasm and evangelism. The late eighteenth and early nineteenth century witnessed a phenomenon that Sarah Crabtree has called the "maturation of the Society of Friends," when a traveling ministry of dozens of Quaker "transatlantic ministers" (also known as "Public Friends") built and consolidated the interaction of widely scattered Quaker communities throughout the British Atlantic area.[4] At the same time, they were becoming wealthier and more urbanized than the average American, and far more so than the typical African American slaves or displaced Native Americans, groups whose status was far more precarious in the national culture. Whereas Quakers had themselves been persecuted during the early period of their religious activities in the late seventeenth century, by the middle of the eighteenth century their wealth and influence was such that their status was relatively secure while other marginalized groups were increasingly becoming the object of Quaker benevolent activities.[5]

During the decades bracketing the Revolutionary War, American Friends came increasingly to be seen as a political and moral force, while at the same time their views on morals, religion, and social arrangements became the object of considerable attention from intellectuals—especially those in Europe—who saw in the apparently harmonious Quaker communities an important precedent and prototype for an emerging democratic politics. However, the idealization of Quaker politics came during a period when Quaker religion was in many respects hardening its dogma and losing the rather flexible theology of the early Quakers. Daniel J. Boorstin perceptively notes, "While the dogma of Quakerism grew more fixed and uncompromising, those of Puritanism tended more and more toward compromise. Puritanism, proverbially rigid and dogmatic—expanded and adapted; while Quakerism—traditionally formless, spontaneous, and universal—built a wall around itself. This is one of the greatest lost opportunities in all American history."[6] Nevertheless, and in spite of their actual abdication—on grounds of pacifism—of political power in Pennsylvania during the Revolutionary period, ideological attention was paid to Quakers by a number of important thinkers who had strong commitments to democratic politics, even though Quakers themselves were by no means monolithic in terms of their own political commitments during the Revolutionary period.

Quakers like Henry Drinker of Philadelphia, husband of the well-known diarist Elizabeth Drinker, was a British loyalist who in 1777 was exiled to Virginia along with nineteen other Quaker men. Left alone with her four children, Elizabeth Drinker was sympathetic enough with the British troops that she provided them room and board during the war. The same year, a Philadelphia Quaker named Sarah Logan Fisher "vigorously supported the refusal of Quakers to accept Continental currency, but professed herself shocked at the subsequent exile of Quaker leaders."[7] Even earlier, debates concerning slavery during the middle and later decades of the eighteenth century marked the arrival of Quakers onto the American political scene, just in time for them to add their voices to debates concerning a new array of political arrangements promised by the impending American Revolution.[8] Because of their reluctance to participate in electoral politics, Quaker activism made its most important impact during this period not in legislative meetings but in the public sphere of print culture, with such important Quaker writers as the itinerant minister John Woolman eventually taking the lead in transforming the Quaker movement into the first religious group to repudiate chattel slavery completely.

Woolman's prescient moral stance on the issue of abolition, particularly after the posthumous publication of his influential *Journal* in 1774—on the eve of the American Revolution—would galvanize American Quakers into a position of national leadership as abolitionists by the early decades of the nineteenth century. Even more remarkably for its time, Woolman's *Journal* also presents a sensibility radically open to and curious about the ways of Native Americans, who in the eighteenth and nineteenth centuries were continuing to endure systematic removal from their American tribal homelands. As he traveled as a missionary in 1761 toward an Indian village in eastern Pennsylvania, he wrote in remarkably sympathetic terms about the Indians he was about to encounter: "I was led to think on the nature of the exercise which hath attended me: love was the first motion, and then a concern arose to spend some time with the *Indians,* that I might feel and understand their life, and the spirit they live in, if haply I might receive some instruction from them, or they be in any degree helped forward by my following the leadings of Truth amongst them."9 Thrust into activism by Woolman's example and a rising tide of abolitionist sentiment, a number of Quakers rose to prominence as participants in the Underground Railroad and as eloquent spokesmen for the cause of antislavery (and later women's rights, with Quakers like Susan B. Anthony in the lead) during the antebellum period. Native Americans remained objects of concern for Quakers, who took the lead during the nineteenth century as one of the U.S. government's favored sources of rural schoolteachers sent to work among Plains Indian tribes who were being forced away from their ancestral tribal lands in order to permit white settlement.

Since the seventeenth-century founding of their sect, Quakers in America and Europe had participated in virulent pamphlet wars concerned with their controversial religious views. American Quakers during the Revolutionary years now entered the political arena, albeit tentatively and with an emphasis on producing new tracts and personal journals representative of maturing Quaker thought and calibrated to achieve political consciousness among the Society of Friends and those with whom they interacted. The Quaker political ethos that emerged during these years, however, did so not only at the hands of

Quakers themselves but also through the influential writings of some non-Quakers who saw in the Society of Friends a uniquely egalitarian and virtuous social collective. The place of Quakers in the national imagination—in this case their role in public exchanges over political ideas—has always been formed through a dialectic involving Quakers as well as interested non-Quakers who saw Quakers religious values as either exemplary or anathema.

In addition to John Woolman's influence and activities as the central figure in Quaker progressivism during this period, other highly visible Quakers made their mark, such as the mercurial tax rebel, pamphleteer, and leader in the Whiskey Rebellion, Herman Husband, along with better-known Quakers as the Pennsylvania educators Isaac Hopper and Anthony Benezet. Hopper and Benezet were influential eastern Pennsylvania activists during the late eighteenth century and stand as exemplary Quakers for their influence in bringing the Society of Friends into the public eye as writers and educators, and especially as educators of freed African American slaves. Their contributions to Revolutionary-era print culture, along with those of Herman Husband, mark out some of the substantial force of Quaker ideology and its relation to key political debates that would continue to infuse the public discourse for many decades to follow.

As had been true since their controversial appearance on the English and American religious scene in the mid-seventeenth century, perceptions about Quakers would be shaped and conditioned by a public discourse constituted by an array of intersecting and competing voices: Quakers, former or birthright Quakers (Thomas Paine, whose English father was a Quaker, being the signal example of a prominent political activist of the period who was born into a Quaker household), and non-Quakers. Each of these discursive subgroups provided viewpoints about the Society of Friends that ranged enormously in intensity and religious commitment. Some articulate writers during the Revolutionary period expressed a large measure of enthusiasm for Quaker values and religiosity. Others, far less sanguine about the kinds of contributions that Friends would make during a volatile period in the nation's history, voiced their grave concerns—concerns that had perennially been expressed by English religious writers—over the disorderliness, lack of patriotic citizenship, and heretical (and possibly non-Christian) spiritualism that Quakers had come to represent in the eyes of many in England and America.

The French-American émigré Hector St. John de Crèvecoeur (1735–1818), famed for having written the enduringly popular *Letters from an American Farmer* (1782) during the years just prior to the American Revolution, is the unlikely source of a major contribution to our understanding of Enlightenment attitudes toward Friends. The most prominent non-Quaker enthusiast of the Society of Friends in America has typically been associated with purely secular ideas about nation building, rather than the discourse of religion as a shaping element in political discourse. That his account of Quaker culture documents aspects of an American community of Friends (on Nantucket Island in Massachusetts) situates Crèvecoeur as a uniquely valuable index to how eighteenth-century thinkers viewed them in relation to nascent American religious and political traditions. Crèvecoeur, who has become best known for inquiring "What is an American" and for having been the first to imagine the incipient American nation as an ethnic "melting pot" for European immigrants to the New World, devotes a considerable amount of attention in his book to Quaker life in colonial America. Preoccupied with finding a way to inhabit the new American polis that would comport with his sensibilities and political biases, Crèvecoeur investigates Quaker culture with a powerful curiosity, although that curiosity and admiration are never compelling enough to persuade him to advocate a national conversion to Quaker doctrine and piety. In the end, though, he provides a representation of Quaker life that stands in ironic contrast to a broader project of colonial development that he documents as a baffling stew of tranquil agriculture, brutal repression of slaves in the Southern plantation economy, and frightening proximity to frontier violence.

The Birth of Quaker Activism: John Woolman, Anthony Benezet, Isaac Hopper

Noted consistently for its demonstration of a graceful English prose style combined with advanced religious and moral views, John Woolman's posthumously published *Journal* (1774) has frequently been assigned representative status because of its clear statement of Quaker religious principles and progressive social critiques.[10] For more than a century, and certainly during the heated abolitionist politics of the antebellum period, this journal stood as one of the major early statements of Quaker opposition to slavery.[11] Early in his career, Woolman had established his progressive credentials by becoming one of the first American writers explicitly to oppose slavery with the publication of his pamphlet *Some Considerations on the Keeping of Negroes* (1754). Woolman was far ahead of his time in this respect, even by comparison with other Quakers, many of whom had owned slaves during the colonial period before the Society of Friends formally repudiated the practice and began to free their slaves. (William Penn, for one, the famous and much-admired Quaker leader who received the land grant of Pennsylvania in 1681 before personally organizing the colony along lines amenable to Quaker settlements, continued to own slaves until his death.) At the same time, though, it is important not to see Woolman as merely a singular prophet of emancipation and moral progress among eighteenth-century Friends. By 1771, according to the Scottish economist and philosopher John Millar (a colleague of Adam Smith), it was becoming obvious that the Society of Friends had turned a corner in the long struggle for slavery's abolition, and some of the best evidence of this progress was occurring among Friends in the American colonies. "The Quakers of Pennsylvania," wrote Millar just a few years before the American Revolution, "are the first body of men who have discovered any scruples" and who "seem to have thought that the abolition of this practice is a duty they owe to religion and humanity."[12] More recently, additional progressive voices— of lesser known Quaker men and women who worked far from the public view—have been added to Woolman's as it becomes clearer that Quakers were a substantial political presence in the colonial and early national periods.

In the public sphere, though, John Woolman was the dominant Quaker figure of his generation, not so much for any promotion of specific principles of religious practice—he was far from a careful theologian—but for his activism on behalf of social justice. More specifically, Woolman aimed his strongest language at two primary evils: poverty and racism—and, of course, the system of slavery that grew out of racial supremacist ideology. Best known for identifying abolitionism with the Quaker movement, it is less frequently recognized that Woolman was at least as powerful in his arguments on behalf of the poor in such works as *A Plea for the Poor* (written in 1763 and published in 1793 under the title *A Word of Remembrance and Caution to the Rich*). Until the publication of Orestes A. Brownson's devastating pre-Marxist treatise on class warfare, "The Laboring Classes" (1840), Woolman's pamphlet on behalf of the lower classes was probably the most radical American statement extant concerning the many injustices associated with enormous class disparities in wealth and privilege. Woolman, character-istically, does not frame his views about class relations in terms specific to Quaker doctrine; in fact, the word "Friend" does not appear at all in his *Plea for the Poor* and shows up in his *Journal* only when he is making reference to like-minded Christians. In other words, Woolman tends to make his claims on behalf of Christian principles in the Quaker faith, but without polemic or specific disputation with other denominations within Protestantism. Woolman sets out his claims in the language of common sense, with no tendency to wishful utopianism that might be expected from other progressive thinkers.

As to the problem of poverty, Woolman begins with moral terms that would be unsurprising from the antimaterialist pen of the nineteenth-century writer Henry David Thoreau: "Wealth desired for its own sake obstructs the increase of virtue, and large possessions in the hands of selfish men have a bad tendency, for by their means too small a number of people are employed in things useful; and therefore they, or some of them, are necessitated to labor too hard, while others would want business to earn their bread were not employments invented which, having no real use, serve only to please the vain mind." Pub-lished only a few years after Benjamin Franklin's secular gospel of hard work, *The Way to Wealth* (1758), Woolman's *A Plea for the Poor* is arresting not only for its concern with disparities in wealth but also for its insis-tence that human beings should work neither too much nor too little. Rather than urge the accumulation of wealth through incessant labor, which is the Franklinian ethos, Woolman took the relatively unusual po-sition that labor should be moderate only; inappropriate disparities in income could thus could indicate a situation in which men "find occa-sion to labour harder than was intended by our gracious Creator." This emphasis on moderate productivity, a point to which he returns repeat-edly in *A Plea for the Poor*, suggests that temperate labor can provide for adequate sustenance and "the leisure to attend on proper affairs of soci-ety," while supporting a contented way of life: "While our strength and spirits are lively, we go cheerfully through business. Either too much or too little action is tiresome, but a right portion is healthful to our bodies and agreeable to an honest mind."[13]

While John Woolman was a significant figure in his own day, his posthumous reputation would become even more burnished during the course of the nineteenth century, as antislavery politics grew stronger and louder during the years leading up to the Civil War. Still later, a few years after the War had ended and the Emancipation Proclamation had finally taken effect, Woolman's works—including the *Journal* and the renamed edition of *A Plea for the Poor*—appeared in print once more for the edification of American readers still traumatized by the terrible struggle over slavery. The re-publication of Woolman's *Journal* in 1871, in time to mark the centenary of its first appearance in print, is in some respects a watershed event. With the Civil War over and the slaves freed, the central political issue that lay at the core of Woolman's life work had finally been confronted, if not resolved. From the perspective of the Reconstruction years, American readers could ponder once more the implications of Woolman's early activism and implacable insistence on ending slavery. Moreover, post–Civil War readers of Woolman had the opportunity to consider a longer history of Quaker activism and representation: the 1871 edition of Woolman's works was given a lengthy introduction by none other than the great Quaker poet of the nineteenth century, John Greenleaf Whittier, who had spent decades as a tireless abolitionist and humanitarian writer.

That Woolman is the essential American Quaker writer of the eighteenth century is unquestionable, but his canonization—he appears as the single Quaker figure in most modern literary anthologies of the period—has to some degree contributed to the neglect of other significant Quaker writers of the period, like his contemporary, the Pennsylvania educator Anthony Benezet. Benezet, who has received extended biographical treatment from Roberts Vaux, was born in 1713 in St. Quentin, Picardy, in France, to a wealthy and distinguished family of Calvinist Huguenots. His father experienced discrimination at the hands of Catholic authorities and subsequently fled with his family first to Holland and then to London, where Anthony received a basic education. As young teen he was apprenticed to a cooper, and by the age of fourteen, Benezet had converted to the Religious Society of Friends, even before emigrating with his family to Philadelphia at the age of eighteen. His subsequent career in and around the Philadelphia area is marked by a long-standing commitment to education, with a particular devotion to the matter of education young African Americans in southeastern Pennsylvania.

After a stint as a printer's proofreader and as a schoolteacher in Germantown, Pennsylvania, Benezet was soon recognized as a talented

Quaker educator Anthony Benezet teaching African American students.

teacher/writer. In 1742 he was called to the Philadelphia public school as an instructor, before eventually establishing a female seminary of his own, specializing in the education of girls from Philadelphia's upper classes.[14] In a teaching career that lasted for more than forty years, Benezet was a radical innovator in educational theory whose equal would not appear on the American scene until the famed A. Bronson Alcott. Alcott, assisted by the equally brilliant Elizabeth Peabody, continued the progressive-minded reform of American education with similar techniques in the Temple School of Concord, Massachusetts, in the early nineteenth century. By all accounts, Benezet's students (like those of Alcott) loved him for his mild and nurturing pedagogy, and especially for his avoidance of corporal punishment, which until then had been a standard schoolmaster's recourse for discipline. Benezet's educational project soon extended beyond the education of wealthy Philadelphia girls to the education—at his own expense—of the city's African Americans; this he accomplished first by means of a self-funded night school and later with a separate school for their instruction. A decade after the American Revolution a French visitor to Philadelphia (one of the numerous students of Quaker morality at that time) wrote admiringly of Benezet's success at educating the African American youths of that city:

I saw in this school a mulatto, one-eighth negro; it is impossible to distinguish him from a white boy. His eyes discovered an extraordinary vivacity; and this is a general characteristic of people of that origin.

The black girls, besides reading, writing, and the principles of religion, are taught spinning, needlework, &c, and their mistresses assure me that they discover much ingenuity. They have the appearance of decency, attention, and submission. It is a nursery of good servants and virtuous housekeepers. . . . It is to Benezet that humanity owes this useful establishment.[15]

Benezet's activism as an abolitionist and as an advocate for the education of African Americans is contemporaneous with that of his fellow Quaker John Woolman. Benezet is notable as well for his publication, presumably intended for non-Quaker English and American readers, of an early version of the Quaker discipline in his pamphlet *A Short Account of the Religious Society of Friends* (1780), which provided concise accounts of the key Quaker teachings on pacifism, the Inner Light, silent worship, unpaid ministry, gender equality, prohibition of swearing, and refusal of sacraments.

In some ways, Anthony Benezet is even more explicit in his advocacy on behalf of African Americans than his abolitionist predecessors among American Friends, and his advocacy went beyond Woolman's concern about the basic immorality of the trade in human beings. Benezet avoided the relatively condescending benevolence of many later abolitionists by making a more radical claim of intellectual equality between the races. Vaux, for instance, cites Benezet as follows, "I can (said Benezet) with truth and sincerity declare, that I have found amongst the Negroes as great a variety of talents, as among a like number of whites, and I am bold to assert, that the notion, entertained by some, that the blacks are inferior in their capacities, is a vulgar prejudice, founded on the pride or ignorance of their lordly masters, who have kept their slaves at such a distance as to be unable to form a right judgment of them."[16] It was egalitarian principles such as these that formed the motive for Benezet's major abolitionist publications of the pre-Revolutionary period, such as *An Account of that part of Africa Inhabited by Negroes* (1762) and *A Caution and Warning to Great Britain and Her Colonies, on the Calamitous State of the Enslaved Negroes* (1767), which were published at his own expense and had a substantial effect on the English antislavery movement. Soon a confidante of the intellectual elite of his day, Benezet expressed similar antislavery views in letters to his friends Abbé Raynal and Benjamin Franklin.

Even more radically, Benezet was extraordinarily prescient in his concern for the Native inhabitants of the American colonies; to them, according to Vaux's assessment, "there flowed from the expanded heart of Anthony Benezet, copious streams of solicitude and sympathy." This sympathy led Benezet to publish a remarkably early defense of Indian rights, especially those displaced by settlements in western Pennsylvania and Ohio, in *Some Observations on the Situation, Disposition and Character of the Indian Natives of This Continent* (1784). Benezet's compassion for the plight of Natives put him in a distinctly minority position among colonial writers, most of whom expressed clear support for the removal of Natives from the receding frontiers in Pennsylvania. Directly criticizing those Quakers who advocated on behalf of Natives, the anonymous pamphleteer "Philopatrius" wrote in 1764 that in fact Quaker activism on behalf of Natives—who had killed a number of colonists at Lancaster, Pennsylvania—was in fact a misguided attempt to assist "Savage Indian Butchers" of the Europeans who wished to establish homesteads on what previously had been Native lands. Instead, "Philopatrius" asks about Quaker sympathy for the slain whites of Lancaster: "Where are the Quakers who have sympathized with them, or pitied their distress?" And he surmises that the Quaker defense of Native rights merely disguises their bald political cynicism: "Why all this Clamour against Quakers? Surely they don't solely govern. True, Thank God they do not: But if a few bad Men in the Administration be very detrimental, what may we apprehend where so many Quakers are intrusted, who have lately prov'd their very Religion to be a political engine, to which they themselves pay no conscientious Regard, but as it suits their crafty Purposes."[17]

Vaux also turns to physiognomy in order to register something of Anthony Benezet's peculiarity, citing a homeliness far removed from the grand physiques among such political leaders as George Washington or Thomas Jefferson. Vaux writes that "The person of Anthony Benezet was small; his countenance was composed of strong and interesting features, and though his face beamed with benignant animation, it was far from being handsome. Of this he was himself sensible, for a friend of his once suggesting a desire to possess his portrait, he did not assign the conscientious objection which he probably entertained on the subject, but thus replied to the request, 'O! no, no, no, my ugly face shall not go down to posterity.'" Upon his death at the age of seventy-one, in 1784 Benezet was celebrated at the largest funeral ever staged in Philadelphia, a crowd of mourners drawn from both the highest and the lower ranks of that community, including "many hundreds of black persons" who testified "by their attendance, and by their tears, the grateful sense they entertained of his pious efforts on their behalf."[18] So it was that one of the leading moralists of the day, nearly a century and a half after the arrival of Friends in America, was accorded the kind of public recognition that would help to solidify the marginal-yet-virtuous status of Quakers in the early republic. With Benezet and Woolman, then, the image of Quakers in the late colonial period of the eighteenth century had finally been completely transformed from that of the early Quakers. In 1742 it was still possible for a distinguished Cambridge minister like Charles Chauncy, then writing with some distress about the new enthusiasms of the Great Awakening, to recall a previous generation of Quakers who had roiled the American religious scene with their fervor and subversiveness. Speaking of the large-scale conversions then in progress, Chauncy compared their behavior to that of a previous generation of Quakers: "Sometimes, [their enthusiasm] may be seen in their countenance. A certain wildness is discernable in their general look and air; especially when their imaginations are mov'd and fired. Sometimes, it strangely loosens their tongues, and gives them such an energy, as well as fluency and volubility in speaking, as they themselves, by their utmost efforts, can't so much as imitate, when they are not under the enthusastick [sic] influence."[19] In place of the disorderly Quaker women of Chauncey's youth, the new public Quaker image conveyed by activists like Benezet or Woolman (or even by Franklin, who was often associated with the Quaker community of Philadelphia[20]) increasingly was aligned less with religious issues per se, and far more with progressive social critique and reformism conveyed by Friends behaving with restraint and decorum.

Benezet's work on behalf of African Americans as an advocate and educator stands with the early antislavery advocacy and class consciousness of John Woolman as among the most significant Quaker political actions that were taken during the years of the early republic. It would be an error, however, to suppose that they alone were performing the work of proto-abolitionism and progressive race politics during that period. Other prominent Quakers were active in the public sphere, creating a widespread sense of Quakers as progressive activists. Benezet's activism enlisted other Quakers with a strong calling to the abolitionist movement, and in at least one case their activism became as famous as that of Benezet himself.

Isaac T. Hopper, a Philadelphia Quaker who served for years as an instructor several nights a week at Benezet's school for African American adults, aided escaping slaves as a participant in the Underground Railroad, wrote narratives of their lives, and provided pro bono legal advice on their behalf—was another early American Quaker who took up the cause of antislavery long before any substantial mainstream of American opinion against human servitude began to hold sway in the North. Born in 1771 near Woodbury, New Jersey, Hopper came from a strongly Quaker background, although his own father had been read out of meeting for marrying outside the sect.[21] Still, his father attended meetings regularly, and the youthful Hopper not only attended Quaker meetings with him but also married a Quaker woman before he himself officially became a convinced member of the Society of Friends at the age of twenty-two. In one of her more hagiographic moments, his biographer, Lydia Maria Child, speculated of the youthful Hopper at the time of his 1793 marriage to his Quakeress cousin and bride, Sarah Tatum, that "It was probably the pleasantest period of his existence. Love and religion, the two deepest and brightest experiences of human life, met together, and flowed into his earnest soul in one full stream."[22]

The particulars of Hopper's career, which had been well known for decades among the Philadelphia Society of Friends, were staged not only in the Philadelphia newspapers of his youth but also for British and American readers in Child's admiring biography, *Isaac T. Hopper: A True Life* (1853), which was published a year after Hopper's death at the age of eighty-one.[23] Child's biography, which also includes reprinted versions of Hopper's seventy-nine "Tales of Oppression" slave narratives that he published as newspaper columns between 1780 and 1843, singles out Hopper as a surprisingly bold abolitionist who worked tirelessly on behalf of escaping slaves. Hopper, like his fellow Quaker Anthony Benezet, worked directly with freed slaves, and as boy living close to the Quaker community of the Delaware Valley, Hopper had frequent contact with some escaped slaves who had made their way into New Jersey and southeastern Pennsylvania. Lydia Maria Child naturally emphasizes the role played by the Society of Friends in shaping Hopper's views, showing how he grew closer to full-fledged membership in the Quakers as his life unfolded. But she also includes in her account a telling episode in the moral education of the future abolitionist, one that figures as a remarkably powerful expression of autobiography from an escaped slave that Hopper meets as a young boy. While driving cows in Woodbury one summer in 1780, the nine-year-old Isaac Hopper had a conversation that would turn shape his career as an abolitionist and advocate for African American slaves:

> When he drove the cows to and from pasture, he often met an old col-
> ored man named Mingo. His sympathizing heart was attracted toward
> him, because he had heard the neighbors say he was stolen from Africa
> when he was a little boy. One day he asked Mingo what part of the
> world he came from; and the poor old man told how he was playing
> with other children among the bushes, on the coast of Africa, when
> white men pounced upon them suddenly and dragged them off to a
> ship. . . . The old man wept like a child when he told how he was fright-
> ened and distressed at being thus hurried away from father, mother,
> brothers, and sisters, and sold into slavery in a distant land, where he
> could never see or hear from them again. This painful story made a
> deep impression upon Isaac's mind; and though he was then only nine
> years old, he made a solemn vow to himself that he would be the friend
> of oppressed Africans during his whole life.[24]

In this narrative it can readily be discerned how the politics of Hopper's career are refashioned by that personal encounter with Mingo the es-caped slave. Not only is Hopper's life story exemplary as a model for vir-tuous benevolence with regard to the matter of slavery, but the Quaker sensibility and Quaker community apparently provided him with the capacity to derive his moral certitude and righteousness not from ab-stract sources or texts but directly from the compelling voice of one of American slavery's victims. As with representations of Quakers through-out American literary history, Friend Hopper takes his lesson in benevo-lence directly from the object of his altruism, with the added suggestion that non-Quakers would lack the ability to do so themselves.

In Child's hands, Hopper's work also emerges as confirmation of the picture of slave life offered by Harriet Beecher Stowe in *Uncle Tom's Cabin* (1852) and as confirmation of the long-standing centrality of Quakers in the work of abolition. Child indicates this by aligning the particulars of the respective accounts provided by Stowe and Isaac Hopper, noting that "The facts, which were continually occurring within Friend Hop-per's personal knowledge, corroborate the picture of slavery drawn by Mrs. Stowe. Her descriptions are no more fictitious than the narratives written by Friend Hopper."[25] Whereas Stowe had provided the most im-portant imaginative account of America's culture of slavery for the ante-bellum years of the nineteenth century, the re-publication of Hopper's writings on abolitionism adds weight to Stowe's representation of Quakers as central actors in the political work of antislavery.

Herman Husband and Revolutionary Politics

While Woolman, Benezet, and Hopper were diligently at work as Quaker activists during the decades before the American Revolution, Friends with more fluid commitments to Quaker discipline were making their own contributions to the Revolutionary ethos of the day. A case in point about the involvement of Friends in a range of Revolutionary-era political debates can be seen in a survey of incidents from the flamboyant career of Herman Husband (1724–95),[26] a sometime-Quaker, revolutionary agitator, pamphleteer, and leader of the Pennsylvania Whiskey Rebellion. Best known for his leadership of the North Carolina Regulators, whose rebellion against British taxation in that colony led to an early skirmish with the colonial authorities, Husband's religious commitments overlapped with his rebellion against centralized government power (first the British government; later the American government). This steadfast champion of American liberty was also, during his younger days, the author of religious pamphlets that described his own ardent conversion to the Quaker faith. Years later, disillusioned with what he saw as the cynical behavior of Quakers in the North Carolina meeting that he had joined, he published criticism of them along with a renewed commitment of his devotion to the Inner Light of divine inspiration.

Born in colonial Maryland to an Anglican family, Husband attended a powerful sermon by the great evangelist George Whitfield and in 1739 converted first to Presbyterianism before becoming a Quaker around 1750, at the age of twenty-six. Years later, he would publish an account of his conversion experience in a pamphlet whose full title emphasizes his commitment to personal experience and direct argument. *Some Remarks on Religion, With the Author's Experience in Pursuit Thereof, For the Consideration of All People, Being the Real Truth of What Happened, Simply Delivered, Without the Help of School-Words, or Dress of Learning* (1761) was published at Husband's own expense in the Quaker stronghold of Philadelphia, just before he left his home in Baltimore for the first of his frontier adventures in central North Carolina. Several years later, after finding himself at the center of some bitter disputes among the North Carolina Quakers, whom he accused of immoral behavior and a formalist overemphasis on the "thee" and "thou" shibboleths of Quaker plain speech, Husband published these accusations as *The Second Part of the Naked Truth; or, Historical Account of the Actual Transactions of Quakers in their Meetings of Business* (1768).

Husband is a notable figure in the history of American Quakerism for his participation in the important pre-Revolutionary events that would eventually lead to the larger conflict with the British forces; he also serves as a useful example of Quaker self-representation during the tumultuous years of political debate that formed the prelude to the American Revolution. After moving to Orange County, North Carolina, in 1762, the always-enterprising Husband had acquired large land holdings and soon became one of the leaders in the Regulator movement, a group of several thousand central and western North Carolina residents who rebelled during the period 1764–71 against the collection of taxes by county sheriffs. The Regulator conflict over perceived unfair taxation has frequently been viewed as a precursor to the impending rebellion against England during the Revolutionary War. Encouraged by the charismatic Herman Husband, the Regulators agreed to allow him (rather than the sheriffs) to collect the correct tax levies from each of them. During a meeting with the state legislature—Husband was an elected state representative—he was reprimanded for nonpayment of taxes by North Carolina colonial governor William Tryon, a reprimand to which Husband replied with a symbolic gesture.

The symbolism of Husband's rebellion against Governor Tryon is clever enough as he had intended it, and it takes on even greater resonance when the scene is described by Husband's twentieth-century chronicler, the North Carolina historian William Edwards Fitch, who published an account of the Regulator controversy in 1905. Several of Fitch's comments about Husband detail not only his leadership during the years leading up to the Regulators' eventual defeat at the hands of British forces, but also the impressive qualities of Quaker identity that marked Herman Husband during his dealings with the much-resented colonial authorities. In facing down the tax reprimand from Governor Tryon during the legislative sessions, Fitch writes, Husband "Walk[ed] to the Speaker's desk with the firmness, plainness, and boldness of a Quaker, and throwing a bag of specie on the table in front of the Governor, Husband replied, 'Here, sir, are the taxes which my people refused your roguish sheriff. I brought it to keep it from dwindling, seeing that when money passes through so many fingers, it, like a cake of soap, grows less at each handling.'" Rebellion blended with Quaker firmness thus characterizes the historical view of Husband in this scene. Fitch continues in this direction by associating Husband with the revolutionary activism of Benjamin Franklin "with whom [Husband] kept up regular communications. Franklin was accustomed to send Husband printed pamphlets, which he copied or printed, and distributed among the people." Fitch's historical presentation, like earlier accounts of Franklin that had falsely presumed his membership in the Quakers, knits together the will to revolt with the austerity of Quaker religiosity, while not taking the more difficult step of becoming entirely persuaded of the practicality of life as a Friend. Even on the frontiers of rural North Carolina, Fitch seems to say, where Friends were present but limited in their numbers, the Quaker pacifist ethos was ironically fanning the flames of Revolution. Quaker defiance of authority suited the spirit of rebellion, according to Fitch, who concludes that "[Husband] was one of those independent Quakers (educated at the honest school of William Penn) who refused to pull off his hat and bow before the minions of despotism."

On May 16, 1771, two thousand Regulators were defeated by Royal Governor William Tryon and one thousand of his soldiers at what became known as the Battle of Alamance. Owing to his pacifist Quaker beliefs, Husband did not participate in the battle and soon moved to Maryland, later making his way to Pennsylvania, where he participated in the Whiskey Rebellion. There he lived in the sparsely settled counties east of Pittsburgh until his death in June 1795. Now a largely forgotten Quaker figure from the American eighteenth century, Harmon Husband lived and embodied many of the qualities that European writers of the period were ascribing to Friends in the young nations.[27]

Crèvecoeur: An American Farmer and the Society of Friends

Perhaps no other major text from the American Revolutionary period has been so consistently misunderstood as Crèvecoeur's *Letters from an American Farmer,* which was first published in London in 1782 and immediately became a literary sensation among readers on both sides of the Atlantic, in French and English editions. Above all, this book describes Americanization as a process by which persons of disparate ethnicities are transformed by means of a "melting pot" into a new breed of agrarian, republican citizen: a citizen entirely different from European precursors. In part because of its rather misleading title, but also because of the way its text is usually edited and anthologized for the general reader, Crèvecoeur's *Letters* has frequently been read as a document that focuses most of its attention on agrarian life in colonial America. Indeed, the passages in *Letters* that focus on the ethos of the American planter and the notion of the "melting pot" are the ones most often quoted, and these same passages are those that divert attention from the subtlety of Crèvecoeur's larger and more complex project, which involves not just a mythic construction of the "American farmer" but also an analysis of social alternatives to the independent agrarian life. The literary historian David Carlson, in an essay that delves into the nuances of Crèvecoeur's legal philosophy, concurs that many of the anthology editors who have excerpted *Letters* "have left their readers with a distorted image of the text." Avoiding the mythical dimensions of Crèvecoeur's Farmer James, Carlson opts instead to examine the legal discourse of *Letters*. He concludes that the Crèvecoeur's descriptions of the Quaker community of Nantucket (like the Native American community that Farmer James eventually joins) should be understood as ironic—and thus a faulty—alternative to the possessive individualism that Crèvecoeur favors, primarily because the "radical communitarian sensibility" of the Quakers failed to resolve the important ideological conflicts of the age. Agrarian life and the concept of an American melting pot are, along with the famous chapters dealing with slavery in Charleston and the Native American–induced "distresses of a frontier-man," crucial elements of Crèvecoeur's unusual book. The overall plan of *Letters*, however, reveals that Crèvecoeur's narrative also has other important themes, but ones that are typically overlooked or underemphasized by historians of early America. Of these, his account of the Religious Society of Friends in America is the most important.[28]

Six of the twelve letters and nearly half of the pages that Crèvecoeur includes in *Letters* are given over to discussion of Quaker life in the American colonies. These *Letters*, taken as a whole, do indeed provide a narrative that makes gestures toward the importance of farming, republican citizenship, American racial identity, and the colonial project. But consider the chapters that intervene between the familiar and often-anthologized "What Is an American" (Letter 2) and his equally famous "Description of Charleston;—thoughts on slavery . . ." (Letter 9). Their titles follow, in the spirit of indicating more accurately the content of Crèvecoeur's book as a whole: "Description of the island of Nantucket; with the manners, customs, policy, and trade, of the inhabitants" (Letter

4); "Customary education and employment of the inhabitants of Nantucket" (Letter 5); "Description of the island of Martha's Vineyard, and of the whale fishery" (Letter 6); Manners and customs at Nantucket" (Letter 7); and "Peculiar customs at Nantucket" (Letter 8). Would it be accurate to suggest, as Carlson has done in his discussion of *Letters* in terms of "Farmer vs. Lawyer" that these admiring descriptions of Quaker life demonstrate "the symbolic and therapeutic role of Nantucket Quakerism for the American farmer"? After the Charleston letter, another letter focusing directly on Quaker life is presented in the form of a fictionalized missive called "From Mr. Iw___n Al___z, a Russian gentleman, describing a visit he paid, at my request, to Mr. John Bartram, the celebrated Pennsylvania botanist" (Letter 11).

This last letter is significant for its attention to John Bartram, a lapsed Quaker who held an official position as botanist to King George II, as well as for its remarkable description of an eighteenth-century Friends meeting. The last piece of correspondence ascribed to the Russian gentleman, which is devoted to discussing Bartram, is also the only place in Crèvecoeur's *Letters* where he deals specifically with the famed Pennsylvania Quaker botanist, who—like other distinguished Americans of the period—had been of specific interest to the French *philosophes* of the eighteenth century. The focus on Bartram by a French writer was no coincidence. As the historian Richard Slotkin states, "The French conceived of America as a stage on which the drama of man's evolution was being replayed for a civilized audience hopeful of its final outcome: the creation of civilization. The New World was a kind of experimental laboratory in which revolutionary theories of human nature and divinity were being tested and proven." In this part of his *Letters*, Crèvecoeur characterizes an exchange between Bartram and the Russian as one during which large, and perhaps hyperbolic, claims are made about sympathetic relations between Quakers and Negroes. In a passage that the Quaker historian Henry J. Cadbury has evaluated as constituting not an exaggeration but an idealization of this relationship, Crèvecoeur claims that John Bartram tells his Russian guest that freed black slaves in America "constantly attend our meetings, they participate in health and sickness, infancy and old age, in the advantages our Society affords." Whether such representations are understood to be exaggerated or merely idealized, the fact remains that Crèvecoeur, like other European intellectuals, focused on Quakers as exemplary American types who serve as a screen upon which to project fantasies of new political arrangements and new modes of racial harmony. This idealization of Quakers occurred for good reason, since Friends were among the first Americans to relinquish their slaves as a matter of religious principle. Still, it should also be remembered that Quakers owned slaves well into the eighteenth century, and some slaves were in the hands of Nantucket Friends.[29]

In crucial ways for European thinkers, and especially for French artists, intellectuals, and politicians of the late eighteenth-century Revolutionary period, Quakers had emerged as representations of a uniquely attractive blend of piety and communitarianism. Moreover, the commercial prowess of Quaker Nantucket gave it a globalist outlook that was unique among the American colonies. As Robert J. Leach and Peter Gow conclude:

> Nantucket Quakers lived in a cosmopolitan world. They grew used to neighbors sailing away and returning from far-off places for trade or in pursuit of whales. Every day Nantucket housewives could see goods being landed from ports around the world even as their husbands, sons, and possibly themselves could speak with familiarity about the household arrangements of fellow Quakers in Philadelphia, yesterday's tavern brawl in Newport, the price of sugar in Jamaica, or the noise in London's streets. A Nantucket Quaker family might regularly host Friends from Quakerism's farthest reaches. A family member might be off playing a similar ambassadorial role elsewhere. That Quaker women were also free (at least within the recognized standards of the religion) to travel in their own right meant that islanders could bear witness to the world through the lens of a unique set of values.[30]

Even the British writer Thomas Babington Macaulay, whose popular *History of England from the Accession of James II* (1848) included acerbic criticism of Quakers generally and Quaker heroes like William Penn specifically, nevertheless saw the powerful imprint of Penn and the other Quaker leaders on the imagination of French thinkers of the Revolutionary period. Macaulay admitted that "The French philosophers of the eighteenth century pardoned what they regarded as [William Penn's] superstitious fancies in consideration of his contempt for priests, and of his cosmopolitan benevolence, impartially extended to all races and to all creeds. His name has thus become, throughout all civilised countries, a synonyme for probity and philanthropy."[31] Quakers in some respects also served as a countertype or cultural alternative to the utopian ideal of the innocent and noble savage as imagined by Jean-Jacques

Rousseau and other influential French thinkers of the eighteenth century. In other ways, the "good Quaker" avoided the more austere aspects secularism in Enlightenment thought. "The good Quaker," concludes Richard Slotkin in his classic study of violence in American culture, "is a figure who mediates between the natural naïve goodness of the savage and the cold wisdom of the European."[32]

There apparently were few limits to the French intellectual idealization of the Society of Friends. As Edith Philips writes in her analysis of the "good Quaker" in French legend, not all American Quakers were understood by French thinkers to embody the highest social and moral accomplishment, but nevertheless, "Pennsylvania outshadowed all the other American colonies in French popular opinion. New England was merely a place where the good Quakers had been persecuted; the South a vague locality where slavery was practiced. Pennsylvania was Utopia itself."[33] To which might be added, Quaker Philadelphia was the primary locus for European analysis of the American Revolution, and Benjamin Franklin—Philadelphia's most famous expatriate—spent the nine years subsequent to the American Revolution living in France. Numerous French intellectuals of the late eighteenth century raised their voices in support and admiration of Quakerism generally, and especially that most successful version established by Quaker emigrants to Pennsylvania and the Delaware Valley region. Some French writers, however, are notable for having made praise of Quakerism a consistent theme in their literary careers. Perhaps the most notable example was the prolific controversialist and Girondin leader Jacques-Pierre Brissot de Warville (1754–92), who was a highly visible figure in the French public sphere until his death by guillotine in 1792. Taking his cue from Crèvecoeur, who had—perhaps unconsciously—devoted such a large portion of his *Letters* to a depictions of nonfarming Quaker communities in New England, Brissot responded to directly to Crèvecoeur (whom he cites in his writings) and other French writers interested in American Quaker life with books such as his *New Travels in the United States of America, Performed in 1788: Containing the Latest and Most Accurate Observations* (1794). *New Travels*, a lengthy and detailed account of the social and economic situation of the early American republic, resembled Brissot's many other publications about America: he included fervent praise for the Society of Friends as well as admiring historical sketches of such American Quaker luminaries as Anthony Benezet and John Woolman. As for Warner Mifflin (a Virginia Quaker and slaveholder who in 1774 apparently became the first American to free his slaves voluntarily and to pay them restitution for their servitude), Brissot goes out of his way to interview him personally during a trip to America and confirms that Mifflin is indeed a paragon of virtue and a model Quaker citizen.[34]

American Quaker life in general is described by Brissot in glowing terms, perhaps because he was a French "conservative republican" by political bent. Visiting a New Jersey village in 1788, Brissot writes, he had in mind the idea that "I wished to see a true American farmer" and then describes his visit to a Quaker farm. The farmer he meets, a thirty-year-old convinced Quaker named Mr. Shoemaker, impresses him greatly, as does his family. Of the Quaker farm women and family life, Brissot observes admiringly that "They are beautiful, easy in their manners, and decent in their deportment. Their dress is simple; they wear fine cotton on Sunday, and that which is not so fine on other days. These daughters aid their mother in the management of the family. The mother has much activity; she held in her arms a little granddaughter, which was caressed by all the children. It is truly a patriarchal family. We conversed much on the Society of Friends." Brissot's curiosity as a journalist brings him much closer to the nuances of Quaker practice, and his insights about Quaker life in America are grounded in his attendance at meetings and funerals and his interviews with a number of Quakers that he meets during his travels. From family life to the arrangement of religious services, Brissot finds the Quakers on a path to utopian possibilities and the attainment of Enlightenment virtues. The Quaker way of silent worship draws his particular attention and praise, even though he observes that the Friends who speak in meeting lack the eloquence usually associated with evangelical preaching:

> The Quakers are of a different character; they early habituate themselves to meditation; they are men of much reflection, and of few words. They have no need, then, of preachers with sounding phrases and long sermons. They disdain elegance as useless amusement; and long sermons appear disproportioned to the force of the human mind, and improper for the divine service. The mind should not be loaded with too many truths of at once, if you wish they should make a lasting impression. The object of preaching being to convert, it ought rather lead to reflection, than to dazzle and amuse.[35]

Having adopted an analysis of American Quaker life that emphasizes the utopian possibilities of their way of religious and community life, Brissot extends and reinforces the opinions of Crèvecoeur, while adding the observation that Quaker faith in America could indicate the welcome development of a thoroughgoing Deism in the young nation.[36]

Although Pennsylvania Quaker life is not a focal point of Crèvecoeur's *Letters*, it is nonetheless clear that he was very much aware of the thriving Quaker communities of Philadelphia and the Delaware Valley. In his unpublished letters, there are numerous instances where he makes direct reference to the Society of Friends in Pennsylvania, and these letters thus supplement and strengthen the esteem he shows for them in his published works. For instance, in his draft letter on "Sketch of a Contrast between the Spanish & English Colonies" (ca. 1787), Crèvecoeur draws sharp comparisons, what he calls "a most astonishing contrast," between the representative communities of the Spanish and English settlements in South and North America, respectively. In sketching his comparison, it is the enormous difference between the Roman Catholicism of Lima and the Quakerism of Pennsylvania that constitutes the most important cultural gap between those two colonies. The usual Protestant critique of Roman Catholicism's mysticism and disproportionate clerical power thus ensues before Crèvecoeur turns to his much-admired Quakers. In Catholic Lima, he writes disapprovingly, the faithful are at the mercy of "a Multiplicity of Priests, dignified clergy, of Fryars Every where spread" while the faithful masses of Peruvians "not only worship the Deity, but Implore every one of its attributes; they dayly Invoque the assistance of Every saint, offer them the greatest adulation by, offerings, Donatives; by Legacies they often make them their Heirs—they sometimes even think of purchasing their favors by Gold & Diamonds, the most precious things they have . . . the Fears of Future Torments are Incessantly held before their Eyes, the Bliss of Heaven is represented to them in the most captivating collours." Nothing could be more different from the religious traditions then coming to maturity in the American colonies, about which he writes "How differrent, how simpler is the system of Relligious Laws, Established follow'd in this country." To the corruptions of priest-ridden Peruvian Catholicism, he suggests, look not only to the American Protestant tradition in general but also "Compare the Fewer & still simpler Tenets of the Peaceable Quakers, with that Voluminous sistem of Bulls, ordinances, Decretals & other Rules observed in [Catholic] S. America. . . . Observe that perfect Equality which prevails amongst them; where there is neither First nor last, neither Priest nor Presbyters, neither Minister nor clerk, neither visible Sacrement, nor outward Form—." The contempt for Roman

Catholicism, which Crèvecoeur expresses with such vigor, is assuaged thoroughly by the refined and egalitarian world suggested by Quaker communities and worship practices.[37]

Barry Levy, one of the few scholars to have noticed Crèvecoeur's attentiveness to the Quaker community of Nantucket, sees Crèvecoeur's interest in the Quakers as part of a broader French admiration for the new forms of egalitarian domestic life such as the one promulgated among the Quaker faithful of Nantucket and elsewhere in the American colonies. Levy notes that the French *philosophes* of Crèvecoeur's generation, influenced by Voltaire's early praise of Quaker prosperity and self-sufficiency, looked to the Quakers as having successfully created a "quintessential republican economy in which domesticated relations united both impressive wealth production and the maintenance and fostering of civic virtue." Edith Philips also points to the early influence of Voltaire in spurring Crèvecoeur and other proponents of the French Revolution to look carefully at the American Quakers as an ideal form of community: "Ever since Voltaire had praised [Quaker] virtues it had been a mark of liberalism and independence of thought to oppose the tolerance, simplicity, honesty and spirituality of the Quakers to the lack of those qualities in contemporary society." Specifically, it is Voltaire's *Lettres philosophiques* (1732) that most likely engaged Crèvecoeur's interest in the Society of Friends and initiated the broader French interest in the mythical "good Quaker." This influential book, with each of its first four chapters titled, "Sur les Quakers," was perhaps the most significant of early French accounts depicting the Quakers as comprising an admirable new social, religious, and political alternative to traditional modes of authority and belief. Voltaire remained impressed all his life with the idea of America "Quaker life as a model for a sustainable and virtuous community, writing in 1754 during his exile from Paris at the age of sixty that "if the sea did not make me unsupportably sick, it is among the Quakers of Pennsylvania that I would finish the remainder of my life."[38]

Crèvecoeur achieved transatlantic literary fame during the generation following John Woolman; Crèvecoeur's descriptions of Quaker settlements among the whaling communities of Nantucket Island and Martha's Vineyard lavish abundant praise on the Quaker way of life (this in spite of the apparent ambivalence about the Quakerism expressed by the Native Americans living on Nantucket[39]). In fact, Crèvecoeur's biographers speculate that some of his relatively progressive attitudes toward slaves and Natives, along with his admiration for

Quakers, may have been shaped to some degree by his reading of Woolman's *Journal,* which appeared posthumously in 1774, almost a decade before the first publication of *Letters.*[40] A more certain influence on Crèvecoeur's views of the clergy and colonialism was Abbé Raynal's *Histoire philosophique et politique des établissements et du commerce des Européens dans les deux Indes* (1770), an influential volume reprinted dozens of times in English and French. Like Crèvecoeur himself, Raynal joined the chorus of enthusiasm for the fledgling religious group by concluding that Quakers are admirable for their social enlightened ways and their democratic orientation. Raynal's skepticism about the European colonial project in America, combined with his anticlericalism, make his views dovetail very well with the Quaker ethos that Crèvecoeur would discover on Nantucket and Martha's Vineyard.

The most astute recent analysis of the complexities and ironies of Crèvecoeur's attraction to life among the Nantucket Quakers belongs to Nathaniel Philbrick, who argues that Crèvecoeur's apparent utopianism and enthusiasm (voiced through his Farmer James, a sensitive and cerebral man who describes himself as a "farmer of feeling") for American life runs aground when he realizes the drawbacks to island life among the Friends. Finding evidence for Crèvecoeur's misgivings in James's shifting narrative voice during the Nantucket sequences, Philbrick sees "evidence that James's attitude to the Nantucket 'utopia' is anything but static; rather, it modulates from an initial enthusiasm to an ever increasing awareness that island life may not be so ideal after all. In this way, the Nantucket sequence subtly and then directly challenges the optimistic vision of the book's beginning and contributes significantly to Crèvecoeur's gradually unfolding tale of disillusionment."[41] As Herman Melville might have agreed, the savagery of whaling considered alongside the pacifism and restraint of Quaker island life made for a profoundly ironic—and to Farmer James decidedly disagreeable—arrangement. Philbrick also observes Farmer James's attentiveness to the Quaker women of Nantucket, who are characterized as happy and healthy, but frequently buffered in their labors not merely by prayer and devotion to the Inner Light but also by doses of opium that allow them to retain their cheerful demeanor through difficult times. Farmer James, notes Philbrick, is also quite favorably impressed by the physical charms of Nantucket's Quaker women, one of whom he escorts to a "house of entertainment" on the island. As James slyly describes this encounter, "I had ... the satisfaction of conducting thither one of the many [Quaker] beauties of that island (for it abounds with handsome women), dressed in all the bewitching attire of the most charming simplicity; like the rest of the company, she was cheerful without loud laughs, and smiling without affectation. . . . We returned as happy as we went; and the brightness of the moon kindly lengthened a day which had passed, like other agreeable ones, with singular rapidity."[42]

Crèvecoeur, through the eyes of Farmer James. was alert in examining Friends for any variance from their stereotypical piety and rectitude, so that any lapse on their part would thus become an implicit criticism of their religious ideas. The Quakeress who is slyly eroticized by Crèvecoeur in this passage thus functions in a way similar to the English Quakers who were described in the seventeenth- and early-eighteenth-century popular press as sexually promiscuous and licentious in their personal behavior. Philbrick is sensitive to this erotic mode in Crèvecoeur's writing, for he notes that "The [Quaker] 'beauty'" described by Farmer James, "does not correspond to the usual notion of a Quaker as a drab, polite, wraith; she is more an ingenuous siren, tempting the Farmer out of his role as an objective observer into a rare instance of personal participation in Nantucket life."[43] In short, Philbrick's account of Crèvecoeur meshes with my general argument about the ways that Quakers had been both harshly attacked, even demonized (during the first decades of the movement), but subsequently admired for their pious virtues. The admiration directed toward Friends, though, as the example from Crèvecoeur shows, just as often devolved into satire or suspicions about the presumed hypocrisy of Quaker claims to virtue and modesty.

Praise for Quakers during the late eighteenth and early nineteenth century was by no means limited to a narrow circle of French thinkers. Focusing on representations of the Quaker legend in eighteenth-century France, Philips has noticed "an almost unanimous chorus of praise" favoring Quakers in the popular press, noting that although Quakers were sometimes attacked by religious reactionaries, "Liberals, freethinkers, 'Encyclopedists,' regarded it as a mark of tolerance to admire the Quakers." Philips also concludes that admiration for American and English Quakers seldom eventuated in religious conversions by French citizens to the Quaker faith: "For the most part, however, the Quaker was regarded as a type to be admired and even idealized, but not imitated. The radicals of the eighteenth century were essentially conservative in conduct. So much deviation from common behavior as is implied in the Quaker's conduct seemed exaggerated and somewhat ridiculous to them."[44] Thus, much of the French enthusiasm for Quakerism lacked intellectual nuance and actual familiarity with Quakerism in either the English or American context, but nevertheless, as Jeanne Henriette Louis concludes, "Quakers were in vogue in pre-revolutionary France, mainly among artists, intellectuals and politicians."[45] Barry Levy, in an overview of late eighteenth-century Quaker family life, also argues that in idealizing the American Quaker, French thinkers of the late eighteenth century overlooked a good deal of the turmoil then rippling through Quaker communities as the Society of Friends experienced considerable restructuring and changes in discipline. New Quaker prohibitions against slaveholding, the withdrawal of Friends from the Pennsylvania Assembly in 1756,[46] and the strengthening of Quaker rules against marriage to persons outside the Society (which in turn led large numbers of the rising generation of Quakers to be read out of meeting for this transgression) complicated the social reality of a group idealized by the *philosophes*.[47] Quakers were not vanishing altogether during the time of their voguish popularity among the French chattering classes, but their numbers were shrinking because of the severe marriage restrictions of the period. Levy estimates that between about 1750 and 1790 Pennsylvania Friends disowned around half of its membership in order to preserve its religious discipline: "After much debate and resistance, Quaker leaders chose to protect their household ideal and disown, in effect summarily, all those who married irregularly." Even as European intellectuals continued to idealize the Quaker communities of America, Quakers were themselves experiencing a crisis in their membership that exposed fault lines within the Society of Friends and would result in limited growth during subsequent generations.[48]

Given the ongoing debates within the ranks of Quakers themselves, Crèvecoeur's sustained attention to the nonfarming Quakers of Nantucket, which occupies so much of a book that ostensibly is concerned with American farm life, is ironic and perhaps even willfully avoids proper attention to the complexities of theological debate then occurring among Friends. But his admiration of Quaker life is consistent with that of Voltaire and numerous other French *philosophes* of the period, all of whom had a lengthy infatuation with aspects of Quaker life that appeared to have produced both individual morality and a prosperous commonwealth in William Penn's Quaker Pennsylvania. For this reason, it is not surprising that although modern historians have focused their attentions on Crèvecoeur's incipient nationalism and agrarian mythmaking, his own contemporaries in France (such as the 1785 reviewer for the *Journal de Paris*) would be equally fascinated by his depiction of virtuous American Quaker life: "Of all imaginable sects this is the one which offers the most constant example of simplicity, justice, gentleness, patience and true humanity. Among them there is neither first nor last. All are equal. They do not swear, they abhor war."[49] With French sentiment during the years just before the French Revolution running strongly in favor of Quaker values, it is perhaps fitting that a group of Nantucket whalers would eventually emigrate to Dunkerque, in the north of France, to begin a Quaker settlement there. Soon after, this small Quaker colony of emigrant Nantucket Islanders were introduced to the young French nobleman Jean de Marsillac, a Friend who would soon write the first French language biography of William Penn (*La vie de Guillaume Penn, fondateur de la Pennsylvanie, premier législateur connu des Etats-Unis d'Amérique* [1791]). The historian Jeanne Henriette Louis has noted that "Thanks to Jean de Marsillac, William Penn's spiritual legacy was present in France during the French Revolution, as well as Benjamin Franklin's ideological legacy."[50] Thus, after considerable high-minded theorizing, the French nation did itself finally accept a tiny dose of the American Quaker community themselves, without ever adopting for French culture in any significant way the religious principles of the Quaker movement.

3

Chronicles of Friendship

Quaker Historiography in the Early Republic

The Quaker of the olden time!
How calm, and firm, and true,
Unspotted by its wrong and crime,
He walked the dark earth through!
Anonymous, "The Quaker of the Olden Time" (1846)

You can discern it in them, illuminating their faces—their whole persons, indeed, however earthly and cloddish—with a light that inevitably shines through, and makes the startled community aware that these men are not as they themselves are,—not brethren nor neighbors of their thought. Forthwith, it is as if an earthquake rumbled through the town, making its vibrations felt at every hearthstone, and especially causing the spire of the meeting-house to totter. The Quakers have come. We are in peril!
Nathaniel Hawthorne, *Main-Street* (1849)

For the first century and a half of their existence, early Quakers in England and America were anything but passive in the face of a steady onslaught of books, broadsides, pamphlets, and articles decrying their religious beliefs and practices. During the early decades of the movement, Quakers and their sympathizers mobilized every aspect of the popular press in order to claim the privilege of following their radical preferences in worship while asserting a host of strikingly anti-authoritarian social claims. The burgeoning print culture of the British Atlantic allowed these claims to circulate in the public sphere at little cost, an advantage for Quaker writers who frequently lacked the financial means to publish in expensive media like bound books. The largest number of what were referred to as "Friends Books," according to the records of writer and pioneering Quaker bibliographer John Whiting (1656–1722) of Bristol, England, who catalogued thousands of these ephemeral documents from the latter half of the seventeenth century, were in fact cheaply produced leaflets, broadsides, and slender pamphlets.[1] Opposition to and persecution of Friends declined slowly, though, and as late as 1708, when their worship and principles had already become far less troubling to the authorities and ordinary people alike, colonial leaders like the eminent Puritan, diarist, and Salem witchcraft judge Samuel Sewall (1652–1730) were still voicing opposition to Quakers. Asked to sign a warrant to authorize a Quaker meetinghouse, Sewall refused and declared that "I would not have a hand in setting up their Devil Worship."[2] Still, legal tolerance, followed by an actual tolerance of Quaker life, was by the early eighteenth century well underway. While the first seventeenth-century Quaker missionaries such as Mary Dyer had been dealt with harshly or even martyred for their cause in colonial Massachusetts, a later generation of highly articulate Pennsylvania Quakers like William Penn and other Philadelphia Friends remained outspoken in defending their faith. They were not just bold in rejecting the written criticisms that appeared for many decades after the founding of the Society of Friends, but also secure financially and politically because of the political and economic power solidifying in the hands of the Quaker leadership in Pennsylvania and the Delaware Valley.

Even before this surge in influence by colonial Quakers had taken full effect, however, it was possible by 1722 for American colonists to peruse the first comprehensive and authoritative history of the Society of Friends, William Sewel's *The History of the Rise, Increase, and Progress, of the Christian People Called Quakers*. First written in Low Dutch in 1717 and then translated into an English edition in 1722, this lengthy book remained in print as a steady seller in England and America until it was superseded finally by English abolitionist Thomas Clarkson's even more comprehensive *A Portraiture of Quakerism* (1806).[3] Some versions of Quaker history had already appeared in England, as with the compilations of Quaker writings under the editorship of important writers like Gerard Croese and George Bishop, whose documentary histories of the Friends appeared in 1696 and 1702, respectively.[4] But Sewel's research on the early Friends, which provided a better sense of the larger Anglo-American Quaker world, was disseminated widely during the eighteenth century, and consequently established itself as the standard account. The American Quaker convert and pamphleteer Herman Husband found Sewel's presentation of Quaker history to be a major turning point in his own convincement as a Friend: "I had a Desire and intended to get Luther's Works; but before I did, I met with Sewall's [*sic*] History, a Book giving an Account of the Rise and Progress of a People called in Scorn Quakers, which was like the Sun breaking out of Darkness into Noon-day."[5]

Although Sewel's history deals only in a very limited way with the American branch of the Quaker faith, it is significant because of its ambitious treatment of the first few decades of Quaker activity in England. Sewel's narrative technique of interspersing scenes of Quaker attempts to establish themselves in New England would have had the effect for colonial Friends of showing their relationship with a larger movement of Quakers in the British Atlantic arena. The narrative patterns and thematic emphases of Sewel and Clarkson, the first major historians of the early Friends, establish the lineaments of official Quaker history as it would have been available to members of the Society of Friends and also to those outside the movement who had a serious interest in understanding its origins and the development of its religious and social practices. Short of convincement and membership in a Friends meeting, these histories provided a richly detailed (if imperfect and somewhat incomplete) and sympathetic perspective on the broader outlines of Quaker history as it emerged during a crucial century of nation building in America.

Sewel's history is valuable because it synthesizes important episodes of the first decades of Quaker life in England and provides a critique of the New England Puritan response to Quaker evangelism. The eclectic quality of his history is indeed somewhat distracting; while he proceeds chronologically and writes clearly and capably, *History of the Quakers* combines historical analysis interspersed with an of anthology of long extracts from early English Quaker writings by prophetic figures like

George Fox. In spite of these shortcomings, the publication of William Sewel's *History* marks a significant narrative milestone in the evolving status of Quakers in England and America. After more than a half century of controversial religious practices that had put the Society of Friends into serious conflict with more dominant established Protestant churches on both sides of the Atlantic, Quakers finally had ready to hand a substantial work of historical scholarship.[6]

In a sense, Sewel's work serves as a foundational history for the Society of Friends in the same way as the much more famous work of ecclesiastical history by Cotton Mather (1663–1728) serves to document, authorize, and reify the activities of colonial Puritans in New England. Like Mather's *Magnalia Christi Americana* (1702), a work imperious in both title and content that is typically translated as "The Ecclesiastical History of New England," Sewel's *History of the Quakers* sets out ambitiously to chart the early development of an important religious movement that began in England and later established itself in the American colonies. Like Mather's ecclesiastical history of the Puritans, Sewel's work appeared first in London and was subsequently published in America, but only after its credibility and popularity had been earned among English Quakers. Having earned status as reliable history by its adoption in England, the smaller and, of necessity, less adventurous American publishers successfully brought an edition of Sewel's history to market in the Quaker stronghold of Philadelphia several years after the first English edition.

A short comparison concerning the relationship of Sewel's *History of the Quakers* to Mather's *Magnalia,* a document that would provide a mighty influence on later historians, is in order here. Although the two books share certain similarities because they were both conceived as sympathetic theological chronicles at approximately the same historical moment, Mather's *Magnalia* and Sewel's *History* follow entirely different principles in setting out their narratives of church origins. The table of contents for Mather's history of the Puritans in New England, which covers the years 1620–98, shows his unmistakable preference for institutional history: he recounts in detail the early days of Harvard College, which would be the training ground for future generations of the ministers and magistrates that populate most of the opening pages in *Magnalia.* These are the individuals, according to "The Reverend and Learned" Cotton Mather's opening pages, who formed the most important part of the Puritan legacy in America: "Governours," "Famous Divines,"

"Magistrates," "Benefactors," and "Venerable Assemblies." By contrast, Sewel's *History* emphasizes not only the bravery but also the marginality and lack of power of the early English and American Quakers, who were repeatedly subject to ridicule, harassment, physical coercion, fines, banishment, and other severe penalties. Although he does show some of the ways in which certain prominent English Quakers, like George Fox—and wealthy ones like Margaret Fell and William Penn—participated in English politics in highly visible ways, Friends in Sewel's *History of the Quakers* are for the most part marginal figures whose names have been lost to history and whose sufferings led to a chronicle of their enthusiasm but did not lead to the establishment of a new province (as was the case with the Puritans in New England). Both Mather and Sewel had in mind for their histories a chronicle of the early years of their respective religious movements, but the distance between their subjects is enormous. Whereas Mather's *Magnalia,* for all of its claims of Puritan rebellion against corrupt Anglican authority, might be fairly described as having followed an authoritarian model of civic and religious affairs, Sewel fixes most of his attention on those whose extreme behavior as Quakers put them in opposition to the law of England and the vigilante justice applied against them by English mobs and bullies during the middle decades of the seventeenth century.

William Sewel's *History of the Quakers* (1717)

The first truly distinguished history of the Quakers was written over the course of twenty-five years by the Dutch lexicographer and historian William Sewel, a Quaker and close associate of George Fox, who in the first part of the eighteenth century brought to completion an eight-hundred-page narrative of the Society of Friends. The elapsed time since Sewel began his research, in the early 1690s, is significant not just for the thoroughness that long years of composition allowed him to apply to his historical narrative, but also because his years of writing the Quaker history were precisely those years when Friends began to transform their early enthusiasms and to regularize their religious discipline for all Quakers. After he had translated the book from Low Dutch into English, it became a standard reference work on the Society of Friends and remained so for more than a century in both England and America. In Massachusetts, for example, when the young Unitarian minister Ralph Waldo Emerson began his own study of Quaker traditions during the 1830s—in the years before publishing his seminal *Nature* (1836) essay—it was to Sewel's venerable history that he turned in order to understand their religious activities in relation to the post-Christian transcendentalism that he was beginning to construct.[7] English readers also held Sewel's book in high esteem. Writing admiringly about the experience of attending a Quaker meeting in an essay reprinted in 1834 by the New Bedford *Mercury,* the English poet Charles Lamb paid his own tribute to Sewel's work: "Reader, if you are not acquainted with it, I would recommend to you above all church narratives Sewel's *History of the Quakers.* It is in folio and is the abstract of the journals of Fox and the primitive Friends. It is far more edifying and affecting than anything you will read of [early Methodist clergyman] John Wesley and his colleagues. Here is nothing to stagger you, nothing to make you mistrust, no suspicion of alloy, no drop or dreg of the ambitious spirit."[8]

As Sewel begins his account of the early Quaker movement, he pays scrupulous attention first to recounting the general atmosphere of persecutions for English martyrs during the Protestant Reformation, which had produced the Puritan movement and other radical dissenting sects such as the Quakers. Concerning the Puritans and their flight to religious liberty in New England, however, Sewel is acerbic and points out the cruel irony surrounding the persecution of colonial dissenters from Puritan orthodoxy (such as the Quakers), when considered in the light of the Puritans' own flight from persecution in England: "Very remarkable it is, that even those [Puritans], of which many in the reign of king Charles I, went to New-England, to avoid the persecution of the bishops, afterwards themselves turned cruel persecutors of pious people, by inhuman whippings, &c. and lastly by putting some to death by the hands of a hangman: a clear proof indeed, that those in whom such a ground of bitterness was left still, tho' it had not always brought forth the like abominable fruits, were not come yet to a perfect reformation; for though the stem of human traditions and institutions sometimes had been shaken strongly, yet much of the root was left."[9] Against the backdrop of American Puritan hypocrisy and religious discrimination, Sewel details the crucible in which an American Quaker ethos was formed and reconstituted out of an English legacy of persecution brought on by charismatic religious expression, which once had threatened the integrity of Protestant orthodoxy.

In much the same way that saints' lives recounted as hagiography in popular earlier works of Reformation martyrology such as John Foxe's enormously influential *Book of Martyrs* (1563),[10] Sewel indicates that extraordinary endurance of insult and pain were essential in order for Quakers to withstand a variety of assaults leveled against their religious principles and, most painfully, against their bodies. In his preface Sewel emphasizes that the early Quakers were on the whole defenseless yet assertive in their religious convictions. Unwilling to take up arms, even against their persecutors, "They, who had not king, prince, nor potentate to protect them, and, who in the beginning had not among themselves any men of renown or literature, but relying on their integrity, and trusting to God alone, have at length triumphed over the malice of their opposers, by suffering (which rose to that degree, that it was at the expense of the lives of many of them) under violent oppression from high and low, and the opposition of learned and unlearned."[11] Set upon by their enemies, Quakers patiently endured "bitter revilings, scornful mockings, rude abuses, and bloody blows from the fool-hardy rabble, but also severe persecutions, hard imprisonments, grievous banishments, unmerciful spoil of goods, cruel whippings, cutting off of ears, smotherings in prison." Examples abound in Sewel's history not only of frequent jailings of leaders like George Fox, but also of physical attacks against those Quakers who were bold enough to hold house-meetings in defiance of the orthodox clergy, who labeled the Quakers "House-Creepers" for their custom of meeting at houses rather than at priestly temples.[12]

Roused and angered, and frequently encouraged in their vigilante anger by orthodox religious authorities, mobs of ordinary English citizens regularly went looking for Quakers who were holding meetings in defiance of church law and assaulted them at will. Sewel makes the connection clear between mob violence and its sponsorship at the hands of the clergy, as in this passage recounting the persecutions of 1658:

> Now there was great persecution, both by imprisonment, and breaking up of meetings; and many died in prisons: for the priests speaking evil of the Quakers, it did kindle the insolency of the rabble not a little, so that they did not stick to throw squibs into the meetings, to cast rotten eggs on those that were met, to beat on drums and kettles, and so to make a hideous noise, and to abuse people most grievously with blows and violent punches. One day there being a meeting appointed near London, they beat and abused about eighty persons that came out of the city to meet there, tearing their coats and cloaks from off their backs, and throwing them into ditches and ponds.

The Quaker response to such vicious treatment, according to Sewel, in many cases took the form of a renewed commitment to their own moral improvement and personal spiritual conviction.[13]

Far from shrinking before discrimination and assault at the hands of the orthodox, colonial Friends (and especially the women of the sect) are shown to hold the ground of their religious views while developing an unprecedented inner strength. Sewel observes that they had been woefully outnumbered in the American colonies and set upon regularly by those offended by the troublingly antinomian doctrine of the Inner Light, but nevertheless he finds that early Anglo-American Quakers remained doggedly resolute in their faith, while simultaneously "among all these vicissitudes, notable instances have been seen of unfeigned godliness, sincere love, much true-heartedness, extraordinary meekness, singular patience, ardent zeal, undaunted courage, and unshaken steadfastness, even among the female sex, which though the weakest, yet in the hardest attacks, showed a more than manly spirit."[14] The "manly spirit," he points out, comes not from adrenaline, delusion, or madness, but from serene confidence in the rightness of their beliefs. For all of his unalloyed admiration of the Quakers and their radical new concepts of the Inner Light's democratic availability, Sewel is careful to avoid harmonizing his view of Quaker piety with the views of those who accused Quakers of being merely mentally disturbed, willfully blasphemous, or at the mercy of idiosyncratic delusions or fantastic dreams. While acknowledging the night-journeying power of dreams within Quaker culture, he cites George Fox on the need to discern between dreams or sensations that are authentic expressions and experiences of the Divine, and those spurious and misleading dreams that lead away from the true faith. In some respects, Sewel admits, Fox's followers were a "dreaming people," and yet he notes that Fox consistently warned his converts that "Except they could distinguish between dream and dream, their observations would be nothing but confusion, since there were three sorts of dreams; for multiplicity of business sometimes caused dreams; and there were whisperings of Satan in the night seasons; and there were also speakings of God to man in dreams." Rather than appearing only as zealots empowered by the ill-gotten courage of psychosis or hysteria, the steely but eloquent resolve of the early Quakers is presented by Sewel as having grown organically from a set of coherent, fervent, and unflinching beliefs.[15]

Eloquence of speech and graceful, written prose characterize the preponderance of recorded communication attributed to the Quaker martyrs in Sewel's history, and Quaker speech—increasingly documented by the authorities themselves as Friends began slowly to establish themselves as a tolerable religious groups—gradually becomes a part of the colonial record. Whether Sewel is examining the letters salvaged from their correspondence, testimony gleaned from courtroom proceedings, or essays written in retrospect about the overt discrimination that Quakers experienced during the first half century of their existence, the power of Quaker oratory and devotional writing is consistently emphasized. Whereas the earliest American Quaker victims of orthodox retribution like Mary Dyer and Marmaduke Stephenson failed even through their powerful use of language to enlist the support of their Puritan accusers, Sewel shows the modest but unmistakable rhetorical inroads established by Quakers defending themselves from charges of blasphemy and sedition. From time to time, wavering and uncertainties could be detected among the orthodox magistrates, who for previous generations had served as unrelenting persecutors of Friends, whom they deemed to be heretics and enemies of civic order. But the example of a self-proclaimed Quaker named Wenlock Christianson serves as a useful example of this new hesitancy about punishments. As with the more notorious case of Mary Dyer's sentencing and execution, Governor John Endicott once again played a central role in the case of Christianson, who came to trial in 1661, only a year after Dyer had finally met her end on the gallows. When his case finally came before the magistrates, some found themselves powerfully swayed by Christianson's articulate and passionate defense of his Quaker beliefs— to say nothing of his sharp reminder to the court that England herself prescribed capital punishment only for *Jesuit* blasphemy not for *Quaker* blasphemy.[16] Sensing a troubling lack of resolve among the lesser magistrates, however, Endicott took it upon himself to override their objections, thereby sentencing Christianson, declaring to the Quaker that he must "be hanged until you are dead, dead, dead."[17] The style of Wenlock's immediate retort to Endicott is replete with the graceful periods and eloquence that had come to characterize much of Quaker preaching, even by the earliest years of the movement:

> Known be it unto you all, that if ye have power to take my life from me, my soul shall enter into everlasting rest and peace with God, where you yourselves shall never come. And if you have power to take my life from me, the which I do question, I do believe you shall never more take Quakers['] lives from them: note my words; do not think to weary out the living God, by taking away the lives of his servants. What do you gain by it? For the last man that you have put to death, here are five come in his room. And if ye have power to take my life from me, God can raise

up the same principle of life in ten of his servants, and send them among you in my room, that you may have torment upon torment, which is your portion; for there is no peace to the wicked, faith my God.[18]

To this remarkable speech, the gathered magistrates responded with consternation and unease, rather than with fury, even though Christianson's trial occurred before Charles II finally expressed his displeasure at the ill treatment of Quakers in Massachusetts.

With Christianson plainly willing to mount the gallows unrepentant and staunch in his religious views, his words seemed in Sewel's judgment to manifest the presence of the Divine: "The holy confidence with which he uttered these words show, and the sequel made it appear plainly, that something supernatural was contained in them." Given this surprising turn of events, Endicott retreated from his imperious sentence and allowed Christianson and twenty-seven other imprisoned Quakers to be released from jail, albeit not before two of the prisoners were singled out for public floggings. Still, even though colonial Friends were not typically subject to capital punishment, much persecution lay in store for those less fortunate Quakers in Massachusetts who had been accused of lapsing from orthodoxy. For reasons that are unclear from Sewel's record, two of Christianson's friends, Peter Pearson and Judith Brown, were both "stripped to the waist, and fastened to a cart's tail [and] whipped through the town of Boston, with twenty stripes apiece." This moderation of punitive force after Christianson's trial and gallows speech marks a kind of turning point—given additional force in September 1661 by Charles II's subsequent protective ruling for the Quakers—indicating that the once-totalitarian power of the colonial orthodox authorities had begun its very slow but inevitable decline. Still, the bitter edge of Sewel's commentary about New England' intolerance toward the Quakers is unmistakable, as is his judgment that the American colonists were less than candid about the harsh treatments to which Quakers had been subjected.[19]

Reviewing the jailings and harsh punishments of the men and women who served as early Quaker evangelists in New England during the 1650s, Sewel concludes that "Such was the entertainment the Quakers first met with at Boston, and that from a people who pretended, that for conscience-sake they had chosen the wilderness of America, before the well-cultivated Old England; though afterwards, when they took away the lives of those called Quakers, they, excuse their cruel actions, did not stick to say, that at first they had used no punishment against the Quakers."[20] He also shows the English Puritans to be much more severe in their treatment of Quakers than, for example, the Swedish settlers in the New World, whose toleration of religious difference is striking by comparison with the cruelty of the "precise New England men." Religious persecution, argues Sewel, was a function not so much of the historical moment in which the Quakers appeared, but of the particularly intolerant strain of the Puritan temperament. While the Puritan "magistrates . . . did glory in cruelty" and were "foolish enough to persuade themselves that their whipping was some kind of meritorious work, "not all American colonists acted in like fashion: "in some places of America lived also Swedes, who in regard of their worship were no less despised by the English, than of old the Samaritans were by the Jews: and yet those Swedes entertained the Quakers, when they came amongst them, far better than the English did."[21]

Sewel's scholarly history of the Quaker movement appeared in England and America at a time when the popular press was still awash with printed materials written in staunch opposition to its principles. Chief among those violently opposed to Quaker beliefs was the tireless Anglican pamphleteer Francis Bugg (1640–1724?), a former Quaker who penned sensationally titled diatribes like *The Great Mystery of the Little Whore Unfolded, and Her Witchcrafts . . . Discovered. Whereby the Quakers Are Once More Set in Their True Light. By Way of Dialogue between First, a Church of England Man. Secondly, a Protestant dissenter. Thirdly, a Right-Bred Quaker* (1705) and *Goliath's Head Cut Off with His Own Sword, and the Quakers Routed by Their Own Weapons: by a Dialogue Tripartite. . . . Whereby the Great Mystery of the Little Whore Is Farther Unfolded* (1708).[22] In an era when Quakers continued to stand well outside the pale of religious orthodoxy, even by the standards of many Puritans and other dissenters from the Church of England, Sewel's historical recapitulation of how the Society of Friends had been established thus served as important material and rhetorical justification for eventually accepting Quakers as tolerated participants in the world of respectable Anglo-American religions. Moreover, his rehearsal of the early years of the Quaker movement delivers a vivid portrayal of the contest between established orthodoxy and the upstart Friends, with their women preachers and their overt and implicit resistance to socioreligious authority in early modern England. Both the founding of the Quaker movement and the contentious debates that swirled in the public sphere are recounted through Sewel's reviews and extracts of early Quaker writings, and his summaries of the resistance to Quaker subversion in the popular press.

Within the pages of his *History of the Quakers,* Sewel devotes a large portion of narrative to the crucial early period of Quaker heresy, especially the years of Oliver Cromwell's rule in 1650s, when Fox and his band of followers were regularly subject to arrest and imprisonment, and the marketplace of print exploded with diatribes against the new religious movement. From this period, Sewel includes large portions of writings by George Fox, especially his *Journal,* excerpts from the works of other prominent early Friends, and anecdotes about early Quaker evangelists in England. As for Cromwell himself, Sewel observes that he made no special efforts to enforce attendance of the general citizenry at the national church or to persecute Quakers in particular, but Cromwell's apparent indifference to attacks upon Friends by their religious enemies created an environment in which Quakers were regularly subject to coercion and violence. As a consequence, "The Quakers, so called, were imprisoned for refusing to swear, or for not paying tithes to maintain the priests; and they were whipped like vagabonds, for preaching in the markets, or in other public places; or they were fined for not taking off their hats before magistrates; for this was called 'contempt of the magistracy'; and when for conscience-sake they refused to pay such a fine, either the spoiling of goods, or imprisonment became their share."[23] In the bustling port city of Bristol, for instance, the established clergy preached vehemently against the Quakers and incited their congregations to take vigilante action against them. Having been given free license to their parishioners to function as unofficial religious police in their districts, Bristol residents began harassing Friends with impunity. With the moral sponsorship of the orthodox clergy, "the riotous multitude did not stick to rush violently into the houses of the Quakers, so called, at Bristol, under a pretence of preventing treasonable plottings." Having urged the magistrates to imprison Quakers for treason and sedition, national church ministers had set the stage for all manner of popular retribution against Friends. Warnings by the traditional clergy in Bristol "instigated the rabble to that degree, that now they thought they had full liberty to use all kind of insolence against the [Quakers]; beating, smiting, pushing, and often treading upon them till blood was shed; for they were become a prey to every malapert fellow, as a people that were without the protection of the law."[24] Added to the vigilante justice administered at street level by opponents of the Quakers, the English courts regularly found Quakers guilty of such crimes as refusing to take oaths, failing to attend orthodox Anglican church services, or otherwise disrupting the conventional social practices of the day; for such offenses, Friends were frequently subject to banishment and were transported to colonial outposts like Barbados or Jamaica to suffer years-long terms of indentured servitude. Even transported across the Atlantic, though, Quakers did not cease advancing their religious doctrines through meetings and evangelism, as may be concluded from a 1676 colonial law passed in Barbados that had the expressed intent of outlawing all Quaker public testimony and preaching. Meetings open to slaves were singled out for special legal scrutiny, and the anti-Quaker statute ordered confiscation of any slave discovered in attendance at a Friends meeting.[25]

Sewel is alert to the role played by gender in the debates surrounding the early Quakers. As the numbers of Quakers increased quickly in London and other large towns like Bristol, women became visible as prominent and charismatic preachers in regular meetings during the Cromwell years. In turn, the women preachers enraged orthodox pamphleteers, who decried them as witches and insisted that they be prevented from assuming ministerial roles. In fact, Sewel specifies that the first "settled meeting" for Quakers was held at the home of one Sarah Sawyer at Aldergate and that soon after, Anne Downer was the first Quaker woman to preach publicly in London. As Quaker meetinghouses were built, the popular press continued to churn out its warnings, and Sewel notes that "Abundance of books were now spread against the Quakers, as seducers and false prophets; and these written by the priests and teachers of several sects; for they[,] perceiving that many of their hearers forsook them, left no stone unturned to stop it." That some of these "seducers and false prophets" were women only stoked the rage of the orthodox.[26]

The centrality of gender to the matter of early Quaker evangelism is evident not only in England, Scotland, Wales, and Holland—the settings in which most of Sewel's history unfolds—but in the fledgling New England colony, where the English Puritan movement had established its most important beachhead. Sewel's historical narrative proceeds with a careful eye trained on developments in New England, highlighting the parallel activities of English and American friends during the middle years of the seventeenth century. The famous trials and martyrdom of Mary Dyer feature prominently in these accounts, but Sewel supplements his portrait of Dyer with vivid portrayals of Mary Fisher and other Friends who suffered at the hands of Puritans and their magistrates during these years. The presence of women is a recurrent theme, although Sewel himself makes no particular assessment of the gender politics implicit in the arraignment and jailing of a remarkably large proportion of women among the Quaker ministry. Typical of these women in Sewel's history is the feisty and surprisingly independent Mary Clark, a London native who left her husband (a merchant tailor) at home to care for their children while she traveled to America soon after the arrival of Mary Dyer. Upon her arrival, Clark scolded the Boston magistrates for their harsh treatment of Quakers, but for her troubles she was summarily sentenced to a flogging followed by twelve weeks of cold winter jail time. "After she had delivered her message," Sewel notes with his usual attention to the minute details of Quaker punishment, "she was unmercifully rewarded with twenty stripes of a whip with three cords, on her naked back. . . . The cords of these whips were commonly as thick as a man's little finger, having each some knots at the end; and the stick was sometimes so long, that the hangman made use of both his hands to strike the harder."[27] Although such accounts of physical violence and jailing are prominent in Sewel's narrative, not all of the early women Quakers appear as victims in scenes of persecution. While Sewel does recount the difficulties encountered by the Quaker missionary Mary Fisher, who had been arrested and jailed after her arrival in Boston during the summer of 1656, he also depicts Fisher as an independent woman of the world.

After her release by the Boston authorities, Fisher traveled extensively as a Quaker evangelist at various ports on the Mediterranean. By 1660 she had managed to reach Smyrna and Adrianople in Turkey, but the English consul learned of her activities and sent her back to Venice. Undeterred, Fisher traveled once more to Turkey and met successfully with the Muslim sultan Mahomet, who along with his religious council apparently listened with interest to her new religious ideas. After delivering her message concerning the Quaker faith, the Turks asked her "what she thought of their prophet Mahomet?"; to this Fisher "answered warily, 'that she knew him not; but Christ the true prophet, the Son of God, who was the light of the world, and enlightened every man coming into the world, him she knew.'" Of the Muslim prophet, she continued in a conciliatory vein, he should be judged "to be true or false, according to the words and prophecies he spoke" and that "if the word that a prophet speaketh come to pass, then shall ye know that the Lord hath sent that prophet; but if it come not to pass, then shall ye know that the Lord never sent him."[28]

According to Sewel, male Quakers fared equally badly at the hands of Puritan magistrates in New England. And their punishments, set out in vivid detail in the form of a historical narrative detailing the first fifty years of Friends' activities in England and America, serve as occasions for his persistent criticism not only of English magistrates and anti-Quaker vigilantes, but of the New England authorities who had themselves been victims of religious discrimination. Special criticism is directed at the Puritan minister John Norton (in a palpably ironic tone, Sewel calls him a "high priest"), whose zeal was so consistently placed on the side of those who would persecute the Quaker minority that he maintained stoutly that physical punishments were entirely appropriate for heretics and other religious miscreants. After a particularly cruel abuse of a Boston Quaker named W. Brend, who had been starved for a week and subjected to extended floggings so that "his back and arms were bruised and black, and the blood hanging as in bags under his arms; and so into one was his flesh beaten, that the sign of a particular blow could not be seen, for all was become as jelly," Norton reacted to complaints about the severity of Brend's beating with the tart rejoinder that "W. Brend endeavoured to beat our gospel-ordinances black and blue; if he then be beaten black and blue, it is by just upon him; and I will appear in his behalf that did so." Sewel is blunt in his assessment of Norton's violent turn, concluding that "It is therefore not much to be wondered at, that these precise and bigoted magistrates, who would be looked upon to be eminent for piety, were cruel in persecuting, since their chief teacher thus wickedly encouraged them to it."[29] With remarks like these, Sewel became one of the first historians to chart the early development of fierce religious intolerance in colonial New England.

Sewel's *History of the Quakers* concludes with a testament to Queen Anne (reigned 1702–17), who, building on the earlier mandate of Charles II, had solidified English toleration of Quakers by 1710, when she addressed the subject of toleration of Friends in an address to Parliament. Approximately sixty years after the first Quakers had begun their journey to a new, mystical faith grounded in their belief in resistance to civil and church authority and wed to a profound experience of the Inner Light, Quakers in the British Atlantic were finally deemed to be members of a tolerable religious group. Calling themselves "protestant dissenting subjects" in a subsequent letter to Queen Anne in June 1713, written just four years before the initial publication of Sewel's history, the Quaker authors (members of the London Meeting) express their gratitude at their newly secure protection under the law of England. Writing at the conclusion of the War of the Spanish Succession, during which England had been engaged in fighting Catholic France in Europe and America (in the colonial theater, the conflict was called Queen Anne's War), the London Quakers compared the new climate of toleration to English intervention on behalf of Protestants in other parts of the world: "We are also under a dutiful sense of the queen's gracious government and compassion manifested towards tender consciences at home, as well as noble and Christian interposition in favour of persecuted protestants abroad."[30] As this carefully timed letter suggests, the London Quakers were taking pains to assure Queen Anne (and, in a subsequent letter, King George I) of their loyalty both to her rule and to the Protestant cause. Sewel's *History* concludes its analysis of the period 1650–1715 by asserting Quaker allegiance to the larger causes of Protestantism and English nationalism.

The early decades of violent encounter and heretical accusations thus are subsumed into Sewel's broader narrative plan, which, as his citation of deferential letters to the monarch shows, situates the Quakers peacefully and loyally as exemplary Protestant subjects. Obviously and persistently at variance with English norms of religion and sociability, the early American and English Quakers of Sewel's imagining negotiate confrontation and belonging, mysticism and pragmatic citizenship. Like all religious movements, though, the Society of Friends evolved as social pressures shifted and its membership inevitably absorbed new personalities, preferences, and desires—and Sewel's history reflects these changes. Another century of religious practice and social adjustment would pass, however, before a more nuanced history of Friends would appear at the hands of Thomas Clarkson, an early nineteenth-century abolitionist and admirer of the Society of Friends. With the benefit of methodologically improved and more balanced scholarship, historical representation of Quakers would achieve greater precision and nuance during a period when their political views were becoming increasingly public and controversial. Quakers would again become iconic in the popular mind not because of a popular familiarity with the particulars of their faith, discipline, and practice, but because their religious and moral views could be forged into useful tools for public debate. Reputed to have produced powerful ideas and moral concerns,

Quakers in the second century of the movement would become attractive public figures in ways unimaginable for the early Friends, while the larger public persisted in keeping a safe distance from the practice of Quakerism itself.

Updating the Quaker Legacy: Thomas Clarkson's *A Portraiture of Quakerism* (1806)

William Sewel's history stood for nearly a century as the standard account of the Society of Friends, until it was superseded in the early nineteenth century.[31] The timing of the next full-scale historical reckoning for the Quaker movement arrived at a propitious moment, when after many decades of quiet obscurity Quakers in England and the United States had begun once more to enter the public consciousness because of their stubborn support for the abolition of slavery. One of Great Britain's most fervent abolitionists, therefore, would write a newly definitive account of the Society of Friends. The English abolitionist Thomas Clarkson's lengthy, three-volume examination of the Society of Friends, *A Portraiture of Quakerism*, is unprecedented in its comprehensiveness, and definitive for its age, in dealing with the nuances of Quaker principles as written into its religious discipline and subsequently enacted on the American scene. It is by far the most thorough analysis of the various aspects of the religion in terms of its theological principles and in its participation in the broader political and social culture of which it had been a part since its origins in the mid-seventeenth century.[32]

With more than 150 years of Quaker history to examine, Clarkson's perspective is a longer and more subtle one, and it comprises a greater variety of experiences for the Society of Friends than did Sewel's. That pioneering history had been researched during the late seventeenth century, when Quakers were still perceived as a clear and present danger for English and American religious and civic life. Updating Sewel's pioneering work by including developments in the Society of Friends, Clarkson's historical work on eighteenth-century Quakerism would not be superseded until the publication of Rufus Jones's *The Later Periods of Quakerism* (1921).[33] Clarkson's history also takes a much more nuanced theological view, while downplaying the sensationalism and hagiography that figured so importantly for Sewel, whose experience of antagonism against Quakers in Europe had been recent and vivid. In addition, *A Portraiture of Quakerism* serves as the most significant re-statement and codification of Quaker values since Robert Barclay, a Scottish theologian trained in

Calvinism and who later became a Quaker, had published his influential Quaker theology in *Apology for the True Christian Divinity* in 1676.

Although Clarkson is perhaps less well remembered than William Wilberforce, his famous ally in the English antislavery movement, he was equally prominent for his tireless activism on behalf of the abolitionist cause. Christian religious principles shaped Clarkson's activism, and he was aware of the Society of Friends as an exemplary community grounded in pious severity and yet active in the public sphere by preaching and publishing the evils of slavery at the same time perennially defending itself against charges of heresy. Clarkson was born the son of a school headmaster, in Wisbech, Cambridgeshire, England in 1760. After a long career of public service and activism, he came late in life to the task of historical scholarship, by means of which he would tell the story of Quakerism in England and America. His study of the Society of Friends, which runs to approximately 1,200 pages, served as the most formidable statement of Quaker religion when it was first published and remained the standard work of its kind for much of the nineteenth century. It is intriguing that such a magisterial treatment of the Quaker faith would emerge from the scrupulous research of a non-Quaker—Clarkson was a staunch member of the Anglican Church—albeit a man deeply impressed by the Friends, of whom he remained a lifelong admirer.

Clarkson had first become aware of the African slave trade while a young student at St. John's College, Cambridge, where he wrote a prize-winning essay condemning slavery. That essay, written as a Latin dissertation for his master of arts degree and titled *Essay on the Slavery and Commerce of the Human Species* (1786), was translated and enlarged with the aid of Clarkson's brother and published shortly after his graduation. With the publication of this early abolitionist text, Clarkson also made his first important contact with the Quaker activist community. In the course of locating a publisher for his dissertation, he encountered a family friend who happened to be a Quaker, and it was through this chance meeting that Clarkson was introduced to a sympathetic Quaker writer/publisher named James Philips, who agreed to edit and publish Clarkson's first work. After meeting Phillips, who also helped him publish his views in a pamphlet titled *A Summary View of the Slave Trade and of the Probable Consequences of Its Abolition* (1787), the young Clarkson was soon introduced to other abolitionists, many of them Quakers as well. The most important of these friendships occurred after Clarkson was invited to participate, along with William Wilberforce and other leading antislavery activists, in a series of parliamentary investigations into the particulars of the slave trade and the nightmarish experience of the Middle Passage. It was Clarkson himself who helped acquire specific documentation in support of the abolitionist cause by helping to interview some 20,000 sailors employed in the slave trade.

After the launch of the English abolitionist movement in 1787, Clarkson became the backbone of its difficult campaigns. Utterly devoted to cause of defeating African slavery, he traveled thousands of solitary miles on horseback in order to muster support; he also was instrumental in organizing a number of community-based antislavery local committees, while continuing to write tirelessly. In addition, he had always been a sympathetic supporter of the French Revolution's fight for "freedom and equality," and when war erupted between England and France in 1793, Clarkson's popularity declined and his campaign against slavery was overwhelmed in the public eye by military concerns. A year after the war with France began, a sick and exhausted Clarkson went into a temporary retirement with his wife at the Lake District farm of his Quaker friend Thomas Wilkinson in Penrith. At this point in his career, despite the fact that he would continue to write prolifically about the abolition of slavery, Clarkson moved toward a new phase of his research to initiate a massive new project devoted to examining the Religious Society of Friends. As a lifelong admirer of Quaker values, which of course centrally included firm opposition to the slave trade, Clarkson would continue his research into Quakerism for many subsequent decades, paying particular attention to Quaker life in America. This phase of Clarkson's work resulted in *A Portraiture of Quakerism* (published in 1806, just before the 1807 parliamentary decision to abolish the slave trade); another dimension of his research resulted some years later with his two-volume *Memoirs of the Private and Public Life of William Penn* (1813).

After he had established his life's work of advocating the abolition of slavery, Clarkson would eventually become an important part of the social world of his generation's most important poets. When the not-yet-famous William Wordsworth and Samuel Taylor Coleridge families moved to the Lake District near Clarkson's home in late 1799, Clarkson and his wife, Catherine, quickly befriended them and were drawn into the social circle of those great English poets, who had just finished composing *Lyrical Ballads* (1798), their landmark volume of English Romantic poetry.[34] In later years, it would be another English poet and member of the Wordsworth circle, John Wilson, who would write the most memorable tribute to Clarkson in verse, with his "On Reading Mr. Clarkson's *History of the Abolition of the Slave Trade*" (1812), in which Wilson memorably described his view of Clarkson's pious resolve: "Deep within his soul, / The groans of anguish, and the clank of chains, / Dwelt ceaseless as a cataract, and fill'd / The secret haunts of meditative prayer."[35] During these years of poetic fecundity for Wordsworth and Coleridge, Clarkson was deeply immersed in the research that would culminate in his lengthy study of the Society of Friends. And it is *A Portraiture of Quakerism* that is Clarkson's most important investigation into the faith and practice of the Society of Friends, which amounts to a definitive religious handbook—it could even be described as a de facto catechism—for the Anglo-American Quaker faithful. In clear prose and with enormous attention to the theological and social principles involved, Clarkson produced in these weighty volumes the nineteenth century's most crucial, as well as the most balanced, statement on behalf of the Society of Friends.

Above all, Clarkson would conclude in the *Portraiture* volumes that Quakers were estimable and distinct from other Christians. What distinguished them was what he saw as their righteousness and moral courage: "This courage to dare to say what they believe to be right, as it was an eminent feature in the character of the primitive, so it is unquestionably a trait in that of the modern Quakers. They use no flattery even in the presence of the king; and when the nation has addressed him in favour of new wars, the Quakers sometimes had the courage to oppose the national voice on such an occasion, and to go before the great personage, and in a respectful and dignified manner, to deliver a religious petition against the shedding of human blood."[36] Furthermore, Clarkson learned from Sewel that Quaker courage had been forged in a crucible of sectarian difference, which in turned necessitated that this persistent group of religious outsiders remain resolute despite the many attacks from the orthodox on the "peculiar" beliefs and activities of Quakers:

> This trait [of courage] is generated again by all those circumstances which have been enumerated, as producing the quality of independence of mind, and it is promoted again by the peculiar customs of the society. For a Quaker is a singular object among his countrymen. His dress, his language, and his customs mark him. One person looks at him. Another perhaps derides him. He must summon resolution, or he cannot stir out of doors and be comfortable. Resolution, once summoned,

begets resolution again, till at length he acquires habits superior to the looks and frowns, and ridicule, of the world.[37]

In the pages of Clarkson's history, it is possible to discern with great precision the prevailing ethos and standard theology of early nineteenth century Anglo-American Quakerism, as they appeared to one of the great admirers of the that tradition. When Clarkson enters the theological scene, a century and a half after Quakers had first emerged as a small, deeply pious group of Christians drawn from the middling classes of northwest England, the Society of Friends had been transformed from a religious practice of dangerous disruptive enthusiasms to a practice of conformity and quietism.

By Clarkson's day, the official Discipline—the principles and catechism for the faithful—had also been made more explicit in such matters as marriage within the faith and other points of division between the faithful and the worldly, with the result that while Quakers increasingly came to be members of the prosperous classes in America and England, their religious rules persistently divided them socially from non-Quakers. In consequence, in the latter decades of the eighteenth century, when Quakers had received tremendous praise from such sources as the French *philosophes,* their numbers were shrinking markedly as the American population surged, and as their own members were frequently "read out of meeting" or otherwise opted out of the Quaker fold because of its tightened Discipline. It is at this juncture, when the Quaker movement had finally reached its later stages of maturity in both England and America, that Thomas Clarkson would commit to print a comprehensive and detailed overview of its piety and social mores.[38]

Until Clarkson's comprehensive treatise on the Quakers appeared, the standard account of Quaker religious views—and the most influential work in terms of its effects on Quaker theology and practice—had been Robert Barclay's *Apology for the True Christian Divinity* (1676). Originally written in Latin and published first in Amsterdam, Barclay's catechism was soon translated into English and by 1703 had gone through five English editions; translations into Dutch, French, Spanish, and Arabic soon followed. Along with his careful explanation of the Quaker doctrine of the Inner Light, Barclay added a formal code of social principles that would be adopted by most Quakers in subsequent years. These are worth citing in full, because it is these new social principles that would immediately identify Quakers as a "peculiar people" whose unusual appearance and behavior flouted the normative social codes of the period. Barclay himself understood the power of these iconoclastic rules, as evidenced by his acknowledgement that, "And because the nature of these [rules] is such, that they do upon the very sight distinguish us, & make us known, so that we cannot hide ourselves from any without proving unfaithful to our testimony: our trials and exercises have here-through proved the more numerous and difficult." As formalized by Barclay, the Quaker code of behavior, appears to be equal parts radically democratic and radically austere. For instance, he proposes:

> That it is not lawful to give to men such flattering titles as, "Your Holiness," "Your Majesty," "Your Eminency," "Your Excellency," "Your Grace," "Your Lordship," "Your Honor," &c., nor use those flattering words commonly called "compliments."
>
> That it is not lawful for Christians to kneel or prostrate themselves to any man, or to bow the body, or to uncover the head to them.
>
> That it is not lawful for a Christian to use superfluities in apparel, as are of no use save for ornament and vanity.
>
> That it is not lawful to use games, sports, plays, nor, among other things, comedies among Christians, under the notion of recreations, which do not agree with Christian silence, gravity, and sobriety: for laughing, sporting, gaming, mocking, jesting, talking, &c., is not Christian liberty, nor harmless mirth.
>
> That it is not lawful for Christians to swear at all under the Gospel, not only not vainly, and in their common discourse, which was also forbidden under the Mosaical law, but even not in judgment before the magistrate.
>
> That it is not lawful for Christians to resist evil, or to war or fight in any case.[39]

Long before Quakers came to be associated with benevolent causes such as the abolitionist movement, and only a few decades after a generation of primitive Quakers had scandalized the orthodox establishment by declaring themselves as individuals capable of experiencing the Inner Light of divinity, Barclay's precepts for Quaker virtue had become the most popular catechism for the faithful as well as providing a useful exposition of the faith for those, like Clarkson a century later, who wanted insight into the Society of Friends.

On the one hand, Clarkson generally writes in a balanced, serenely nonjudgmental mode about the Religious Society of Friends, scrutinizing the religious world of the Quakers with authentic curiosity and true admiration. On the other hand, he never felt the need to convert entirely to their faith and practice, or even to explain fully his own esteem for them as a religious movement per se as opposed to an activist sect working to end slavery. Avoiding the hyperbole and mystifications of Christian hagiography, which were rampant in the popular English press during the earlier decades of the eighteenth century, Clarkson delineates the theological world of Quakerism as faithfully as possible, calling attention to both the numerous strengths and occasional shortcomings of Quaker life. Although not a Quaker himself, he "was thrown frequently into the company of the people, called Quakers" in the course of his activism on behalf of enslaved African Americans. Even before he became intimately familiar with Quaker life, he had produced a prescient abolitionist tract while a student at Cambridge University, where his daring, prize-winning Latin essay of 1786 (*Essay on the Slavery and Commerce of the Human Species*) shows the direct influence of John Woolman's *Journal* and the Quaker Anthony Benezet's *Some Historical Account of Guinea* (1771). Clarkson mentions both Woolman and Benezet specifically as crucial influences on his antislavery position, and singles out the American Quaker movement generally for having been the earliest and most influential of Christian groups to renounce, in no uncertain terms, the holding of slaves: "I have the pleasure of being credibly informed that the manumission of slaves, or the employment of freemen in the plantations, is now daily gaining ground in North America. Should slavery be abolished there (and it is an event, which, from these circumstances, we may reasonably expect to be produced in time) let it be remembered, that the Quakers will have had the merit of its abolition."[40]

The consistent theme of Clarkson's first volume is the various forms of personal restraint that characterized the Quaker life at that time, and the limits and strictures of their religious principles are spelled out under several broad headings: "Moral Education," "Discipline," and "Peculiar Customs." In all of these sections, it is striking to note the marked transformation of the early Quaker enthusiasms. No longer a religion of spiritual enthusiasts and exuberant rebels, according to Clarkson, Quaker practice had seemingly become more than anything else a grammar of probity, rectitude, and sobriety. Clarkson's observations about the transformation of enthusiasm into sobriety buttress the later claims of Jack Marietta and Barry Levy, historians who have described the last half of the eighteenth century as a substantially more subdued, less public period of Quaker practice, during which time the Society of

Friends made several important additions to its rules for discipline while generally undergoing a phase of bureaucratization that hardened its organizational structure. Levy also points to the tensions disruption created within the Quaker community as this bureaucratization and codification were occurring. Pennsylvania Quakers, for example "disowned 50 percent of the rising generation of Quaker children, they abolished slavery within the Society of Friends, and the Quakers withdrew from government [to avoid official involvement with the Revolutionary War effort]." Much of this turmoil among late-eighteenth-century American Quakers has been overlooked by their contemporary admirers, such as Crèvecoeur and the French *philosophes,* who had imagined Quakerism to be a viable model for community building under new democratic political arrangements. But prosperity and community growth, combined with the explosive growth of the broader middle Atlantic region inhabited by most American Quakers, had fostered intractable difficulties in maintaining a pious faithful population. For example, as the Delaware Valley region grew more densely populated, socially complex, and thus more difficult to control, the elders chose to hew to the letter of the Quaker discipline and to maintain strict rules for membership in the Society. This hardening of the Society's doctrines in turn led inevitably to the reading out of meeting of many of its rising generation of young people.[41]

Privileged to know them well because of his common cause with their work as abolitionists, Clarkson claims to have arrived at "a knowledge of their living manners, which no other person, who was not a Quaker, could have easily obtained." From these comments alone, we can see that Quakerism was perceived at that historical moment to be somewhat impenetrable to those who were not members themselves. Clarkson's loyalties are such that he feels obliged to describe the particulars of their faith while he is still alive to do so, believing that "if I were not to put my hand to the task, the Quakers would probably continue to be as little known to their fellow-citizens, as they are at present."[42] He intends to provide a faithful portrait of a community that he admires, and yet he presents them consistently something of a mystery to the world that they inhabit. Specifically, Clarkson has great admiration for the orderly domestic habits of Quaker families, contradicting much criticism of the Quakers then emanating from the popular press of England, which objected vociferously to their egalitarian family arrangements even as their patterns of worship grew less enthusiastic and more restrained. One such criticism was aimed at defending the patriarchal structure of the traditional English family. For example, in the venerable *Edinburgh Review* a certain Lord Jeffrey had opined in an 1807 review of Clarkson's *Portrait of Quakerism* that Quaker families were dysfunctional to the extent that the children were "inwardly chilled into a sort of Chinese apathy by the restraints in which they are continually subjected" so that as they became adults they also became "very stupid, dull, and obstinate . . . in conversation; and tolerably lumpish and fatiguing in domestic society: active and methodical in their business, and narrow minded and ill informed as to most other particulars."[43] The burden of Clarkson's history thus included the fairer portrayal of Quaker family life.

Amazed by the persistence of the Quakers in the abolitionist movement, Clarkson aims to write a respectful and admiring moral history, but there are other motives as well in what will become three detailed volumes devoted to the Religious Society of Friends:

> I believed I should able to exhibit to the rest of the world many excellent customs, of which they were ignorant, but which it might be useful to them to know. I believed too, that I should be affording to the Quakers themselves, some lessons of utility, by letting them see, as it were in a glass, the reflection of their own images. I felt also a great desire, amidst these considerations, to do them justice; for ignorance and prejudice had invented many expressions concerning them, to the detriment of their character, which their conduct never gave me reason to suppose, during all my intercourse with them, to be true.
>
> Nor was I without the belief, that such a history might afford entertainment to many. *The Quakers, as every body knows, differ more than even many foreigners do, from their own countrymen.* They adopt a singular mode of language. Their domestic customs are peculiar. They have renounced religious ceremonies, which all other Christians, in some form or other, have retained. They are distinguished from all the other islanders by their dress. These differences are great and striking. And I thought therefore that those, who were curious in the development of character, might be gratified in knowing the principles, which produced such numerous exceptions from the general practices of the world.[44]

Quakers appear to be *in* America but not *of* America; because they are "resident aliens," persons who are distinctively visible while remaining ciphers to the uninitiated, they are ideal subjects for a moral anthropologist like Clarkson, who was sympathetic with Quakerism, although "not in name; but I hope in Spirit; I was nine parts out of ten of their way of thinking."[45]

Under the rubric of "Moral Education," Clarkson focuses first on the Quaker discipline's prohibition against popular amusements: dancing, music, fiction, and games of chance (including stock market speculations). As always, Clarkson is careful to avoid characterizing Quakers as extremists in these matters and points out that while these prohibitions are enforced for adult members of the community, some latitude is allowed for the playful activities of children, whose natural exuberance requires that they be permitted to enjoy the amusements and games that would be prohibited for adults who had grown into the role of "moral beings." Nevertheless, Clarkson describes the incubation of a moral being through careful training, so that "Quaker children are rebuked for all expressions of anger, as tending to raise those feelings, which ought to be suppressed."[46] This firm regulation of the passions is naturally of a piece with the Quaker prohibition against games of chance and their attendant excitements, which militate against spiritual life and give free rein to debasing earthly amusements. Similar prohibitions are detailed with regard to enjoyment of music, about which Clarkson wholeheartedly agrees with Quaker discipline to the extent it prohibits music as a wasteful diversion from responsibility, and in particular the kinds of responsibility that he felt to be the province of women. Dismayed by what he felt to the inferior education of women during his lifetime, he often pleaded for them to have better and less frivolous training: "The education [women] receive marks the inferior situation for which they are considered to be designed. Formed like dolls or playthings, which are given to children to captivate by outside appearances, they are generally rendered incapable of exhibiting great talents, or of occupying an important station in life . . . it seems to have been reserved for the Quakers . . . to insist upon that full practical treatment and estimation of women which ought to take place wherever Christianity is professed."[47] Clarkson's view of Quaker women, in particular, as occupying a separate sphere of moral and social life had become a familiar one by the time he came to write his study. As Phyllis Mack suggests: "The Quaker woman was symbolic of Quaker values in their undiluted state because the values of Quakerism itself were feminine values. Restraint, benevolence, privacy, domestic order, passivity: all of these, familiar enough to observers of Victorian womanhood, evolved in the early eighteenth century as attributes not only of women but of the saintly Quaker man."[48] In *A Portraiture of Quakerism*, it is women's musical frivolity that seems to be Clarkson's primary concern in this regard, and he goes so far as to describe it as "a criminal waste of time," which is "more to be deprecated, because it frequently happens, that, when young females marry, music is thrown aside, after all the years that have been spent in its acquisition, as an employment, either then unnecessary, or as an employment, which amidst the new cares of a family, they have not leisure to follow." Music, charges Clarkson—echoing the precepts of Quaker discipline as he understands them—is also a sedentary activity that damages the human constitution, with particularly dangerous consequences for young women. "Hence," he claims, "the females of the present age, amongst whom this art has been cultivated to excess, are generally found to have a weak and languid constitution, and to be disqualified, more than others, from becoming healthy wives, or healthy mothers, or the parents of healthy progeny." The pleasures of worldly entertainments, eschewed by the Quaker faithful, are seen in this light as detrimental to both propriety and the progressive feminist cause.[49]

Even more severe than the suppression of instrumental music, according to Clarkson, are the prohibitions that Quakers had placed on vocal music. Like instrumental music, vocal music is problematic because of its strong appeal to the senses and its capacity for aesthetic pleasure. But the nondiscursive quality of instrumental music renders it somewhat more benign than vocal music. While instrumental music is "considered as incapable, on account of its inability to articulate, or its inability to express complex ideas, of conveying either unjust or impure sentiments to the mind. Vocal music on the other hand, is capable of conveying to it poison of this sort." For instance, "if . . . words in a song are in themselves unchaste, if they inculcated false honour, if they lead to false opoinions, if they suggest sentiments, that have a tendency to produce depraved feelings, then vocal music, by which these are conveyed in pleasing accents to the ear, becomes a destroyer of morals." Whether they be hunting chants, martial anthems, or drinking songs, all vocal music thus carries with it a morally corrosive tendency that must be avoided in order to promote spiritual experiences above sensual indulgence.[50]

As with the immoral influence of theatergoing and dancing (which traditionally were proscribed by the Quaker discipline), claims Clarkson, it is the Quaker view that amateur singing or even amateur musicianship thus engenders worldliness and, through lyrics that are unchaste, a decline in personal modesty. No longer merely the province of elite connoisseurs and professional troubadours, music and its attendant urge for new modes of artistic expression breeds both aesthetic energy and rank consumerism. Once "Musical people"—and now this includes an enormous group of middle-class amateurs as well as professionals—"have acquired skill and taste" they "are desirous of obtaining every new musical publication, as it comes out. . . . The professed novel reader, we know, waits with impatience for a new novel. The politician discovers anxiety for his morning paper. Just so it is with the musical amateur with respect to a new tune." Theatricality and musical expression, then, are rightfully forbidden by the Quakers because of their tendency to corrupt the religious mind, and especially the malleable minds of the young.[51]

The distress shown by Clarkson as he harmonizes with Quakerism and its reluctance to adopt modern principles, as with his criticism of music and dance, has much to do with a wildly proliferating discursive culture (song, theater, print) in English and American life. He predictably argues that popular novels—the preeminent form for middle-class expression and consumption—should be cause for grave consternation. In this consternation about mass print culture, Clarkson is not alone; the warnings about the dangers of fiction reading had been legion since the eighteenth century and would continue unabated into the late nineteenth century. Once again, as with a good deal of Clarkson's discussion of moral education, it is *women* who must be protected from the influence of the unseemly aspects of print culture: "Females, on account of the greater delicacy of their constitutions, are the more susceptible of such impressions. These effects the Quakers consider as particularly frightful, when they fall upon this sex."[52]

While all Christians can be damaged morally by fiction reading, for women the dangers are physical as well. Noting the illicit urges and powerful excitements produced in the novel-reader, Clarkson notes that his research had led him to "a physician of the first eminence" who confided in him that "music and novels have done more to produce the sickly nervous habits of our highly educated females, than any other causes that can be assigned. The excess of stimulus on the mind from the interesting and melting tales, that are peculiar to novels, affects the organs of the body, and relaxes the tone of the nerves, in the same manner as the melting tones of music have been described to act upon the constitution."[53]

After detailing these principles of moral education, the first volume of Clarkson's *Portraiture of Quakerism* continues with a careful analysis of Quaker discipline, as developed through the practice of "meetings for discipline" as instituted first by George Fox. Intended both to form precise rules of conduct and also to admonish (and thereby reform) those individuals who have gone astray of Quaker morality, these meetings are founded on the principle that no effort should be spared in the attempt to bring the offending person back within the pale of correct Christian behavior. Instruction, rather than punitive measures, undergirds the Quaker discipline, which is applied by Quakers to their membership.

Here, Clarkson inserts a discourse about the lack of religious instruction in American prisons and on capital punishment's failure to reduce crime. When applied to the issue of capital punishment, Quaker doctrine is thus quite clear in its position that all judicious means must be attempted to reform the criminal, to return him to the community of the faithful, rather than resorting to execution for all crimes except murder (a legal principle codified, for example, in Pennsylvania when William Penn—over the strenuous objections of Queen Anne—formed colonial laws based on these Quaker principles).

This discussion of the Quaker principle of using all available resources to *reform* rather than to *harm* the criminal leads Clarkson to a discussion of that radical Quaker innovation, the Philadelphia penitentiary, with its emphasis on renovating the moral character of those there imprisoned.[54] For instance, in a major break with prison tradition, the Philadelphia penitentiary stipulated that "As reformation, again is now the great object, no corporal punishment is allowed in the prison. No keeper can strike a criminal. Nor can any criminal be put in irons. All such punishments are considered as doing harm. They tend to extirpate a sense of shame. They tend to degrade a man, and to make him consider himself as degraded in his own eyes." Clarkson exuberantly approves of the new Quaker-inflected institution, noting also the Philadelphia penitentiary's principles of gender segregation, silence, temperance, chaste language, cleanliness, and useful labor.[55]

Volume I concludes with a careful account of what Clarkson calls the "peculiar customs of the Quakers," beginning with one of the best available descriptions of early nineteenth-century Quaker clothing. What is most illuminating here is the way that Clarkson demonstrates that the development of Quaker habits of dress grew out of specific circumstances of class stratification in fifteenth- and sixteenth-century England. What to nineteenth-century Americans appeared as a peculiar unwillingness on the part of English and American Quakers to wear colors grew out of the visible status that clothing conveyed in Renaissance

England. Consequently, in Quaker communities, "The men wear neither lace, frills, ruffles, swords, nor and any of the ornaments used by the fashionable world. The women wear neither lace, flounces, lappets, rings, bracelets, necklaces, ear-rings, nor anything belonging to this class." It was during the seventeenth century in England when expensive household furnishings and elaborate clothing—including types of clothing once permitted only for persons of high rank and fortune—increasingly became available to members of the emerging middle classes, who began to avail themselves of fashions once worn only by the nobility. As Clarkson points out, in 1652, during the same decade that saw the formation of the early Quaker community in England, a foppishly dressed cleric, the eminent John Owen, dean of Christ Church and vice chancellor of Oxford, could be seen "wearing a lawn-band, as having his hair powdered and his hat curiously cocked. He is described also as wearing Spanish leather-boots with lawn-tops, and snake-bone band-strings with large tassels, and a large set of ribbands pointed at his knees with points or tags at the end."[56]

Clothing, of course, was only the most visible of peculiarities that set Quakers off from the larger world during the nineteenth century. Along with their plain attire, Clarkson observes a general sense of restraint and thrift, which was reflected in sartorial habits but also in somber domestic spaces with a striking lack of artwork or portraiture, even among the prosperous classes of Quakers.[57]

Clarkson also reminds his nineteenth-century readers that what might appear as a quaint linguistic anachronism was in fact tied to the anti-authoritarian bent of early Quakerism. Directing a "thou" toward the authorities in those years of savage religious discrimination could have dire results: "Many magistrates, before whom [Quakers] were carried in the early times of their institution occasioned their sufferings to be greater merely on this account. They were often abused and beaten by others, and sometimes put in danger of their lives. It was a common question put to a Quaker in those days, who addressed a great man in this new and simple manner, 'Why you ill bred clown do you thou me?'" Citing William Penn's similar reluctance to use the flattering "you" for individuals because of Penn's view that "The word you . . . was first ascribed in the way of flattery, to proud Popes and Emperors, imitating the heathens vain homage to their gods, thereby ascribing a plural honour to a single person; as if on Pope had been made up of many gods, and one Emperor of many men; for which reason you, only to be addressed to many, became first spoken to one," Clarkson shows convincingly that the peculiarities of Quaker language were in fact based on a radically and stubbornly democratic view of human value, which eventuated in a Quaker religious culture in which the obeisance and servility signaled by bowing, scraping, and removal of hats before superiors were seen as honors of the world and thus anathema. This protodemocratic impulse was based on their belief in the sole sovereignty of God and conveyed by refusal to adopt the flatteries of conventional social address. Quakers since the time of Fox had abandoned the symbolically (and sometimes literally) servile use of such terms as "sir," "madam," "master," "mister," "my lord," "saint," and "your excellency" in favor of the plain forms of "friend" or "neighbor"; they avoided drinking honorific toasts at dinner; and replaced the pagan calendrical names for the days and months with numbered designations ("first month" for January; "first day" for Sunday, etc.).[58]

The full-scale, scholarly monographs by Sewel and Clarkson were by far the most comprehensive histories of the Quaker movement during the early decades of the republic, but early American readers could also read inexpensive pamphlets like Anthony Benezet's *A Short Account of the Religious Society of Friends, Commonly Called Quakers* (Philadelphia, 1814). This gracefully written twenty-eight-page booklet, which was composed 150 years after the first arrival of Quakers in America, first paints a brief but reverential overview of George Fox's seventeenth-century work as a missionary Friend. Before turning the particulars of theology, though, Benezet's history spells out concisely the behaviors and habits that had characterized its members since the early years of the movement and showed them visibly and audibly to be differentiated from the larger community:

> These converts to the Light of Christ in the Soul of Man, were distinguishable for a grave, sedated deportment; singular uprightness in their dealings; punctuality in the performance of their promises; a sparingness in discourse; great temperance and frugality at their tables; and plainness and simplicity in their dress and behaviour. They declined servile and fantastical gestures, compliments and other forms of salutation, such as putting off the hat, scraping the foot, bending the knee, drinking healths, &c., esteeming them to be violations of that sincerity and seriousness which becomes Christians; yet considered it their duty to treat all men with gentleness and respect.[59]

The brief history of Quakerism offered by Benezet focuses its attention on personal manners, behavior, and etiquette. Not merely a religion concerned with "the Light of Christ in the Soul of Man," the *Short Account* describes a whole repertoire of social signs and behaviors meant to indicate church membership. Language, diet, clothing, bodily gestures, facial expression: all of these categories of human behavior thereby are written as essential signs of Quaker belonging. So too with the ascetic Quaker attitude toward amusements, which Benezet describes as hindrances to "an inward communion with God"; his history of the movement indicates a collective decision that "the pursuit of worldly fashions and diversions, such as gaming, dancing, stage playing and other amusements of the same baleful tendency, are to be refrained from, as evidently tending to raise the human mind, which is prone to vanity, above the preserving fear of God."[60] Only after showing a wide range of visible signs and manners common to Quakers does Benezet finally turn to the particulars of doctrine and worship for the Society of Friends.

Quaker historians like the educator and historical pamphleteer Anthony Benezet regularly made attempts to remind those outside the faith of how the Society of Friends had come to maturity in the American colonies and the early republic, thereby providing the perspectives and narrative involvement of writers living sympathetically within the Quaker community. Equally important and powerful, though, and especially as the print cultures of books and periodicals evolved during the nineteenth century, were the historically based accounts of Quaker life available to British and American readers in the popular press. History as it related to the world of Quakers in America became available to the popular imagination not exclusively or even primarily through the systematic histories of professional historians like William Sewel or Thomas Clarkson, but also by means of images and narratives produced in novels and magazines: the stuff of an ordinary (but nonscholarly) reader's literary and intellectual life. The way Quaker history infiltrated the periodicals of the eighteenth century and continuing until the World War II years needs to be mentioned in order to acknowledge the far greater number of American readers who learned their national history by reading such magazines as the *Atlantic Monthly* and *Harper's New Monthly Magazine*, whose pages did much to produce middle-class values and sensibilities during the latter decades of the nineteenth century.

Many of these articles and essays, which in the post–Civil War years provided general historical overviews of Quaker life and customs, almost certainly had a great deal more impact on the general reader than works of theology or religious controversy. Such accounts of the Society of Friends were produced by both members and nonmembers of the sect. Mrs. J. L. Hallowell, a member of a Quaker family, used her essay "A Quaker Woman" (1872)—published in the *Atlantic Monthly*—not only to praise the homely virtues of Quaker life but also to point out some of its errors and shortcomings. "The great defect in Quakerism," she wrote, "which even the monastic ascetic escaped of old, is that it takes no account of the impulse and craving for beauty, the art instinct in human nature." Her other complaints take a similar course by observing what she perceived to be the fatal lack of an aesthetic sense in areas such as the drama and music, both of which had long been frowned upon due to Quaker principles of restraint and spiritual focus. History of Quaker life often took an even milder form, in which the Society of Friends is associated with the colonial past and is described in terms familiar to the local color literary movement of the late nineteenth century. Thus, Howard Pyle's long essay on the colonial Delaware River Valley communities, "Old-Time Life in a Quaker Town" (1881), turns away from any specific discussion of religious life or principles, while treating Quaker life as yet another rather trivial and mostly vanished dimension of the national culture; as such, the Quaker communities he discusses comprise "not the great events that affect the destiny of the nation, but rather the homely every-day life of the last century."[61]

Perhaps the grandest statement of American history to appear in the late nineteenth century was written by George Bancroft, the distinguished statesman-scholar whose monumental *History of the United States* (1834–76) appeared in ten volumes (later revised as a six-volume edition) during the crucial middle decades of the century. In recounting the religious controversies of the colonial period, it is striking that Bancroft's history elevates the Quaker ethos to such a degree, by comparison with the bigotry that he sees in early Puritanism. By 1658, Bancroft writes, it was becoming evident that "The union of church and state was corrupting both." He acknowledges the need for the Puritan colonial authorities to keep order in the fledgling colony, but he also conveys a sense of admiration for the rebellious spirit of the Quakers, as well as for the sincerities of their piety and faith:

The early Quakers in New England appeared like a motley tribe of persons—half fanatic, half insane, and without definite purposes. Persecution called them forth to show what intensity of will can dwell in the depths of the human heart. . . . Some [Quakers], who had been banished, came a second time; they were imprisoned, whipped, and once more sent away, under penalty of further punishment if they returned again. . . . A payment of ten shillings was the penalty for being present at a Quaker meeting, of five pounds for speaking at such a meeting. In the execution of the laws, the pride of consistency involved the magistrates in acts of extreme cruelty. But Quakers swarmed where they were feared.[62]

He is even more enthusiastic in his praise of what he describes as a "paradise of Quakers" in America: the community of Friends that had settled in coastal Carolina during the late eighteenth century. Of this community, he attests, "Here were men from civilized life, scattered among the forests, hermits with wives and children, resting on the bosom of nature, in harmony with the wilderness of their gentle clime. With absolute freedom of conscience, reason and good-will to man were the simple rule of their conduct." Seen from Bancroft's perspective, Puritan New England's violent history of religious persecution against dissenters stands in sharp contrast to the utopian possibilities adumbrated by Quaker values of the sort manifested in the Carolina paradise.[63] Bancroft's admiration of Quakerism's religious principles is evident in his *History*, but it rises to enthusiasm in a chapter focusing on "The People Called Quakers in the United States," in which he traces the history of George Fox and the Quaker movement, and then delineates the moral ground upon which the sect rests. There's little doubt that Bancroft's esteem for them promotes them above any other religious group, even though his historical model leaves no room for cultural dominance or even significant moral influence by Quakers.

Despite the increasing quietism of Quaker practice in Britain and America after the seventeenth century—which many historians have associated with their increasing prosperity and prominence in the colonial business sphere—the long-standing tradition that began with early Puritans describing the "attacks" by Quakers on religious and social orthodoxy was repeatedly inscribed into historical narratives by successive generations of American historians. Even in the late nineteenth century, almost two hundred years after American Quakers had transformed their religious expressiveness from their earlier enthusiasms to a far more restrained and orderly piety, historians were still trying to separate truth from propaganda in the matter of antagonisms between Puritans and Quakers in colonial New England. One important example is Richard P. Hallowell's *The Quaker Invasion of Massachusetts* (1883), a sympathetic, but far from one-sided, account of Quakerism. The book sums up the conventional history of the early American Quakers: "The main charge in the indictment of the Quakers, and the one upon which Puritan apologists most rely to justify their own clients, is that Quakerism manifested itself here in the persistent and frequent lawlessness and indecent conduct of its adherents. We are taught to believe that the Puritans were exasperated beyond endurance, and that the solution of Puritan persecution is to be found in the extravagances of the Friends. Will this plea bear the test of examination?" Hallowell singles out Cotton Mather's *Magnalia Christi Americana* as perhaps the most influentially damaging "storehouse of ammunition for [Puritan] apologists," and a source of grave distortions about Quaker history.

Mather also attacked New England's Quakers in some of his lesser known works, such as *Little Flocks Guarded Against Grievous Wolves* (1691), an incendiary pamphlet in which he railed specifically against the charismatic Quaker evangelist and pamphleteer George Keith. But his attack on Keith contained a more general assault on the Quaker doctrine of the Inner Light and its implication that salvation could be available to each individual person, an idea whose radicalism is obvious when placed in stark contrast to the prevailing Calvinist belief in the innate depravity of humanity. The prejudices that Mather held against Quakers, though, also disclose his view of grace and salvation as being mainly the province of European Christians and their colonial proxies. Mather takes the view that Quaker doctrine appears to undermine the racially coded Christian supremacy that he had spent his career defending: "So then the *Quaker* hold that the *Indians* and *Negroes,* and the *Pagans* beyond *China,* have *Sufficiency* of *Grace* and *means* of salvation. . . . He must [therefore] hold that there is not in the darkest corner of the *Indies* a man that is . . . reprobate."[64] Mather's opinions would of course find their way into the most dominant and influential histories of English settlement in New England, and along the way his anxieties about the Quaker movement would become accepted as a reliable guide to the eccentricity of the Society of Friends. As Hallowell rightly argues, because Puritan leaders like Mather and others had remained the standard accounts of religious controversy in the Massachusetts Bay Colony, their undeniable prejudices and self-interested distortions about early relations between the Puritans had too often been reproduced and thereby converted into widely accepted historical dogma, despite the efforts of historians sympathetic to the Quaker way, such as Sewel and Clarkson.[65]

4

Quaker Biography in Transatlantic Context

Quaker biography is a record of immaculate devotion, as untrue as it is uninteresting.

> Sarah Greer, *Quakerism: or, the Story of My Life* (1851)

My first afternoon, on reaching New Bedford [in 1838], was spent in visiting the wharves and viewing the shipping. The sight of the broad brim and the plain, Quaker dress, which met me at every turn, greatly increased my sense of freedom and security. "I am among the Quakers," thought I, "and am safe."

> Frederick Douglass, *My Bondage and My Freedom* (1855)

We are not champions for Quaker faith, but we are for Quaker character. No class of community is more thrifty, more industrious, or more charitable, none produces better citizens or better men than the peace loving, law abiding Quaker. Heaven knows that we should all be better if we had more Quaker sentiment and Quaker practice in our everyday walk and conversation. It is too late in the age to call Quakers either fools or lunatics.

> Editorial, *Flake's Bulletin* (Galveston, Texas, 1867)

In the early years of the English Quaker movement, especially during the decades immediately following its founding by George Fox and

his allies in the mid-seventeenth century, an intense pamphlet war ensued in which numerous vicious attacks against Quakerism were published by those concerned to prevent Friends' activities from disrupting
the prevailing religious orthodoxy. These published assaults made use of
a myriad of intellectual tactics and rhetorical modes, ranging from the
most scripturally learned and abstruse theological argumentation to the
wilder and more populist expressions that made their way into leaflets
or cheap broadsides, such as "The Four-Legg'd Quaker: To the Tune of
the Dog and Elder's Maid, or, the Lady's Fall" (ca. 1664). Published
anonymously in London, "The Four-Legg'd Quaker" incites violence
(castration) against Quakers while accusing them of heathen behavior
and bestiality. This anti-Quaker print artifact, clearly intended for broadside posting and public amusement, is illustrated with images showing
male Quakers alternately appearing as fearsome devils, Quaker-hatted
centaurs, and in lustful pursuit of a mare, the refrain to each of the song's
verses warns merrily that: "Help, Lords and Commons, once more
help, / O send us Knives and Daggers! / For if the Quakers be not gelt, /
Your Troops will have the Staggers." This strain of harsh antipathy
against the early Quakers, however, gradually subsided during the first
half century after the founding of the sect. During the period from
approximately 1650 to 1700, the Anglo-American Quaker movement
evolved from a highly visible and confrontational sect into a more quietistic and reclusive religious group, and as a result printed attacks on Quakers both in Britain and America eventually grew less frequent and certainly less vituperative. Shifting political winds also contributed to the
newly moderated posture taken toward Quakers from the eighteenth
century on; subsiding anger directed toward Friends in public discourse
could perhaps signal recognition of the obviously progressive moral positions they had taken on the question of slavery.

Since the late eighteenth century had seen most Quakers turn to a
staunch opposition to slavery on both sides of the Atlantic, Quakers became known in the Anglo-American public sphere far more as agitators
wed to the cause of abolition than as a group of subversive enthusiasts
armed with blasphemous or disruptive religious practices. After the
Civil War this tendency toward tolerance of Friends continued, so that
by the late nineteenth and early twentieth century the pendulum of
concern had swung entirely away from the fierce persecutions of the
seventeenth century. Instead, representations of Quakers had become
rather comic, with little suggestion that Quaker beliefs or customs

amounted to anything approaching a sustainable religious threat or a dangerous cultural force. In short, the debunking of Quaker theology and piety had become a moribund practice by the middle decades of the nineteenth century. Indeed, in what could be described as one of the major reversals of American public sentiment directed at a religious group, by the one-hundredth anniversary of the Quaker arrival in New England, anxiety about Quaker heresy had evaporated in the print marketplace. New literary representations of benevolent and otherwise admirable Quakers continued in full force as Friends' ethical convictions gradually came to stand for much of what the American public aspired to attain in terms of morality.

Outside the Society of Friends, the lives of Quakers could be (and were) imagined in fictional narratives, but American readers in the nineteenth century also had available for their perusal numerous publications, such as Quaker memoirs and journals, many of them modeled explicitly or implicitly on those of the great eighteenth-century diarist and pamphleteer, the Quaker abolitionist John Woolman. During the rapid expansion of the print marketplace during the nineteenth century, American readers interested in either ordinary Quaker lives or the lives of increasingly prominent Quakers who were activists in the debates about slavery also could certainly avail themselves of a variety of other literary resources in order to learn about Friends. The works of well-known and historically important Quakers like George Fox, William Penn, Elizabeth Ashbridge, and John Woolman remained in print owing to the burgeoning print marketplace and thus were widely available to Quakers and non-Quakers alike. For example, a new edition of John Woolman's *Journal* (originally printed in 1774) was published under the editorship of Quaker poet John Greenleaf Whittier (1807–92)[1] in 1872, only a few short years after the end of the Civil War.

This chapter considers several examples of nineteenth-century Quaker biography—texts that illuminate and document Quaker lives. These biographies suggest something of the range of representations of the Religious Society of Friends available to American readers during the antebellum period, and this chapter focuses four in particular: (1) a popular biography of the colonial leader William Penn by Mason Locke Weems (2) an anti-Quaker autobiography by a young Irish woman named Sarah Greer (3) a memoir by Thomas Battey of Quaker missionary life among the Great Plains Indians, and (4) a brief critical biography of John Greenleaf Whittier published in the *Atlantic Monthly* by

Harriet Prescott Spofford. While making no claim to comprehensive coverage of the field of nineteenth-century Quaker biographical writing, these examples denote some of the ways Quaker lives and religious practices could be imagined during a significant period for American biography.

That the antebellum period figures significantly in the gestation of American biography can be illustrated by a number of key developments.[2] The decades of social turmoil before the Civil War and wrangling over the concept of geopolitical "Manifest Destiny" (a term coined in the 1850s) were also crucial years of debate and consolidation around the idea of an authentically American cultural identity, with a corresponding desire for a suitable and distinctive American literature to advance the ethos of a newly solidified nation. This remarkable literary ferment, involving such writers as Herman Melville, Ralph Waldo Emerson, Nathaniel Hawthorne, Henry David Thoreau, Harriet Beecher Stowe, Emily Dickinson, and others, has been amply documented by a host of critics, perhaps most prominently by F. O. Matthiessen in his influential literary history of the period, *American Renaissance: Art and Expression in the Age of Emerson and Whitman* (1941). The broader literary scene of the period, which expanded well beyond the world of fiction and poetry in the process of working toward the notion of "Young American" literature during the Manifest Destiny era, also reinforces the idea that representative American lives were becoming a signal theme in mass print culture and the American literary marketplace.[3] To take one important instance, systematic representations of ideal American lives during the antebellum years took encyclopedic form at the hands of Harvard historian and Unitarian minister Jared Sparks, who served for many years as general editor of the monumental *Library of American Biography*.[4] Sparks himself contributed profiles of Ethan Allen, Benedict Arnold, Marquette, La Salle, Count Pulaski, Jean Ribault, Charles Lee, and John Ledyard. Perhaps most tellingly for the prospects of biography as a genre, Ralph Waldo Emerson chose the mid-nineteenth century, at the time of his greatest fame, to compose his profiles of six great historical figures for an attentive American audience with the publication of *Representative Men* (1850).[5] Given this kind of impetus for American biography in general, it is easy to see that biographies of Quakers would find a ready market among a large readership already preoccupied with political and religious aspects of national belonging. Although it is true that novels in many respects allow for a more free-ranging and imaginative depiction of such stock characters as Quakers, the more "truthful" genres of autobiography, biography, memoir, eulogy, and reminiscence also provide revealing accounts of the ways in which this religious subgroup can be narrated into the political and moral imaginary of a national literary tradition.

Without making any claims as to comprehensiveness, given the very large number of possible examples of American Quaker memoir and biography, this chapter will illuminate some of the issues and themes that shaped Quaker biography during the nineteenth century. It is here that we examine a genre that is most concerned with delineating actual lives of Quakers. Whereas other chapters have dealt with such issues as the early threat to Puritan orthodoxy during the colonial period, the allure of Quaker community and family life during the tumultuous Revolutionary years, the historiographical challenge of documenting the faith and practice of Quakerism by the first major historians of the movement, and the multifarious forms of characterization and fictional representation of Quakers during the nineteenth century, this discussion of biography stays close to the principle of analyzing the life narratives of several Quakers through some examples of autobiography and biography that would have been easily available to nineteenth-century American readers.

Perceptions of denominational leadership have been a significant factor in the discourse about religions found in American mass-print culture. From the time-honored legends of Puritan forebears like John Winthrop and Cotton Mather to the controversial and sometimes scandalous Mormon prophet Joseph Smith to the many fearful anti-Catholic depictions of popes and priests, the nineteenth-century world of print featured numerous publications that narrated the debates about American religious culture. In order to see how representations of Quaker leadership might fit into this tradition, the first example of Quaker life writing is a popular biography written by the famed author, Episcopal clergyman, and book peddler, Mason Locke Weems, titled *The Life of William Penn* (1829). Like George Washington, the subject of another famous book by Weems, the Pennsylvania Quaker leader seemed an ideal subject for this brief biography by the prolific and enterprising bookman. An advocate of religious freedom whose tolerance for other faiths was many years ahead of his time, as well as a pacifist during colonial years in Pennsylvania fraught with violence and conflict, William Penn (1644–1718) was the kind of historical figure ripe for the kind of popular mythmaking in which Weems specialized. It was Weems, after all, whose fifth edition of *The Life and Memorable Actions of George Washington* (1806) had first produced the legendary tale of George Washington and the cherry tree, among other durable aspects of the Washington myth.[6]

The second example, published the decade before the Civil War by a former Irish Quaker named Sarah Greer, illustrates an ongoing tension between Quaker separatism and the desire on the part of many of its members to rejoin the larger community. It also demonstrates that, for all their high-profile work on behalf of human rights, even as late as the middle years of the nineteenth century, Quakers were far from being universally admired in Ireland, England, and America. Published in antebellum America in 1852, this autobiography also serves as a reminder of the transatlantic dimensions of the ongoing public discourse about Quaker culture, a civic dialogue that reached a boiling point as a result of abolitionist rhetoric in the years before the Civil War.

The third example is not a full-scale biography per se but instead is a biographical memoir published in 1875 during the Reconstruction years by a missionary to the Great Plains Indians. *The Life and Adventures of a Quaker among the Indians* comprises an account of a Quaker schoolteacher named Thomas C. Battey. It appeared as the American South was being remade with considerable turmoil, and when the Native Americans that Battey worked so closely with in the southwest territory of Oklahoma were undergoing yet another phase of their relocation onto grim reservations far from their ancestral homelands. Battey's career, typical of many young Quaker schoolteachers of his generation, adumbrates the central role of Quakers in many different benevolent organizations, while also illustrating some of the unique influence that Quakers, because of their uncommon respect and tolerance directed toward Native Americans, had always had among Native communities.

The fourth and final example is more a biographically inflected critical essay, written in 1884 by Harriet Prescott Spofford, about the famed American Quaker poet and abolitionist John Greenleaf Whittier. Shorter than the other examples examined here, Spofford's account of Whittier's impact on American literary culture was nevertheless highly visible within postbellum print culture because of its appearance in the influential and popular *Harper's New Monthly Magazine* (then under the editorship of George William Curtis). Then, as now, this extremely influential and widely circulated magazine was an organ of mainstream

Northern opinion, broadly construed. Despite its brevity, though, Spofford's essay is striking for its insistence on a powerful correspondence between the very idea of American identity and Whittier's own distinctive Quaker identity and poetics.

The Life of William Penn (1822): Quaker Biography as Propaganda

Until the rapid expansion of mass-print culture after 1840, when successful New York–based entrepreneurs like Nathaniel Parker Willis and Evert Duyckinck came into prominence as leaders in the world of literary publishing, there is perhaps no one individual who influenced the American book trade more than Mason Locke Weems (1759–1825). Notable primarily for a popular, though somewhat inaccurate biography of George Washington (ca. 1800), Weems spent the better part of thirty years writing and selling inexpensive chapbooks, while working as an agent for the Philadelphia publisher Mathew Carey. Not only did Weems earn fame as a purveyor of brief biographies of George Washington, Benjamin Franklin, and Revolutionary War general Francis Marion, he also capitalized on the religiously tinged moralizing texts that had become a vital part of the American print marketplace during the first half of the nineteenth century. Some of these popular tracts spoke directly to personal morality and sexual restraint, as may be seen from such titles of Weems-authored tracts as *Hymen's Recruiting Sergeant* (ca. 1799), *God's Revenge Against Murder, or, The Drown'd Wife* (1814), and *Revenge Against Adultery* (1815). Others, like his biography of George Washington, promoted ideal models of civic and political virtue for a growing national audience of readers apparently eager to find their way to a national identity in part through reading.[7]

Given the broader outline of his career in bookselling, then, the decision by Weems to produce an admiring account of the founding political leader of the Pennsylvania Quakers comes as little surprise. Penn's fame as a settler of Pennsylvania and as a man of sincere Christian piety would be burnished by Weems for a new generation of American readers, and this book fit perfectly with Weems's previous career as a chronicler of the good and great men of the new nation. Published in 1822, *The Life of William Penn* resembles Weem's earlier biography of George Washington, which was unabashedly written to elevate the first president to near-mythical status. It seems clear that Weems was planning to capitalize on the earlier success of the Washington biography, which continued to sell steadily, thanks in part to continuing advertisements for that book in the back pages of *The Life of William Penn*. Weems spent much of his time in Philadelphia and would have been quite familiar with the Society of Friends, although he was not a Quaker but an ordained Episcopal priest who claimed to have enjoyed the presence of George Washington himself as a parishioner in the Mount Vernon parish where had once been temporarily assigned.

Weems presents his American readers with a William Penn in glowing terms, beginning with an account of the Pennsylvania founder's genealogy, which is notable in *The Life of Penn* for the virtues ascribed to both of Penn's parents and also for the sturdy traits that mark Penn himself as an exemplary Englishman and ideal American immigrant. The bravery requisite for a colonial founder of seventeenth-century Pennsylvania Weems traces directly to Penn's father, a distinguished commander who had served in the Royal Navy, sat in Parliament, and before his death had expected to receive a peerage from the Crown. According to Weems, the piety and devotion of the zealous convert to Quaker faith—William Penn's associates in England viewed Quakers as crazed heretics—can be attributed directly to the Christian nurture of Penn's mother, whom he characterizes as a careful teacher and a sincerely faithful, religious woman. Characteristically for Weems, whose writings are notable for their rather overwrought prose style, he describes Penn's childhood relationship with his mother in grandiose terms: "As the Parent Eagle calling her young to his native skies, when she sees the breaking forth of the sun over all his golden clouds, thus did this tender mother improve the precious hours of the nursery to sow the seeds of religion in the soul of her son."[8] Christian nurture at the hands of a doting mother eventually leads to a profound conversion experience for Penn that Weems describes in reverent terms. Weems uses the occasion of narrating William Penn's youthful conversion as an opportunity to promote a more general set of ideas about the presence of God in the life of the Christian faithful, "Besides, is not every man and woman on earth daily receiving *visitations* from God, and calls to the honours of a pious life? What is every transport which the soul feels in obtaining victory over lust, but a visitation of God? What is every secret blush of shame, or palpitation of heart from guilt, but a visitation from God, and a strong call to a good life?"[9] With this kind of generalized account of Penn's religiosity as being congruent with that of other non-Quaker Christians, Weems's biography has the effect of showing Penn and the Quakers at once to be distinct from, and analogous to, other Protestant believers in America.

Rather than showing William Penn's Quaker faith as being estranged from the beliefs of mainstream Christian faith and practice, Weems aligns Penn with the core values and moral principles of all righteous Americans and does so by emphasizing the secular dimension of Penn's life in Pennsylvania. Weems traces the life of Penn through a number of crucial episodes, including his expulsion from university as a result of his conversion to Quakerism, as well as his period of incarceration in England for similar reasons. Other facts from Penn's biography are presented in more straightforward fashion. Notable among these details is the depiction of Penn's arrival in the American territories granted to him by Charles II as payment for a large debt the king had owed Penn's late father. Despite his well-known incompetence as an administrator and political leader, Charles II—himself a controversial figure in England because of his tolerance for Roman Catholicism—is granted an important role in *The Life of Penn* because of his careful instructions to William Penn on the subject of religious tolerance in the Pennsylvania territories: not only would Penn be given freedom to establish a community for Friends, but Charles II directed him to maintain an atmosphere of religious tolerance for all persons, orthodox members of the Church of England or not. Weems also associates Penn with culturally tolerant attitudes: the long letters of advice Penn had written to his children in England and the surprisingly amicable relationships that formed between Penn's Quaker community and the Native population living in eastern Pennsylvania around the time that Penn was planning and implementing his designs for a major city in Philadelphia.

The overall effect of Weems's attempt at writing William Penn into the annals of American popular history is that Penn's life is distinguished not for any peculiarity of faith or radical dissent from the religious orthodoxy that held such powerful sway during his life. Instead, here Penn is first and foremost a talented and virtuous colonial leader, a pious family man who left his beloved Pennsylvania in 1701 before meeting his end in 1718, long after he had laid the groundwork for the successful colony that would bear his name. The concluding gesture of *The Life of Penn* is also tinged with morality, as Weems includes a long appendix of Penn's reflections and maxims, most of which bear not on specific religious topics per se, but resemble more the manner of Benjamin Franklin's Poor Richard, albeit absent the Franklin wit. Devoid of nearly any hint of how deeply held Penn's religious radicalism might have been, Weems's biography demonstrates the extent to which Quaker faith had in many ways become domesticated as yet another curious, but ultimately harmless and probably laudable, aspect of an increasingly diverse religious culture in the United States.[10]

The Hazards of Friendly Piety:
Sarah Greer's Flight from Quaker Faith

For a glimpse into the fading genre of the anti-Quaker pamphlet or exposé, we turn to one of its final examples, which was published in the perennial Quaker stronghold of Philadelphia in 1852. Its Irish author, Sarah D. Greer, had first published her memoir, *Quakerism; or the Story of My Life* (1851), under a pseudonym in Ireland, calling herself simply "A Lady Who for Forty Years Was a Member of the Society of Friends." Response to Greer's best-selling account was immediate in Britain, as evidenced at length by an anonymous review of the book in the Anglican quarterly magazine *The Christian Remembrancer.* The same review was also reprinted verbatim in the popular Boston weekly magazine *Littell's Living Age* in late 1851, in which it would have been read by large audiences in New York, Boston, and Philadelphia, among other cities. The British reviewer is skeptical about certain aspects of Greer's narrative of Irish Quaker life, but he emphasizes what he sees as the emptiness of Quaker piety, its ritual trappings of language, dress, and propriety shrouding a hollowed out and desiccated faith. All that remains, according to the review, are the visual and material aspects of Quaker tradition, without the fervor of belief that characterized its early enthusiasts. As Greer's memoir shows, he writes, "There is nothing more to learn [about Quaker religion] than what we see, nothing left but externals; the system has decayed from within, and left only an outer shell—a course of observances and traditions of men. The omissions of a former age are the *acts* of the present; the negligences of a wild enthusiasm are transformed into rigid requirements, and the relaxations of two hundred years are the bond, and fortress, and dependence of today."[11] These familiar criticisms of Quaker life are similar to those expressed by many other nineteenth-century commentators, but it is striking that the reviewer, like Greer herself, is able to write at such great length about the status of Quakers in the decade before the American Civil War without once mentioning the critical importance of Quakers to the abolitionist politics of the day. These are deeply ironic omissions because

Quakers would have been most visible to the average citizen reader in England or the United States, not so much for the nuances of their faith and practice within the Society of Friends but for their public pronouncements about the evils of slavery.

Greer's decision to describe Quaker life while avoiding discussions about Quaker political activism has corollaries in the work of her contemporaries among American writers. The Friends who populate Melville's *Moby-Dick* (which like Greer's memoir was published in both England and the United States in 1851) are eerily silent about the institution of slavery as they conduct their hunt for the great white whale, but Melville's decision to include Quakers as important members of the whaling crew nevertheless appears to address in oblique fashion the ongoing political and social conversations about slavery and abolition, in which Quakers participated with amplified voices. Although Greer herself does not allude directly to these political or social debates as she begins her memoir, any book featuring Quakers prominently and published in the decade leading up to the Civil War would have touched a nerve with British and American readers, many of whom would have been well aware of Quaker activism then underway in abolitionist circles. So it is in this unacknowledged context of Quaker alignment and sympathy with the cause of slaves that Greer voices her insistence that she has published her autobiography because of a desire to make known the "truth" about Quaker life and at the same time to improve the Society of Friends:

> So very little is known of the mystery of Quakerism, and so established is the character of the Society for respectability and morality, that I am quite prepared to find myself accused of ungenerous and malicious motives for writing; but persuaded that truth is after all the most powerful weapon which can be employed to accomplish any purpose, I have endeavoured to place it conspicuously forward, and on it alone I rely. . . . As a fire which has not been stirred, will burn away, and become so choked up with ashes as to be incapable of yielding warmth or light, and requires not merely a gentle application of the poker, but a strong and vigorous stirring up, to dislodge the burnt out, and rekindle the good coals, so I conceive the Society of Friends now needs a thorough good rousing; for the ashes have accumulated, and well nigh put out the fire.[12]

Greer frames her critique in religious terms, which in certain ways resemble a jeremiad, ostensibly taking the Society of Friends to task not for their political allegiances but for their having fallen away from righteous

Christianity. "To consider the Society of Friends as a religious body, is a monstrous stretch of imagination," Greer insists, "Respectable, active, intelligent, benevolent, useful, wealthy and influential, they undoubtedly are; but a man may be all this, and yet devoid of that religion, without which, he can never hope for life eternal." Greer's concern about the spiritual well-being of Quakers has mainly to do with her observation they have insufficiently regarded Scripture as the primary revelation of Christian truth. Having avoided a proper reverence for biblical truth, Quakers had forced her to hope that "a determination may spring up to refuse the silly babblings of those incapable preachers who now infest the Society, and to insist on the Bible being read, and its truths preached."[13] She claims, moreover, that Quaker censorship of writings by its members had led to an inaccurate picture of their religious lives. The principled objections that she makes to contemporary Quakerism, however, are set aside for much of her memoir in favor of a remarkably detailed account of daily life for a wealthy and privileged Quaker girl in Ireland.

The early chapters are filled with sketches of characters from the Quaker community, including dismal and tedious preachers, prosperous Friends who have become so obese from overeating that they are unable to stand during testimony at Meeting, and young women chafing at the Society's prohibitions about such matters as ostentatious clothing. She also describes a world that lacks sufficient stimulation of the imagination, so that when a friend conspires to let her borrow a copy of Walter Scott's popular novel *Ivanhoe* to read, the young Sarah Greer, "gladly agreed" and gave little heed to the Quaker prohibition against novel reading. This transgression is even more notable in that earlier in her autobiography she had looked askance at one of the household nursemaids who was less than devout in her piety, but spent much of her free time buried in novel reading. Greer notes that her own father, an upstanding member of the Irish Quaker elite, had himself owned a small collection of Portuguese, Spanish, and even a few English novels (although, she said, he did not read them). As to popular English books, one of which was Samuel Richardson's epistolary novel *Sir Charles Grandison* (1754), the rebellious young Sarah admitted that she "read them over and over again; partly because I liked them, and partly because I so often heard Friends preaching against reading novels; who, whilst they acknowledged generally having themselves been very fond of so doing, warned us of the danger, because they were so very fascinating.

Therefore I craved after them, and in a way I little expected, my desire was gratified to its full extent." The secretive pleasure she takes in the romantic world of fiction is echoed in her subsequent comment that "whether it was because stolen waters are sweet, or because of the exceeding fascination of the book itself, certainly no one ever enjoyed a book [*Ivanhoe*] more than I did, and some more of the same delightful author's works, which I obtained in the same manner. When reading it in the arbour or in the study, I always took care to provide myself with either an Atlas or Sarah Grubb's Journal; and then if either one of the Mistresses or one of the spy girls came in sight, the Novel was popped under, and the Atlas or the Journal looked innocent or edifying."[14]

Quakerism; or, the Story of My Life is of course an autobiography that primarily sets out a version of the Quaker experience in an Anglo-Irish setting, rather than detailing the specifics of Friends in America. Still, there are a number of compelling reasons for viewing Sarah Greer's personal story in connection with religious and social developments in the United States. In the first place, the history of Quakerism constitutes a record of a postcolonial culture: one in which important developments on each side of the Atlantic were recorded and transmitted across the ocean in print or oral form. Added to this fact of a rich transatlantic discourse—some of it ardently supporting the Society of Friends, but much in harsh opposition—the story of Greer's life was deemed significant enough to be published in Philadelphia, the de facto nerve center of American Quaker life. The timing of her publication came at a time when Quakers were very much the center of attention in American literary life. The story of Greer's life appeared in the print marketplace at exactly the same moment that depictions of Friends were playing a major part in runaway best sellers like Harriet Beecher Stowe's *Uncle Tom's Cabin* (1852). While Stowe's antislavery novel was telling the dramatic tale of Quaker benevolent work with the Underground Railroad, Herman Melville was exploring vastly darker aspects of the Quakerish soul with his depictions of the raging and vengeful Captain Ahab and his Quaker whaleship officers in *Moby-Dick* (1851).

Joining the mostly Irish cast of *Quakerism*, a key character in the autobiography is the American traveling missionary, James Flannil, who plays a substantial role in Greer's merciless critique of Irish Quaker life. Friend Flannil, introduced to the Greer family by two young members of the Meeting, has traveled to Ireland as a missionary and arrives at the prosperous Greer residence in company with an English Quaker minister who has been serving as Flannil's escort during the mission trip. Although Greer claims that her characters are thinly disguised versions of actual Quaker persons, she resorts to caricature in describing Flannil as aversion of an American giant: "He was six feet four inches high, large boned, and coarse looking in the extreme. A great shapeless white cloth coat, lined with light green, covered him all over. His feet were enveloped in huge moccasin boots, and his countenance was indicative, in a remarkable manner, of crossness and discontent." Like Daniel Boone, Huckleberry Finn, or other legendary frontier characters, Flannil is a larger-than-life figure, whose crude personal manners, grimy dishevelment, and rustic appearance combine to make him an unlikely sight as he enjoys a respite in the tastefully arranged parlor of the Greer family: "The trowsers were drawn up to the knees, . . . a curious garter, made of the bark of a tree and twine, was thrown down on the rug, and the stockings deliberately taken off, exhibiting to our wondering eyes, two of the very dirtiest and biggest feet I had ever beheld."[15]

Greer's consternation with what she takes to be the decline and corruption of a once-worthy mode of Christian practice grows more vehement and reaches an angry pitch at this point, as she takes stock of the ignorant and unseemly Friend Flannil who has invaded her household:

> It was seeing such a man honored—a man who seemed not to possess one redeeming trait of virtue or amiability—who was entirely ignorant of the Scriptures—who was as ignorant as he was selfish, and as selfish as he was knavish and cunning; it was seeing such a disgrace to the name of Christianity honored, and almost reverenced, by the whole body of Friends in America, England, and Ireland; it was seeing this, that first inclined me to think it possible that Friends might be in error, and conviction that they were mistaken in one point, gradually opened the way to look at others, until at length, and not without thought, and prayer, and research, and years of careful study, I am now clearly of opinion, that Quakerism is not what it professes to be—a pure form of Christianity; but a deep and subtle delusion; where some truth is mixed up with great error—where the most soul-deluding doctrines are clothed in the garment of superior sanctity—where imagination is substituted for inspiration—where spiritual pride assumes the form of mock humility, and external forms take the place of dedication of heart-where the ignorant and the hypocritical take the lead, and where the substance, the life of religion—faith in the blood of Jesus Christ, is never mentioned.[16]

The turning point in Greer's repudiation of her life as a Quaker thus appears to occur during her assessment of Friend Flannil, a quintessentially American representative of the faith. When he demonstrates himself to be slovenly, bumbling, and inarticulate as a person and as a preacher, he usefully confirms and links both the crude backwardness of American culture and the lamentable quality of the Quaker ministry. The extremity of her caricature of America through her representation of the boorish Flannil serves well to highlight her self-interested notions of cultural superiority. Greer's opinion is questioned by an editor's note appended to the review of her memoir in *Littell's Living Age.* Judging her lampooning of Friend Flannil to be a distortion of reality, the editor counterbalances Greer's invective by insisting that "Having well known and dearly loved many members of this Society in the United States, we are unable to give credit to an anonymous writer [Sarah Greer] who makes such strange attacks upon Joseph Gurney and Elizabeth Fry,[17] 'whose praise is in all the churches.' And the story of the American minister seems too monstrous and absurd to be true. Everybody who knows anything of the Quakers knows them to be eminently neat and decorous."[18] The memoir, its subsequent review, and the attached editorial commentary thus insert themselves into various arguments in a complex discourse in which Quakers were on the one hand perceived as a spiritually bankrupt and perhaps willfully insincere religious group, but on the other hand as at the very least "eminently neat and decorous" and possibly as the religious group most progressively oriented in their view of slavery, which was by far the most pressing political, social, and moral issue of the day.

When *Quakerism* was published in London in 1851 (the American publication followed in 1852), the American print marketplace, responding mainly to the controversial influence of Friends in the debates surrounding slavery, had already established a tradition of using Quakers as stock fictional characters. The largest religious issue then being confronted by print culture, however, was not related to the Religious Society of Friends for their radical position with regard to the plight of African American slaves. Instead, the literature of the antebellum period was immensely preoccupied with the rise of Roman Catholicism in the United States. Following the devastating Irish potato famine of the 1840s, Irish immigration created huge numbers of new Americans who were, at least nominally, Roman Catholic. And this wave of new immigrants created much animosity, particularly among residents of East Coast cities, where there quickly arose concern over the religious destiny of the United States and the potentially problematic tension between national loyalty and allegiance to the pope. American pamphleteers and novelists soon took of the matter of Roman Catholicism and its purportedly un-American bias to create a vast genre of anti-Catholic writings that extended and revised the long-standing European pattern of animosity between Protestant and Catholic.

Some of the force of Greer's autobiography, which of course has anti-Quakerism at its heart, depicts the Society of Friends as embodying dangers equivalent to those posed by the Roman church: "There is a great similarity between Quakerism and Popery. Both are the religion of the priests, and the people are compelled to an outward conformity. The domineering influence of the Friends who take part in the discipline, over the body, is exactly a counterpart of that which the priests exercise over their flocks. The one requires obedience, because they are inspired, they tell us; the others call themselves the Church, and demand it. The spirit is the same in Both!"[19] The distinctive vestments worn by Roman clergy she sees as analogous to Quaker strictures about plain attire, which she dismisses as "Popish mummeries."[20] Whereas Quakers since their earliest years had claimed plain dress as a sign of their commitment to the religious life and their repudiation of all that is worldly, Greer criticizes the peculiar dress of Quakers as yet another sign of their arrogance and vanity. Once again, it is the decadent customs of Roman Catholicism that serve in her argument as the most fitting analogy to those of the Quakers, as she notes that "The adoration with which the Friends regard their peculiar dress, often exposes them to imposition. I do not mean that they actually worship their garb; but the morbid sensitiveness with which they regard it, is similar to that feeling with which the Romanist regards, or professes to regard, the pictures and relics of saints."[21] What is ironic here is that the Quaker movement, known among Americans as the Protestant sect with perhaps the greatest liberty of personal religious expression, comes under criticism here as tending toward the kind of overreaching ecclesiastical authority that led to the Protestant Reformation in the first place. Rather than conceding that the relatively decentered authority of Quaker church leadership worked to democratize its proceedings, most notably by granting women the right to preach and otherwise minister to Quaker congregations, Greer insists that a calcified leadership had come to apply its authority and discipline without reasonable warrant and to the detriment of the membership.

It should be understood that Sarah Greer's voice, despite the sustained critique to which she subjects the Society of Friends, belonged to a distinct minority view in the nineteenth century. Much more common in literary and critical representations were laudatory or admiring comments, with many narratives of Quaker life (especially those authorized by Quaker movement) written as hagiography. So it is that Greer's biography was immediately subjected to criticism by reviewers who were at pains to indicate a more balanced religious and moral view of the Society of Friends. By the conclusion of Greer's tale, it becomes transparent that her primary objective is to provide a conversion account: the story of her return to the established Church of England, whose preaching, reliance on biblical revelation, tithing, and more liberalized social precepts were more fulfilling to her. Thus, it is fair to evaluate her life's story not only as biography but as a work of religious controversy that means to elevate the Church of England's teachings over those of its radical dissenting sect, the Quakers.

The anonymous reviewer for London's *Athenaeum,* in an article that appeared just after the first edition of *Quakerism: or, the Story of My Life,* faulted Greer for her narrow perspective on the purported follies and formalities of her community of Quakers, remarking acerbically that "Our emancipated Quakeress"—that is, Greer herself—"might have pointed out the sound kernel" of the Society of Friends "as well as the rotten husk." The reviewer insists on a balanced view of religious failings, while criticizing Greer for singling out Quakers for her attacks. "The lady who issues [*Quakerism*] proceeds apparently on the assumption that the sect which she has quitted monopolizes all the vulgarity, greediness, worldliness, and inanity which disfigure the world of high professors," insists the anonymous reviewer. At the same time he alludes to the single-mindedness with which Greer focuses on the errors of Quakerism: "There is scarcely a world of exception or qualification— scarcely an indication of the solid worth and sincere, if narrow, self-sacrifice which must also be credited to Quakerism, else it must long ere this have crumbled to nothing out of its own sheer rottenness." Still, once having taken Greer to task for her one-sidedness, the reviewer turns to his own view of the impractical nature of Quaker life and values. In supplying his own critique to supplement that of Sarah Greer, the reviewer notes the too-lofty idealism of Friends, alongside what he deems as their failure to abide by the letter of their own strict Discipline. After citing Greer's comment that "It is really a very difficult thing for a

Quaker to be consistent with his own principles; and even the most rigid are often found swallowing them whole," the reviewer assents to her judgment about the impossibility of following the Quaker way. "The cardinal difficulty of the Society [of Friends], wherein lie the seeds of its decay . . . [is that such] nonconformity as its statues of discipline profess is not merely at variance with every rule of nature and common sense, but, if honestly carried out, is totally incompatible with the simplest transactions of life." By "transactions of life" the reviewer (and Greer) mean to imply the financial transactions that frequently gave the lie to Quaker discipline, as when a prosperous Quaker merchant considers it a sin to indulge in fashionable clothing or jewelry, and yet has few qualms about selling such items at a handsome profit to those outside the Society of Friends. To understand this contradiction, the reviewer joins Greer in analogizing with respect to the Roman Catholic tradition: Quaker discipline followed to the letter—which it rarely is according to this analysis—would require its membership to live with rules "stricter than that of the strictest monastic asceticism, without monastery walls to shut him away from the vain world, and the religious ceremonies to supply that want which 'knocks loud' at the heart of every human creature who has been born with an iota of imagination."[22]

Thomas Battey: A Quaker among the Indians

As with distinguished American Quaker writers such as John Woolman and William Bartram before him, the nineteenth-century Quaker schoolteacher Thomas C. Battey took the measure of early American life on the outer edges of the national frontiers. Battey's earnest work took place among the Southern Plains Indians just after the Civil War, during a period of rapid westward expansion in the United States. To facilitate the ethnic cleansing of Indian removal, U.S. military forces supervised and enforced Native displacement from ancestral tribal lands. The story of Indian removal from the North American Plains is well known to historians, but an aspect of their removal less frequently described is the role of American Christian groups in partially ameliorating the condition of Natives there and in other regions of the United States and its territories during these years. Although U.S. policies toward Natives made it inevitable that they would indeed be removed from their ancestral homelands, to be replaced primarily by white settlers, Quakers during the early decades of the nineteenth century played an important role in providing some measure of service to displaced

Natives and their children. Such contact between Quakers and at-risk Native tribes in America was nothing new. Karim M. Tiro states in his discussion of interactions between Quaker missionaries and Oneida natives in the first half century of the early republic, "The Quakers were key figures at the inception of the federal Indian policy that guided every administration from Washington to Jackson." In central and western New York State, the Seneca tribes of the Iroquois nation had previously been targeted by President Washington, who "recommended Quaker instruction for Seneca children," and federal agent Timothy Pickering "encouraged the Quakers to intensify their contacts with the Iroquois at treaties he convened in the early years of [the 1790s]."[23]

Schools managed by Indian agencies on the Northern Plains were generally assigned to the Protestant Episcopal Church, while schools and agencies on the Southern Plains were placed under the direction of the Quakers. Quaker schoolmasters frequently filled the ranks of these Indian schools, especially those instructors who had been trained in the excellent Quaker primary and secondary schools of the Middle Atlantic states. Their success as pedagogues among the Native tribes in various regions of the American territories has been quite convincingly attributed to their focus on the acquisition of skills in literacy and farming. In New York State, for instance, writes Tiro, "The Quaker strategy . . . emphasized training natives in plough agriculture and the English language rather than preaching the gospel and seeking converts."[24] It was from such a background that Thomas C. Battey would arrive on his first assignment among the Natives of Oklahoma. Descended from a family of Rhode Island colonists, Battey was itinerant by disposition. After a childhood spent on his uncle's Vermont farm, Battey later attended a Quaker school in eastern Pennsylvania, near Philadelphia, and for a time harbored dreams of pursuing a career in medicine. When financial hardship put medical school out of his reach, he turned to the work of school teaching and promptly set off for a series of teaching stints. First, he taught in schools in northern Vermont, and later in the small community of Viola, Iowa (now called Springville). Eventually, Thomas Battey would turn at age forty-three to teaching among displaced Natives in the area of Anadarko, Oklahoma, thanks to the offices of the Wichita (Indian) Agency, who hired him as an instructor in 1871.[25]

Traveling with his wife and young son by horse-drawn wagon, muleback, ambulance, and foot from Iowa to the Southern Plains of the Oklahoma territory, Battey's began his first assignment among Natives:

an eight-month tour of service with the long-suffering Caddoe tribe. When Battey's superintendent at the Wichita Agency, a fellow Quaker named A. J. Standing, assigned him to the Caddoes, the tribe had already been displaced not only from their homeland of Louisiana, but had been removed later to southeastern Texas and then central Texas, before arriving in Oklahoma. Their traumatized condition was palpable, for as Alice Marriott suggests, "The sufferings of the Caddoes on their forced march northward exceeded the better-known agonies of the Five Civilized Tribes [Iroquoian-speaking Cherokee and the Muskogean-speaking Chickasaw, Choctaw, Creek, and Seminole] on the Trail of Tears westward. By the time the Caddoes reached their agency, they had become deeply suspicious and profoundly afraid of almost all white men, and with good reason. This was especially true when their agent, on whom the Caddoes had greatly relied during their removal, was murdered by white Texans within a few months of the establishment of the agency."[26]

"Thomissey"—as Thomas Battey became known to the Natives with whom he worked on the Southern Plains—several years later also worked as a trusted emissary to the rebellious Kiowa tribe. Long harried by enemies, the Kiowa had been removed in the eighteenth century from the Black Hills after battles with their rivals among the Arapaho, Cheyenne, and Dakota (Sioux). With their sometime rivals, the Comanches, the Kiowa would go on to create much disruption in the form of raids on white settler communities in Texas and New Mexico during the mid-1870s, and Thomissey was summoned from Oklahoma to Texas by the Indian agency in order to help negotiate the peace. It was the Quaker Thomissey, alone among the negotiators dealing with the Kiowa, who finally established a peace between these Natives and the white settlers who were intent on opening tribal lands for farming and timber clearing.

Battey's frontier work was perhaps typical in many respects for rural educators during the nineteenth century, with additional complications because of the cultural and linguistic divide between white and Native. Wages were extremely modest, supplies such as slates and chalk were scarce, and many of the children at the small boarding school attended sporadically and sometimes disruptively. In lieu of permanent school buildings, Battey frequently traveled with a canvas tent, which served him as a school for the one or two dozen Native students assigned to his care, and also as his residence on the prairie. Runaway students were

common, and violence among the students often revealed both ado-
lescent conflict and cultural differences between white and Native be-
havioral norms. Thomissey describes one of these conflicts among his
young Kiowa "scholars":

> This morning, while a couple of our small boys were at play, one of
> them became suddenly angry, and seizing a sharp-cornered club, dealt
> the other a hard blow on the head, inflicting a severe scalp-wound.
>
> The blow, very fortunately, fell upon a thick portion of the skull, or
> he might have been killed. I sewed up the wound, dressed it with cam-
> phor and sugar, and put him to bed. The other boy was locked up in the
> chamber, and kept there all day, food and water being carried to him.
>
> In the course of the day, [Kiowa] Captain Black Beaver came in
> and talked to the scholars in the school-room, then went into the cham-
> ber and talked to our little prisoner.
>
> He told him how badly it made him feel when he heard what he
> had done. "That his teachers feel badly, the agent feels badly, his chief,
> and all his friends, when they hear what he had done; and more than
> that, his Father in heaven was displeased. He sees us all the time, He
> knows all the time—all we do, all we think. He does not like to see his
> children get angry—quarrel, and hurt each other. You ought to be very
> sorry. Your teachers do right to lock you up, so you think how bad you
> [have] been, and not do so any more. You ought to live like brothers,
> and love each other; then you feel good, make your teachers, your chief,
> and your friends feel glad, and God will make you happy." A Christian
> sermon from an Indian.[27]

A number of elements distinguish Thomissey's brand of education
from that practiced in other quarters of the United States, but perhaps
the most obvious is his transmission of the Quaker ethos to the Kiowa
leader. In this way, the Quaker precepts of gentle correction, self-
examination, and "penitence" take the place of any form of corporal
punishment, as Thomissey would explain to the boy's mother. Here,
Thomissey carries into his educational program some of the central
values that in 1790 had gone into the Quaker-backed creation of the
first American penitentiary. As with Philadelphia's Walnut Street Jail,
Thomissey had enacted in his school a system whereby transgressions
are punished not with violence but with solitary confinement and an ac-
companying program of personal reform for the inmate.

The benevolence expressed through the career of Thomas Battey
and other Quakers working in the Indian agencies of the nineteenth

century, a well-intentioned Christian benevolence is nevertheless problematic both in its representation and in its politics. Self-conscious about his role not only as an educator but as a kind of Christian missionary (albeit one in service to government policies of Indian removal), Thomissey's religious certainty, voiced periodically in his account of life on the Southern Plains, brackets and conditions the compassionate service that he provides for the Natives. And while he does occasionally refer to the prayer life of the Quaker meeting itself, more often the spiritually energized passages in Battey's account focus on his desire to alter the beliefs and social practices of the Natives whom he has been serving. While Battey's view of Natives could be understood in certain ways as a charitable one, there are real limits to the progressiveness of his attitude toward them. These limits to his vision are legible, for example, when he prays, "May these lofty hills, these beautiful valleys, and these wide-spreading plains, which have been for ages silent witnesses of atrocious deeds of blood, re-echo with high and living praise, from how blaspheming tongues, to thee, the Almighty Creator and Preserver of all things, and the redeemer of a fallen race from sin and the wages of it."[28] Put another way, the historical recognition of Quakers as selfless workers on behalf of the most progressive causes, an acknowledgment that is both overdue and fitting for many reasons, should not obscure the moral limits within which even those Quakers with the finest of intentions were operating.

Battey repeatedly describes the condition of Natives without giving full voice to their concerns. His representation of the misbehaving boy placed into solitary confinement unfolds as a scene of moral instruction and Christian ethos, but it also renders the Natives as nameless abstractions, whose own circumstances and individuality remain blank. His prayers at meeting extend this sense of the Quaker missionary's tendency to see himself not as preserving a Native way of life but as *transforming* that life—through his altruistic intervention—into a life of Christian holiness. Far from advocating for the value of Native customs, language, and beliefs, Battey prayed for "the growth in grace of such as may have experienced that birth in which they can grow in grace, and that those who may not yet have come to it may be brought forth in the newness of that life which is eternal; particularly these poor deluded, benighted, and superstitious heathen children."[29]

Although such comments reveal him to be condescending toward Native culture, it is apparent from his memoir that a good deal of

Thomissey's effectiveness as a negotiator among the Natives came from his own gifts as a communicator combined with an ability to enlist the support of key Native intermediaries. One of the English-speaking Natives, a Delaware named Captain Black Beaver, is described as having arrived at Thomissey's Oklahoma reservation in order to calm those Kiowa and Comanche who had been disrupting white settler communities with their raids. In Thomissey's view, Captain Black Beaver had been invaluable for his work to advance U.S. government policy, and with the added benefit that he convinced the Natives living on the reservation to "stop raiding, send their children to school, settle down, and do as their friends the Quakers wanted them to do." Judging by such a scene of negotiation, governmental Indian removal policy, implemented in part by the Indian agencies and schools in frontier locations like the Oklahoma territory, has been provided leverage in two different ways. Thomissey provides a brief transcript of Captain Black Beaver that illustrates this dual leverage:

> "The Quakers," he said, "are your friends; they made a treaty with the Indians more than two hundred years ago, in which both parties had bound themselves, and their children after them, to be friends to each other forever. This treaty has never been broken. The Indians have never taken any Quaker's blood, and the Quakers have always been true friends to the Indians.
>
> "Our grandfather at Washington [D.C.] knew this, and for this reason had sent the Quakers among us. He knew that they would do right by his red grandchildren. He sent two of them among us to build us a school; they made us a good school, and we know that they are good men, love the Indians, and will take good care of the Indians' children."[30]

Based on the evidence provided by this kind of mediated exchange between colonizer ("Washington") and colonized (Kiowa and Comanche), the figure of the Quaker—embodied by "Thomissey" but imagined for the Native audience through the intermediary narrative of Captain Black Beaver—has thus become a paradoxical sort of cultural agent. On the one hand, the well-intentioned Friend Thomissey selflessly provides education to Southern Plains Natives whose world had been turned upside-down by policies of Indian removal. Arriving early and staying long to assist Natives in the work of acculturation and conformity to white settlement, Quakers like Thomissey and his family sponsored and enacted a form of altruistic work for American Natives, indigenous peoples whose circumstances would conceivably have been far more desperate without Quaker intervention. On the other hand, as can be observed within the pleading of Captain Black Beaver, Quakerism has become an important figure of help and concern deployed on behalf of non-Native colonial power in America: a non-Native colonizing force that goes merely by the name of "Washington" when Black Beaver speaks. Partially screened by the moral force of Quakers at work on behalf of Natives, and doubly credited through the testimony of a friendly Native like Black Beaver, Quakers do indeed work for the benefit of the unfortunate indigenous tribes. But their moral credibility simultaneously credits their political sponsor, the U.S. government, with the capacity for directing to the Natives some portion of concern and justice.

The Representative Quaker Poet:
John Greenleaf Whittier

Life writing from Quaker authors such as the recovering Quaker Sarah Greer or the activist Quaker Thomas Battey are useful as documents that reveal the perceptions, values, and behavior of persons with an immediate stake in the Society of Friends. They provide a view of Quaker life that avoids the tendency to depict Friends as caricatures of either prudish moralism or virtuous perfection. While these accounts differ in their presentation (favorable for Thomas Battey, highly unfavorable for Sarah Greer) of the lived experience of Quakers, they indeed avoid some of the cartoonlike qualities attributed to Quakers during the later nineteenth century and early twentieth century. At times, even publications by Quakers themselves created the unintended impression that Friends were strange, freakish, simply maladapted to normal, modern lives, or even physically remarkable. For instance, the English giant, Robert Hales (1820–63), who stood over seven feet tall and who published his *Memoirs of Robert Hales: The English Quaker Giant, and His Wife, The Giantess, The Tallest Pair in the World* (1849) about the time he was being featured in circus shows staged by P. T. Barnum, is perhaps the most notable case in which the popular media of the day used sensationalism to represent actual Quakers as bizarre types.[31] Aside from anomalies like Robert Hales, though, many Quaker biographies of the nineteenth century (unlike many of the novels focusing on Quakers) provided fairly reasonable and relatively noncontroversial views of Quaker religious life. Although the texts they produce were undoubtedly mediated in various ways, and thus provide only partial and to some degree biased accounts of Quaker life, the biographies of Greer and Battey are the kinds of autobiographical documents that show the movement anthropologically, saturated as they are with the flavor of lived experience within the parameters of a specific religious tradition.

A somewhat different biographical view was available later in the nineteenth century in the form of accounts of Quakers written by non-Quakers who produced these life narratives for the local color-inflected magazines of the post–Civil War era. The most broadly influential of these biographies appeared within the pages of widely distributed American magazines such as *Harper's New Monthly Magazine* and the *Atlantic Monthly*. Decades after the critical historical moment when Quakers had become boldly visible to all Americans because of their unflinching positions on the subject of abolitionism, the media could reflect at its leisure upon the cultural importance and the enduring legacy of Quaker history and life in the United States.

A singular example of the phenomenon by which Quaker life and values were made available to an enormous readership during these years appears as a detailed 1884 review/essay on the life and accomplishments of the Quaker poet, abolitionist, and Massachusetts legislator John Greenleaf Whittier, published in the pages of *Harper's New Monthly Magazine*. Harriet Prescott Spofford (1835–1921), an essayist, poet, novelist, and short story writer from Maine, titled her essay simply "The Quaker Poet," no doubt because by the time of its publication, John Greenleaf Whittier had become perhaps the most famous Quaker writer in the world. The example of Whittier is an instructive instance of lived Quakerism serving as a powerful impetus for the formation of American regional and national identity. Frequently grouped with the other popular "Fireside Poets" of the antebellum period—James Russell Lowell, Henry Wadsworth Longfellow, and Oliver Wendell Holmes—Whittier stands apart from more enduringly canonical nineteenth-century poets like Walt Whitman, Emily Dickinson, and Herman Melville because of his lifelong popularity. Far from being a protomodernist writer in the mold of these other poets, Whittier nevertheless enjoyed wide readership, as evidenced by his many successful volumes of poetry, including an oft-reprinted collected poems published by the venerable Ticknor and Fields (later the Riverside Press) of Boston. While Whitman could write longingly, in his preface to *Leaves of Grass* (1855) that "The proof of a poet is that his country absorbs him as affectionately as he has absorbed it," it is Whittier whose public reception in the nineteenth

The Quaker Giant Robert Hales and the Quaker Giantess on display at Barnum's Museum in 1848. Hales, the son of an English farmer, weighed 460 pounds and stood over seven feet tall.

century comes closer to meeting that description. Nevertheless, Whitman's opinion about Whittier's accomplishment was decidedly mixed: "Whittier's poetry stands for morality . . . as filtered through the positive Puritanical and Quaker filters; is very valuable as a genuine utterance. . . . Whittier is rather a grand figure—pretty lean and ascetic— no Greek—also not composite and universal enough (doesn't wish to be, doesn't try to be) for ideal Americanism."[32]

By 1884, several crucial periods of Quaker history had receded into the past and beyond the recollection of many American readers: long, antagonistic years of theological controversy and discrimination; decades of colonial and later national uncertainties during the American Revolution, when Quakerism was understood by some as a template for progressive politics; and finally many years before and during the Civil War when Quakers returned to prominence as vocal abolitionists and activists in subversive activism such as the Underground Railroad.

Distilling her impression of the Quaker tradition and John Greenleaf Whittier's central role within that tradition, Spofford sees him as an iconic instance of distinguished human morality embodied in a magnificent physique:

> At seventy-six years and over one can be said to have the beauty only of age, striking as that is in Mr. Whittier's case, with the dark eye and the full beard, where black lines still appear among the silver, while his form is as straight and his step is as firm and elastic as ever. But the poet's youthful beauty is reported to have been extraordinary: very tall, erect, and well knit, with fine features, dark skin, and a flashing deep-set black eye, he could not have looked the Quaker to any extent; and in fact we think he is more of a Quaker in habit and affection than anything else.[33]

Much could be said about Spofford's unalloyed reverence for the physical charisma that the elderly Whittier embodied well into his eighth decade; it is a fascination with Quaker physical beauty that bears some resemblance to Harriet Beecher Stowe's portrayals of the handsome and virtuous Quakers in *Uncle Tom's Cabin,* in which the Halliday family at the Quaker settlement exude wholesomeness and vigor into middle age and beyond. The overall tenor of Spofford's remarks, however, emphasizes the extent to which the handsome and accomplished Whittier in many ways is not fully a Quaker in any conventional sense.

Spofford's view differs somewhat from the usual description of Whittier's Quaker identity, which can be observed in the biography of Whittier written years later by Thomas Wentworth Higginson, who pointed directly to the Quaker moral background in order to understand the excellence of Whittier's character and poetry:

> Whittier had . . . the early training of a spiritual aristocracy, the Society of Friends. He was bred in a class which its very oppressors had helped to ennoble; in the only meetings where silence ranked as equal with speech, and women with men; where no precedence was accorded to anything except years and saintliness; where no fear was felt but of sin. This gave him at once the companionship of the humble and a habit of deference to those whom he felt above him; he had measured men from a level and touched human nature directly in its own vigour and yet in its highest phase.[34]

Far too attractive to be the stereotypical Quaker of Higginson's imaginings, Whittier strikes Spofford as having the peculiarities of Quaker tradition in favor of a more tolerant image and manners. Spofford takes note as well of his adherence to Quaker customs of silent worship and plain language, but also is careful to indicate that "he dresses so nearly like men of the world in cut and color that only practiced eyes could detect the slight difference in the shape of his coat" and that "his feelings about such matters are entirely liberal." To Spofford's relief, even in the matter of clothing his family members, Whittier avoids the austere stringency of Quaker custom while striking a tolerant chord, as he gives his blessing to a young niece so that she may wear a fashionable cape.

Spofford provides a genealogy of the poet that traces him back to the early years of the great migration from England to the Massachusetts Bay Colony, when John Greenleaf's ancestor Thomas Whittier arrived in Haverhill in 1647. The "sweet lyricism" to which Whittier is heir, speculates Spofford, might in fact with some poetic justice be associated with the Thomas Whittier's importation of his own hive of honey bees into the Haverhill settlement. It is a savory lyricism that runs through his work, she argues, and his artistry comprises a body of poetry that serves to express the myth of America in comprehensive but gentle terms. Along with his abiding sweetness as a poet, there are numerous important themes in his work that she emphasizes as characteristic not only of his work but as national themes that his work tends to highlight. Spofford's way of naming these national themes is to call them "ancestral murmurs" of the Calvinist legacy in America; in his verse the ancestral hum voices moral principles — "hatred of tyranny, contempt for wrong, the idealism of peace, and love of man, be he white, red, or black."[35]

From the perspective of the twenty-first century, what is perhaps most surprising is Spofford's assessment of Whittier's gifts as a poet, for which she has nothing but the highest praise. It is true that the staunch traditionalism and didactic flavor of the Fireside Poets has, since the nineteenth century, become much less studied than the more innovative, paradigm-shifting verse of protomodernist poets like their contemporaries Walt Whitman and Emily Dickinson. Spofford's assessment of Whittier's accomplishments as a poet, an evaluation that appears nearly thirty years after the first publication of Walt Whitman's *Leaves of Grass* (1855), leaves no doubt as to her view of Whittier's importance. Just a few years before Spofford's essay in *Harper's New Monthly Magazine,* however, an anonymous reviewer for the *Catholic World* had not only judged Whittier's poetry to be weak but also found his writing and persona to be contrary to American values and character: After complaining first about the lack of a suitable American national literature, the reviewer grumbles specifically about Whittier's faults as a poet and as an American, concluding that his work would ultimately be of interest and value only to his fellow Quakers, who seem to be out of step with the American ethos:

> Now, whatever idea we may form to ourselves of the typical American, or whether we think such a being exists at all, no one would ever imagine him to be a Quaker.
>
> The American is eager; the Quaker is subdued. The American is loud, with a tendency to boastfulness and exaggeration; the Quaker is quiet and his language sober. He shuns the conflict and the battle, does not over-estimate his strength; while the American would fight the world, catch the Leviathan, swim the ocean, or do anything most impossible. The Quaker is cautious, the American reckless. The American is aggressive, the Quaker is timid. A great poet is held by no bonds. His eye glances from earth to heaven—the infinite is his home; and that Whittier should be only a Quaker poet is of itself sufficient evidence that he is not a great poet.[36]

Spofford's assessment of Whittier's poetic achievement reaches an entirely different conclusion. Hearing a profound lyricism in his work leads her to conclude that "no poet since [Robert] Burns has so abounded in music," Spofford concludes that he stands not only as a crucial writer in the Quaker faith or even the New England tradition, but as a central figure in the canon of American poetry, and even as "perhaps the most peculiarly American poet of any that our country has produced."[37]

Spofford was far from alone in her evaluation of the Quaker poet's centrality in the American literary canon.

Only a few years after Spofford's essay on Whittier, the *Brooklyn Eagle*
reported on a ceremony commemorating Whittier's eightieth anniversary and celebrated before an assembly at All Souls Universalist Church
on South Ninth Street, Brooklyn. This event, which featured a "fine,
handsomely framed portrait of the Quaker poet surrounded by the national colors," was headed by the Universalist pastor Alman Gunnison,
whom the *Brooklyn Eagle* reported as singling out Whittier for his highest
praise and citing him not merely as Quaker pacifist or as a religious poet
of fragile sensibilities: "There is nothing that is artificial or weak about
him, but there is much which is just as dainty and delicate as it is virile."
For Gunnison, as with Spofford, Whittier was "The most distinctively
national poet that has lived and sung in the history of our country. . . . a
man so wide and generous in sympathy, so alive to the genius of the nation that did we follow English precedence he would be the suffrage of
the people be made the laureate of America." In short, Gunnison points
to Whittier as an exemplary American poet embodying masculine integrity and strength, while at the same time displaying the kind of sympathetic nature worthy of recognition as the nation's poet laureate.[38]

In differentiating Whittier from the Fireside poets, for example,
Spofford insists that "The woods and waterfowl of [William Cullen]
Bryant belong as much to one land as to another; and all the rest of our
singers—Emerson, Longfellow, Lowell, and their brethren—with the
single exception of [Quaker poet] Joaquin Miller, might as well have
been born in the land of Shakespeare and Milton and Byron as in their
own. But Whittier is entirely the poet of his own soil." So much so that
his poetic works, despite their origins in the Quaker faith, a persistently
minority religion in the United States, could in significant ways constitute and narrate the very history of the New England colonies. Spofford views Whittier's achievement as a kind of time capsule—a uniquely
American moral and historical archive distilled into verse form, "It
is hardly an exaggeration to say that if every other record of the early
history and life of New England were lost," she writes, "the story could
be constructed again from the pages of Whittier. Traits, habits, facts,
traditions, incidents—he holds a torch to the dark places, and illumines
them every one."[39] It is to these same Quaker traits, facts, traditions,
and incidents—both real and imagined—that fiction writers of the
same era would turn.

5

Representing Quakers in American Fiction

The representations of Quaker manners which have been popular of late, in novels, are most ludicrous travesties of the reality.

Francis Frith, *The Quaker Ideal* (1894)

Every Quakeress is a lily.

Charles Lamb, "A Quaker's Meeting" (1843)

Nathaniel Hawthorne was among the most prominent of antebellum American writers to observe the seriousness with which Quakers could approach their reading lives. In 1849, just before completing his masterwork, *The Scarlet Letter* (1850), Hawthorne received an unexpected visitor at his Concord home. She was, Hawthorne records in his *American Notebook* for that year, "a lady, rather young, and quite comely, with pleasant and intelligent eyes, in a pretty Quaker dress":

> She offered me her hand and spoke with much simplicity, but yet in a ladylike way, of her interest in my works, and her not being able to resist a desire to see me, on finding herself in my vicinity. I asked her into the sitting-room, to enjoy our back view; and we talked of the scenery, and of various persons and matters. Lowell, Whittier, Mr. James, and Herman Melville, were more or less discussed; she seemed to be a particular friend of Whittier, and had heard of his calling on me, two or three

years ago. Her manners were very agreeable indeed; the Quaker simplicity, and the little touch of Quaker phraseology, gave piquancy to her
refinement and air of society. She had a pleasant smile, and eyes that
readily responded to one's thought; so that it was not difficult to talk
with her;—a singular, but yet a gentle freedom in expressing her own
opinions;—an entire absence of affectation. These were the traits that
impressed me; and on the whole, it was the only pleasant visit I ever experienced, in my capacity as author.[1]

The young woman who so impressed Hawthorne with her intellect
and breadth of reading did not introduce herself until the time of her
departure from the Old Manse, when she gave her name as Elizabeth
Lloyd, whom Hawthorne later discovered to be a minor Philadelphia
poet with ties to the Quaker poet and abolitionist John Greenleaf Whittier. The irony of a Quaker visiting the Old Manse to pay her respects to
him must have been powerful in its effect on Hawthorne, though, whose
Salem ancestor William Hathorne had been closely involved in the sentencing of several seventeenth-century Quaker women to be flogged
through the streets of Salem, Massachusetts.

That Quakers can be described as avid serious readers, however,
constitutes only one aspect of their role in American literary culture.
That Quakers had become known as avid readers but also as popular
characters in antebellum fiction can be seen readily in the era's most
popular and influential novels, usually during an episode of the highest
drama. One of the more memorable scenes from Harriet Beecher
Stowe's *Uncle Tom's Cabin* (1852) occurs during Eliza Harris's flight from
slavery, after she arrives at the safe domestic haven of Rachel and
Simeon Halliday, members of a devout Quaker household who have offered her temporary lodging on behalf of the Underground Railroad. It
is in this orderly place of cleanliness, courtesy, thrift, good will, and piety
that the fugitive slave Eliza finally is able to sleep soundly and subsequently to dream "of a beautiful country,—a land, it seemed to her, of
rest,—green shores, pleasant islands, and beautifully glittering water;
and there, in a house which kind voices told her was a home, she saw her
boy playing, free and happy child." Upon waking the next morning,
Eliza finds herself reunited with son and husband in the antebellum
social oasis that is the Quaker settlement. If *Uncle Tom's Cabin* may be
understood, in part, as promoting an idealized form of American family life, then surely the Quaker Halliday family is one of the preeminent
examples of that domestic sphere.[2]

Temperate and serene, the men, women, and children in Stowe's Quaker settlement exude Christian virtue, moral gravity, robust health,[3] and personal strength; for them, social justice begins at home, and the Quaker doctrine of an "inner light" for each believer manifests itself in an environment of mutuality, candor, and dignity. Here, age is respected and venerated, especially among the women, whose beauty seems to ripen with the years rather than fade. No youthful beauty, the carefully coiffed and plainly dressed Rachel Halliday possesses "one of those faces that time seems to touch only to brighten and adorn."[4] Here, too, the authority of patriarchy largely gives way to the guiding genius of cheerful and industrious women. Simeon Halliday, "a tall, straight, muscular man," speaks few words and stands clear of the more-important kitchen labors of the household's women, who bustle about creating "an atmosphere of mutual confidence and good fellowship." A rare moral exemplar among Stowe's male characters in the novel, however, it is Simeon who chastens his young son for hating the slaveholders who would have prevented George and Eliza from living in peace. Instead, the fictional Quaker patriarch serenely insists upon unconditional love and benevolence, and that he "would do even the same for the slaveholder as for the slave, if the Lord brought him to my door in affliction."[5]

However, despite all of their admirable morality—which extended to the all-important notion of equality for women—Stowe's novel does not linger among these Friends of the Quaker settlement. For all the optimism expressed about these believers in the "inner light" of Quakerism, *Uncle Tom's Cabin* does not directly advocate a turn to Quakerism as a solution for the problem of American social ills. As one critic has noted, while highlighting the otherness of Quaker clothing and dialect, Stowe's novel also clearly indicates her admiration for the humanitarianism of Quakers. There are limits to her representations, however, for "No Quaker refers to the Inner Light, no Quaker discusses or even alludes to an inner awareness of spirituality, no Quaker refers to Christ."[6] Quakers in this novel are fashioned as exemplary figures of Christian virtue, but do not dominate the narrative as a whole; they are presented as model Americans, but just as clearly their religious world seems to be little more than a fantasy, or an impossibility on the larger scale that interests Stowe. In this way, Stowe follows a formula that would become familiar over the course of the nineteenth century. Quakerism's representation in fiction as a set of exemplary American religious and social practices appears alongside its failure to attract large numbers of follow-ers. Consistently in the socially progressive vanguard, and commonly used in fiction as one of the highest expressions of Christianity, Quakers in early American fiction are deployed for our admiration but also enlist our recognition of their broader failure to capture American religious enthusiasm in any significant way. Quakers are equally notable as an-gelic representations of an unrealizable social and moral ideal: partici-pants in a version of religious practice that inevitably will lie outside the popular reach.[7]

When the abolitionist movement intensified during the years before the Civil War, Quakers like Stowe's Halliday family demonstrated and embodied the ideals of domestic stability and racial benevolence that *Uncle Tom's Cabin* sponsors.[8] These Quaker ideals, it is important to note, were voiced by antebellum writers who themselves were Quakers and also by those, like Stowe, who admired and emulated certain values and traits of the Quakers without adopting every article of their faith. An-other of these Quaker sympathizers, Benjamin Rush Plumley, an asso-ciate of the abolitionist William Lloyd Garrison and later a staff officer for Union general John C. Fremont, probably used his experiences grow-ing up among the Quaker faithful near Philadelphia in Bucks County, Pennsylvania, as the inspiration to write his *Lays of Quakerdom* (1853–55). Writing under the pseudonym "Ruth Plumley," Benjamin Rush Plum-ley's *Lays of Quakerdom* consisted of three narrative poems of Quaker hagiography, which he published first in the *Knickerbocker* magazine dur-ing the years leading up to the Civil War. The *Lays*, which describe the piety of three icons of seventeenth-century Quakerism, appear along-side brief, sympathetic histories of their subjects but with no commen-tary about nineteenth-century political and social problems. Each about two hundred lines in length, the poems bear the following titles: "The Execution of Mary Dyer," "Visit of Mary Fisher to Sultan Mohammed IV," and "James Parnell, the Quaker Proto-Martyr." Two of them mar-tyrs for their faith (Mary Dyer in New England, James Parnell in Lon-don) and one of them an intrepid traveler to the court of the Turkish sultan who urged Christian faith among the Muslim leadership, all of Plumley's subjects are unstintingly brave and radiant in their faith. Plumley wrote that much of Mary Dyer's force as a radical Christian de-rived from her ability to speak clearly of her beliefs before her vindictive opponents:

> Startled by the transformation
> Sate the rulers proud;
> Wondering at her awful beauty
> Gazed the vulgar crowd;
> While her words went through the stillness,
> Ringing clear and loud.[9]

Like many of the abolitionists who would follow these early Quakers to the American public square two centuries later, Plumley's martyrs demonstrate both public morality and personal restraint in working toward social justice. The crisis of slavery and the attendant discourses of abolition that emerged in the late antebellum period provided an ideal opportunity for revisiting—imaginatively—the colonial period. Just as Plumley's contemporary Nathaniel Hawthorne was turning to the historical theater of colonial Puritan life in his short fiction and *The Scarlet Letter* (1850) in order to critique and problematize the origins of American religious and national identity, writers like Stowe and Plumley were reinscribing Quaker faith within the larger American culture so as to provide a harsh critique of such matters as the nation's long history of racial bigotry and religious intolerance.

Decades later and continuing well into the twentieth century, when American regionalists and local colorists turned consistently to representations of the quaint, the picturesque, and the historically curious, Quakers were prominent among the stock figures that conjured up a sense of a uniquely admirable and yet uncannily repellent American tradition. Whereas early Puritan theologians, as recalled acutely in novels like Nathaniel Hawthorne's *The Gentle Boy* (1839), had understood how the Religious Society of Friends could engender fanaticism and religious strife, by the late nineteenth and early twentieth century, Quakers came to be understood as rather ineffectual, anachronistic figures: Americans who are morally correct and yet insufficiently equipped to wrestle with modernity.[10]

One of the earliest American novels to depict Quakerism as an ideal form of American worship and moral practice, Elizabeth B. Lester's *The Quakers; A Tale* (1818), applied Quaker values to some durable fictional themes: romance, seduction, and adultery. In choosing such topics, Lester situated her novel firmly within established thematics of the popular English novel, with the steadily selling precedent of Samuel Richardson's *Clarissa: or the History of a Young Lady* (1748) as perhaps the preeminent example of this kind of fiction aimed at readers in England

and America. Novels specifically focused on the idea of Quakers in love had also begun to appear in the Anglo-American world of print, in English novels such as *The Quaker. A Novel, in a Series of Letters, by a Lady* (1785), which, like many early novels, was published anonymously and in epistolary form. As these eighteenth-century examples demonstrate, English and American writers alike had begun to find in the intersection of secular modernism and Quakerish traditionalism a rich lode of romantic possibilities, which typically pitted matched Friends—who apparently seemed far more likely as subjects for such a test than Anglicans, Baptists, Catholics, Jews, or Calvinists—against their own stated principles as well as against the corrosive forces of emerging forms of middle-class morality.

Kezia Brooks, the beautiful and wealthy young Friend at the center of Lester's *The Quakers,* speaks little of spirituality or the Inner Light, and instead harbors only the most diluted version of Quaker theology or religiosity; she "was mildly religious; a Christian in practice, rather than theory." Still, the novel makes clear that without her veneer of Quaker modesty and propriety, she would have been instantly subject to libertinism as well as her own vanity. The plot of *The Quakers,* which focuses on the courtship and married life of Kezia Brooks, shows her to be slightly vain, but otherwise good-hearted and loyal (largely because of her Quaker training). After she chooses unwisely to marry the rakish Robert Honour, the downward spiral begins. A brief period of wedded bliss is followed by Honour's descent into a profligate life of gambling, drinking, financial irresponsibility, and marital infidelity—all of which is tolerated and abetted because of Kezia's naïve Quakerish "desire to please universally." When Honour's infidelity finally comes to light, at the end of the novel, he impulsively agrees to a duel with one of his enemies and is mortally wounded. At this point, Lester chooses to end her novel with a turn to sincere Quaker faith. With a chastened and newly devout Kezia by his side, the dying Honour undergoes a deathbed conversion to Quakerism. The Quaker ideal, absent for most of the novel, thus makes a critical appearance as the novel concludes—when the incorrigible libertine discovers Quakerism as salvific—but only as his own demise becomes inevitable. Once again, as with Stowe's admirable and yet apparitional Quakers in *Uncle Tom's Cabin,* the literary function of the Society of Friends and its members has much do with attesting to the values of Quaker morality versus other moral practices. But mostly

Quakerism exists outside the frame of the narrative itself: for Harriet Beecher Stowe, the fleeting glimpses of the Halliday clan at the Quaker settlement; for Elizabeth B. Lester, the suggestion that true Quaker faith can exist only after an unseemly tale ends in tragedy.[11]

American fiction dealing with Quakers frequently assigns considerable blame to those groups, religious or otherwise, who had persecuted the Quakers for their beliefs or actions. This is most abundantly true in the case of Puritans in colonial New England, for whom the Quakers were such a notable threat to the indivisible church-state tradition of the "New England Way." With their lack of centralized clerical authority and their openness to the lay ministry of women, colonial Quakers represented heresy at its most subversive for the Puritans who controlled all aspects of church and government in crucial places like the Massachusetts Bay Colony. The faults of colonial Puritanism had quickly made their way into a range of popular American novels produced in the early nineteenth century.

One of these novels, *Rachel Dyer: A North American Tale* (1828), was written by the Maine-based popular novelist, lecturer, feminist, one-time Quaker, and reformer John Neal.[12] Based partly, albeit inaccurately, on New England colonial history, *Rachel Dyer* returns to the notorious Salem witch trials by connecting the tales of two persons who, several generations apart, were convicted and executed for witchcraft and heresy in colonial Massachusetts: the infamous Quaker Mary Dyer, and George Burroughs, who had been accused and executed for witchcraft in 1691, several decades after Mary Dyer had been executed by the Puritan authorities. By fancifully blending the stories of Mary Dyer and George Burroughs—and by creating the purely fictitious Rachel Dyer as a granddaughter of the Quaker prophet and martyr Mary Dyer—Neal proceeds with a historically minded account of colonial religious persecution. The conflation of the stories of Quakerism and witchcraft also produces a clear genealogy of New England Quakerism that can be traced from the ardent faith of the legendary Mary Dyer to her daughter, the fictional tradition-bearer Rachel Dyer.

Neal introduces Rachel only in the latter half of his novel, after a series of colonial courtroom scenes in which falsely accused witches are tried and then executed, despite the best and bravest efforts of George Burroughs to exonerate them. When Burroughs himself is falsely accused and brought forward to face charges before the Puritan magistrates during the first half of the novel, Rachel Dyer is alluded to only as a mysterious but unidentified presence in the courtroom. As the final movement of the novel explains, Rachel at that time had been living without the protection of men, on the dangerous wilderness frontier. Her mysterious appearance at the trial of George Burroughs is followed by her courageous testimony, which pitted her support of George Burroughs against the witchcraft charges of his many accusers. Rachel's appearance and demeanor conform with one of the more popular ways of representing Quaker women: as heroic but homely paragons of virtue. As Neal first describes her, "If God ever made a heroine, Rachel Dyer was a heroine—a heroine without youth or beauty, with no shape to please, with no color to charm the eye, with no voice to delight the ear." Later, when she appeared before the witchcraft tribunals, she is once again uniquely courageous but also notable for her physical unattractiveness: "It was Rachel Dyer—the red-haired witch—the freckled witch—the hump-backed witch they saw now—but they saw not her ugliness, they saw not that she was unshapely or unfair. They saw only that she was brave."[13]

The example of Rachel Dyer, who ultimately avoided death at the hands of Puritan authority only by dying in her jail cell—Bible in hand—on the night before her scheduled execution, provides yet another instance of a fictional representation of Quakerism that serves to critique the main currents of Protestantism in America. As Neal noted with regard to Mary Dyer's earlier execution, "The Quakers died in their belief as the great always die—without a word or a tear; praying for the misguided people to their last breath, but prophecying [*sic*] heavy sorrow to them and theirs."[14] Through her peaceful engagement with Native Americans on the colonial frontier, her ability to live independently in a household without men, her willingness to speak out boldly against fraudulent criminal charges, and her sincere piety, Rachel embodies a kind of American antitype, a living model of how religious enthusiasm might be deployed in America for progressive causes and real justice.

Harriet Beecher Stowe, initially through a youthful encounter with the Quaker activist Angelina Grimké in 1831, had long been fascinated with the Society of Friends and its work on behalf of abolitionism and women's rights. Well before the publication of *Uncle Tom's Cabin*, Stowe had begun to use the device of the "good Quaker" in her fiction, as with her 1845 sketch "Immediate Emancipation," in which a runaway slave in Cincinnati is allowed to go free, thanks to the intervention of a

Quaker who convinces the slave's master of the evils of human bondage. However, like *Uncle Tom's Cabin,* this early sketch stops well short of advocating a conversion to Quakerism among Stowe's enormous readership. In this regard, Stowe turns to Quaker ideals in much the same way as did her contemporary Margaret Fuller, whose protofeminist tract *Woman in the Nineteenth Century* (1845) appeared the same year as Stowe's "Immediate Emancipation."[15] For Fuller, Quakers—although mentioned only briefly in *Woman in the Nineteenth Century*—provided a key model for blending femininity with participation in the public sphere. Like the great female stage performers of her day, writes Fuller, nineteenth-century Quaker women had already made important advances on behalf of the feminist cause: "we should think those who had seen the great actresses, and heard the Quaker preachers of modern times, would not doubt, that women can express publicly the fullness of thought and creation, without losing any of the peculiar beauty of her sex." Of course, Margaret Fuller pointedly does not conclude that Quaker religiosity constituted anything resembling a sufficient feminist paradigm. Like Stowe's Quakers, who are unmistakably feminine, Christian, and politically progressive, the Quaker women in Fuller's estimation suggest all of these traits, while nevertheless also appearing implicitly to be radically "other," and perhaps not entirely assimilable to the American political and social context.[16]

In their eagerness to shed their inherited (typically Unitarian) faith, New England transcendentalists like Margaret Fuller saw in Quakerism an important dimension of religious practice that would affirm the value of individual spirituality while extending that spiritual practice into the realm of practical power and social reform. Ralph Waldo Emerson, the central thinker in American transcendentalism, enriched his own rapidly changing philosophical and religious views by immersing himself in a study of English and American Quaker thought. His journal indicates that during his vacation in New Hampshire's White Mountains in July 1832, he had with him a copy of William Sewel's influential history of the Quakers and Tuke's *Memoirs of the Life of Fox.* Emerson's lecture on George Fox, which grew partially out of the notes he took during that July, was delivered on February 26, 1835, just a year before the publication of his landmark "Nature" essay in 1836.[17] The lecture formed a part of his six lyceum lectures on biography, presented before the Society for the Diffusion of Useful Knowledge at Boston's Masonic Temple. His great esteem for the early Quaker leader can be discerned by the other four historic, representative men included with Fox during that season of Emerson's lecture career: Milton, Michelangelo, Luther, and Edmund Burke. Each of these men, Emerson wrote, "Towers above his [Fox's] contemporaries and is not one man in a thousand men, but one man in a thousand years."[18] As for his own affinities for the Society of Friends, Emerson admitted to at least one friend who inquired about the Concord sage's religious identity that "I am more a Quaker than anything else. I believe in the 'still, small voice,' and that voice is Christ within us."[19] Emerson's view of Quaker life generally, and George Fox's accomplishments specifically, emerges from Emerson's appreciation for their application of the "Religious sentiment," which he delineates as being somewhat akin to the transcendental, religiously creative, and spiritualizing principle of the "Reason" in his "Nature" essay of 1836.

A similar view of Quakers as having worked in the vanguard of the religious sentiments, thereby supplying a vital link between ancient Christian impulses and the antebellum turn toward benevolence and spiritual sentimentality, can be seen not only in Emerson but in many of his contemporaries in transcendentalist circles and others with progressive political leanings. It is perhaps fitting, then, that the great abolitionist and popular novelist Lydia Maria Child (1802–80) would not only write favorably about Quakers in her published letters but also would have her collected letters edited by the famed Quaker poet and novelist John Greenleaf Whittier in 1883. Although Child presciently noted the decline of the Society of Friends during the nineteenth century and thought that "The Friends as a society may become extinct," she also was convinced of their moral importance and that "not in vain did they cast forth their great principles into everlasting time." Child wrote in no uncertain terms about the shared egalitarian and spiritually humane ethos among those who worked for both secular democracy and Quaker religious values during the years since the inauguration of the Quaker movement in the seventeenth century: "No truth [the Quakers] uttered shall ever die; neither shall any truth that you or I may speak, or express in our lives. Two centuries after William Penn brought indignation upon himself by saying 'thou' to the Duke of York, the French revolutionists, in order to show that they were friends of equality, wrote in their windows, 'In this house we "thou" it.' And this idea, dug up by the Friends from the ashes of early Christianity, has in fact given rise to the doctrine of 'spiritual brotherhood,' echoed and reechoed from [English Unitarian

founder Joseph Priestly] to [American Unitarian minister William El-
lery] Channing."[20] It is especially intriguing here to see Child, who was
herself not a Quaker, indicating the vital importance of Quaker thought
and spirituality to the highly influential Anglo-American Unitarian
movement and, by implication, the American transcendentalist movement with Ralph Waldo Emerson at its center and apex.

For all of her ecumenical spirit, however, Child was always careful to
indicate her strong preference for less radical forms of Protestant Christian religiosity. In her 1856 novella, *The Catholic and the Quaker*, a romantic
tale of the wartime courtship of an Irish youth and his Quaker lover,
Child concludes by observing the complaints about the marriage by
both Quakers and Catholics, "Both [of whom] prognosticated evil consequences of such a union." Such dire consequences from the presumed
incompatibility of Quaker and Catholic never come to pass, but Child
ends the novella by pointing to what she understood to be the grave religious errors on each side: "The worst that happened was, Alice learned
that there might be superstition in the cut of a garment, as well as in ven-
eration for an image; and Camillo became convinced that hatred and violence were much greater sins than eating meat on Fridays." In this way,
Quakers and Catholics thus are used as elements in a mutual critique, a
critique that ultimately turns the young couple into liberal Christians of
the sort that the Unitarian Lydia Maria Child could approve.[21]

The convergence of mass print culture (with its attendant professional-
ization of authorship) and the increasingly complicated religious scene
in the antebellum United States appears to have sponsored an environment in which imagined Quakers could stand as the authentic, purified
form of Protestant radicalism. During the antebellum decades, serious
interest in the Quaker ethos was not limited merely to Unitarians like
Emerson, whose training in divinity school would have equipped him
very well with a sense of the significant place of Quakers in Protestant
theology, and whose turn to Romantic transcendental philosophy placed
him in sympathy with many of the principles of Quaker individualism.
James Fenimore Cooper, whose entire career as a writer of violent frontier novels—most significantly the five volumes published between 1823
and 1841 that comprise the Leatherstocking Tales—stands as a refuta-
tion of Quaker morals, was himself from a Quaker background. References to Quakers appear occasionally, perhaps most prominently, in the
first of his Leatherstocking tales, *The Pioneers* (1823), whose events unfold

in central New York State in 1793. Judge Marmaduke Temple, the protagonist of that novel, is a retired Quaker merchant and prosperous landowner (not unlike Cooper himself) whose father "Old Marmaduke" had been a friend of William Penn in what Cooper calls the "peaceful and unenterprising [Quaker] colonies of Pennsylvania and New Jersey" (ch. 2). His probity and good character, the narration soon makes clear, stem from a combination of wealth and secularized Quaker principles, although he enjoys fine clothing and ostentation that would have been abhorrent to Quakers of that era. Most useful for Cooper's purposes is the implication that Quaker genealogy can be tied to moral excellence, even as Quaker practice appears to be both strange and picturesque. As one character explains to Marmaduke Temple's wife, Elizabeth (who did not come from a Quaker background): "I've always set store by the Quakers, they are so pretty-spoken, clever people, and it's a wonderment to me how your father come to marry into a church family; for they are as contrary in religion as can be. One sits still, and, for the most part, says nothing, while the church folks practyse all kind of ways, so that I sometimes think it quite moosical to see them; for I went to church-meeting once before, down country" (ch. 15).

The evidence from nineteenth-century American novels seems to support Henry Seidel Canby's comment that "The Quaker has been unfortunate in fiction and drama," which appears to argue that there has been a pattern of negative portrayals of Quaker lives in the nation's fiction.[22] Nevertheless, the fictional portrayals continued unabated as did the dramatic portrayals of Friends, and not all of the portrayals were negative. Fictional representations of American Quakers typically follow Stowe's narrative pattern of admiration for their piety and justice, while stopping well short of proselytizing on behalf of the Society of Friends, who usually appear to comprise a preternaturally gifted subset of humanity—ethereal savants of benevolence. We see this ambivalence about Quakerism not only in Harriet Stowe's writings but in those of other writers as well. In Rebecca Harding Davis's remarkable novella of the laboring classes, *Life in the Iron Mills* (1861), the nameless woman who rescues the lowly Deb Wolfe from dire impoverishment and criminality, turns out to be a Quaker, but one of nearly supernatural serenity and virtue. Just after her companion, the ill-fated working-class sculptor Hugh Wolfe, dies in jail of tuberculosis, the deformed and miserable "Deb" finds comfort and recuperation at the hands of this Quaker woman, who appears miraculously at the moment of crisis. It is the

Quaker woman, "a homely body, coarsely dressed in gray and white," who attends to the wretched laborer in her hour of mourning and cares for the tragically dead sculptor's body. Eternally modest and yet teeming with Christian virtue, the homely Quaker woman serves here as an example of the sort of noble creature that Walt Whitman had in mind when speaking of laudable women in the Society of Friends, such as the abolitionist Lucretia Mott. "Do you know the Quaker women?" Whitman once inquired of his companion Horace Traubel, "The women are the cream of the sect. It was not Lucretia Mott alone—I knew her just a little: she was a gracious, superb character, but she was not exceptional." Whitman spoke not only of his high estimate of Friends as exemplary people but also of his own identification with them. During his final days in Camden, New Jersey, Whitman explained to Traubel that "A curious affinity exists between me and the Quakers, who always say, this is so or that is so because of some inner justifying fact—because it could not be otherwise. I remember a beautiful old Quakeress [probably Hannah Whitall Smith of Camden] saying to me once 'Walt—I feel thee is right—I could not tell why but I feel thee is right!'—and that seemed to me to be more significant than much that passes for reason in the world."[23] The extreme otherness suggested by the Quaker woman's willfully drab attire in Davis's novella, worn in a society of increasingly conspicuous consumption, also highlights the alterity of her benevolent actions in assisting the hapless Deb. Thus, the astonishing and gratifying scene of human rescue, when understood from the perspective of Davis's readers, creates a moral and logical impasse: rescuing the victims of brutal industrial labor becomes a desirable and necessary act, and yet the burden of rescue is borne by a phantomlike Quaker rather than by society as a whole.[24]

Consequently, although *Life in the Iron Mills* presents a devastating antebellum picture of the working poor of industrialized America, Davis offers very little in the way of practical remedy for the dire material circumstances of her impoverished millworkers.[25] The upper-class characters in the story range from profoundly empathetic to coarsely indifferent, but none of them extends anything other than mere sympathy and prayers to the oppressed victims of subsistence wage-slavery. In short, the novel's bold exposé stops well short of advocating broad social change or substantial intervention to alter the condition of the hapless workers. Instead, Davis allows her nameless Quaker woman to appear as a deus ex machina, appearing suddenly by the side of the bereaved woman to "solve" Deb's problematic life. The woman rescuer—angelic, pious, and serene like the Friends in Stowe's Quaker settlement—figures then as both a superhero of benevolence and as a social impossibility: ordinary human beings find themselves incapable of aiding the poor, while the imaginary Quaker does what only Quakers can apparently do.[26]

Even her description of her home partakes of this fantasy of altruistic perfection: "Thee sees the hills, friend, over the river? Thee sees how the light lies warm there, and the winds of God blow all the day? I live there,—where the blue smoke is, by the trees." The tranquility and moral steadfastness exuded by the Friends of Stowe's Quaker settlement in *Uncle Tom's Cabin* are reproduced by Davis's solitary Quaker woman in her pastoral abode, to which Deb retreats after her own three-year imprisonment for theft. Once again, what is striking about Davis's narrative strategy and commentary here is that she provides for a Quaker intervention precisely at the moment when things seem darkest for the oppressed laborer, a moment—it must be acknowledged—that coincides with the novella's clearest failure to propose a more thorough consideration of practical solutions for the plight of an American underclass. As Davis herself admits, "Three years after, the Quaker began her work. I end my story here." The work of the Quakeress, which amounts to a slow transformation of human neglect and criminality, then proceeds in a location that could not be more different from the bleak industrial landscapes of the iron mills:

> There is no need to tire you with the long years of sunshine, and fresh air, and slow patient Christ-love, needed to make healthy and hopeful this impure body and soul. There is a homely pine house, on one of these hills, whose windows overlook broad, wooded slopes and clover-crimsoned meadows,—niched into the very place where the light is warmest, the air freest. It is the Friends' meeting house.

Turning away from landscapes of urbanization, and evading any concerns for the vexed matter of industrialization and its attendant problem of the laboring classes, Davis effectively allows the Quaker woman's intervention—at once admirable and yet clearly a fantasy—to substitute for a broader conversation about such matters as social responsibility and workers' rights.[27]

Although she points to the dire need for social reform and especially workers' rights in her fiction, Rebecca Harding Davis's rescuing Quaker angel of *Life in the Iron Mills* demonstrates simultaneously the inability of non-Quakers to seize the moral high ground of charitable intervention. In this way, Davis shares with Stowe the implicit critique of an antebellum reformist movement that could never quite measure up to the standards set by Quaker idealism. But Quakers in American fiction also sharpened perspectives on the colonial past. For example, during the antebellum years Quakers were frequently used as stock characters, as historical antitypes, for the purpose of expressing a certain amount of regret about America's Puritan past. Decades after the Revolutionary period, according to Lawrence Buell, American writers sometimes used the time-honored habit of criticizing New England's Puritan past—a habit that Nathaniel Hawthorne developed into high art in the creation of such works as *The Gentle Boy* (1839) and *The Scarlet Letter* (1850)—to create fiction in which "Quakerism is used as stick with which to beat the Puritans." Buell points to the heroine of Eliza Buckminster Lee's novel *Naomi* (1848) as one instance of this retrospective dichotomy of colonial Puritans and Quakers. Naomi, a young English Puritan immigrant to colonial Massachusetts, becomes an exemplary figure for her resistance to Puritan authority and her resolute adherence to the Quaker doctrine of the Inner Light instead of mere biblical revelation. Jailed briefly for her heresy, she triumphs eventually in Quaker marriage, settling in New Jersey with a Harvard graduate who shares her Quaker beliefs. Buell goes on to suggest, however, that the conclusion of *Naomi*, which depicts a newly founded and apparently blissful Quaker family, amounts to far less than a wholesale endorsement of the Society of Friends. Although Naomi adopts certain key aspects of Quakerism in the course of her resistance to the provinciality and repression of her Puritan elders, her own persistent characterization of Quakers as "ignorant," "vulgar," and "illiterate" signals a narrative tactic that elevates Quakerism as an abstract or didactic concept while disparaging Quakerism as a lived religion. In the end, remarks Buell, although Naomi takes on the apparent religious identity of Friends (and especially their religious individualism), she nevertheless "finds most [Quakers] in appallingly bad taste." The example of *Naomi* is far from a unique instance of the tendency of American fiction writers of the nineteenth century to utilize the history of Friends as a means of criticizing the more predominant strains of colonial religious practice. For example, in a discussion of Rebecca Gibbons Beach's historical novel *The Puritan and the Quaker: A Story of Colonial Times* (1879), an anonymous reviewer for the *Nation* magazine acerbically noted the purposeful theme of that book:

"to rehabilitate the Quakers of colonial times, or, if it does not vaunt the discretion of the Quakers, to make clear the ferocious tyranny of the Puritans."[28] The persistence of Quaker representation in historical fiction, long after the conclusion of the Revolutionary War and the Civil War—both conflicts during which Friends had important roles as noncombatants and as abolitionists—gives some sense of how deeply Quaker history and principles had been registered within the moral structures of American literary culture.[29]

The development of Quakers as stock types in nineteenth- and early twentieth-century fiction should also be understood in the context of denominational growth and population change during those years. The shifting patterns of religious affiliation and regional demographics lessened the attention paid to the Quakers who had come so early to the fight against the involuntary human servitude. Although by the mid-eighteenth century, English Quaker immigration—especially to the Delaware Valley region—had resulted in rapid growth to the point that Quakers had become the third-largest denomination in the colonies, the multifarious Christianization of America soon moved the Society of the Friends to the margins of religious discourse and practice in the United States. In demonstrating this decline in the prominence of Quaker religion, whose primary contribution to American morals the historian David Hackett Fischer views as the concept of "reciprocal freedom," he notes that whereas "in early America, the Friends were not a small sect,"

> After the mid-eighteenth century the number of Quakers in British America continued to rise in absolute terms, but began to fall relative to other religious groups. Among all American denominations, Quakers slipped to fifth place by 1775 (with 310 meetings); ninth place by 1820 (350 meetings); and sixty-sixth place by 1981 (532 meetings).

The marginalization of Quaker practice that these numbers suggest, however, seems not to correspond to a decline in imaginative engagement with fictional characters who exemplified various aspects of the mystical and protolibertarian ethos associated with the Society of Friends.[30]

Enthusiasm for Quakers in fiction was not simply a matter of admiration for their abolitionist positions on slavery. Consequently, as the nineteenth century unfolded, with its rapidly shifting religious demographics, the notion of American Quakerism as a quirkily admirably religious

ideal lent itself persistently to the development of various stock fictional
characters, which both Stowe, Davis, and numerous other writers readily adopted for a range of purposes. Herman Melville, the most prominent antebellum novelist to make significant use of Quaker characters,
does so explicitly in *Moby-Dick* (1851), which features the Quaker island
of Nantucket as its early setting. During the several years before the
publication of that novel, however, Melville's awareness of Quaker values and costume were already on display in *White-Jacket, or the World in
a Man-of-War* (1849), a novel that presents his most direct challenge to
the violence and authoritarianism then typical aboard seafaring vessels.
Before Melville turned to the world of tight-fisted, seafaring Nantucket
Quakers in *Moby-Dick* (1851), he developed something of a Quaker pacifist sensibility in *White-Jacket*. Opening with a description of the endlessly useful and paradoxical white jacket worn by the narrator, Melville
goes out of his way to alert his readers to its links with Quakerism, remarking that the garment has a "Quakerish amplitude about the skirts."
Later in the narrative, Melville sardonically footnotes the concept of a
military cannonade for the benefit of a "Quaker reader": that unusual
or perhaps imaginary reader who would not have understood one of
the basic concepts of naval artillery.[31]

Melville's preoccupation with the perplexities of American Quaker
life grew only more intense over the next few years. As Wynn M. Goering has remarked about *Moby-Dick*, Melville's novel focuses on "a
thoroughgoing Quaker enterprise, with a Quaker-owned vessel shipping
from a Quaker port, guided by a Quaker first mate and a mysterious
captain whose 'thee's' and 'thou's' reveal his religious heritage."[32]
Shrewd businessmen and sailors, Quakers like Captain Peleg and Captain Bildad introduce the youthful Ishmael to the business of whaling
during the initial chapters of the novel. And Bildad's sister, Aunt Charity, embodies the charitable ideal of Quakerism that Stowe and Davis
express in their own fiction. Attending to the needs of sailors in port,
Aunt Charity, "a lean old lady of a most determined and indefatigable
spirit, but withal very kindhearted, . . . seemed resolved that, if *she* could
help it, nothing should be found wanting in the Pequod, after once fairly
getting to sea."[33] Like the nameless Quaker in Davis's *Life in the Iron Mills*,
Aunt Charity conforms to the putative moral excellence of American
Friends, providing endless nurture and care for those within her domestic sphere (in this case a ship rather than a cottage): "And like a sister of
charity did this charitable Aunt Charity bustle about hither and thither,

ready to turn her hand and heart to anything that promised to yield safety, comfort, and consolation to all on board [the] ship."[34]

At the center of *Moby-Dick*, Captain Ahab of Nantucket stands as the one character most powerfully wrought from an amalgam of religious and philosophical discourses, among them the Inner Light of Quakerism. Like Peleg and Bildad, he "retain[s] in an uncommon measure the peculiarities of the Quaker, only variously and anomalously modified by things altogether alien and heterogeneous." The furthest thing from the pacifist tradition, Ahab and his fellow Quaker whaling captains are "fighting Quakers; they are Quakers with a vengeance." Bildad, not to mention Ahab, embodies the contradiction between Quaker pacifism and the bloody hunt for whales; it is he who "though a sworn foe to human bloodshed, yet had . . . in his straight-bodied coat, spilled tuns upon tuns of leviathan gore." With its biblical cadences, Ahab's soaring language owes a measure of its grandeur to the "thee" and "thou" of the Quaker idiom, but Melville is careful to indicate that Ahab's personality and character, along with those of the other Nantucket captains, are aggressive mutations of Quakerism whose peculiarities only result "from another phase of the Quaker, modified by individual circumstances."[35] In any case, Melville conforms to typical nineteenth-century attitudes about Quakerism by emphasizing their "peculiarity" or "queerness" (terms he uses frequently to describe the New Bedford and Nantucket Quaker whalemen), indicating their curious moral force while marginalizing them as decidedly quasi-American types.

The clearest precursor to Melville's use of Quakerism as an admirably pacifistic religious tradition—but one that nevertheless harbors and sometimes discloses extremely violent urges—appears in Robert Montgomery Bird's widely popular historical novel, *Nick of the Woods; or, the Jibbenainosay* (1837).[36] Sharing Captain Ahab's pathologically inverted Quakerism, with its enormous appetite for revenge and violence, the brutal Indian-killer Nathan Slaughter figures the American Friend's impossibility in two separate ways. On the one hand, Bird represents Nathan (a Quaker) in the early scenes of the book as a morally problematic person because of his extreme pacifism even in the face of imminent Indian attacks. He apparently does what no self-respecting American frontiersman may do during the troubling Kentucky border wars of the 1780s: he refuses to fight and kill Natives, even if his own life is in jeopardy. By turns fearful and genocidal, the purportedly noble young hero Roland Forrester describes their adversaries in bestial terms, as "yonder crawling reptiles,—reptiles in spirit as in movement" and urges Slaughter to fight. Slaughter concurs with Forrester's assessment of the Kentucky Indians but nevertheless responds pacifically to a disbelieving Forrester: "does thee think to have *me* do the wicked thing of shedding blood? Thee should remember, friend, that I am a follower of peaceful doctrines, a man of peace and amity." In the context of the novel (and in accord with his own opinion), Bird suggests that Quaker pacifism of this sort should be unthinkable for an American frontiersman confronting the perpetrators of murder, who, far from being heroic warriors, typically return from battle "laden with the scalps of miserable squaws and babes."[37]

On the other hand, and equally unthinkable, are Slaughter's acts of retribution against the Natives; as the novel eventually discloses, Nathan Slaughter's alter ego, Nick of the Woods, has been clandestinely performing horrific acts of vigilante murder, scalping, and mutilation against the encroaching Natives. It is here, then, that Bird highlights a second key aspect of the American Quaker's impossibility. Just as only a devout Quaker could have resisted the urge to combat and slay Indians during the conquest of the frontier, so too only a renegade Quaker—one like Nathan Slaughter, whose wife and children had been killed by Natives—could muster the urge to dispatch Indians with such enthusiasm. A disturbed Quaker gone beyond the bloody logic of mere colonialism, Nick/Nathan exhibits a gluttony for murder and a thrill for carnage that places him well beyond the pale of "ordinary" frontier warfare. Having been revealed as the fervently willing executioner of Kentucky's Indian population, the violently warped Quakerism of Nathan Slaughter also suggests the radical fissures in his moral condition; "his appearance and demeanor were rather those of a truculent madman than of the simple-minded, inoffensive creature he had so long appeared to the eyes of all who knew him." Insane or not, however, and in a pattern that would be rehearsed by the imaginary Quaker champions of wage-laborers and slaves in Davis and Stowe's fiction, Bird's sinister yet admirable Friend, Nick of the Woods, operates outside the conventional American moral compass, while serving to buffer conventional American morality from one of its most lamentable failures: the violent elimination of Native Americans.[38]

Setting aside, for the moment, the dark and aggressive Quaker countertypes developed by Melville and Bird, nineteenth-century American writers usually imagined Friends in a much more favorable and benevolent light. The nearly unanimous literary admiration for Quakers would be marred only occasionally by criticism of this religious group, who of course had been the subject of intense and often-violent discrimination by the Puritans during the early American colonial period. But ironically, one of the more prominent voices of criticism came from the poet and novelist Bayard Taylor, the product of a Kennett Square, Pennsylvania, Quaker family (though not a Quaker himself). The social world of Quaker Pennsylvania depicted in Taylor's novels, such as *Hannah Thurston: A Story of American Life* (1863) and *The Story of Kennett* (1866), reveals characters who are less notable for their charity and virtue than those depicted by Stowe and Davis. In Taylor's view, Quakerism had come to stand for excessive propriety and emotional restraint, which in turn led to Quaker families marked by a lack of intimacy and affection. When considering marriage, Hannah Thurston, the protagonist of the eponymous novel, is admonished by her mother to choose a husband capable of expressing himself authentically, without the strictures of Quaker self-control. *The Story of Kennett*, which directly concerns an affluent Quaker family, even scrutinizes the religious practices emblematic of the Friends' meeting, with its apparently spontaneous expression of the Inner Light. Suggesting a certain intellectual impoverishment in the sect, Taylor remarks of a Quaker speaker at a meeting that "A close connection of ideas, a logical derivation of argument from text, would have aroused their suspicions that the speaker depended rather upon his own active, conscious intellect than upon the moving of the spirit; but this aimless wandering of a half-awake soul through the cadences of a language which was neither song nor speech was, to their minds, the evidence of genuine inspiration."[39]

Despite his sometimes harsh assessment of bourgeois Quaker life and religious practice, Taylor also shares with other nineteenth-century fiction writers the tendency of assigning to Quakers certain stereotypical characteristics. As his modern literary biographer, Paul Wermuth, has suggested, Taylor's four novels share a number of stock characters, most notably, "the fatherless boy living with an older woman, usually his mother [or] an aunt, who is usually a Quaker" (in *Hannah Thurston*, the female character lives alone with a Quaker mother).[40] Along with Stowe and Davis, Taylor emphasizes the feminine practice of Quakerism and especially the idealized qualities of Quaker domesticity and ethical identity. It is true that Taylor finds fault with certain aspects of Quaker life, but he also retains a highly favorable view of them as virtuous

citizens—exemplary (if possibly misguided) figures of Christian benevolence.[41] What is crucial in this regard is the way Taylor's Quaker legacies inevitably give way to more "up-to-date religious" and social alternatives. Quakerism in Taylor's fiction figures not only as goodness but as
strangely anachronistic with relation to modern life. We can observe this
contradiction in terms of narrative patterns: just as the fleeing Eliza in
Stowe's novel pauses only briefly to linger among the comforts of the
idealized Quaker Settlement, so too does Bayard Taylor place his characters on a trajectory moving away from Quakerism, a religious spirit
which he associates with a no-longer-relevant American past.

The legendary "Fighting Quakers" of the Revolution, who reput-
edly put country before faith to defend American liberty, were given new
life during the Civil War by writers like John Townsend Trowbridge,
whose popular novel *Cudjo's Cave* (1864) was published at the height of
the conflict. A New Yorker by birth, Trowbridge had already been active
in Boston and New York literary circles, where he came under the influence of writings by transcendentalists like Orestes Brownson, A. Bronson Alcott, and Ralph Waldo Emerson. His close personal friendships
with Walt Whitman, Theodore Parker, and Harriet Beecher Stowe serve
as further evidence of his position close the center of intellectual life in
New York and Boston, where he would have been aware of the powerful
new currents of philosophy and literature that were fueling the American Renaissance. After publishing some novels and a good deal of
other writing for an eclectic assortment of antebellum periodicals—
from the cheap, ephemeral weeklies then booming in his adopted home
of Boston to contributions to early numbers of the *Atlantic Monthly*—
Trowbridge's longest and most popular novel turned to the problem of
race in the American South through the character of Penn Hapgood, a
fictional Quaker. A loosely constructed tale of wartime adventures on
the east Tennessee frontier, *Cudjo's Cave*'s main protagonist is another in
a long line of caricatured Quakers who figure in so many novels of the
nineteenth century. Like so many other fictional Quaker characters, the
Quaker schoolteacher Hapgood is comically rendered but also (nearly)
endlessly sincere in his religious convictions about social equality, plain
talk, and pacifism.

The extent of Penn Hapgood's pacifism comes early in the novel,
when he is attacked by a mob of Rebels who brutally tar and feather
him for his unflinching support of the Union cause. The rest of the
novel follows the exploits of Hapgood as he is taken into the care of two

slaves, who provide a hiding place for him in a secret cave. After a long series of adventures and escapes from the Confederate patrollers, Hapgood eventually comes face to face with the enemy, whom he confronts along with a motley band of allies, including the slaves Cudjo and Pomp, who had harbored him and nursed him back to health after the tar-and-feathering. The long sequence of scenes with the pacifist Hapgood shown first as a pathetic victim of sadistic mobs and later as a passive ward of the fighting slaves finally culminates in a turn to violence of his own. Trowbridge writes of Hapgood's conversion from nonviolent spectatorship to adrenalized and violent participation in hand-to-hand combat against the rebel army:

> Pomp bounded upon the rocks and over them, with a yell which the rest took up as they followed, charging headlong after him. Cudjo, brandishing his sword, leaped and yelled with the foremost—a figure fantastically terrible. Penn, with the fiery Stackridge on one side and his beloved Carl on the other, forgot that he had ever been a Quaker, hating strife. Not that he loved it now; but, remembering that these were the deadly foes of his country, and of those he loved, and feeling it a righteous duty to exterminate them, he went to the work, not like an apprentice, but a master,—without fear, self-possessed, impetuous, kindled with fierce excitement.

Soon after, during an especially brutal scene of combat, Penn Hapgood gravely wounds an enemy soldier. Only a subsequent mishap involving stray gunfire, which kills the wounded soldier, permits Hapgood to avoid ultimate responsibility for having killed another human being and allows him to stand over the fallen enemy's body while saying "I am glad I did not kill him." And yet for all of Penn Hapgood's conscientious regret at the soldier's death, he has clearly undergone the necessary conversion of Quaker noncombatant into confident American patriot. Setting aside his earlier plans to marry the beautiful Virginia (for *Cudjo's Cave* is also a tale of sentimental romance), Penn Hapgood, who had unflinchingly accepted tar and feathers without violent reaction, finally takes up arms for good and assumes the military leadership of a Pennsylvania regiment. He became a valiant fighter "known as the 'Fighting Quaker,' and distinguished for that rare combination of military and moral qualities which constitutes the true hero."[42]

After the Civil War, as slavery receded and industrialization (with its continuing problems for the laboring classes) became an inescapable fact of American life, representation of Quakers in fiction came to signify once again an ethos weighted with concerns about women's rights, domestic thrift, pious behavior, and virtuous citizenship, but it was an ethos that no longer required the commitments of abolitionism. This shift to the less overtly politicized Quaker domestic sphere can be seen in a number of post–Civil War novels. For example, yet another elderly Quaker woman plays a pivotal role in Louisa May Alcott's novel *Work* (1873), which, through the life of its young heroine, Christie Devon, takes on the subject of "that large class of women who, moderately endowed with talents, earnest and true-hearted, are driven by necessity, temperament, or principle out into the world to find support, happiness, and homes for themselves." Though not a Quaker herself, the twenty-one-year-old Christie comes under the influence of Quaker culture at a critical point in her life. As its title suggests, *Work* considers the question of labor—especially women's labor—but the novel is distinctive for the way it blends Alcott's concerns for promoting a strong work ethic and for anatomizing the question of marriage for working-class women. Eminently marriageable, and yet orphaned and financially insecure, Christie Devon shuttles from one humble job to the next: household servant, actress, governess, and laundress. Her life of menial labor appears to be inescapable until finally she accepts a service job in the household of old Mrs. Sterling, a widow and the mother of thirty-one-year-old David Sterling, a kind but unambitious florist.

In *Work,* the Quaker household is represented, in accord with nineteenth-century literary tradition, as a model of domestic tranquility. During her first meeting with the angelic Mrs. Sterling, for example, Christie notices that her "kitchen was tidy with the immaculate order of which Shakers and Quakers alone seem to possess the secret."[43] Her son, David, whom Christie eventually marries, also retains certain Quaker traits and habits, although he maintains that "I wear drab because I like it, and say 'thee' to [Mother] because she likes it, and it is pleasant to have a little word all our own." The decline of Quakerism thus figures prominently as a theme in *Work,* but what links the novel most strikingly to the long tradition of Quakers in American fiction is its exposure of non-Quaker characters to the world of Quakers in order to educate them in certain avenues toward virtue. In Alcott's hands, as for so many other American novelists, Quakerism is administered homeopathically, temporarily, and often by Quaker women in scenes of domestic perfection. Almost always, though, Quaker life is described as illusory or untenable but somehow necessary in small doses in order to create a virtuous citizenry. In the case of Christie Devon, marriage into a Quaker family stimulated her to a life of feminism and social activism after her husband's death in the Civil War. In *Work,* the influence of Quaker morality spawned by the elderly Mrs. Sterling, but not the practice of Quaker religion in any strict sense, produced two ideal types of liberal American. The first, David Sterling, whom Alcott presents as having served as a noble warrior for the antislavery North: "In spite of his Quaker ancestors, he was a good fighter, and, better still, a magnanimous enemy, hating slavery, but not the slave-holder, and often spared the master while he saved the chattel." Slavery having been vanquished, the second ideal type, Christie Devon, emerges in middle-aged widowhood as a community activist for women's rights, a woman transformed from a youthful life of menial labor to a Quaker-influenced adult who stands at the center of "a loving league of sisters, old and young, black and white, rich and poor, each ready to do her part to hasten the coming of the happy end."[44]

The device of using Quaker characters as angelic models of altruism and Christian virtue continued to be used regularly during the late nineteenth century and well into the early years of the twentieth.[45] The Philadelphia physician and novelist S. Weir Mitchell based his most popular historical tale, *Hugh Wynne: Free Quaker* (1897), on the character of an adventurous young Quaker who eventually became involved in the Revolutionary War. A somewhat conventional romance, constructed as a *Bildungsroman* in which a young Friend is expelled from the Philadelphia Quaker Meeting for youthful indiscretions such as drinking, carousing, gambling, and dueling, combined eventually with his desire to fight in the Revolutionary War (a moral impossibility for a devout Quaker), Mitchell's novel produces a relatively rare character in American fiction: a Quaker who stands as the central character in a novel. The fictional Hugh Wynne, who became one of the legendary Free Quakers (also known as "Fighting Quakers")[46] who set aside the Quaker code of nonviolence and willingly fought for American independence, has all the classic qualities typically associated with a romantic hero: wealthy, handsome, clever, and brave. But in nearly every important respect, he diverges from the qualities that had long been associated with Quakerism: piety, thrift, selfless benevolence, and refusal of worldly activities. As one critic as suggested, Hugh Wynne's demonstrated resistance to Quaker doctrine only reinforces the prevailing attitude toward this religious sect in America: "the non-Quaker writer seems to be interested in the

Quaker hero only when he is at odds with the Society that produced him."[47]

Inevitably, Hugh Wynne's actual Quakerism drains inexorably away, only to be replaced with a more generalized, nonsectarian virtue that works in the service of American independence during the crucial years of the Revolution. His representation by Mitchell uses the convenient vehicle of literary Quakerism: its substantial moral heft but not its profound spiritual content and deeper religious commitments. Hugh Wynne's adoption of the Free Quaker code, as narrated within Mitchell's historical novel, aligns him more squarely within an American political culture (and national memory) that prized violent resistance to colonial authority more highly than it did the inwardness and nonviolent ethos of traditional Quakerism.[48]

By World War I, however, and in part due to doctrinal changes and modernization within many branches of the Society of Friends itself, the stereotypical Quakers used by Stowe, Davis, Mitchell, and others came to be used much less frequently in American fiction. In fiction, if not in religious practice itself, Quakerism had apparently begun to out-live its usefulness as an exemplary counterpoint to "mainstream" values. As the charms of local color writing gave way to the new seriousness of naturalist and then modernist fiction, literary portrayals of Quakerism as a primal (if always quaint, retrograde, and unrealizable) form of American virtue began steadily to disappear.

Given the general decline in the use of Quaker fictional characters during the early twentieth century, it comes as something of a surprise to discover that Quakerism's literary epitaph would be written by Theodore Dreiser, one of America's most important and influential natural-ist writers, and a novelist who had long been famous as a chronicler—in works such as *Sister Carrie* (1900), *Jennie Gerhardt* (1911), and *An American Tragedy* (1925)—of the human encounter with modernism, secularism, and materialism. Dreiser's remarkable posthumous novel, *The Bulwark* (1946), stands near the conclusion of a long tradition of using Quakers as exemplary figures in American fiction. Because of its deeply sincere representation of an authentically devout Quaker, *The Bulwark* reverses a good deal of the cynicism about the possibility of Quaker morality that Dreiser had demonstrated in *Sister Carrie*, published fifty years ear-lier. In Dreiser's far more famous novel, the young Carrie Meeber—an amoral theatrical celebrity in the making—not only enacts the fakery of a new, more marketable name ("Carrie Madenda"), but also finds her greatest stage success by taking on the role of a character who could be seen as her moral opposite: the "little Quakeress." When Dreiser finally turned to narrating a tale based on Quaker virtue, his angle of view changed in favor of a radical sympathy for Quakerism. His protagonist in *The Bulwark,* a banker named Solon Barnes, is the scion of a prosperous Maine farmer who moves to New Jersey to care for family members. Marking the shift from the agrarian to the urban, Barnes is consequently a liminal character but nevertheless a sincere and devout Quaker who continues to embody all the traditional values endorsed by his religion: thrift, modesty, rigorous honesty, charity, and sobriety.[49] Always circumspect in financial matters, especially about his own financial success, Barnes is the sort of Quaker—like those constructed by nineteenth-century novelists—whose virtue seems unattainable by others. As one of his friends, herself a lapsed Quaker, remarks to one of Barnes's sons, that Solon Barnes is "Too religious. . . . All the Barnes . . . have been too set in the matter of religion and duty. They've hung onto their Quakerism until they're almost extinct as human beings—that is, all but the doctor and myself. Now, I haven't a thing against Quakers. I love them dearly. If I could live as they do, and keep my place in society, I'd do it. But it can't be done, Stewart. I can't do it. No one can."[50]

Set in the early decades of the twentieth century, *The Bulwark* chronicles the grim failure of Quakerism, in the person of the admirable Solon Barnes, to resist the forces of modernity. Refusing the tendency of certain earlier American novelists to view Quakers as unchanging pillars of virtue—as reliable but imaginary Friends existing at the margins of an unfriendly and morally debased nation—Dreiser's novel illustrates the tectonic power of modernity to overwhelm even the most virtuous individual and the most exemplary religious tradition. For all of his firm probity, Barnes is eventually shattered by the enormous moral deteriorations that pervade the world around him: financial chicanery and criminality in his own bank, sexual and bisexual promiscuity by his children, and, finally, a downward spiral of larceny, rape, murder, and suicide by his youngest son. Before his death from cancer at the end of the novel, Solon Barnes enjoys a minor reconciliation with some of his remaining children, but the elegiac tone pervading the book signals the wholesale waning of Quakerism—especially the austere version preferred by Solon Barnes—as a practical antidote to the troubles of modernity. Paradoxically, much of the difficulty in viewing the Quaker ideal as a helpful social and spiritual remedy, according to Dreiser, lay in its

almost unimaginable virtuousness. Describing the placid Barnes home-
stead, for example, Dreiser seems to fault their tidy life for its failure to
reflect the contingency and rough-cut difficulty of the actual world. In
his view, "the atmosphere surrounding them seemed too fixed, too still.
It was all too well ordered, too perfect for frail, restless, hungry human
need."[51]

Failed or not as a religious tradition capable of salvaging modern
morality, however, it is nevertheless clear that Quakerism had captured
the imagination of yet another major American novelist, and this time
one who had long been wary of organized religions. More specifically,
The Bulwark's religious thematics also disclose that by the latter part of
his career, Dreiser had immersed himself in the study of canonical
Quaker writings. It is a novel that takes Quakerism with great seriousness, often using the stubbornly antimodern Solon Barnes to voice quotations from the Quaker *Book of Discipline* and from John Woolman's
eighteenth-century *Journal*. Dreiser therefore appears on some levels to
be overtly promoting the Quaker tradition, serving as evangelist for a
faith that he construed as embodying a program of resistance to a range
of moral quandaries, including materialism, sexual promiscuity, and
market capitalism. But Dreiser, like the many other American novelists
who found rich literary and moral resources within the Quaker tradition, never went so far as to adopt the Quaker faith himself, thereby following in the footsteps of his nineteenth-century predecessors, who similarly found in American Quakerism a religious practice that was at once
both virtuous and impossible. For many decades Dreiser had been wres-
tling in his fiction with a family legacy of puritanical German Catholicism inherited from his own father, but this secular urge was balanced
against his own manifest desire to substitute some form of spiritual experience for the chaotic shallowness of twentieth-century life. Perhaps because of his deep commitment to realism—and to expressing the social
world in its actuality—Dreiser found himself seeing, recognizing, and
accepting the moral force of Quakerism but without entirely adopting it
wholeheartedly as his own religious, moral, or practical perspective.

F. O. Matthiessen, who, along with Lionel Trilling, was one of the
few contemporary critics to examine *The Bulwark* in any detail, describes
and defends this gradual turn to Quaker religiosity in Dreiser's work,
finding in it evidence of Dreiser's moral synthesis of politics (Marxist)
and religion (generic Christian): "One might say that he was an old
man, untroubled by inconsistencies that subsequent events would have

made obvious. But . . . he had found—if more essentially in Woolman than in Marx—beliefs that he was convinced the world could no longer afford to ignore." As for Trilling, Dreiser's consideration of Quakerism was apparently complete but, nevertheless, deeply troubling. In the course of his full-scale attack on Dreiser's fiction in the opening pages of *The Liberal Imagination* (1950), Trilling insisted that the "blank pietism" of *The Bulwark* supplied proof that "Dreiser's religious affirmation was offensive; the offense lies in the vulgar ease of its formulation, as well as in the comfortable untroubled way in which Dreiser moved from nihilism to piety." Whatever the merits of Trilling's harsh assessment of Dreiser, what his criticism leaves out of consideration is Quakerism itself, not to mention its deployment in American fiction for more than a century. In *The Bulwark*, Dreiser had chosen not simply a turn toward generic Christianity or "blank pietism"; instead, he nominated Quakerism *specifically* for the religious paradigm in a novel that reversed many decades of secularism in his fiction.[52]

For writers of local color stories, historical fiction, and regionalist novels, there have been clear advantages to enlisting the stereotypical Quaker in the service of delineating norms and dominant values in American culture during a century and a half of the nation's most rapid growth and development. But Quakers in fiction also came to stand for the best people that most Americans could never become. The formulaic representation of American Quakers does indeed produce characters with unimpeachably rigorous Christian faith, living domestic lives of order and harmony. These quaint figures appear to embody and to manifest the whole range of social virtues—charity without condescension, complete egalitarianism, unshakable pacifism, and flawless rectitude in business affairs—to an admirable degree. Admiration, of course, did not always imply imitation, because practical concerns frequently dampened enthusiasm for Quaker discipline. As Walt Whitman admitted in an editorial that he wrote for the New Orleans *Daily Crescent* in 1848 on Friends' refusal to bears arms, "Quakerism can never become the creed of the race; and you might as well expect all men to adopt the straight-cut coat and plain phraseology of the followers of [George] Fox, as to hope that the principles of peace will ever become the law of men's opinions and actions."[53] In popular American fiction, though, and particularly for those genres operating in the didactic or reformist mode, such characters were used as a device for calibrating the moral urgency of the narrative. In essence, however, the American literary

representation of what I have been calling "imaginary Friends" con-
structs two separate frameworks for understanding and evaluating
human conduct. The first, inhabited by Quakers—but multiply indexed
in terms of its alterity and practical impossibility—calls implacably for
justice, peace, benevolence, restraint, equality, and a religious ethos motivated by the Inner Light resident in each believer. But the second
framework, just as clearly suggested by the Quaker fiction under review
here, implicitly concedes the higher moral and religious ground to
Quakers, while nevertheless insisting upon the intrinsic goodness and
virtue of its own radically more limited suggestions for American social,
political, and religious improvement.

6

Staging Quakerism

Theater and Cinema

Oh we're plain and sober folks as you may see,
With the world we've naught at all to do!
Yes we pass the time away quite soberly
And our quiet life pursue.

We care for nothing but the simple joys,
Nor a smile and joke like other girls and boys!
O, the very modest things for us suffice,
As for dancing, Oh, it's naughty but it's nice.

Yet I'd like to shake a toe my dear,
Yea verily, dear! Yea verily, dear!
O, I'd like to dance with you my dear,
For it's naughty, yea it's naughty but it's nice.

When the spirit moveth us what can we do?
We must only willingly obey!
O, I think we're doing wrong now love don't you?
Shall we to sports give way?

There can't be harm in only doing thus,
So why should we incline to make a fuss?

O, we trip the 'light fantastic' once or twice,
Tho' it's naughty, very naughty, yet it's nice.
Charles E. Pratt, "The Dancing Quakers" (1873)

QUAKERESSES WORE MASKS
A very unique reception was given on Wednesday evening by the
Unique Euchre club of Prospect Heights. It took place at the home of
Mr. and Mrs. J. Perry, 676 President Street. The women were dressed
as Quakeresses and wore masks.
Brooklyn Eagle (March 1, 1896)

The use of Quaker characters on stage as stock characters had become a commonplace almost from the earliest years of the establishment of the Society of Friends in the middle of the seventeenth century, and deployment as both comic and serious types in the theater in many ways resembles the use to which Quaker stock types were used in fiction of the same period. Before the stage drama gave way to the increasingly influential genre of film in the late nineteenth century, the representation of Quakers on the American stage was partially diverted and extended into new forms of public theatricality on the lyceum stage and within the high-stakes drama of abolitionist oratory and politics. Later, as film decisively took the place of legitimate stage performances as the most popular dramatic medium for American audiences, Quaker characters were given substantial roles in the development of early twentieth-century American cinema, including films made in the silent era.

Before the increasingly intense nineteenth-century politics of abolition prompted Friends to make forays into the public sphere, they had been perceived and represented by many non-Quakers as peculiar types of religious believers, those whose stringent moralizing and piety embodied both explicit and implicit critiques of the more popular forms of Anglo-American Christian practice. Quakers had in various ways always fashioned themselves dramatically, and as self-consciously recognizable members of a socially marginal but morally iconic tribe who manifestly spoke and dressed differently than non-Quakers. Thus, a kind of daily and commonplace theatricality was frequently associated with the religious world of the Society of Friends, not just for pious moralizing but also for their peculiar dress and speech in the quotidian theater of

daily social interactions. Thus, they also quickly became useful stock figures on the eighteenth-century British and American theatrical circuit.
Quakers as dramatic types readily became staples, first, of the American
stage repertory and, later, of twentieth-century American film dramas.

From the postcolonial era after the Revolutionary War ended in the
late eighteenth century until approximately 1950, near the conclusion
of yet another violent decade in world politics, the figure of the Quaker
has retained a firm hold on the moral imaginary in American culture.
In working through a range of sociopolitical problems in American life,
dramatists and filmmakers in America often turned to the idea (but not
usually the reality) of Quakers in order to assess moral problems and set
the perceived limits of "mainstream" values into sharp relief by distinguishing those values from those of Friends. In these cases, Quakers are
rarely depicted with great sympathy but always with an eye toward
using them as tools to differentiate between tenable morality and a
morality that could only be the province of a "peculiar people."

By 1795 in postcolonial Philadelphia, and only a few years before
a lapsed Quaker and famed novelist named Charles Brockden Brown
had begun producing some of the first important American fiction,
the comic dramatist John Murdock (1748–1834) was busy writing about
Quakers for theatrical audiences. During the period when American
colonies solidified their victory over the British in the Revolutionary
War, the colonial theater was vibrant with numerous amateur and professional performances, and as in England, comedy was an exception-
ally popular genre. Drawing on a decades-long tradition of using Quakers for comic dramatic effect, a tradition that appears to have begun
in early eighteenth-century England with Charles Shadwell's *The Fair
Quaker of Deal; or, the Humours of the Navy* (1715), Susanna Centlivre's *A
Bold Stroke for a Wife* (1718), and Richard Wilkinson's *The Quaker's Wedding:
A Comedy* (1723), Murdock staged a loosely constructed farce about the
romantic world of American Quakers in *The Triumphs of Love* (1795). In
selecting the Quakers for comic treatment, Murdock was also possibly
following the more recent example of renowned English actor, dramatist, and prolific song-writer Charles Dibdin (1745–1814). Dibdin's enduringly popular romantic comedy *The Quaker: A Comic Opera* (1777) had
been staged first on the London and Dublin stages before audiences,
and then at least as early as 1794 in Boston and perhaps for other audiences in the American colonies. Susanna Centlivre's romantic comedy
of Quaker life, *A Bold Stroke for a Wife* (1723), enjoyed a similar revival of

popularity in America, with performances in many cities on the Atlantic coast such as Baltimore (1783), Annapolis (1783), and Boston (1794).

The late-eighteenth-century Irish stage had also taken advantage of the popular interest in comic representations of Quakers, as evidenced by John O'Keefe's *The Young Quaker: A Comedy* (1784). When it was staged at Boston's Haymarket Theatre in September 1797, O'Keefe's play was advertised by the slightly different title, *The Young Quaker; or, The Fair American*, thus revealing a deft sense of marketing for American audiences. Although the script for *The Young Quaker* seems not to have survived, we can guess that its scenario involved a certain amount of sexual innuendo and perhaps a seduction story: the same broadside advertisement also mentions the opening play of the evening at the Haymarket Theatre, a pantomime in two acts called *Don Juan; or, the Libertine Destroyed*. Dibdin's *The Quaker*, a fairly conventional romantic comedy, features a young woman named Gillian torn between her commitment, on practical grounds, to a prosperous old Quaker farmer named Steady, and her authentic and passionate love for a handsome young man named Lubin. Its dramatic representations of Quakers follow the tradition set out by earlier Anglo-American efforts to show Quakers as inordinately peculiar people who are made ridiculous in their efforts, based largely on their traditional insularity as a sect, to resist the forces of romantic love. Steady the Quaker farmer, though, is not shown as a cuckold or a dupe. Instead, he is gently led by his firm moral principles to act virtuously, but against his own interests as a passionate (if aging) lover in pursuit of the beautiful young Gillian. As the play concludes, old Steady renounces his love for Gillian and grants the happy couple his sincere blessing: "Verily, my heart warmeth unto you both: your innocency and love are equally respectable. And would the voluptuous man taste a more exquisite sensation than the gratifying his passions, let him prevail upon himself to a benevolent action."[1]

This kind of comedy applies its force in several directions at once, with a Quaker stereotype as its fulcrum. Old Steady relinquishes his claim on Gillian only to acquire the greater moral stature that accrues to the perpetrator of a benevolent act, in this case the self-effacing refusal to pursue his own wishes in marriage. True romance ensues, and a happy conclusion is produced for the comedy—but only at the cost of any desires that the Quaker might possess with regard to an attractive young woman. And, finally, Steady's actions confirm what so many representations of American Friends insist upon: Quaker values are those that have the capacity of cementing the bonds of community (in this case an marriage between appropriately matched persons), but the Quaker himself, so long as he adheres carefully to the letter of his religious views, appears from the perspective of non-Quakers as a relatively unattractive and socially disabled human being, albeit one whose values are estimable.

For a variety of reasons, theatrical productions were highly controversial and even outlawed during the American colonial period, and variations in local ordinances often meant that plays staged in one city could be censored as inappropriate or unlawful in others. The theater in Philadelphia had during the early years of the colony been perceived as a troublesome, rabble-rousing, immoral, and licentious institution, and both the Pennsylvania colonial assembly and the Philadelphia authorities of the early eighteenth century attempted repeatedly to prevent the staging of any sort of theatrical event in that important city. These restrictions on American theatrical productions have long been understood as being related to the perceived threat on civic authority posed by plays that sometimes called the fragile authority of the colonies into question. It has not often been noticed, however, that much of the concern about theatrical regulations in Philadelphia grew out of Quaker power in the Pennsylvania colony, and that the Quaker characters who were both praised and lampooned in the theater of the early republic often gave Quaker authorities a goodly measure of consternation. Detailing the legal struggle over the colonial Philadelphia theater, historians Odai Johnson and William J. Burling describe a flurry of laws passed by the Quaker-dominated Pennsylvania assembly, laws that were repeatedly struck down by Parliament: "In 1700 the Assembly of Pennsylvania passed a law prohibiting 'stage plays, masks, revels.' In 1705 it was repealed by Parliament. The following session, the prohibition against playing was once more enacted in the Pennsylvania assembly. In 1709 it was again repealed in Parliament. In 1711, the Quaker Assembly in Pennsylvania passed their prohibition for the third time, which in 1713 was a third time repealed in Westminster."[2] Having possessed for nearly a century the legal right to present stage plays, actors and playwrights aimed their poison darts at some of their favorite targets: the very Quaker authorities who had once denied them the right to provoke Philadelphia's citizens with theatrical performances.[3]

In John Murdock's *The Triumphs of Love* (1795), for example, the Quaker families of George Friendly Sr., and Jacob Friendly Sr.

provide the domestic setting for a series of farcical episodes in post-Revolutionary Philadelphia. The civic, religious, and moral problems that the families confront are treated in comic fashion, but the seriousness of the issues they face is plain: they are the same problems spawned by the turmoil of a Revolutionary War that had established a tenuous system of representative government, rule by law, and declaration of the equality of all citizens under the law. The farce presses political conundrums into its breezy and raucous scenes. Young Irish servants named Patrick and Jenny shed bright light on the circumstances of recent immigrants in the new republic, chafing under the harsh rule of their capricious Quaker household employers, while providing a class-based counterpoint to the circumstances of the slave servant Sambo, who is eventually freed by his Quaker master in what historian Joseph Boskin has described as "one of the earliest examples of abolitionist politics."[4] That the elder Friendly brothers have so little control over the daily activities and marriage choices of their children highlights the fragility of a social order in the process of transforming itself from a traditional, paternalistic model of authority to a new model of authority established on the basis of republicanism.

A profligate Quaker youth (George Friendly Jr.) and his dutiful Quaker brother (Jacob Friendly Jr.) illustrate these tensions vividly as they venture into new roles in the early American republic. Lapsed from his Quaker traditions to the dismay of his father, George Jr. scoffs at the strictures of his family's Quaker principles, preferring a rakish life of carousing, seductions, masks, farces, and slapstick impersonations (some of them cross-dressed). Marriage outside of the Quaker faith is a question that lies at the center of the play as George Jr. opts to marry a non-Quaker, thus disappointing his father to some extent, but, ironically, his marriage also has the salutary effect of curing him finally of his dissipated and rakish habits. A similar matrimonial quandary is faced by George Jr.'s sister Rachel, who must defy the paternal authority of her Quaker father in order to wed Major Manly, a non-Quaker who is nevertheless a highly virtuous man and an acknowledged hero of the American Revolution.

Several observations may be made about the circumstances of Quaker life in Philadelphia as related in John Murdock's *The Triumphs of Love*. The play provides, for one thing, a useful barometer of status for the Society of Friends nearly 150 years after the first arrival of Quakers in the American colonies, and in the geographical location (Philadelphia) that had, since William Penn's founding of the colony in 1681 as a haven for Friends, been the epicenter of their social and cultural influence. Murdock uses the play as a comic treatment of the issue of social class, a theme that the fledgling American dramatic tradition had inherited from its English theatrical forebears. To these typical class battles, Murdock adds important new themes such as the presence of African American slavery (Sambo) and a small but growing cohort of Irish working-class immigrants (Patrick and Jenny). The story of social life in America that the play narrates suggests that divisions of were of considerable concern among prosperous Quakers, who now held considerable power in Philadelphia and the region surrounding the Delaware River Valley. No longer the reviled apostates or members of an isolated or persecuted minority, as they had been during the first half-century of Quaker activity in England and America (1650–1700), late eighteenth-century Quakers like Murdock's good citizens figure as part of the dominant cohort in Philadelphia society, whose financial privilege and marital boundaries are steadily under siege at the hands of poor immigrants, slaves chafing under their servitude, and attractive non-Quakers (Major Manly) who assault the Quaker tradition of marital endogamy. Membership in the Society of Friends, while understood by this period of American history as conferring to the individual a relatively high moral status, is besieged by doubts as to its generational durability (young George Jr. is a rake and a frivolous trickster), its astringent social habits (Friend Peevish is a man every bit as humorless as his name would suggest), and its threatened superiority as an organization presumed to be filled with surpassingly virtuous members (Major Manly, an authentically virtuous non-Quaker, is the truly exemplary man in the play).

Family turmoil serves as an index and guide to Quaker social instability in *The Triumphs of Love*. Both of the two Friendly brothers (and both of the sons, who are cousins) are nominally Quakers but only one part of the family—Jacob Sr., and Jacob Jr.—hews closely to the letter of Quaker discipline. When Jacob Sr. objects on religious grounds to the possibility of brave Major Manly pursuing a courtship with his daughter, Rachel Friendly, George Sr. admonishes him for his rigidity: "Is it because he is not one of us? I'd maintain it, Jacob, . . . it is a dev'lish arbitrary law of your society, that you won't permit a connection with other sects of Christians." Hearing this, Jacob Sr., who is described throughout the play as fighting a rearguard action against encroaching outsiders threatening to taint the purity of Quaker family and culture, responds tartly that, "It is vain to reason with thee, brother—thou art so violent in what thou dost undertake; our society has had its rules of long standing; which have kept the church together, from generation to generation." At this point, it is left for Quaker to critique Quaker, in a critique that unfolds in a sequence of dramatic dialogue between the two brothers. During this exchange, Murdock's script appears to suggest a fracture within the Society of Friends and initiated by its own memberships, rather than any besetting or persecuting force outside the religious fold that might have the capacity to erode the stability of a formerly close-knit Quaker community. The final salvo in this debate about Quakers versus the larger community is left to be launched by George Sr., who is himself a birthright Quaker but one possessing only moderate piety and relatively relaxed attitudes about social mingling with worldly others. After listening patiently to his brothers pious views about the need to remain separate and exclusionary in relation to the larger social order, George Sr. responds with heat, "Psha, psha—don't tell me about your generations and generations: you are a virtuous, valuable people; but you should not set yourselves up, in opposition to other people, so much," thus laying bare one of the enduring objections to Quaker values: from outside the Society, Quaker discipline, with its strong moral code and separatist ethos, appears not only virtuous but also smug, self-satisfied, and overly convinced of its own good conduct.[5]

Perhaps the most ambivalent critique of the Society of Friends in *The Triumphs of Love* appears with regard to the situation of the character Sambo, who is enslaved by the George Friendly Sr. family as the play opens but is eventually freed because of the insistent idealism of George Jr. Murdock displays an ambivalent attitude toward Quakers and their increasing reluctance to hold slaves—a nascent abolitionist position for the Society of Friends that had been inspired in particular by John Woolman's moral leadership on the issue since the publication of his influential *Some Considerations on the Keeping of Negroes* (1753, 1762) and his posthumous *Journal* (1774), which included additional arguments against slave-owning and the slave trade. Woolman's principled opposition to chattel slavery, as well as the significant opposition to Woolman's ideas on the part of those who believed Africans incapable or unworthy of independence as free citizens, may have been on Murdock's mind as he created the memorable Sambo to play his rather small but important part in a scene that allows for the expression of African aspirations and a Quaker benevolence that quickly is revealed to be naive. The crucial scene in which Sambo is finally freed opens with George Jr. secretly observing Sambo as the black servant examines his own face in a mirror and thinks aloud about the state of his life and his attitudes about himself. This scene is also notable for Sambo's use of exaggerated language and comic manners that in subsequent decades would become standard fare on the blackface minstrel stage: "Why black foke sold like cow or horse? He tink de great somebody above, no order tings so. — Sometimes he tink dis way—he got best massa in e world. He gib him fine clothes for dress—he give him plenty money for pend; and for a little while, eh tink himself berry happ. Afterwards he tink anoder way. He pose massa George die; den he sold to some oder masssa. May be he no use him well. When Sambo tink so, it mos broke he heart."[6] Upon hearing this moving speech, George Jr. admits the cruelty and injustice of slavery, even under the relatively benign circumstances in which Sambo had been living (as a servant to a kindly Quaker family).

At the very center of Murdock's play, then, stands this primal scene of moral accounting, in which a young Quaker sees, and feels profoundly, the grave error of his family's choice to own slaves: "The untutored, pathetic, soliloquy of that honest creature, has more sensibly affected me, than all I have read, or thought, on that barbarous, iniquitous slave-trade." Having concluded that he must act on Sambo's behalf, George Jr. does so immediately, even though he has lingering doubts about the wisdom of his decision when seen against the backdrop of a larger American social scene. "Yet how many thousands of the poorer class of whites are there, whose actual situation are vastly inferior to [Sambo's]; he has no anxious cares for tomorrow, no family looking up to him for protections—no duns at his doors."[7] Moreover, George Jr. wonders about Sambo's ability to conduct himself properly without the supervision of strict, watchful, and temperate owners like the Friendlys, whose Quaker values had long been imposed on their servants and slaves as well as themselves. As readily becomes apparent in subsequent scenes, George Jr.'s concerns about Sambo's self-control are well founded, as at his very first opportunity Sambo (not unlike George Jr. himself earlier in the play) drinks heavily with the regular tipplers at a local public house and appears on stage to be completely drunk (albeit still happy about his new freedom). George Jr. remains steadfast in his commitment to Sambo's new life, however, and does not try to reverse his decision to liberate his slave.

The Quakers who populate Murdock's farce are shown evidently to be dissolving the rigid boundaries that once had prevented their members from intermarrying with persons outside the rather limited world of the Society (in this, Murdock is faithful to the actual history of increasing Quaker intermarriage during the eighteenth century), while at the same time, these few Quakers are shown to be at the epicenter of a vastly more important social issue of their time—the abolition of slavery. On the one hand, committed Quakers are depicted as being comical or even ridiculous because the elder generation of Friends is by turns cynical and rigid about the traditional discipline that limits their social choices, and because the younger generation as a whole is driven more by romance than by religious principle. On the other hand, it is the lapsed Quaker George Jr., a birthright Quaker converted away from piety to the secular, hedonistic life of a boulevardier, who makes the critical decision to free Sambo. Quaker values thus provide the moral gravity that sponsors the decision to allow Sambo to go free, while secular, non-Quaker values definitively shape the moral and social world of both George Jr. and the life of freedom that Sambo is beginning to experience not as a Quaker but as a church-less free man of color.

Anticipating by a half century Theodore Dreiser's decision, in his masterwork *Sister Carrie* (1900), to provide his young protagonist Carrie Meeber with a lucrative stage career as a pretty and flirtatious Quaker girl, James T. Fields (one of the founding partners in Boston's distinguished literary publishing house Ticknor and Fields) composed the light-hearted song "The Quaker Girls" (1851) and published it the same year as Stowe's *Uncle Tom's Cabin,* that crucial antebellum American novel that, not coincidentally, featured fictional Quakers active in the more serious pursuit of assisting escaping slaves. Fields, who before turning to a long career (1861–71) as editor of the *Atlantic Monthly* had written both songs and poetry, produced the lyrics like the following, which in a number of ways set the tone of romantic comedy for the many popular songs and theatrical representations of Quakers that would appear over the following century: "Who loves not the Quaker girls! / I'm thinking of a fair one now, / With tresses dark, and sunny brow—/ As stately as a nun." Unlike Stowe, whose Quakers are shown to be warm and hospitable, serious and devout, Fields's lyrics suggest the possibility of the demure Quakeress as an object for sly romantic fantasy. The transformation of this particular Quaker representation is quite remarkable between the eighteenth and nineteenth centuries: from stodgily pious theatrical figures—who would surely avoid any sort of musical entertainment—into the loveliest girl of Philadelphia who also sings the most melodious songs.

There is something almost willfully perverse about Fields's effort to write a song in which Quakers could be written into a rather trivial confection of verse that evades any mention of their religion or politics. Whereas Quakers in 1851 were widely known as ardent sponsors of the Underground Railroad and as leading lights in the abolitionist movement, Fields attends not to political matters but instead to the "dazzling form" and "fairy voice" of Helen Hay, his fictional young Philadelphia Quakeress. Specifically, what Fields shares with a long tradition of imagining Quakers in American literary culture, however, is his presumption that the mere identification of a character as a Quaker will suffice to mobilize a constellation of conventional views about Friends, so that his representation can then function as either a smoothly functioning stereotype or, in the case of "The Quaker Girls," as a sly, ironic departure from type. In this way, the designation "Quaker" functions as do most stock literary characterizations or stereotypes ("Sambo," "Negro," "Irishman") that appear frequently in songs and stage plays. But as a religious stock characterization, the term "Quaker" or "Quakeress" has been unique. Other religious groups in American history have certainly been stereotyped and conventionalized in our literature, but it is difficult to find comparably blunt literary designations for individuals such as "The Catholic Girl" or "The Baptist." Thanks to the unique power of Quaker stereotyping, the label would continue well into the twentieth century to be a usefully overdetermined designation suggestive of an extraordinary blend of piety, modesty, thrift, pacifism, sobriety, rectitude, and passivity. But the label also continued to be deployed critically or ironically as a marker of those traits that Quakerism was understood to minimize, conceal, or otherwise negate: sexuality, physical beauty, musical enjoyment, avarice, comedy, and flexible morality.

The popular songs of writer-composers like James T. Fields undeniably contributed to popular impressions of the Society of Friends, but far more important in shaping the views of many elite readers may have been the poetic writings of Field's close friend and famous publishing client, Henry Wadsworth Longfellow, who during second half of the nineteenth century was at the very pinnacle of his fame. During his lifetime, and especially following the publication of his major works,

Evangeline (1847), *The Song of Hiawatha* (1855), *The Courtship of Miles Standish* (1855), and *Tales of a Wayside Inn* (1863, 1872, 1873), Longfellow was a household name for American and British readers and had become the sort of poet whose works were regularly memorized in classrooms across the nation. This kind of artistic stature, which had remained elusive to now-canonical figures like Walt Whitman and Herman Melville during the nineteenth century, elevated Longfellow to an enormously influential cultural position nearly akin to being the nation's official poet laureate. If Henry Wadsworth Longfellow had opinions about the Quaker life in America, a vast and typically well-educated reading audience was prepared to listen respectfully to his views.[8]

Although he has rarely been mentioned or even noticed as a dramatist by American literary historians, primarily because his dramatic works were never produced for the stage, Longfellow's most extended statement about Quakers in American life appeared in the pages of one of his closet dramas, specifically his verse drama *John Endicott* (1868). This is not to say that Longfellow had entirely neglected the impact of the Society of Friends in America during his career. Twenty years before *John Endicott* appeared, Longfellow had already indicated his interest in Quakers and his admiration for their moral and social effects on the nation in his best-selling *Evangeline* (1847), a long historical poem written during his years as a professor of languages at Harvard College. In *Evangeline*, the memorable heroine, a Roman Catholic girl named Evangeline Bellefontaine, is exiled from her native home in Acadia and travels through many parts of America on a frustrating journey during which she attempts both to find a new homeland and to discover again the embrace of her lost Acadian lover and fiancé. Gabriel Lajeunesse, the Acadian youth from whom Evangeline had been separated when their Acadian homeland was attacked and then destroyed by English forces (an attack that dates to 1755), follows a separate path of exile with his father. Gabriel is unable to find Evangeline on a journey that takes him to Louisiana, where he lives for most of his life. The many years of her own difficult exile frustrate Evangeline's search for Gabriel until, near the end of her life and travels, Longfellow has her travel to Philadelphia, the city where Evangeline—now working for the poor as a Sister of Mercy—finally will be allowed a brief reunion with the now-elderly Gabriel. It seems highly significant, though, that Longfellow chooses to have his long poem of unrequited love conclude not on the desolate plains of Canada or the West, nor near religious sites such as the "Tents of Grace of the Moravian Missions," nor even in the new Louisiana homeland, but instead in the Delaware River Valley heartland of the Religious Society of Friends: the city of Philadelphia. Longfellow describes an aged Evangeline (still nominally a Roman Catholic) as experiencing a fitting respite from her many years of lonely exile in the city of Quakers, which he compares in its moral ambiance and geographic beauty to the lost lands of French Acadia:

> In that delightful land which is washed by the Delaware's waters,
> Guarding in sylvan shades the name of Penn the apostle,
> Stands on the banks of its beautiful stream the city he founded.
> There all the air is balm, and the peach is the emblem of beauty,
> And the streets still reëcho the names of the trees of the forest,
> As if they fain would appease the Dryads whose haunts they molested.
> There from the troubled sea had Evangeline landed, an exile,
> Finding among the children of Penn a home and a country.
> There old René Leblanc had died; and when he departed,
> Saw at his side only one of all his hundred descendants.
> Something at least there was in the friendly streets of the city,
> Something that spake to her heart, and made her no longer a stranger;
> And her ear was pleased with the Thee and Thou of the Quakers,
> For it recalled the past, the old Acadian country,
> Where all men were equal, and all were brothers and sisters.[9]

Longfellow places Evangeline and Gabriel in an idyllic American Quaker setting already equipped with linguistic and social markers that had shaped their utopian existence in Acadia. Although the two aging lovers are buried in a small Catholic graveyard in Philadelphia, Longfellow's dramatic point is clear enough: there is a kind of congruency between the peculiarly Quaker life of Philadelphia, which stood as a prosperous symbol of the Society of Friends long after the religious intensity of the Quakers had been abandoned to modernity and its prosperities, and romantically lost colony of French Acadia.

Longfellow's verse drama *John Endicott* would eventually be included as part of Longfellow's sequence of lengthy religio-historical poems in *Christus* (1872); the often-overlooked work was published first as one of two companion verse dramas in *The New England Tragedies* (1868). The second verse drama, *Giles Corey of the Salem Farms,* unfolds as a critique of the persecutions enacted during the late-seventeenth-century Salem witch trials, while *John Endicott* opens in Boston in 1665 and focuses on a fictionalized tale of Quaker persecutions, which in many respects is modeled on the legendary Quaker martyr, Mary Dyer. The name John Endicott would have been familiar to any reader conversant with the early history of Massachusetts, when Endicott served a term as colonial governor in the years before the arrival of John Winthrop in 1630. In addition, readers of Nathaniel Hawthorne's works, such as his early collection *Twice-Told Tales* (1837), would have recalled the name because of Hawthorne's memorable description of the Puritan leader's merciless persecution of religious dissenters in his story "Endicott and the Red Cross."

In *John Endicott*, Longfellow adapts and revises the historical record of persecutions against Quakers in colonial Massachusetts in order to heighten his dramatic presentation of the encounter between Puritan and Quaker. In addition, he is able to idealize more completely his invented Quaker characters, especially his central protagonists, the pious Friends Wenlock Christison and his daughter Edith Christison. Another key fictional device is the title character himself, who for the purposes of the play is *not* the historical John Endicott (who governed colonial Massachusetts with an iron hand) but instead a fictional son by the same name who rebels against his father out of sympathy for the serene and virtuous Quakers. Longfellow adds a number of historical elements, such as an appearance by the fiery orthodox Puritan divine John Norton, author of the virulently anti-Quaker tract *The Heart of New England Rent* (1659). In the opening scene of act I in *John Endicott*, it is Norton who delivers an impassioned sermon against heresy; he is confronted as he preaches by young Edith Christison, who enters barefoot, disheveled, and clothed in sackcloth, with other Quakers following her down the meetinghouse aisle. As the congregations roils in confusion at the entrance of the Quakers, Norton curses the young Quakeress and orders her to desist: "Be silent babbling woman! / Saint Paul commands all women to keep silence / Within the churches." To this harsh injunction, Edith replies with equal scriptural confidence that "the women prayed / And prophesied at Corinth in his day; / And, among those on whom the fiery tongues / Of Pentecost descended, some were women!" Norton, playing the merciless persecutor to the fullest, will have none of Edith's defiance, and he replies scornfully before directing the congregation to drive the Quakers away: "Away with all these Heretics and Quakers! / Quakers, forsooth! Because a quaking fell / On Daniel, at beholding of the vision, / Must ye needs shake and quake?" As the Quakers are forced out of the meetinghouse, Norton, citing the book of

Deuteronomy's instruction about merciless punishment of those who promote false gods, reminds the elder Endicott of his duty to enforce the community's religious purity by declaring that "heresies turbulent must be suppressed / By civil power." Thus fortified, Endicott eventually brings Edith Christison before the court and sentences her to be "Scourged in three towns, with forty stripes save one, / Then banished upon pain of death."[10]

The flogging meted out to the mystically inclined Edith Christison has the effect of mobilizing young John Endicott in defense of the Quakers. It is he who identifies morally and emotionally with the Quakers, and after a bitter argument with his father about his treatment of the humble Friends, young Endicott is banished permanently from his family home. Endicott's friend Upsall tries to reason with him and urges loyalty to Governor Endicott because, in his view, the governor is only slightly flawed: "He is an upright man and a just man / In all things save the treatment of the Quakers." But having pleaded with his father about Edith's having been stripped naked to the waist before being flogged in several Massachusetts towns, the idealistic young Endicott concludes bitterly that "I have found him cruel and unjust / Even as a father. He has driven me forth / Into the street; has shut his door upon me, / With these words of bitterness. I am as a homeless / As these poor Quakers are." Eventually—and true to the history of how toleration for Quakers was finally mandated by English law after Charles II was installed as monarch after the death of Cromwell and the end of the Protectorate—Charles II reasserted his power in the colonies by mandating in 1661 that Quakers be tolerated in Massachusetts Bay colony, thus permitting them to follow their religious beliefs. The concluding scenes of *John Endicott* show Governor Endicott finally bending to the will of the crown by conceding his obedience to the writ of mandamus presented to him by courier from London.[11]

The tragedy that Longfellow presents thus is constructed from a set of intertwining themes related to American tolerance for Quakers. On one level, he imagines the pressure exerted on Governor Endicott by his own family, in the person of a fictional son, John Endicott Jr. Old Endicott, a paradigmatic American Puritan who is portrayed in many ways sympathetically as a man of moral integrity and skilled leadership, is revealed on another level to manifest the intolerance and inherent cruelty of the orthodox religious polity in seventeenth-century Massachusetts. The inexorable conclusion of the tragedy features the death of Governor

Endicott and marks the end of a supremely intolerant era in American history. During the unhappy days leading up to his death, while conceding the authority of the English monarch to permit Quakers to live peaceably in the colony, old Endicott could see nothing in the case of liberated Quakers but the erosion of necessary civic authority, while the leading minister, John Norton, registers Charles II's writ of tolerance as intrusion into colonial politics that would harm orthodoxy irreparably by permitting cursed tolerance to hold sway over religious authority, insisting that "There is no room in Christ's triumphant army / For tolerationists."[12]

The governor's tragic experience involves both the permanent banishment of his son from his family, the death of John Norton soon after the receipt of the king's writ of toleration, and the profoundly unsettling recognition at the moment of his death that his son John Jr. represented an entirely new attitude toward the community of faith, as can be seen in his dying words, "O Absalom, my son! I feel the world / Sinking beneath me, sinking, sinking, sinking! / Death knocks! I must go to meet him! Welcome, Death!" The religious orthodoxy that Governor Endicott had spent his career preserving must now give way to the vertiginous, and for him ultimately fatal, experience of considering toleration for religious minorities. Finally, the tragedy centers on John Jr.'s pursuit of Edith Christison, who has been banished to the wilderness after having been flogged nearly to death by order of his father. Earnest and well-intentioned to the last, John Endicott discovers Edith sojourning alone in the wilderness, content with her natural surroundings and overcome with a mystic reverie in which she voices her continuing obedience to the command of the Inner Light, while laying plans to return to the colonial settlements: "O cruel town! I know what waits me there, / And yet I must go back; for ever louder / I hear the inward calling of the Spirit, and must obey the voice." Edith's Quaker resolve and piety— to say nothing of her bloody nakedness—mark her as nothing if not a saint, but one whose mystical bearing and wraithlike qualities quarantine her away from any lasting connection with John Endicott, who seems to represent the slowly evolving moral center of a New England conscience.[13]

Attention to Quaker theatricality persisted into the twentieth century. Much of this attention appeared in the observations of writers and illustrators who detailed—either for serious or comic effect—the "peculiarity" of a sect that dressed austerely and produced an aesthetic for domestic life reflecting the otherworldliness of their spiritual values. At the beginning of the twentieth century, with the publication *Sister Carrie* (1900), his great naturalist novel of social modernity, urban life, and market capitalism, Theodore Dreiser became the most prominent American writer of his generation to have made use of the oddities of traditional Quaker clothing. Dreiser, though never a member of the Society of Friends, resembled many other Americans by remaining ambivalently fascinated by Quaker life. Although twentieth-century Quakers had to a large degree already begun to abandon their customary plain attire in favor of popular fashions, they were still frequently used as instances of the kind of antimoderns who retained a commitment (either sincere or fraudulent) to plain dress even in the face of Gilded Age prosperity and its inevitable tendencies toward ostentation and display. More hints of the ambivalence with which some theatrical representations depicted Quaker culture can be seen in a brief theatrical review of the musical comedy "The Dancing Girl," published in the *Brooklyn Eagle* in 1902, only a few short years after Dreiser's fictional description of Carrie Meeber's success playing the part of a Quakeress in the New York theater district. In the title role of "The Dancing Girl," which was staged at Corse Payton's Lee Avenue Theater on September 1, 1902, according to the reviewer, "Miss Etta Reed Payton again demonstrated that she is a thoroughly capable actress. As the demure and coquettish Quakeress or as the dancing girl, capricious, self willed and soulless, she found ample scope for her talents."[14]

This sort of appropriation of an imagined variety of Quaker woman for the purposes of comedy was far from a rarity. Only a few seasons earlier, the *Brooklyn Eagle* had run a similar review, for another production at the Lee Avenue Theater under the title "The Prodigal Daughter," noted by the reviewer to be a "revival production." During this performance, "The electric fans kept the audience cool, in the face of the many exciting entanglements of the melodrama. The plot of 'The Prodigal Daughter' is too well known to need elaboration. Charles Barringer, as the villain, played conscientiously and with force, and was complimented throughout the performance by some strong hissing. Mr. Payton played the part of Lord Banbury, a wild fellow with a good heart, who is converted to live quietly by a Quakeress, whom he weds."[15] Likewise, it is a conveniently sly maneuver for Dreiser to show the theatrical success of his protagonist Carrie Meeber—an enthusiastically modern character if ever there was one—enabled by her talent at

playing the part of a demurely dressed, but still enticing, young Quakeress. The austere Quakeress, Dreiser seems to suggest, will inevitably
and inexorably be subject to the forces of modernity, even as the plainly
clothed Friend demonstrates and displays a moralized alternative to the
Gilded Age culture of consumption.

Representation of Quakers continued uninterrupted as the motion
picture era began to supplant the legitimate stage as a popular venue for
drama in the late nineteenth and early twentieth century. The visual
media began to transform radically the possibilities for representation,
but the currents of American thought concerning Quaker religion remained remarkably stable, as the psychologist William James, who in his
seminal work *The Varieties of Religious Experience* (1902) had concluded—
despite his own personal ambivalences about religion and spirituality—
that "The Quaker religion . . . is something which it is impossible to
overpraise. In a day of shams, it was a religion of veracity, rooted in
spiritual inwardness, and a return to something like the original gospel
truth than men had ever known in England."[16] The "original gospel
truth" that James highlights as a central aspect of the early Quaker
movement, however, is not exactly what the dramatists and filmmakers
of the twentieth century would emphasize in their treatments of the Society of Friends. Dreiser's remarkable Carrie Meeber, with her infamous portrayal of the pretty young Quaker girl, certainly situated that
protagonist well within the mainstream of theatrical performances and
other fictional works of the era, which included characters meant to
embody the "peculiar" traits and perceived idiosyncrasies of Friends. As
a suitably antimodern, premodern, and un-urban type, Quakers could
usefully be deployed to ironic effect in theatrical settings shaped by the
pressures and transformations wrought within late nineteenth-century
American culture. However, stage performances were diminishing in
importance and social influence as the motion picture entered its first
era of maturity, with their widespread dissemination first in the form of
silent films, and by the 1920s with soundtracks added for enhanced realism and verisimilitude.

A significant portion of early film history is inaccessible to modern
scholars because extant cinematic archives are, in general, limited. As is
well known to film historians, only a small number of silent films survive
from the late nineteenth and early twentieth century. The fragility and
rapid disintegration of nitrate film stocks, combined with a lack of attention by archivists and conservationists, resulted in a situation in

"The Little Shaking Quakers" (1883). Sheet music by Frank L. Bristow. Library of Congress.

"I Like Your Apron and Your Bonnet and Your Little Quaker Gown" (1911). Sheet music by John F. Harrington and Alfred J. Lawrence. Haverford Library collection.

which perhaps more than 90 percent of the thousands of silent films produced during the pre-1915 era have been lost permanently. Nevertheless, what is known of the titles and scenarios of some of these films can shed some useful light on the perpetuation of Quaker culture as a source of archaic religious character types and anachronistic cultural curiosity during a period of rapid modernization in the United States. We do know that the silent film era produced at least several works that take Quaker life as their subject, among them *A Quaker Mother* (1911, silent, Vitagraph Company of America); *The Quakeress* (1913, silent);[17] *Bred in the Bone* (1915, silent);[18] *The Dancing Girl* (1915, silent);[19] and *Beauty's Worth* (1922, silent).[20]

Somewhat more is known about the Harry Millarde silent film production of *The Quack Quakers* (1916), a short feature film, which has been lost to viewers but survives in summary form, thanks to a detailed scenario of the film published soon after its release in a *Moving Picture Stories* magazine. According to the scenario provided by the magazine writer Montayne Perry, *The Quack Quakers* is a short comedy hinging on the premise that a Broadway leading man named Tom Perkins (Victor Rottam) is searching desperately for a beautiful dancing showgirl—"a queen to lead the bunch"—for a chorus line that has already been assembled for a musical titled *Peaches and Cream*. Having surveyed all the showgirls currently at work on Broadway, the gruff stage manager sends Perkins off to find the perfect leading lady, insisting that he scour the city in order to "Find me a girl that's pretty enough and that can dance like a tornado!"[21]

Thus instructed by Isaac Morris, his manager, Perkins embarks on his star search almost immediately, finding on one of the city's beaches a stunningly beautiful young woman named Rosie Pinkham, who, conveniently enough, confesses to Perkins her desire to become a stage actress. She invites him to see her dance later that day at her home, where she lives with her father, Peter Pinkham, an amiable man who has "No prejudice against the stage" and "likes his bit of fun himself." All seems well with the planned audition until Perkins and Morris arrive that evening at the Pinkham residence, only to discover that Rosalind (the former Rosie) and Peter Pinkham are now dressed in traditional, plain Quaker garb and are in the company of Rosalind's Uncle Ezra, a devout Quaker who is paying the family a visit. Instead of the scantily clad bathing beauty of the previous day, they are presented with Rosalind in a completely different light, as she appears to be entirely transformed, "standing in the full glare of a great chandelier, a demure, gray-gowned, white-kerchiefed Quaker maiden, who cast her eyelids down, folded her hands in an attitude of meekness and dropped them a demure courtesy."[22] In place of their budding star, Rosie had apparently been turned into an antithesis of the provocative showgirl whom Perkins had hoped to hire. The explanation for the Pinkhams' sudden transformation is soon revealed, but not before Morris and Perkins stand amazed at the thought of an upright Quaker family having anything at all to do with the stage. The first instinct of Morris is to scold Perkins for having been so obtuse as to believe that a Quaker girl would be a likely candidate for stardom: "You thought a Quaker was going on the stage? That's your Peach? Tom, my boy, the heat has gone to your head. You lead me up here on a wild goose chase to meet a family of Quakers!" To which, Tom Perkins can only muster a befuddled reply, protesting "But they weren't Quakers this afternoon . . . they were just regular folks, just as I told you." Isaac Morris is every bit as surprised by the transformation, and as he and Perkins depart the Pinkham's house in confusion, he wonders aloud about whether Perkins has lost his sense of judgment, asking him "'Does the Quaker church have Billy Sunday?' he asked, 'If they do, that explains it. They run into him on the way home from the beach and hit the Quaker trail. Otherwise, my boy, you're either crazy now or your were drunk this afternoon.'"[23] Neither religious conversion nor intemperance were the solution to the mystery of the Pinkhams having suddenly adopted Quaker manners and clothing.[24]

To their eventual delight, Tom Perkins and Isaac Morris discover that Uncle Ezra had not visited the Pinkhams in their New York home for twenty years, and the Quaker costuming was only a sly and calculating performance intended to deceive their devout Quaker relative. As Rosie explained to a relieved Tom Perkins, the Pinkhams had been trying to maintain appearances: to deceive Uncle Ezra into believing that their faith remained intact, impervious to the corruptions of modernity. When they learned of Uncle Ezra's plans to visit, she admits, "Well, we just scurried around to get ready. We hid all the cards, and covered the pool table, and screened the pictures and draped the statuary, and dressed ourselves up and got it all done just in time. You see, he's an old man and daddy couldn't bear to hurt his feelings. Besides, he's awfully rich!"[25]

The ironies of performance and religious identity in *The Quack Quakers* thus run in several directions. Although she has never been on stage before, Rosie Pinkham, who is assessed by the gimlet eye of Tom Perkins to be the ideal woman for playing the part of a sexy chorus girl, is revealed and in the end turns out to surpass all expectations. An instinctive actress, she so convincingly performs the part of a devout and observant Quaker that even Perkins and Morris—who are experts at stagecraft and shrewd veterans of the theater—do not understand at first that she is merely acting a part. When the truth of her performance is revealed to Tom, he is stunned by her persuasiveness as an actress: "And that little scene was all acting!. . . . Why, you never flickered an eyelash. You looked like the real article, all right." Morris and Perkins locate their ideal actress in the person of a young woman with no experience but with an instinct for what seems to be a counterfeit identity. Part of the irony in this scene is connected to the erotic charge produced in the men (and by extension the audiences that they imagine) when the chaste Quakeress is revealed be merely playing a part. When Morris discovers Rosie's ploy, he "was at first incredulous, but when he was convinced that the Quakerism had been a clever bit of acting he was both highly amused and genuinely excited." In conceding his excitement, Morris rehearses the logic of representing Quaker faith as a embodying a repressed sexual response: one that is all the more alluring once it is released from the grip of faith. This logic can be traced to its conclusion as Rosie's parlor audition with Perkins and Morris continues and they observe her abilities as a dancer:

> Demure and quiet as Rosie had been as a Quakeress, as a dancer she was a veritable whirlwind. It was a wild gypsy dance she had chosen, and after the first moment she lost herself entirely in the spell of the music, and became a child of nature, of fire and ice and flame, of gay October forests and howling prairie gales, of wild birds calling across the marshes and wild beasts howling through tropical jungles. Morris whistled under his breath. . . . "She's a regular Class A, twelve-cylinder, self-starting human cyclone!" he said as she finished. "Young lady, I'll give you three hundred a week, straight, and your costumes."[26]

Admitting to a dramatic expertise that she had used for deluding her wealthy uncle, Rosie had previously told the men demurely but revealingly that "I'm of Quaker blood, you know," as a way conceding that skill at acting could have its uses on the stage (for entertainment of audiences) or in the family (for cynically keeping up appearances about religious devotion). Her deception and cynicism also suggest the potential for a broader cynicism within the Quaker movement as a whole, especially as its well-known traditional practices encounter the decadent urban scene

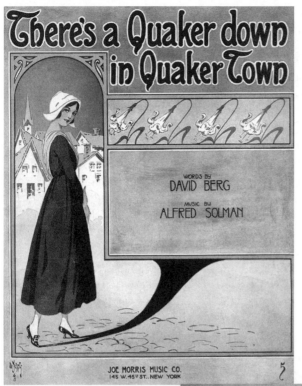

"There's a Quaker Down in Quaker Town" (1916). Sheet music by David Berg and Alfred Solman. Haverford Library collection.

"All the Quakers Are Shoulder Shakers (Down in Quaker Town)" (1919). Sheet music by Bert Kalmar, Edgar Leslie, and Pete Wendlindg. Haverford Library Collection.

that is represented in *The Quack Quakers* by the fast-moving and somewhat jaded world of twentieth-century musical theater. The film seems to suggest that, given the magnetic appeal of musical theater and other urban pleasures, perhaps even Uncle Ezra himself (who insists that he has "no desire to see more of thy city or thy friends") might have been persuaded eventually to set aside his plain clothes, archaic talk, and old-fashioned piety in favor of a rollicking trip down Broadway.

American attention to the role of Quakers in the national imaginary survived the transition from stage to short silent film to the longer film narratives of the later silent films and talking motion pictures. Bridging these rapidly shifting phases of mass media history is one of the classics of the silent era, *Down to the Sea in Ships* (1922). Starring the popular actors Raymond McKee (as Thomas Allan Dexter, a non-Quaker suitor) and Clara Bow (as the beautiful young Quakeress Dot Morgan), this remarkable silent film highlights the once-great nineteenth-century Quaker whaling community of New Bedford, Massachusetts, with vivid sequences showing Friends at worship and doing business, all dressed in authentic plain dress and shown at worship in a traditional meeting house. Seventy years after the publication of Herman Melville's *Moby-Dick* (1851), with its memorable descriptions of Quaker sailors and ship-owners in New Bedford and Nantucket, *Down to the Sea in Ships* updates some of Melville's fictional scenes for an audience of early film viewers. Produced in New Bedford, financed by "The Whaling Film Corporation," and distributed by the aptly named "Wholesome Film Service," the film, under the direction of Elmer Clifton, even makes a number of direct references to Melville's notions about the religious and social world inhabited by the whalers. For example, Clifton quotes directly from Melville: "The Nantucketer, he alone resides and rests on the sea; he alone, in Bible language, goes down to the sea in ships; to and fro ploughing it as his own special plantation. There is his home; there lies his business, which a Noah's flood would not interrupt, though it overwhelmed all the millions in China" (*Moby-Dick*, "Nantucket" chapter). The rest of the film's intertitles are similarly loaded with many quotations from *Moby-Dick* and a number of other whaling books.

The alterity of American Quaker life, exemplified especially by its archaic and plain costuming, comprises one of the main themes of Clifton's film, which in one of its early scenes provides a detailed re-creation of worship at the Apponagansett Quaker Meeting House. Much is made in this scene of the separation of men and women for worship, who sit

on opposite sides of the meeting house; the separation is doubly emphasized at the conclusion of the meeting when a wooden partition is drawn
between the male and female sections of the room and each side continues in single-gender privacy. After worship concludes, it is notable that
the business transacted by the men's meeting (with the acquiescence but
not the participation of the women's meeting) has to do with the "reading out of meeting" of a Quaker who had transgressed the discipline of
the Society of Friends, a decision that the film states bluntly: "In accord-
ance with their strict 'Discipline,' the Quakers read a young man 'out of
meeting' for marrying a girl who is not a Quaker—severing all family,
religious, and social ties."

Produced as a silent sea spectacle, with stowaways, lovers pursued
by a villain, and an appropriate piano score, the film gives its central position to the wealthy and commanding Quaker patriarch William W.
Morgan (played by William Wolcott), a devout Friend and ship-owner
whom the film describes as "Austere, and proud of his American ances-
try, glorying in his fleet of whale ships, a strict Quaker and a careful
businessman." After a young man has been read out of the New Bedford meeting for marrying a non-Quaker, Morgan takes the opportunity
to command his own un-wed daughter, Patience, to remain similarly
loyal, to the life of a whaleman's wife (and implicitly to the life of the
Quaker faithful): "Patience, thee is a whaleman's daughter. Promise thee
will never be any but a whaleman's wife." Morgan is likewise at pains to
police the boundaries of the clannish Quaker community when he confronts Patience's suitor, the young and handsome Thomas, who has
announced his willingness to convert to Quakerism in order to marry
his beloved Patience. For the elder Morgan, however, only the blend of
Quaker and experienced whaleman will be sufficient for any man bold
enough to attempt marriage into his Quaker family. As he declares
to Dexter after his marriage proposal to Patience—and despite the
fact that Morgan, having tragically lost a son of his own to the seas, is
desperately eager to have a male heir in the family—"Patience is a
whaleman's daughter. Unless thee has thrown a harpoon into a whale,
take thy story of love elsewhere. It can never be. Never!" So it is that
Thomas Dexter subsequently embarks on a whaling adventure of his
own, resulting in a breathtaking sea voyage and successful hunt that allows him at the end of the film to marry his true love, Patience.

The Quaker granddaughter, Dot, though, played by Clara Bow to
represent the younger generation as a far less controllable young

woman, seems very likely to be the sort of secularizing Quaker girl who will resist the kind of patriarchal control that the elder Morgan insists upon for Patience, whom he scolds for wearing a too-ostentatious dress when her wedding day finally arrives. As for the irrepressible Dot Morgan, William Morgan admits that while he exercised some control over his daughter, "It was difficult for him to understand his granddaughter, a restless, mischievous daughter of the sea." This misunderstanding is thus emblematic of what will be the inevitable fracturing of a well-disciplined community of Friends. The narrative logic of *Down to the Sea in Ships* eventually discloses the rigidity and virtue of the eldest generation of Quakers, the relative flexibility of the second generation of Quakers, and finally the presumed secular turn of the spirited granddaughter, whose lively demeanor turns to scandal midway through the film: "It is reported that Dot Morgan and Dexter have joined the Oregon Wagon Train and are 'heading west'!" Dexter, of course, has taken on the brave and necessary task of embarking on a successful whaling voyage, which, after putting bravely suppressing a mutiny and saving the ship from being hijacked, allows him to join the Quaker clan and to marry Patience as the film concludes. The young Quakeress Dot, however, is never heard from again by her New England Friends as she has indeed fled for the secular West.

As World War II raged in Europe and the Pacific with no peace in sight, and with German bombs dropping regularly on London, Quakers appeared once more: this time in the British and American film release *The Courageous Mr. Penn* (b/w, 1942).[27] This film offered a deeply respectful portrayal of the London years of William Penn, a Quaker pacifist who became the first leader of the religiously tolerant Pennsylvania colony in America. Directed by Englishman Lance Comfort and with an original story and screenplay by Anatole de Grunwald, the film centers almost entirely on an idealistic portrait of the a dashing young Penn (Clifford Evans), who came of age at a time when his father, an admiral in the English Navy was at the peak of his influence in the court of Charles II. Before turning to the chain of events that led William Penn to found a new colony in America, however, the film opens in the year 1667 with several brief scenes meant to show the dire Quaker persecution then ongoing on the London scene.

Throughout the film, richly dressed, elaborately bewigged, and overfed hangers-on from the court of Charles II, along with the equally decadent and promiscuous Charles II himself, set up a sharp contrast in class status and manners alongside the commoners who populate the filthy streets and raucous taverns of early modern London. The early Friends represented in *The Courageous Mr. Penn* are both dignified and serious, and they (with William Penn in the lead) go about their business earnestly and with due propriety, while their tormentors are portrayed in a much less flattering light. Persecution against the Quaker movement appears in the film to have come from all quarters of seventeenth-century England's class-stratified society, although that aimed at Friends is variously motivated. Both the courtiers and the commoners in the film look upon the Quakers as a dangerously strange and subversive presence, but whereas the courtiers are made uneasy by the Quaker refusal of political power and social privilege, the commoners look askance at those, like George Fox, who abstained from the quotidian pleasures of sporting and drink. One of the first scenes presented shows a strapping young George Fox being dragged into a tavern, where the drinkers insist that he join them in a riot of toasts and debauchery. When he refuses to do so, the mob in the tavern seizes him and dunks him repeatedly into a barrel of beer; after each dunking the stoic Fox merely thanks them oddly and does nothing at all to resist their bullying. Observing this scene, the dashing young William Penn seizes the opportunity to rescue Fox by staring down the drunken mob and forcing them to release the silent and dripping Fox. In another criticism of the Quakers, one of several wealthy and finely dressed tipplers, who has been viewing this entire scene from the safety of a small balcony in the tavern, notes that Fox's Quakers refuse to comply with traditional structures and habits of authority, complaining that "They belong to the common mob, yet they refuse to take off their hats to their betters." Uneasy with the time-hardened privileges of wealth and class, chafing under systems of traditional authority, and eschewing the merriment and rough pleasures of the common Londoner, Quakers in this film come to stand for an ideal colonial type: perfectly fitted to emigrate to distant lands and to populate a new world of virtue and true Christianity, far from the mean streets and palace intrigues of old London.

Even the premature death of Penn's wife, who had taken ill during one of his expeditions to Pennsylvania, fails to dim the lights of his colonial leadership, and he returns to his administrative duties readily, although not without a sentimental scene as he sits in his colonial office reading his wife's old love letters before the final credits roll. *The Courageous Mr. Penn* concludes with an intertitle quotation from Penn: "In essentials, unity—non-essentials, liberty—in all things, charity. Out of our unity will come the greater unity to Europe and the world." By the middle of the twentieth century, then, American and British film audiences were able to imagine the Society of Friends from the perspective of its great colonial administrator; with William Penn figured as an ideal type of Quaker settler, these audiences could see in Quaker life a strong inclination toward tolerant religious practices, an unabashed affection for the material aspects of the comfortable American life, and a romantic turn that figures Penn less as a deeply pious man of religion than as a dashing and sentimental lover.

This particular cinematic version of religious Quaker principles, highlighted by the exemplary William Penn as Quaker avatar and spokesman, was presented to American and British audiences just as the terrible battles of World War II were tearing through Europe and the Pacific. The activities of the modern Religious Society of Friends, of course, makes no appearance in this historical tale of the primitive Quaker movement, but their legacy of pacifism would have been familiar to any viewer of this film in 1942. What the film presents is not primarily a citation of the modern Quaker faith, for which pacifism had become a central premise and the best-known public aspect of Friends' religion. Instead, the role of William Penn is written and performed such that his leadership of a persecuted people and his role as a benevolent colonizer are emphasized above all else. Although the mystical George Fox is indeed portrayed with some sympathy in *The Courageous Mr. Penn,* he and his visionary experiences lie at the margins of the narrative. The Inner Light of Quaker belief is not once mentioned as a substantial or significant aspect of what Penn works to promote during his life in England or America. Setting aside mysticism and piety, the film offers instead a William Penn who espouses rather secular forms of egalitarian virtue, instinctive altruism, and capable (but never fanatical or pious) management of family and colony. Having presented Penn in this way, *The Courageous Mr. Penn* succeeds at constructing its Quaker protagonist as a Churchill-like leader who in a later era might have been fitted to wrestle with the geopolitical turmoil brought on by Nazism and fascism and their attendant persecutions and misappropriations of social power.

The devastating world wars of the twentieth century, both of which were protested by Quaker activists, form a significant part of the historical social context within which Quakers were viewed. If we consider these two major armed conflicts as having shaped world opinion about questions of pacifism and nonviolence, for instance, it is useful to consider that the two most public scenes of Quaker activism during that period were, first, the formation of the American Friends Service Committee (AFSC) in 1917 and, second, the awarding of the Nobel Peace Prize thirty years later (1947) to that organization (along with its sister organization, the British Friends Service Council) on behalf of all Quakers worldwide. The AFSC had been founded in 1917 by a group of Philadelphia Quakers whose original concern was the provision of nonviolent wartime service for conscientious objectors. Their presence as peace activists on the world stage was magnified tremendously after World War II with the awarding of the Nobel Peace Prize, which the organization received just as the brutal details of the Holocaust were becoming widely known in the media.

Given this prominence of Quaker activism in opposition to the major armed conflicts of the early twentieth century, it is therefore not surprising that representations of Quaker life and values would resonate powerfully during that time. And of course no genre of American film resonated more powerfully than the mythic gunfighter nation inscribed into film representations by popular Westerns during those years. It is in many ways ironic that John Wayne, the epitome of the Western gunslinger, would elect to focus on a Quaker family in the very first film for which he was credited as producer.[28] *Angel and the Badman* (1947), a genre Western film that appeared only a few years after the conclusion of World War II, features an itinerant gunslinger named Quirt Evans (John Wayne) who learns to give up his violent ways after he meets Penelope Worth, a pious and beautiful young Quaker woman (Gail Russell). In this popular film, written and directed by James Edward Grant, the gunslinger Quirt is first seen riding at a tremendous gallop across the desert when his horse finally collapses while crossing the farmland of a Quaker farm family headed by patriarch Thomas Worth (John Halloran), and they manage to prevail upon him to enjoy their hospitality. Evans responds to the Quaker family's invitation by insisting breathlessly that he must reach the telegraph office at the nearest town, and they oblige him by rushing him by wagon to the telegraph office, where he, too, collapses after sending a hasty message that stakes his claim to some prize land in the territory. The kindly Friends immediately bring the rugged gunslinger home, where their doctor discovers that Evans had been shot. Evans is required to place himself under the care of the plainly dressed Quaker family, and they readily welcome him into their family, despite stern warnings from their doctor—who knew Evans's reputation to be that of a brutal killer—to beware of the legendary and dangerous outlaw.

The Quaker farmers carefully nurse Quirt Evans out of a two-day delirium and finally back to robust health, and the gunslinger's reputation gradually becomes familiar to them. They learn the lurid details of his criminal background, such as his having survived a shootout with the Dodge City lawman Wyatt Earp and his genius as a quick-draw artist; he is known, they discover, as a man of ruthless courage and raw animal magnetism, and the attraction between the young Penelope Worth and Quirt Evans is immediate and obvious. According to the star-struck telegraph operator during the opening sequences, Evans is a dangerous man, but one with immense charisma and the ability to charm both sexes: "He's closed the eyes of many a man, and opened the eyes of many a woman." The life of the gunslinger, filled with danger, rugged travel, physical risk, and an evidently powerful eroticism—as exemplified by the handsome but deadly Quirt Evans—stands for everything that Quaker life was presumed to have refused and repudiated. The telegraph operator who had spoken of the gunslinger's reputation gives some sense of what general attitudes toward Quakers might have been during the post–World War II era, when he remarks about their odd disapproval of violence: "I've heard about you people, how you don't believe in guns or anything like that, only doing good."

The story unfolds somewhat predictably as an action-filled Western tale centered around the budding romance the two stars, but it soon becomes evident that the Worth family's Quaker identity is no mere incidental aspect of the film, which moves a considerable distance from the usual parameters of the Western film genre. Instead, all members of the Worth family are used to articulate carefully the Quaker principles of pacifism, benevolence, hospitality, and profound concern for the salvation of themselves and others. The film thus becomes a vehicle for articulating the lineaments of the Quaker life, while making problematic those aspects of its discipline that make it unsuited for life on a violent frontier. This is also not a narrative in which Quaker values are easily dismissed or ridiculed, even as the obvious irony sinks in for the viewing audience: cowboy icon and all-around tough guy John Wayne encounters a situation in which his typical projected ethos of violence and assertiveness must negotiate with Quakers in order to earn the affection of a beautiful Quaker woman to whom he is increasingly attracted. Although the comic structure of the film requires that Evans/Wayne provide a foil to the Quaker tradition of pacifism and nonviolence, Quaker values receive an evenhanded articulation, analysis, and defense. After Evans learns of the ongoing drought on the Quaker farm, one pivotal scene shows the gunslinger intimidating a selfish new neighbor who has diverted a communal irrigation stream into sharing the water once more with the Worth family farm. But first, Evans asks Penelope and her mother about her own approach to the water theft by their new neighbor:

> *Evans:* Well, what did you do about [the water being diverted by
>   the neighboring rancher, Frederick Carson]? Don't tell me you
>   prayed . . .
> *Mrs. Worth:* Of course.
> *Evans:* Did it get you any water?
> *Penelope:* We didn't pray for water. We prayed for Frederick Carson.
> *Evans:* Carson turned off the water, and you prayed for him?
> *Penelope:* Of course.
> *Mrs. Worth:* Don't you see? By committing an evil act, the poor man
>   injured his soul.
> *Evans:* I'm glad there's a well.

In the exchange portrayed in this scene, Evans is depicted as laconic, relaxed, and gently good-humored, but behind the veneer of comedy lurks the implicit menace of frontier Just as "Quaker" comes to signify restraint, modesty, and pacifism in *Angel and the Badman*, "gunslinger," especially as acted by John Wayne, signifies the latent threat of violence and overwhelming force.

As with many of the Western characters played by Wayne during his long and prolific career as an actor, the outlaw Quirt Evans resembles in many respects the laconic and ruthlessly violent Natty Bumpo in James Fenimore Cooper's Leatherstocking Tales. Likewise, Quirt's cleverness and resiliency, forged in the crucible of frontier America, produces in him the distinctively American ethos that the historian Frederick Jackson Turner claimed as a deeply inscribed set of national traits: "That coarseness and strength combined with acuteness and inquisitiveness; that practical, inventive turn of mind, quick to find expedients; that masterful grasp of material things, lacking in the artistic but powerful to effect great ends; that restless, nervous energy; that dominant individualism, working for good and for evil, and withal that buoyancy and exuberance which comes with freedom—these are traits of the frontier, or traits called out elsewhere because of the existence of the frontier." We can see that the Quaker piety that stands directly in opposition to the sort of marauding frontier competitiveness that Quirt Evans exemplifies also explicitly contravenes the notion of national identity that Turner promoted with such success during the twentieth-century expansion of American power. If Quirt Evans/John Wayne is cast as a prototypical American character, what else could the earnest and gentle Quaker family be other than a threat to a nation's virtues?[29]

That a friendship or romance could be possible between Penelope Worth and the violent outlaw Quirt Evans at first seems the unlikely in the extreme, and the physician who ministers to the wounded Evans during the opening sequence has a sober conversation with her in which he attempts to dissuade her from allowing Evans to stay at the farm any longer than is absolutely necessary. The doctor makes his argument on the grounds that it would be "unrealistic" to think of Quirt Evans as anything other than a dangerous criminal. At this point, Mrs. Worth (Irene Rich) responds in terms that voice an ethical position that harmonizes perfectly with Quaker teaching, even as her words strike a serious moral tone that seems remarkably discordant with one would expect in the screenplay of a mass-market Western film: "Doctor, we are sure that you will finally realize that realism—untempered by sentiment and humanity—is a mean, hard, cold outlook on life, a frightened outlook." To this, the doctor responds incredulously that the atmosphere of the Worth farmhouse "feels like Never-Never land." This sort of disbelief at the presumed naiveté the Worths, who, having migrated to the West from Quaker-dominated Philadelphia, is echoed in the views expressed by Quirt Evans to Penelope Worth as their romance begins. A good deal of their conversation entails an exposition of the Quaker faith in clear theological terms, with Quirt Evans serving as the interlocutor who poses a set of standard queries about the Society of Friends:

Penelope: We're Friends.
Quirt: Of who?
Penelope: Of all. The Society of Friends. Many people call us Quakers.
Quirt: Oh, it's a religion?
Penelope: It's a belief.
Evans [pointing to a large, inscribed plaque mounted on the parlor wall]: That on the wall . . . [reads] "Each human being has an integrity that can be hurt only by the act of that same human

being and not by the act of another human being." Is that Quaker stuff?

Penelope: It's a Friends' belief.

Evans: Well, supposing somebody whacks you over the head with a branding iron? Would that hurt?

Penelope: Physically? Of course. But in reality it would injure only the person doing the act of force or violence. Only the doer can be hurt by a mean or evil act.

Evans: Are there very many of you Quakers?

Penelope: Very few.

Evans: I sort of figured that.

Despite Evans's wry comments and good-natured resistance to the religious dimension of his blossoming relationship with the Penny Worth, though, as the film progresses Quirt Evans inched ever closer to accepting the reality that the beautiful young Quaker has no intention of abandoning her faith. After Quirt is presented with his own Bible at the Quaker meeting, he goes off on a brief series of wild escapades, but he soon returns and agrees to marry Penny. From this point in the film, Quirt Evans is rehabilitated as a new kind of hero: one who remains charismatic and confident in himself, but absent the criminality that had in the past made him a legendary figure.

It is not entirely clear that Evans has joined the Quakers so wholeheartedly or so completely that he resembles the Worth family in benevolence and piety. Nor is it clear that he has been transformed sufficiently to become a Quaker convert, with the attendant beliefs in pacifism, gender equality, and the always crucial experience of the Inner Light. Nevertheless, the logic of this unusual Western film traces a pattern that ascribes authentic moral force to the example of Quaker lives sincerely lived. Once a type of the mythical bandit, a dangerous prototype of what Shakespeare might have described as an "extravagant and wheeling stranger" on the American Western frontier, Quirt Evans finds himself willingly albeit gradually reconstituted as a man of peace and as a law-abiding family man. The film makes it plain that the John Wayne/ Quirt Evans cowboy does not in any sense become a religious enthusiast, but it makes equally obvious that the ex-criminal's acceptance of his young wife's Quaker practice shapes him ineluctably into a man for whom violence will henceforth be a final resort. As Evans concludes placidly, after leaving his well-used revolver in the dust, and just before the final credits roll, "From now on, I'm a farmer."

The historically based profile of William Penn in *The Courageous Mr. Penn* (1942) and the mythically oriented John Wayne vehicle *Angel and the Badman* (1947), both of which were produced during or just after the upheaval of World War II and thus rely on stereotypes about Quaker life in order to present important narratives about the American colonial endeavor and the problematics of national frontier, utilize Quaker religious scenes and principles in order to triangulate "authentic" American identities that could be understood as virtuous but not exceedingly pious or mystical. Quaker separatism, mysticism, and asceticism are to a large degree downplayed in these films, which have as their leading concerns the presentation of moderated and blunted Quaker theology: radical religious ideas that are made less fervent through prosperous and stable family life, steadily eroded by modern forces, or absorbed into postreligious forms of secular moral principle. In *Angel and the Badman,* Quirt Evans, for example, marries into a Quaker family, but there are no signs that he will adopt Quaker religiosity wholeheartedly or even in a limited way; his concession to his Quaker wife and her steadfast moral outlook is that he will renounce the life of a gunslinger for the stable (but not necessarily pious) life of a family farmer. So too, in a somewhat different way, is the Quaker identity of the historical William Penn shaped by his representation in *The Courageous Mr. Penn,* in which his religiosity and piety are deferred or overlooked in favor of his qualities as a civic leader and as a prosperous founder of what would become a colony of bourgeois American Friends.

Although they are films devoted to understanding the place of Quakers in American culture, though, and considered solely on the merits of their artistic achievement, neither *Angel and the Badman* nor *The Courageous Mr. Penn* can fairly be accorded a central place in the canon of twentieth-century films. Much more influential as a film with the Quaker ethos at its center, both among audiences and film critics, was *High Noon* (1952), which won the Academy Award for Best Picture and which has often been named on movie critics' lists of best American films.[30] This Western classic, starring film icons Gary Cooper and Grace Kelly, has an equally well-known plot, in which the frontier marshal Will Kane (Cooper) is preparing to retire from law enforcement after a long career of service in the fictional community of Hadleyville. He is about to marry the beautiful, and much younger, Quakeress Amy (Grace Kelly), who has asked Kane to give up law enforcement in deference to her religious beliefs. Before he can turn in his badge for good, though, Kane learns that the criminal Frank Miller, whom he had sent to prison previously, has been released and is due to arrive in town on the noon train. The rest of the film involves the building of suspense as the narrative unfolds according to the railroad clock, which indicates that about one and a half hours remain (the same time remaining in the film itself) before the feared arrival of the gunslinging Frank Miller.

Until the final confrontation between Will Kane and the Frank Miller gang, the plot involves Kane's futile attempts to enlist the support of other townspeople in order to put down Miller when he arrives. All of the townspeople except his Quaker wife, a drunken man, and an underage boy refuse to do so; the latter two are dismissed as inappropriate deputies, however, and the gun battle eventually ensues with only Kane's wife Amy lending support to his brave confrontation with the outlaw. The townspeople avoid violence and any form of participation in the fight against Frank Miller, even though they are met (in church) by Will Kane. There, he asks them explicitly to act in the best interests of the town. The refusal of the townspeople to defend themselves by arms is by no means a sign that they have adopted the Quaker ethos of nonviolence and pacifism: making no mention of religion or higher principles of morality, the community merely decides, with the clergyman's apparent blessing, that a gunfight of any kind—even in self-defense—would be "bad for business." After confrontations with the local preacher and the new marshall, the Hadleyville railroad clock ticks inexorably toward the fateful hour and the inevitable confrontation with the villainous Miller, whom Kane finally meets in the center of town after the arrival of the high noon train.

That Kane triumphs over the evil Miller and his gang, thereby making the town of Hadleyville safe once more for bustling commerce and secure domestic life, comes as little surprise, but the presence of Amy Kane—an apparently devout Quaker—in the final scene is a crucial element in the symbolism of this mythic American tale. Miller is killed with a shot from Kane, but the shot is fired while Miller is using the suddenly brave Amy as a human shield. Just before Kane fells Miller, Amy is inspired by the heat of the moment to act violently and against her stated Quaker principles. This occurs during a crucial moment in the gunfight, when only she is in a position to fire a fatal shot at one of Miller's men; significantly, she not only kills the man instantly but manages to do so instinctively and brutally, with a single shot into his back from very close range.

Given these starkly violent events and the circumstances of individual valor triumphing over pure evil, coupled with the willingness of the masses to capitulate morally when their material well-being is threatened, *High Noon* has frequently been interpreted as a political allegory. Richard Slotkin has suggested that this film can easily be read as "an allegory, from a leftists perspective, of Hollywood's surrender to McCarthyism" so that "Miller's return is a metaphorical way of identifying McCarthyism with Fascism: the same people who in an earlier and less prosperous time had risen up to defeat the enemy have now grown too comfortable or complacent to risk their lives and fortunes for the public good."[31] While such a reading surely illuminates a good deal of the film's allegorical content, however, *High Noon* also perpetuates a centuries-long American conversation about the Quaker faith, which is embodied by Amy Kane, whose moral transformation occurs in the heat of battle, when instinct apparently overrules her lifelong piety and she chooses to kill mercilessly in order to save the community and her husband. As with so many fictional narratives of American Quaker life since the colonial period, *High Noon* uses a Quaker stock character as both a moral beacon and an opportunity for converting the moral beacon to a new character who is willing to exercise power and violence, when necessary, in order to advance the American project (in this case, settling a frontier town for the sake of commercial stability). In a situation like the one in which the Kane family finds itself, violence trumps pacifism, with even the most devout of Friends—a young woman whose Quaker beliefs are seemingly unchallengeable—discovered in the end to have violent, retributive, and actionable impulses written into the core of her being.

Epilogue

Any cultural study that presumes to survey a period of three centuries in American life, as this one has done, is bound to have a large number of weaknesses and shortcomings, even when its focus is relatively narrow and concentrates on a small religious group. Another potential problem is associated with how the scholar of religion is situated with respect to the religious discourses being investigated. In any study of religious experience and representations, group membership and personal commitments matter a great deal. Because I am not a Quaker (nor a member of any religious group), my analysis of the discourses surrounding American Quaker religious culture has been shaped, structured, and inevitably limited by my perspective as an outsider, one whose occasional attendance at Quaker meetings in Massachusetts and North Carolina admittedly places me only at the periphery of the religious world of Friends. Moreover, because the three hundred years of Quaker representations that this study takes as its object do not attend satisfactorily to the various and complex communities of Quaker life that have existed in America, it avoids many of the particulars of theology and religious practice that have created both bonds and schisms among Quakers over the years. Although non-Quakers have seldom noticed or remarked upon doctrinal differences and religious incongruity among the various communities of Quaker faithful, there are indeed very substantial differences among Quaker communities; that various commentators on Quaker life over the centuries have presumed that

Friends can be spoken of as an undifferentiated group is a point that this study has emphasized repeatedly, but one that is at odds with the actual varieties of American Quaker experience. In short, as should not be surprising to scholars of religious experience, not all Friends see Quaker religion exactly the same way.

My research in this project pays frustratingly little attention to most of the journals and letters produced by generations of ordinary Quakers, the kinds of documents in which the substance of lived religions comes most fully and vividly to life. This is yet another sign that much more work on the social and intellectual history of American Quakers remains to be done. Nor has this study delved into representations of Quakers beyond the mid-twentieth century, when most Quakers had abandoned the plain clothing and distinctive language that made them iconic figures for previous generations of Americans. In part because of limitations like these—but more especially because of the radical challenge that Quaker theology continues to direct toward the larger American Christian enterprise and toward the American national and imperial projects— discourse by and about the Religious Society of Friends will continue to be a fertile topic for research in American studies.

My aim in attempting to follow multiple strands of discourse about Friends since their arrival in America in the mid-seventeenth century has not been to document in a truly comprehensive way the nuances of Quaker life but instead to suggest the unique role of Quakers—actual Quakers and imagined Quakers—in the formation of American national identity. In order to provide this kind of perspective on the meanings of Quaker religion and identity as they relate to American identities and values more broadly, it has been necessary to attend to Quakerism's long history in America and to representations of Quaker life across a variety of literary and visual genres. The evidence in this study was sifted from research in the areas of theological debates, records of missionary work, political theory, documentary history, biography, fiction, poetry, theater, and film. All of these fields of discursive practice have been useful and illuminating in charting the impact of Quaker religion on American life. Radical inventors of the Quaker movement like the seventeenth-century evangelists Mary Dyer and George Fox contributed in seminal ways to the patterns of these discourses, but perhaps just as crucial for understanding the place of Quaker culture in the national imaginary have been fictional representations of Quaker characters, such as Harriet Beecher Stowe's depiction of Underground Railroad workers at a Quaker settlement or Grace Kelly's performance of embattled Quaker virtue in the popular film *High Noon*. Whereas fully committed and impassioned early Friends like Fox and Dyer supply the perspective and authenticity of religious insiders, the scenes of Quaker religious and social experience offered in media such as fiction or film (frequently produced by non-Quakers) speak with tremendous authority because of the publishing leverage and wide circulation of mass media forms. In this way, as has been seen numerous times in this study, the representations of Quaker life as circulated in mass media come to stand for the essence of Quaker experience even when those representations partake—intentionally or not—in caricature or distortion.

The preceding chapters, however, demonstrate that the American historical archive reveals a continuing engagement between Quaker life and its religious values in conversation with the life and values of the nation as a whole. The territory of this engagement includes a number of issues that bear directly on the history of Quaker religious commitments and social behaviors. First, as the earliest history of their activity in England and America has shown, the Quaker threat to conventional religion and social arrangements was judged to be a serious matter not merely because of the number of Quaker converts but rather because of their sometimes fierce questioning of religious and civic authority. For instance, in an age when religious and civic authority overlapped extensively in the Anglo-American world, the early Quaker rebellion against clerical power in favor of a democratized ministry based on the Inner Light of personal revelation amounted to a breathtaking assertion of the popular will. Against rigidly hierarchical models of church and civic authority, the early Quaker movement posed alternatives that offered, albeit imperfectly, the beginnings of a discursive space to all those Americans, including women, who felt the call to express their religious views. In addition, long-standing Quaker testimonies against heedless materialism, alcohol and tobacco use, and worldly amusements have consistently placed devout Friends at the margins of American social life, whose parameters have for much of the population been configured toward norms of conspicuous consumption and entertainment culture. Quaker opposition to slavery, which hardened gradually in the eighteenth and nineteenth centuries into a central tenet of Quaker abolitionism and commitment to social justice, can be understood as one of the most important and influential consequences of the desire within the Society of Friends to participate in the world of commerce while resisting the damaging lure of excess materialism and the opportunistic exploitation of other human beings.

These same relatively austere principles, espoused by a religious group that for much of its history in America has been equally conspicuous for its idiosyncratic language, plain clothing, peace testimony, and restricted marriages, have made Friends appear to espouse a paradoxical blend of something like reactionary antimodernism infused with radically advanced positions on moral issues and religious practice. This tension between expressions of Quaker conservatism and Quaker radicalism has remained at the core of American fascination with representations of Friends, who for centuries have been documented by non-Quakers and Quakers alike with ambivalence at certain times, animosity at other times, but just as frequently with surpassing admiration. It is clear from the available documentary evidence that American Quakers have persistently entered the national imaginary because of their tendency to sketch something like a narrative of resistance to widely accepted norms in the nation's religion and culture: personal experience of divinity's Inner Light, pacifism instead of violence at junctures of social conflict, sexual equality rather than sexism, and "peculiarity" rather than adherence to pervasive cultural norms.

Notes

Introduction

1. Quakers are members of a religious group also known as Friends or as members of the Religious Society of Friends. The terms "Quaker" and "Friend" are equally accepted by many members of this religious group and will be used interchangeably throughout. It should be noted, however, that some evangelical Friends reject the term "Quaker" and use only "Friend" because it has a scriptural basis and "Quaker" does not.

2. For a survey of scholarly attitudes about religion among literary historians, see Franchot, "Invisible Domain," esp. 834–38.

3. Tocqueville, *Democracy in America,* 45.

4. Bercovitch, "The Ritual of Consensus," 48.

5. Rourke, *American Humor,* 213–14.

6. Moore, *Religious Outsiders,* viii.

7. Ibid., xiii.

8. For discussions of Quaker ambivalence about—and participation in—American military conflicts since the Civil War era, see Jacquelyn S. Nelson, *Indiana Quakers Confront the Civil War,* and Thomas D. Hamm et al., "The Decline of Quaker Pacifism in the Twentieth Century."

9. The Friends World Committee for Consultation puts membership for the Americas at 177,560, with worldwide membership totaling 367,808 (cited in Dandelion, *Introduction to Quakerism,* 177–80).

10. On the various forms of Quaker practice, see Dandelion, *Introduction to Quakerism.* A similarly useful profile that focuses on American Quaker life is Hamm, *Quakers in America.*

11. Templin, "The Quaker Influence on Walt Whitman," 165.

12. Parrington, *Main Currents in American Thought,* vol. 1, 9.

13. Gura, *Glimpse of Sion's Glory,* 5. After a joint meeting of Quakers, Baptists, and Ranters in 1655, Fox succeeded at converting some to the Quaker faith but wrote that he was shocked at Ranter dancing, singing, and affection for drink and tobacco, noting that they "were very rude, and stirred up the rude

people against us. We sent the Ranters to come forth, and try their God. Abundance of them came, who were very rude, and sung, and whistled, and danced; but the Lord's power so confounded them, that many of them came to be convinced" (qtd. in Cohn, *Pursuit of the Millennium*, 289).

14. Bercovitch outlines his theory of a persisting Puritan influence on American cultural identity in *Puritan Origins of the American Self*.

15. Gura, *Glimpse*, 11.

16. The name "Quaker" and "Friend" will be used interchangeably in this study, although the earliest Quakers were ambivalent about accepting a title that was originally meant to have pejorative meanings. Quaker historian William C. Braithwaite asserts that the first usage of the word "Quaker" as a pejorative term occurred in 1647, when the word was directed at Muslim women in Southwark, England (*Beginnings of Quakerism*, 12). The first published catechism of the English Quaker movement used several expressions in referring to members of the new religious movement: "children of Light," "Friends in the Light," "Friends in Truth," and "Friends (A. R. Barclay, "The Advices of the Elders at Balby" in *Letters & c. of Early Friends*, 277–82). The official name "Religious Society of Friends" was not established until the early nineteenth century (Dandelion, *Introduction to Quakerism*, 19).

17. Tweed, *Crossing and Dwelling*, 151.

18. Kundera qtd. in Rorty, *Philosophy and Social Hope*, 20.

19. Fox, *Declaration from the Harmless and Innocent*, n.p. Fox's letter to Charles II confirmed the Quaker commitment to peace that had been outlined the year before by Margaret Fell, the wealthy and prominent early Quaker convert who would marry Fox years later, after the death of her own husband. Several months before Fox's letter defining the Peace Testimony, Fell published a pamphlet addressing King Charles. She asserted that "We are a people that follow after those things that make for peace, love, and unity . . . and do deny and bear our testimony against all strife, and wards, and contentions" (qtd. in Mack, *Visionary Women*, 220).

20. The Quaker historian Jerry Richmond explains the Quaker linguistic tradition as an emblem of its radical democratic impulses: "This practice goes back to the social situation of the 1650s, when the Society was founded and requires a measure of linguistic insight. At that time, as is paralleled in the German language even today, there were different forms for the singular and plural second person pronoun. The plural form was 'you' and the singular form was 'thee' or 'thou.' Again as in German, the 'you' was also the proper and correct singular form to show respect and formality. In German, which closely parallels English in a number of ways, the 'du' is singular, the 'Sie' is plural or singular and formal. . . . The Quakers held that the use of 'you' as a formal pronoun was a contravention of plainness and that no one spoken to was that worthy of respect" ("Quaker Beliefs and Customs").

21. More so than other Quakers, members of the Conservative Quaker (so named even though they are theologically moderate) branch of the Religious Society of Friends have continued to perpetuate traditions of archaic Quaker speech and plain dress. At this writing, Ohio appears to have the largest number of Conservative Quakers continue to hold to the old, plain ways.

22. Levenduski, *Peculiar Power,* provides an excellent account of Ashbridge's life and career as a Quaker minister.

23. Loughran, "The Romance of Classlessness," 324.

24. James N. Green's study of print culture in the Middle Colonies from 1680 to 1720 observes that Quakers in America were exceedingly skilled at advancing their cause by means of printed materials, following their earlier successful experiences of establishing a clandestine system of book publishing in England, and attempted with some success to replicate their methods in Pennsylvania, especially. Green includes a thorough discussion of the Quaker printer William Bradford's career ("The Book Trade in the Middle Colonies," 200–223).

25. William Bradford, *Of Plymouth Plantation* (1651); Cotton Mather, *Magnalia Christi Americana* (1702).

26. Thomas Clarkson's centrality to the British antislavery campaign is vividly recounted in Hochschild, *Bury the Chains.*

27. A full-scale history of American religions would not be attempted until Robert Baird's *Religion in America* (1842), a popular compendium that emphasized the centrality of revivalism in American Protestant culture.

28. Early Quaker leaders like John Woolman are rightly credited with preaching against slavery, but many Quakers were slow to adopt clear antislavery positions. Care must be taken in articulating the differences between the antislavery politics of Quaker visionaries like Woolman and the general reluctance of eighteenth-century American Quakers to do without slave labor, which was a necessary and planned prerequisite for the Philadelphia and the Pennsylvania colony's existence. William Penn, the founder of Pennsylvania, kept slaves on his estate. Quaker merchants in America were involved in the slave trade for generations. Thomas Richardson, clerk of the New England Yearly Meeting from 1728 to 1760 was a slaver, as were prominent colonial Pennsylvania Quakers such as James Logan, Jonathan Dickinson, and Isaac Norris. The Philadelphia Yearly Meeting delayed until 1774 before making involvement in the slave economy a cause for disowning.

29. In his study of the role of economic development in the transformation of American print culture, Ronald J. Zboray observes that in antebellum America "Speech communication, whether on the political platform, Protestant pulpit, or minstrel stage, retained its importance, but in a time before mechanical reproduction of sound such orality emphasized the local present. By contrast, type was well suited to the work of constructing a national identity; imprints simply endured unmodified beyond the exigencies of time and space.

The same text could go everywhere and at any time and encourage (but not decree) a common reading experience" (*Fictive People*, xvi).

30. Another important and highly regarded film about American Quakers, *Friendly Persuasion* (1956), was based on a book by the popular Quaker author Jessamyn West, whose Quaker cousin Richard Milhous Nixon would occupy the White House some decades later.

Chapter 1. Quaker Religion in Colonial New England

1. On Puritan (and Quaker) radicalism in colonial America, including see Gura, *Glimpse of Sion's Glory*, esp. 144–52. The "populist" dimensions of religious enthusiasm during the seventeenth century are investigated more fully in Michael Heyd's excellent review-essay, "The Reaction to Enthusiasm."

2. Catie Gill provides the estimate of 60,000 English Quakers by the end of the 1650s; at the same time, she cautions that those identified as Quakers at that time were anything but uniform or consistent in their religious beliefs and practice and that "the [early] movement remains characterisable only by its diversity" (*Women in the Seventeenth-Century Quaker Community*, 12). Keith Thomas estimated that although they were the largest of the many dissenting sects that appeared during the English Civil War, Quakers had attracted only thirty to forty thousand members by 1660 (*Religion and the Decline of Magic*, 146).

3. Daniel J. Boorstin's chapter "The Inward Plantation" in *The Americans* focuses on both Quaker idealism and Quaker rigidity of belief during the seventeenth and eighteenth century, which he describes as their "bizarre and dauntless spirit" ("The Inward Plantation," 37).

4. Thomas, *Religion and the Decline of Magic*, 59.

5. Patricia Appelbaum explains the modern Quaker church organization as follows: "Local bodies, called Monthly Meetings, may include one or several worship groups. Monthly Meetings are affiliated in larger Quarterly and Yearly Meetings. Since the late 19th century, most Yearly Meetings have been organized into conferences. All these bodies make decisions by spiritually based consensus" ("Quakers," 1320).

6. While it was not printed as a book during his own lifetime, Fox's *Book of Miracles*—the manuscript of which was lost during the eighteenth century—was reconstructed from other references by the Quaker historian Henry J. Cadbury, who compiled and edited a modern edition, *George Fox's Book of Miracles* (1948).

7. Bercovitch, *Puritan Origins*, 29.

8. Sievers, "Awakening the Inner Light," 237.

9. For a carefully nuanced account of the first several years of confrontation between Quakers and Puritans in colonial Massachusetts, with particular reference to Puritan anxiety about the implicit Quaker threat to patriarchy, ecclesiastical authority, and social order, see Pestana, "City upon a Hill under Siege"; Karlsen, *Devil in the Shape of a Woman*, 122.

10. Pestana, "City upon a Hill," 342–43.

11. Ibid., 328.

12. That Quakers were less significant in terms of their religious influence per se is not to say that their activities were going unnoticed in the civic realm. Perhaps the most important development of this kind was the founding of the Philadelphia-based American Friends Service Committee (AFSC) in 1917, during World War I, which had as its aim the assistance of civilian victims of warfare. In addition, the AFSC was instrumental in creating the category of "conscientious objector" and alternative military service for Friends and members of other peace churches such as the Mennonites, Brethren, and Amish. In later years, the members of the AFSC remained active in the areas of promoting civil rights and opposing the proliferation of nuclear weapons.

13. Ahlstrom, *Religious History of the American People*, 176. Parrington, *Main Currents in American Thought*, 2:361–62.

14. Damrosch, *Sorrows of the Quaker Jesus*, 14.

15. Margaret Fell (1614–1702) herself is an important figure in seventeenth-century Quaker religion, and one who is worthy of further study. A beloved leader of the sect, she authored numerous letters to Friends, published pamphlets, and was jailed a number of occasions for failing to take oaths and for holding Quaker meetings. She eventually married George Fox in 1669, eleven years after the death of her first husband, Thomas Fell, a prominent judge who had also served in Parliament. As one of the few Quakers from the gentry, Margaret Fell was frequently called upon to intervene politically on behalf of persecuted Friends.

16. There is a good deal of scholarly evidence that George Fox had a form of lexical agraphia or perhaps dyslexia that prevented him from spelling words correctly. Pink Dandelion, among other historians, suggests that Fox's journal may not be entirely reliable because of the extensive editing done to the dictated account of his religious views (*Creation of Quaker Theory*, 14).

17. On the remarkable career of James Nayler, a well-known Quaker preacher, who in Bristol, England, in 1656 reenacted Christ's famous Palm Sunday arrival in Jerusalem, see Damrosch, *Sorrows of the Quaker Jesus*. Damrosch's account of the prolific and charismatic Nayler includes much helpful historical background on the English context for the rise of Quakerism, in addition to specifying the ruthless punishments meted out to those, like Nayler, who were convicted of "horrid blasphemy." As Damrosch recounts the punishment, Nayler was immediately arrested and after conviction was "brutally punished: the skin was flayed from his back by more than three hundred lashes, his forehead was branded with the letter B (for 'blasphemy'), and his tongue was bored through with a red-hot iron" before he was consigned to Newgate Prison. William Sewel quotes an eyewitness to Nayler's savage flogging, which had been preceded by several hours of punishment in the pillory, as writing that "there was not the space of a man's nail free from stripes and blood from

his shoulders near to his waist, his right arm sorely striped, his hands much hurt with cords, that they bled, and were swelled" (Sewel, *History of the Rise, Increase, and Progress,* 163).

18. For a deeply researched and nuanced account of Quakers in the English print marketplace of the middle seventeenth century, see Kate Peters, *Print Culture.*

19. Qtd. in Gaskill, *Witchfinder,* 174.

20. Pestana, "City upon a Hill," 331–32.

21. Croese, *General History of the Quakers,* 5.

22. Pestana, "City upon a Hill," 328.

23. Levy, *Quakers and the American Family,* 5. Anti-Quaker pamphlets quoted in Gummere, *Witchcraft and Quakerism,* 31. The *Bibliotheca Anti-Quakeriana* (1873), Joseph Smith's compendium of two centuries of anti-Quaker titles (nearly all published in England and Ireland) includes literally thousands of virulently anti-Quaker pamphlets and books. Most of these publications appeared between 1650 and 1750. Gummere argues that Quaker attitudes toward magic and witchcraft were typical for that era, with no disproportionate enthusiasm for magic (*Witchcraft and Quakerism,* 50). For more complete accounts of the durable beliefs in magic and superstition among seventeenth-century American and English Christians, see David D. Hall, *Worlds of Wonder, Days of Judgment,* and Keith Thomas, *Religion and the Decline of Magic,* respectively.

24. J. Taylor, *Account of Some of the Labours,* 4.

25. *Several Laws and Orders,* 1.

26. Sewel, *History of the Rise, Increase, and Progress,* 1:222–23.

27. Norton, *Heart of New England,* 54, 83.

28. According to an analysis of Quaker punishments by Raymond Ayoub, there were at least twenty specific offenses that brought Quakers into conflict with the seventeenth-century English legal code, including but not limited to refusal to swear oaths and refusal to tithe. Ignoring holy days, publishing Quaker books and pamphlets, going "naked as a sign," refusing to serve in the armed forces, and many other transgressions of the social order eventuated in the punishment of Quakers (see "The Persecution of 'An Innocent People,'" 51, for a complete list of these offenses).

29. The custom of banishing Quakers began in the English courts of the seventeenth century, when "banishment" frequently meant forced transportation to colonies like Jamaica or Barbados (ibid., 49).

30. Boorstin, *Americans,* 39.

31. Sewel, *History of the Rise, Increase, and Progress,* 266.

32. The day before William Leddra was led to the Boston gallows to be executed, he wrote to his fellow Quakers an extraordinary letter, in which he urged: "Take heed of receiving that which you saw not in the light, lest you give ear to the enemy. *Bring all things to the light,* that *they may be proved, whether they be wrought in God*" (qtd. in ibid., 313–14; italics in original).

33. Miller, *New England Mind*, 125. Writing in 1717, William Sewel took a similar view of Charles II's personal misadventures (such as his fourteen illegitimate children born to seven mistresses) and administrative failures, concluding that "tho' Charles the second was inclined to voluptuousness, yet he was good-natured, and the persecution [against Quakers] in his reign proceeded chiefly from the instigation of other malicious men" (*History of the Rise, Increase, and Progress*, 308).

34. Ayoub, "The Persecution of 'An Innocent People,'" 46; a significant number of books written by Quakers to record their persecutions at the hands of the orthodox are included in Joseph Smith, *Descriptive Catalogue of Friends' Books* (1867 [1970]), which in turn drew upon the earlier bibliography of Quakeriana in John Whiting, *A Catalogue of Friends Books* (1708).

35. Sewel, *History of the Rise, Increase, and Progress*, 604.

36. Levenduski, *Peculiar Power*, 21. The survey of persecutions against Quakers here relies on Levenduski's helpful overview of this topic; see esp. 1–15. For a more detailed list of punishments enacted against Quakers in New England, see Joseph Besse's sympathetic account in *Collection of the Sufferings*, xxx–xxxii. Jonathan Chu provides a thorough analysis of the legal issues involved in colonial persecutions of Quakers in *Neighbors, Friends, or Madmen*, including chapters specific to Boston, Salem, and Kittery, Maine.

37. Whittier, "The Pennsylvania Pilgrim," *Poetical Works*, 262.

38. Qtd. in Hallowell, *Quaker Invasion of Massachusetts*, 186; italics in original.

39. Chu, *Neighbors, Friends, or Madmen*, 41.

40. Damrosch, *Sorrows of the Quaker Jesus*, 246.

41. During the mid-to-late seventeenth century, Barbados had a relatively large Quaker community that included many slaveholders; before the island's "sugar revolution" in the mid-seventeenth century, tobacco was an important cash crop. For an account of an especially active English Quaker missionary's travels between England, Barbados, and New England during the latter decades of the seventeenth century, see J. Taylor, *Account of Some of the Labours* (1710). Notable in Taylor's account of his travels in West Indies, Newfoundland, New York, England, and Ireland is his comment upon meeting the missionary Quaker Mary Dyer, who had traveled to Barbados after her first sojourn in Massachusetts. Taylor recalls her to have been "a very Comely Woman and a Grave Matron, and even shined in the Image of God" (8).

42. In his recent study of early modern England, *Witchfinders*, Malcolm Gaskill documents numerous instances in which persons (most of them women) accused of witchcraft were interrogated at great length, sometimes tortured, and nearly always stripped naked for examination by female midwives and male magistrates. The intrusive examination of the Quaker women in Boston Harbor is thus in keeping with long-standing English anxiety over the physical manifestations of such devilish witchery as genital growths or oddly-placed "witch's teats."

43. Russell, *History of Quakerism*, 40. In her discussion of seventeenth-century English and American Friends, Naomi Baker observes that "Quaker literature dealing with foreign 'others' . . . exhibits the complexities entailed in a specific Quaker identity which conceives of itself as at once powerful and powerless, included and excluded, as it asserts its exclusive claim to universal truth, while simultaneously celebrating its marginality" ("'Men of Our Own Nation,'" 21).

44. Karlsen, *Devil in the Shape of a Woman*, 123. Christine Leigh Heyrman notes that by the time of the notorious witchcraft indictments and trials of 1692, "a substantial number of the witches accursed by Salem Village's 'afflicted girls' came from families or households that included Quaker members" and that, "the general characteristics displayed by or ascribed to many of the accused [witches] — the caviling questioning of authority, the refusal to confess error in spiritual loyalties and, among women, publicly dominant, assertive behaviour in dealing with men — were all traits familiar to Essex County residents and magistrates in the context of their experience with Quakerism" (*Commerce and Culture*, 112–16).

45. Though the number of books carried by these Quaker missionaries seems large for a nascent religious movement, Kate Peters has shown that the early English Quakers were extraordinarily adept at publishing and distributing their writings: "Quaker leaders began to publish their ideas in tracts and broadsides in late 1652; by the end of 1656, nearly 300 titles had been printed, an average of more than one new Quaker book each week" (*Print Culture*, 1).

46. Sewel, *History of the Rise, Increase, and Progress*, 184.

47. See Mather, *Magnalia Christi Americana*, and Norton, *Heart of New England Rent*, for typical seventeenth-century Puritan attitudes toward Quakers. In *Witchcraft and Quakerism*, Amelia Mott Gummere argues that despite witchcraft accusations leveled against Quakers in the seventeenth and eighteenth century, Quakers generally opposed witchcraft and admonished those Quakers whose spirituality led them to sympathy with persons interested in witchcraft and alchemy. For a discussion for the English law basis for seizure of Quakers on the grounds that magistrates traditionally held the authority to "regulate the movements of strangers within their jurisdictions," see Chu, *Neighbors, Friends, or Madmen*, esp. 35–57. In her study of witchcraft in colonial New England, Karlsen argues that Quakerism and witchcraft were conflated by Puritans during the seventeenth century, noting that Long Island's Mary Wright was the only Quaker to be tried as a witch (in Massachusetts), "the informal connection between witchcraft and Quaker belief persisted" (*Devil in the Shape of a Woman*, 124).

48. Chu, *Neighbors, Friends, or Madmen*, 38–39.

49. *Acts and Laws*, 48.

50. Adams, *Summary History of New-England*, 103. For instance, Elijah Parish and Jedidiah Morse, whose *Compendious History of New England* (1805) competed with Adams's 1799 *Summary History of New England*, contradicted Adams's view of Quaker persecution by blaming Quakers as "enemies to government, unless administered by Quakers" (qtd. in Buell, *New England Literary Culture*, 224).

51. Rhode Island's decision to permit Quakers to enter its ports and to take up residency was complicated by both religious and political considerations. As Jonathan Chu notes, "To pass any anti-Quaker legislation would have required the agreement of influential Antinomian exiles in Newport like William Coddington and John Coggeshall, who were about to become Quakers. The imminent conversion of such men suggested not only sympathy for the sect but dramatic illustration that Quakers were not inherently destructive to order" (*Neighbors, Friends, or Madmen*, 39).

52. Miller, *New England Mind*, 124.

53. "Philopatrius," *Quaker Unmask'd*, 8.

54. "Philanthropos," *Quakers Assisting to Preserve the Lives of the Indians in the Barracks*, 14.

55. The matter of Quakers insisting on the right to "affirm" rather than swearing oaths to God for legal purposes would remain a contentious issue well into the twentieth century in the United States.

56. A comprehensive and nuanced analysis of the roots of Quaker pacifism may be found in Weddle, *Walking in the Way of Peace*. Weddle traces the particulars of the Quaker pacifist obligation in a range of seventeenth-century English and American settings to show that Friends in the early period of the movement held a range of positions with regard to avoiding violence, while describing the many tensions they experienced between private belief and public duty.

57. Budd, *Testimony*, 1–12. For the most influential general discussion of the relationship between criminality, public execution, and corporal punishment in the years before the European Enlightenment, see Foucault, *Discipline and Punish*, in particular his extended discussion of torture and executions as theatrical events bearing both judicial and political weight.

58. Braithwaite, *Beginnings of Quakerism*, 152.

59. Ziff, *Puritanism in America*, 139.

60. Hamm, *Quakers in America*, 28.

61. Hicks, a native of Long Island, New York, had become an itinerant Quaker minister after a religious conversion he experienced in 1774, after which he became a pivotal figure in the so-called Hicksite branch of the Society of Friends, a populist Quaker movement that opposed missionary agencies and trained clergy while returning to the founding doctrine of the Inner Light and personal revelation. Although he was not quite a birthright Quaker himself, Walt Whitman's paternal grandfather and father, who lived on Long

Island, were both friends of Elias Hicks. For a comprehensive discussion of the Hicksite schism in the nineteenth century, see Ingle, *Quakers in Conflict*.

62. Edwin Bronner, introduction to *Early Quaker Writings*, ed. Hugh Barbour and Arthur Roberts, 5.

63. Russell, *History of Quakerism*, 79. Peters also notes the concentration of Quaker authorship in the hands of a relatively small number of writers: "eight men (James Nayler, George Fox, Richard Farnworth, James Parnell, Edward Burrough, Francis Howgill, William Dewsbury, and Richard Huberthorne) individually wrote more than half of all Quaker publications" before 1656 (Peters, *Print Culture*, 21–22).

64. Mack, "Religion, Feminism, and the Problem of Agency," 161.

65. Sievers, "Awakening the Inner Light," 247.

66. Anon., *Edinburgh Review*, 202, 207.

67. For a discussion of the disruptive aural expressivity of "singing Quakers" and "Ranters," see Rath, *How Early America Sounded*.

68. Hoskens, *Life and Spiritual Sufferings*, 27–28. Joanna Brooks points to the autobiography of Jane Hoskens as an example of the American Quaker turn toward a "literature of sufferings" during the eighteenth century, which resembled the literature of sufferings produced in seventeenth-century hagiographies of English Quakers. Hoskens's autobiography, in Brooks's view, had a powerful effect on Quaker identity: "Her story of 'sufferings physical, spiritual, and socioeconomic formed the core of a new American literature of sufferings which—like the literature of sufferings produced in seventeenth-century England—constructed Quakerism as an oppositional and persecuted minority identity" ("Held Captive by the Irish," 39).

69. Margaret Askew Fell Fox, who married George Fox in 1669, also provided the English Quakers with their first headquarters by allowing the group to use her estate, Swarthmore Hall. After her death, a tribute to her work in the first generation of Friends was published (see Fell, *Brief Collection of Remarkable Passages*).

70. Dandelion, *Introduction to Quakerism*, 54; for a helpful summary of Barclay's *Apology*, see Dandelion, 54–57.

71. Turford, qtd. in Beebe, *Garden of the Lord*, 42.

72. Although there were frequent accusations about sexual libertinism among Quakers in the seventeenth- and eighteenth-century popular press, Quakers themselves remained ambivalent about the new gender performances made possible by their religious views. For example, Pestana argues that all the heretics described in John Norton's early tract attacking the Quakers, the *Heart of New England Rent* (1659), "shared a belief in direct revelation, a denial of Scriptures, and a propensity of lascivious behavior and the communal ownership of property (Pestana, "City upon a Hill," 341). While women were indeed empowered to speak at meeting and to criticize men in the process, Quakers

also remained concerned to control the "womanish part" of their expressive selves—the phrase they often used to describe the urge for sensual or otherwise worldly pleasures (see Sobel, *Teach Me Dreams*, 144–46, and Achinstein, "Romance of the Spirit," 415).

73. Dove, *Quaker Unmask'd*, 8.

74. Qtd. in Beebe, *Garden of the Lord*, 10; Myron Goldsmith, qtd in ibid., 11; Samuel Bownas, *An Account of the Life of Samuel Bownas* (Philadelphia, 1759), qtd. in Heyrman, *Commerce and Culture*, 133–34.

75. R. P. Hallowell, *Quaker Invasion*, 98.

76. Levy, *Quakers and the American Family*, 82–83. The preceding paragraph draws extensively on Levy's observations about anti-Quaker writing and his general arguments about the radical transformation of Quaker families in England and America during the seventeenth and eighteenth centuries.

77. Ibid., 230.

78. R. P. Hallowell, *Quaker Invasion*, 106.

79. Qtd. in Kimber, "The Treatment of Quakers," 39.

80. Qtd. in Hallowell, *Quaker Invasion*, 104.

81. Ibid., 98.

Chapter 2. Political Theory and Quaker Community in the Early Republic

The Thomas Jefferson epigraph at the beginning of this chapter is from a letter to "Judge Cooper"; qtd. in Koch, ed., *Jefferson and Madison*, 246–47. I am grateful to Paul Boyer for bringing this statement by Jefferson to my attention.

1. Mack, "Religion, Feminism, and the Problem of Agency," 161.

2. Richter qtd. in Tiro, "'We Wish to Do You Good,'" 365.

3. Boswell, *Life of Johnson*, 327. In 1776, Boswell notes, Samuel Johnson remained opposed to Quaker theology but admitted affection for certain Quakers: "He liked individuals among the Quakers, but not the sect." For Boswell's part, he admitted that "I have always loved the simplicity of manners, and the spiritual-mindedness of the Quakers; and talking with [a Quaker acquaintance], I observed, that the essential part of religion was piety, a devout intercourse with the Divinity; and that many a man was a Quaker without knowing it" (702–3).

4. Crabtree, "'A Beautiful and Practical Lesson of Jurisprudence,'" 54. Crabtree's discussion of the late-eighteenth-century transatlantic Quaker ministry arrays them explicitly in opposition to the broader imperial forces at work during the period, observing that "In forging a community unified by religious and political ideology rather than geopolitical borders, Quakers implied that national/imperial governments were worldly and thus corrupting forces in the modern world" (57).

5. Although African Americans become the object of Quaker benevolent activities, especially during the nineteenth century when the question of slavery became a focal point of Quaker activism, African American membership in the Society of Friends has always been quite limited. For a thorough discussion of African American participation in the Society of Friends, see Cadbury, "Negro Membership," 151–213.

6. Boorstin, *Americans,* 41.

7. This discussion of Elizabeth Drinker and Sarah Logan Fisher is drawn from Linda Kerber, *Women of the Republic,* 63, 76. See also Drinker, *Extracts from the Diary,* for a wealth of details about her life during the Revolutionary War.

8. Cadbury, "Defoe, Bugg and the Quakers," 152.

9. Woolman, *Journal and Major Essays,* 127–28.

10. John Woolman's *Journal* is by far the most famous and widely read of American Quaker journals, but it is only one of many visionary journals produced within the Quaker faith. As Carla Gerona has shown in her recent study of dreams in Quaker culture, "Because ministers could expect their journals to be circulated and perhaps printed after their death, authors self-consciously styled their journals—and their dreams—to instruct future Quakers. In some ways, largely because of this culture of letters, individuals could hardly be thought of as freely shaping the analysis of their dreams. Quaker dreamwork was a collective endeavor that involved multiple members of the community to deploy mass circulation of dreaming" (*Night Journeys,* 28–29). Orally communicated dreams and other unpublished Quaker dreams, however, would remain unregulated for the most part. For a discussion of dreams and abolitions in John Woolman's *Journal,* see White, "A 'Consuming' Oppression" (esp. 9–14), who places Woolman's antislavery views in the context of the West Indian sugar trade.

11. While Woolman has become a canonical figure in the American literary tradition, he was not the first or only Quaker to promote antislavery views. Precedence in this regard goes to William Burling of Long Island, New York, who was the first Quaker to publish antislavery writings. As the black historian Carter G. Woodson (citing Thomas Clarkson's history of the Quakers) describes Burling's visionary antislavery position: "He wrote several tracts to publish to the world his views on this great question. His first tract appeared in 1718. It was addressed to the elders of the Friends to direct their attention to the 'inconsistency of compelling people and their posterity to serve them continually and arbitrarily, without any proper recompense for their services'" ("Anthony Benezet," 37; see Clarkson, *History of the Rise, Progress, etc.,* 1:146–47).

12. Qtd. in Gay, *Enlightenment,* 408.

13. Woolman, *Journal and Major Essays,* 238, 248.

14. For a profile of Benezet's educational and philanthropic career, see Woodson, "Anthony Benezet."

15. Brissot de Warville, *New travels,* 1:221.

16. Vaux, *Memoirs of the Life of Anthony Benezet*, 22.

17. "Philopatrius," *Quaker Unmask'd*, 4, 5, 11.

18. Vaux, *Memoirs of the Life of Anthony Benezet*, 134.

19. Chauncy, "Enthusiasm Described and Cautioned Against," 231–32.

20. Benjamin Franklin lived in France from 1776 to 1785, and his reputation in France was strengthened by his association with Quaker Philadelphia, even though he himself was not a Quaker. As Jeanne Henriette Louis has noted, however, Franklin's family background reveals a number of Quaker connections, including a number of cousins, among his ancestors who lived on Nantucket Island. In addition, Franklin's "maternal grandfather, Peter Folger, who had been a key figure in the British settlement of the island, was the spiritual leader of Nantucket Quakerism. Many descendants of Peter Folger who had stayed on the island had become active Friends there" ("The Nantucket Quakers' Message," 15).

21. Isaac Hopper's mother was also a convinced Quaker and eventually became a regular preacher at meeting; his father, Levi, though he had been read officially out of meeting for marrying the a wife who was not yet a convinced Quaker, saw his business suffer during the Revolutionary War years because of his objections to the fighting and for his refusal to pay required military taxes.

22. Child, *Isaac Hopper*, 43.

23. A novelist of some renown and an important Massachusetts abolitionist, Lydia Maria Child (1802–80) made her early reputation as an abolitionist writer with *An Appeal in Favor of that Class of Americans Called Africans* (1833) and later her published *Correspondence* (1860) with the governor of Virginia.

24. Child, *Isaac Hopper*, 24.

25. Ibid., vi. A modern scholarly edition of Hopper's *Tales of Oppression*.

26. The spelling of Herman Husband's name was also rather fluid. Some of his pamphlets were published under the name "Hermon Husbands."

27. Fitch, *Some Neglected History*, 51–52, 107.

28. Richard Slotkin's analysis of Crèvecoeur's *Letters* is an important exception to the general neglect of Crèvecoeur's writing about Quakers (see *Regeneration through Violence*, 259–68). In a wide-ranging essay on Crèvecoeur, Norman Grabo perceptively highlights the analogy that *Letters from an American Farmer* draws between the virtues of the "ideal plowman" and Quakers, such as the Nantucket Friends or the botanist John Bartram ("Crèvecoeur's American," 168–69); in this way, Grabo's analysis conforms to the broader argument presented in this study about representations of Quakers in America as being simultaneously structured as idealizations and as caricatures (see Carlson, "Farmer versus Lawyer," 259–60).

29. Slotkin, *Regeneration through Violence*, 203; Cadbury, "Negro Membership," 167–68. And some of the slaves in question were not black but instead

were members of the Native American population. Nathaniel Philbrick observes that although Nantucket Quakers "might have declared their opposition to slavery in 1716 . . . that did not prevent their men's meeting clerk, Nathaniel Starbuck, Jr., from willing 'all my Indian men with their debts' to his wife in 1753" (*Abram's Eyes*, 171).

30. Leach and Gow, *Quaker Nantucket*, 38.

31. Macaulay, *History of England*, 1:299.

32. Slotkin, *Regeneration through Violence*, 204.

33. Philips, *Good Quaker in French Legend*, 202–3; Carlson, "Farmer versus Lawyer," 267.

34. For additional perspective on Brissot's political and literary intrigues, and evidence that he may have been a spy, see Robert C. Darnton, "The Grub Street Style of Revolution."

35. Brissot de Warville, *New travels*, 1:163–64.

36. Ibid., 1:153–54.

37. Crèvecoeur, *More Letters*, 82–84. In the decade after the publication of Crèvecoeur's *Letters*, Brissot de Warville made a similar observation about the stark contrast between Catholic and Quaker religiosity: "What a difference between the simplicity of [Quaker services] and the pomp of the Catholic worship! Reformation, in all stages, has diminished the formalities: you will find this regular diminution in descending from the Catholic to the Lutheran, from the Lutheran to the Presbyterian, and from thence to Quakers and Methodists. It is thus that human reason progresses towards perfection" (*New travels*, 1:164–65).

38. Voltaire, *Philosophical Dictionary*. For an alternate view of Voltaire's *Lettres philosophiques* that examines the complexities of his attitude toward Quakers, which he expressed rhetorically through both admiration and criticism of Friends, see Reisler, "Voltaire's Quaker Letters as Strategical Truth," 433ff.

39. Nathaniel Philbrick suggests "indirect evidence" about this apparent Native ambivalence toward Nantucket Quakers by citing the eighteenth-century Puritan Daniel Gookin as having recorded the following description of a meeting between Quaker missionaries and some Indians on Martha's Vineyard: "The Quakers . . . told the Indians, that they had a light within them, that was sufficient to guide them to happiness. . . . The Indians heard all this discourse patiently; and then one of the principal of them that could speak English, gravely answered the Quakers after this manner, "You tell us of a light within us, that will guide us to salvation, but our experience tells us that we are darkness and corruption, and all manner of evil within our hearts. . . . We cannot receive your counsel, contrary to our own experience of our ancient and good teachers . . ." (Gookin, qtd. in Philbrick, "The Nantucket Sequence," 169–70).

40. Allen and Asselineau, *St. John de Crèvecoeur*, 73.

41. Philbrick, "The Nantucket Sequence," 415.

42. Qtd. in ibid., 422.

43. Ibid.

44. Philips, *Good Quaker in French Legend*, 17.

45. Louis, "The Nantucket Quaker's Message," 10.

46. In an early expression of their pacifist principles, Pennsylvania Quakers withdrew from state government after the 1756 declaration of war against the indigenous Delaware and Shawnee Native groups.

47. Levy, *Quakers and the American Family*, 15.

48. Levy, "Tender Plants," 116.

49. Philips, *Good Quaker in French Legend*, 102, 202; Crèvecoeur, qtd. in ibid., 113.

50. Louis, "The Nantucket Quaker's Message," 15.

Chapter 3. Chronicles of Friendship

1. The scope of Quaker discourse in the public sphere of late-seventeenth-century England and America is difficult to measure precisely, but John Whiting's catalogue of "Friends Books" lists approximate 3,000 titles for the period 1650–1708. Whiting's publishers, the Sowle family of London, appear to have been the printers and sellers of a great deal of the early Quaker literature. In the obituary of Jane Sowle's husband, Andrew, he is remembered as having printed Quaker books; his printing materials were several times seized and broken to pieces, and on one occasion a thousand reams of printed books were taken from him by magistrates.

2. Qtd. in Miller, *New England Mind*, 167.

3. Another lengthy (4 vols.) history of the Quakers was published in Ireland at the end of the eighteenth century by John Gough, an English Quaker who served for many years as a schoolmaster in Ireland. Gough's *History of the People Called Quakers* drew heavily upon Sewel's history and would be superseded by Thomas Clarkson's history of the Quakers published in the early nineteenth century.

4. Bishop, *New England Judged*; Gerald Croese, *General History of the Quakers*. Before being issued in an English translation, Croese's history had been published in Latin.

5. Husband, *Some Remarks on Religion*, 22.

6. Thomas D. Hamm is surely correct in asserting that Quaker historiography would not mature entirely until the late nineteenth century, when more balanced historical writing about the Quaker tradition began to appear at the hands, first, of Robert Barclay of Reigate, whose *The Inner Life of the Religious Societies of the Commonwealth* (1876) set a standard of scientific scholarship that would not be superseded until the publication of major early-twentieth-century Quaker historiography. The "scientific" histories that Hamm points to as the main examples of improved historical research into Quaker religion by

Quakers are those by Rufus Jones (1914), William C. Braithwaite (1912, 1919), and Elbert Russell (1942) (Hamm, "George Fox and the Politics of Late Nineteenth Century Quaker Historiography," 11).

7. See Tolles, "Emerson and Quakerism," for a more complete discussion of the relationship between transcendentalism and Quaker religious principles.

8. Charles Lamb's *Essays of Elia* (1822–23) had a wide readership in England and America; his chapter titled "A Quaker Meeting" was reprinted in an 1834 issue of the New Bedford *Mercury;* Lamb, *Essays,* 4.

9. Sewel, *History of the Rise, Increase, and Progress,* 10.

10. Although Foxe's lavishly illustrated history of Christian and especially Protestant martyrs (a volume intended as an attack on the Roman Catholic Church) came to be known popularly as the *Book of Martyrs,* the full title is *Actes and Monuments of these Latter and Perilous Days, Touching Matters of the Church.* In tracing the psychology and rhetoric of Quaker martyrology, Ann G. Myles argues that seventeenth-century Quakers, like all English Protestants, "would have had Foxe's *Book of Martyrs* and similar works ingrained deeply as a pattern for understanding both her own and Friends' collective experience" ("From Monster to Martyr," 14).

11. Sewel, *History of the Rise, Increase, and Progress,* v.

12. Ibid., 219.

13. Ibid.

14. Ibid., 26.

15. Ibid., 35. For a brief summary of the events surrounding the trial and execution of Mary Dyer, see Myles, "From Monster to Martyr," 4–8.

16. Sewel's account of seventeenth-century Quakers shows them frequently to have been accused of being Papists, an accusation meant for those who were sympathetic to the Roman Catholic Church. Although Quaker and Catholic theology were, and are, radically different, suspicions about Quaker allegiance to Rome or Quaker identification with Catholic principles were likely caused by suspicions that Quaker resistance to the orthodox English church placed them in essentially the same subversive position as Papists.

17. Sewel, *History of the Rise, Increase, and Progress,* 318.

18. Ibid.

19. Ibid.

20. Ibid., 184.

21. Ibid., 389.

22. Occasionally, a defender of the Quakers would write in opposition to Bugg's invective, as with Daniel Defoe, who, though not a Quaker himself, was sympathetic enough with the movement that he published an anonymous pamphlet called *A Friendly Rebuke to one Parson Benjamin* (i.e., Bishop Benjamin Hoadley) in 1719, listing the author as "By One of the People called Quakers." For more background on Defoe, Bugg, and Quakerism, see Cadbury, "Defoe, Bugg and the Quakers," 70–72.

23. Sewel, *History of the Rise, Increase, and Progress,* 96.

24. Ibid., 97.

25. The colonial injunction against Quakers in Barbados specified six months imprisonment and forfeiture of one thousand pounds of sugar for any permanent resident who dared to "publicly discourse or preach at a meeting of the Quakers." The law further encouraged informants to advise the Barbados authorities of any Negroes in attendance at Quaker meetings or schools, promising one-half of the proceeds of seizing the slave to be awarded to the informant (ibid., 611).

26. Ibid., 97.

27. Ibid., 198.

28. Ibid., 294.

29. Ibid., 224–25.

30. Ibid., 796.

31. During the eighteenth century, Sewel's pioneering work on the early Quakers was followed by a number of sympathetic histories that supplemented his aim of showing the origins of the Friends movement in the best possible light. Notable among these are the hagiographies of Quakers collected in Joseph Besse, *Collection of the Sufferings* (1753), and the four-volume anthology of early Quaker documents in John Gough, *History of the People Called Quakers* (1789).

32. Clarkson's *A Portraiture of Quakerism* was published in English and American editions in 1806; in 1820 a French edition was published and helped to rekindle discussions about the figure of the "good Quaker," which during the French Revolution had been the subject of much admiration by the *philosophes.*

33. Although published nearly a century ago, Jones's *The Later Periods of Quakerism* is still the best single historical study of Friends in the eighteenth century, and it emphasizes the mystical elements of Quaker life worship. For a recent review of historical works on eighteenth century Quakers, see David J. Hall, "Study of Eighteenth-Century English Quakerism," especially 106–8.

34. Catherine Clarkson shared her husband's deep interest in the Quaker movement. Her attendance at Quaker meetings in the Lake District and her study of George Fox's journal apparently led to a marked change in her religious views, to the point that one of her friends observed that "She is become a religionist and a believer. Her faith receives little or no aid from written revelation— but god has spoken to her heart in a most sublime and mystical manner. In short, she is a species of Quaker" (qtd. in Ellen Wilson, *Thomas Clarkson,* 104).

35. John Wilson, "On Reading Mr. Clarkson's History of the Abolition of the Slave Trade," 357.

36. Clarkson, *Portraiture of Quakerism,* 3:184.

37. Ibid., 3:186.

38. The standard biography of Thomas Clarkson is Ellen Gibson Wilson's *Thomas Clarkson.* Adam Hochschild's superb study of the eighteenth-century British antislavery movement, *Bury the Chains,* features an extended

discussion of Clarkson's alliances with prominent Quaker abolitionists and argues that it was Clarkson's moral zeal—far more than that of the his better-remembered abolitionist colleague William Wilberforce—that galvanized the movement.

39. Robert Barclay, *Apology*, 515–16.

40. Clarkson, *Essay on the Slavery and Commerce*, ix–x.

41. Levy, *Quakers and the American Family*, 16.

42. Clarkson, *Portraiture of Quakerism*, 1:i, iii.

43. Qtd. in Levy, *Quakers and the American Family*, 7.

44. Clarkson, *Portraiture of Quakerism*, 1:ii, emphasis added.

45. Qtd. in Beck, "'A Witness Lasting, Faithful, True,'" n.p.

46. Clarkson, *Portraiture of Quakerism*, 1:53.

47. Qtd. in Wilson, *Thomas Clarkson*, 91.

48. Mack, "Religion, Feminism, and the Problem of Agency," 164.

49. Clarkson, *Portraiture of Quakerism*, 1:62–63.

50. Ibid., 1:70–71.

51. Ibid., 1:78.

52. Ibid., 1:131, 133–34.

53. Ibid., 1:135.

54. For a full-scale discussion of the ramifications inherent in modern prisons developed on the model of the Philadelphia penitentiary, see Foucault, *Discipline and Punish*.

55. Clarkson, *Portraiture of Quakerism*, 1:201–2.

56. Ibid., 1:244.

57. Barnard, *Dorothy Payne, Quakeress*, 97. Barry Levy points out that during the decades immediately before and after the American Revolution (1750–90), a period that coincided with an increased bureaucratization of the Society of Friends and a corresponding hardening of the Quaker discipline, about half of the rising generation of young Quakers was read out of meeting for marrying outside the sect or for other infractions against the faith. These were also the decades when the Society abolished slavery among its membership and began to withdraw from active participation in government (*Quakers and the American Family*, 16).

58. Clarkson, *Portraiture of Quakerism*, 1:277–78, 280, 286.

59. Benezet, *Short Account of the Religious Society of Friends*, 5.

60. Ibid., 6.

61. Mrs. J. L. Hallowell, "A Quaker Woman," 225; Pyle, "Old-Time Life in a Quaker Home," 190.

62. Bancroft, *History of the United States of America*, 1:313.

63. Ibid., 1:312, 422–23.

64. Mather, *Little Flocks Guarded Against Grievous Wolves*, 19.

65. Richard P. Hallowell, *Quaker Invasion of Massachusetts*, 72, 75.

Chapter 4. Quaker Biography in Transatlantic Context

1. Whittier, although typically remembered as a poet and abolitionist, also tried his hand at historical fiction in 1849, when Ticknor and Fields published his only work of fiction, *Leaves from Margaret Smith's Journal in the Province of Massachusetts Bay, 1678–9*, a semifictional romance of Quakers and Puritans set in Colonial Massachusetts during the witchcraft era.

2. For an excellent discussion of biographies in American print culture of the nineteenth century, see Casper, *Constructing American Lives.*

3. The classic account of the antebellum New York literary and cultural nationalist movement is Perry Miller, *The Raven and the Whale.* Edward Widmer's *Young America: The Flowering of Democracy in New York City* comprises an even more nuanced account of the personalities and politics involved in the antebellum drive for an American national literature.

4. A specialist in the history of the American Revolution, Jared Sparks also served as president of Harvard University from 1849 to 1853. The *Library of American Biography* itself was published in two series: ten (1834–38) and fifteen (1844–47) volumes, respectively.

5. Emerson's representative men are Plato, Swedenborg, Montaigne, Shakespeare, Napoleon, and Goethe.

6. His more than twenty years of itinerant bookselling led Weems on extensive travels by horse-drawn cart through early America, including the South, preaching and peddling as he went. Along with biographies of George Washington, Benjamin Franklin, William Penn, and Francis Marion, Weems also authored a number of tracts that focused on sexual morality. Another notable best seller among Weems's customers in the 1790s was his reprinted edition of the eighteenth-century English antimasturbation tract, *Onania.* Commenting on Weems's lucrative blend of moralizing and base pandering to readers, the literary historian David S. Reynolds concludes that his "tracts display a new amoral *exploitation* by a bookseller who was attentive above all to salability" (*Beneath the American Renaissance,* 60; emphasis in original).

7. For a more thorough discussion of the process by which nineteenth-century Americans used reading to form political allegiances and national identities, see Zboray, *Fictive People,* and Anderson, *Imagined Communities.*

8. Weems, *Life of William Penn,* 23.

9. Ibid., 26.

10. William Penn remained a popular subject for biography, as evidenced by a more reliable biography of the Quaker leader by Samuel M. Janney (1801–80), a Hicksite Quaker minister from Virginia, which he published in 1852 and which subsequently was reprinted many times. Janney, who in 1853 also published a popular biography of George Fox, drew considerable criticism from some Quakers of that era who objected to the Hicksite interpretations of

Quaker theology that he included in these biographies. The Harvard historian Jared Sparks also included George E. Ellis's excellent 1847 biography of William Penn in *The Library of American Biography*, under Sparks's general editorship.

11. Anonymous review of *Quakerism*, 337.

12. Greer, *Quakerism*, viii.

13. Ibid., xi.

14. Ibid., 31, 58.

15. Ibid., 58–59.

16. Ibid., 103–4.

17. Joseph John Gurney (1788–1847) was a banker in Norwich, England, and a prominent Quaker minister. He was the brother of Elizabeth Gurney Fry (1780–1845), a Quaker reformer whom he joined in an effort to end capital punishment and improve prison conditions. He also was the brother-in-law—through his sister Hannah—of Thomas Fowell Buxton, an antislavery crusader.

18. Anonymous review of *Quakerism*, 387.

19. Greer, *Quakerism*, 117.

20. Ibid., 250.

21. Ibid., 307.

22. "Quakerism" [*Athenaeum*], 233.

23. Tiro, "'We Wish to Do You Good,'" 355, 357.

24. Ibid., 358.

25. Background information on Thomas C. Battey in this and the following paragraphs is drawn from Alice Marriott's introduction to the 1968 reprint edition of Battey's *Life and Adventures*.

26. Ibid., ix–x.

27. Ibid., 65–66.

28. Ibid., 64.

29. Ibid., 89–90.

30. Ibid., 253–54.

31. Hales was apparently paid £800 for his appearances on behalf of Barnum, who presumably had the idea of marketing the huge Englishman as a sideshow attraction not only for his size but for his "peculiar" religion. As a teenager during the 1830s, Hales made appearances at local fairs in England, billed as "The Norfolk Giant," along with his seven-foot two-inch sister, Mary. While working for Barnum, he participated in a sham marriage to one Elizabeth Simpson, an Irish woman from County Cork who toured with the circus and whose advertised height was eight feet. Together, they were dressed in plain Quaker clothes and marketed for two years in Barnum's circus as "The English Giant Quaker and His Wife, The Giantess, The Tallest Pair in the World."

32. Qtd. in Parrington, *Main Currents in American Thought*, 2:367.

33. Spofford, "The Quaker Poet," 183.

34. Higginson, *John Greenleaf Whittier*, 2.

35. Spofford, "The Quaker Poet," 171.
36. Anonymous, *Catholic World*, 437.
37. Spofford, "The Quaker Poet," 178–79, 172.
38. "Quaker Poet's Anniversary," 2.
39. Spofford, "The Quaker Poet," 179.

Chapter 5. Representing Quakers in American Fiction

1. Hawthorne, *American Notebooks*, 225.
2. Harriet Beecher Stowe, "Immediate Emancipation: A Sketch," 222. The most recent writings to examine representations of Quaker in American literature, Glenn N. Cummings, includes an excellent discussion of the Quaker settlement section of *Uncle Tom's Cabin* ("Exercising Goodness," 134–81). See also Howard W. Hintz, *The Quaker Influence in American Literature;* Thomas Kimber, "The Treatment of Quakers as a Character in American Fiction, 1825–1925"; and Philip Keith, "The Idea of Quakerism in American Literature."
3. Just before the Civil War, Catherine Beecher reported most American women to be frail and unhealthy but made an exception in the case of certain Quaker women: "The proportion of the sick and delicate to those who were strong and well was, in the majority of cases, a melancholy story. [But] . . . a lady from a country-town, not far from Philadelphia, gave an account showing eight out of ten perfectly healthy, and the other two were not much out of health. On inquiry, I found that this was a Quaker settlement, and most of the healthy ones were Quakers" (*Letters to the People on Health and Happiness*, 132). Barry Levy concludes that as early as the seventeenth century Quakers were more fertile, more happily married, and healthier than their non-Quaker counterparts. In Quaker families, "Surveillance, voluntary marriage, spiritualized love, [and] closeness in age led to higher fertility and better health" (*Quakers and the American Family*, 88). Not all observers, however, reached the same conclusion about Quaker health. After a visit to Philadelphia and other mid-Atlantic states with large Quaker populations, the eighteenth-century French journalist J.-P. Brissot de Warville concluded that while moderate diets, comfortable attire, and temperance gave Quaker women certain advantages in health, they were substantially less physically active than their non-Quaker counterparts: "To preserve good health, a female should have the gaiety of a woman of fashion, with the prudence and precaution of a Quaker" (*New travels*, 1:298).
4. For a detailed account of American Quaker dress, see Leanna Lee-Whitman, "Silks and Simplicity." Lee-Whitman also traces the transformation in Quaker apparel from the eighteenth century, when "Quakers often wore stylish clothing in gay colors," to the nineteenth century, when Quakers typically adopted "the standard drab uniform" that has so often been associated with the "plain" sect.

5. Stowe, *Uncle Tom's Cabin*, 215, 223, 224. Henrietta Buckmaster has speculated that Stowe's characters Rachel and Simeon Halliday were in fact based upon the Underground Railroad activists Levi and Catherine Coffin, Indiana Quakers who worked for decades on behalf of escaping slaves and whom Stowe would have known after their move to Cincinnati in 1847 (*Let My People Go*, 90). The benevolent, aging, and wise Quakeress is seen frequently in American fiction of the second half of the nineteenth century, possibly as a result of Stowe's success in depicting Friends in *Uncle Tom's Cabin*. Such characters may be seen in works as Mrs. Joseph H. Hanaford's *Lucretia, the Quakeress* (1853) and Osgood Bradbury's *The Fair Quakeress* (1857), in which the wisdom of an elderly Quaker aunt serves as mentor and matchmaker for a young woman torn between two potential suitors.

6. Betty Jean Steele, "Quaker Characters in Selected American Novels," 123.

7. Jack Marietta, *Reform of American Quakerism*, provides the most complete account of late-eighteenth-century bureaucratic restructuring of the Society of Friends. For a helpful brief summary of the institutional development of the Quaker religion in America, see Butler, *Awash in a Sea of Faith*, 118–20. On the orthodox Quaker movement of the nineteenth century and its split from the Hicksite sect, see the thorough account provided in Hamm, *Transformation of American Quakerism*. For a narrower, but helpful, examination of Quaker schisms in Philadelphia since the Hicksite controversy, see, Baltzell, *Puritan Boston and Quaker Philadelphia*, 433–51.

8. Despite the kind of praise that Stowe provides for Quaker households like that of the Halliday family, and while eighteenth- and nineteenth-century Quakers were widely admired by many non-Quakers for the cohesiveness and harmony of their domestic arrangements, Barry Levy counters that for all their apparent tranquility, within the Society itself "Quakers were ambivalent about domesticity itself. They alone had experienced domesticity's moral and economic ambiguities" (*Quakers and the American Family*, 17). In spite of these qualifications about the functioning of Quaker households, however, Levy goes even farther in claiming the centrality of Quakers in establishing patterns of morality-based domesticity in America and argues that "the Pennsylvania Quakers originated and established the institution of the morally self-sufficient household in American society" (22).

9. Plumley, *Lays of Quakerdom*, 9.

10. In a recent study of the radical Christian tradition in American writing, *Identifying the Image of God* (2002), Dan McKanan writes of Quakers in nineteenth-century fiction as examples of "liberal interlopers" who "model a practice of liberal faith and devotion independent of violent social structures" (McKanan, 34. For a nuanced discussion of "the liberal encounter with Puritan violence" in fiction of the nineteenth century, see ibid., 11–45).

11. Elizabeth B. Lester, *Quakers: A Tale*, 10, 147.

12. Born in Maine to Quaker parents but trained as a boxer and fencer, Neal had been read out of Friends meeting for brawling.

13. Neal, *Rachel Dyer*, 148, 226.

14. Ibid., 36.

15. Brian Harding argues that Fuller's sympathy for Quaker ideas was conditioned largely through the influence of the renowned Unitarian minister William Ellery Channing, whom Fuller cited in *Woman in the Nineteenth Century* as insisting that women were "souls . . . each of which had a destiny of its own . . . whose leading it must follow, guided by the light of a private conscience" (qtd. in Harding, introduction to *The Scarlet Letter*, by Nathaniel Hawthorne, xxvii).

16. Stowe, "Immediate Emancipation: A Sketch." For analysis of the Stowe/Grimké encounter, see Joan E. Hedrick, *Harriet Beecher Stowe*, 65–66; Fuller, *Woman in the Nineteenth Century*, 24. Fuller also advances the example of "the pure and gentle Quaker poetess" Mary Hewitt, who along with her husband, William, had attained a level of literary accomplishment that had earned her a place "among the constellation of distinguished English-women" (67).

17. On Emerson's study of Quakerism, see F. B. Tolles, "Emerson and Quakerism" and M. C. Turpie, "A Quaker Source for Emerson's Sermon." Turpie finds notable Quaker influence on Emerson's important sermon and points to Thomas Clarkson's historical summary of Quaker views on the Christian practice of the Lord's Supper. Emerson had borrowed Clarkson's volumes from the Boston Athenaeum library and studied them carefully while traveling in the White Mountains before delivering the Lord's Supper sermon (97–98).

18. Emerson, "George Fox," 165.

19. David Green Haskins, *Ralph Waldo Emerson: His Maternal Ancestors, with Some Reminiscences of Him* (1886), qtd. in Tolles, "Emerson and Quakerism," 142.

20. Child, *Letters*, 28.

21. Child, "The Catholic and the Quaker," 142.

22. Canby, *Classic Americans*, 115. Canby, himself born into a Quaker family, nominates a possible exception to the unfortunate fate of Quakers in fiction by citing James Fenimore Cooper's Natty Bumpo (in Leatherstocking Tales) as embodying the core of the Quaker ethos that Cooper had inherited from his own Quaker father: "It is Quaker morality, Quaker spirituality, and Natty is the best Quaker in American literature" (114). Canby's contribution to Quaker fiction was *Our House* (1919), the story of an American Quaker family at the end of the nineteenth century, which detailed the struggle of a son to become a successful writer.

23. Rebecca Harding Davis, *Life in the Iron Mills*. Whitman qtd. in David S. Reynolds, *Walt Whitman*, 219, and Gary Schmidgall, *Intimate with Walt*, 24. For a detailed account of Quakerism's impact on Whitman, see Lawrence Templin, "The Quaker Influence on Walt Whitman."

24. Lee-Whitman, "Silks and Simplicity," 9. The sketches in Sarah M. H. Gardner's *Quaker Idyls*, document the changes in Quaker clothing from the perspective of a late-nineteenth-century Quaker woman. For background on evolving Quaker attitudes toward portraiture in the nineteenth century, see Beck, "'A Witness Lasting, Faithful, True.'"

25. Poor relief had been a staple of Anglo-American Quaker doctrine since the mid-seventeenth century. As Auguste Jorns observes, "The Quakers in England laid the foundations for modern social work long before the abortive character of public poor relief as actually practiced had been recognized at all" (*Quakers as Pioneers in Social Work*, 235).

26. Iconic Quakeresses can be found in myriad nineteenth-century texts, and frequently they appear to have been based upon impressions of abolitionist Quaker women such as the famed Lucretia Mott. Mott had an enormous impact on those, like Frederick Douglass, who had the opportunity to hear her preaching at an antislavery meeting: "[Lucretia Mott] was attired in the usual Quaker dress, free from startling colors, plain, rich, elegant, and without superfluity—the very sight of her, a sermon. In a few moments after she began to speak, I saw before me no more a woman, but a glorified presence, bearing a message of light and love from the Infinite to a benighted and strangely wandering world, straying away from the paths of truth and justice into the wilderness of pride and selfishness, where peace is lost and true happiness is sought in vain" (Douglass, *Life and Times*, 904). Douglass further acknowledged in his final autobiography the role of Quakers Ann Richardson and Ellen Richardson in raising the funds to purchase of his freedom (at a cost of $750) after his escape from slavery (987).

27. Davis, *Life in the Iron Mills*, 63. Davis's later novel *Waiting for the Verdict* (1867) also presents Quakers in a positive light and as progressive voices for racial conciliation.

28. "Recent Novels," 114.

29. Lee's distaste for Quakerism comes as little surprise, when her link to New England Puritanism is understood. A native of Portsmouth, New Hampshire, she was a descendant of the seventeenth-century poet and staunch Puritan Ann Bradstreet (Steele, "Quaker Characters," 55–56). Lawrence Buell, *New England Literary Culture*, 249–50.

30. Fischer, *Albion's Seed*, 422–23. On the broader Quaker influence on the development of American social and political values, see the extended discussion in Fischer, 419–603.

31. Melville, *White-Jacket*, 3, 65.

32. Goering, "'To Obey, Rebelling,'" 519.

33. Melville, *Moby-Dick*, 105.

34. Ibid. For an extended discussion of Melville's use of the Quaker motif in *Moby-Dick*, see Goering, "'To Obey, Rebelling.'"

35. Melville, *Moby-Dick*, 82.

36. After its publication in Philadelphia in 1837, *Nick of the Woods* eventually appeared in at least twenty editions. A year before the book was published, Bird had already satirized the Quaker call to benevolent social activism and philanthropy in his novel *Sheppard Lee* (1836).

37. Bird, *Nick of the Woods*, 131–32, 9.

38. Ibid., 386.

39. Bayard Taylor, *Story of Kennett*, 79. As Steele has pointed out, in *The Gilded Age*, Mark Twain and Charles Dudley Warner include a romantic subplot involving a young Quakeress named Ruth Bolton, and she too chafes at the strictures of "her tradition-bound life"; like S. Weir Mitchell's Hugh Wynne, Ruth's father had been expelled from the Quaker Meeting for not following Quaker customs (Steele, "Quaker Characters," 709; Twain and Warner, *The Gilded Age*, 157).

40. Wermuth, *Bayard Taylor*, 96.

41. Occasionally, practicing Quakers produced their own fictionalized accounts of missionary work and activism, as in Nellie Blessing-Eyster's *Chinese Quaker*, which details Quaker missionary work in San Francisco's Chinatown during the 1880s.

42. Trowbridge, *Cudjo's Cave*, 446–48, 502.

43. Louisa May Alcott, *Work*, 11, 221.

44. Ibid., 266, 386, 442.

45. Caulfield's *Quakers in Fiction* lists several hundred twentieth-century English and American novels with Quaker themes and characters, along with an equal number of juvenile novels concerned with Quaker life.

46. When state militias sent out their calls for help during the American Revolution, a number of Quakers—like the fictional Hugh Wynne—responded to their call to assist in the war against the British and were subsequently expelled from the main body of the Quaker religion. In Philadelphia, a group of approximately two hundred Free Quakers founded their own meetinghouse in Philadelphia, which operated until 1834, when the meetinghouse was closed by its last two members, one of whom was the flag maker Betsy Ross.

47. Steele, "Quaker Characters," 50–51.

48. Mitchell had already written extensively about the "problem" of Quakerism in an earlier novel, *Hephzibah Guinness*, in which he presented a forbiddingly austere Quakeress whose arrogance and rigidity as guardian of a beautiful sixteen-year-old girl cause the younger woman to seek life beyond the Quaker meeting (see Steele, "Quaker Characters," 103–5, for a more detailed discussion of this novel). N. P. Runyon's *Quaker Scout*, which centers on a heroic New York soldier during the Civil War, provides yet another fictional treatment of wartime valor by a fighting Quaker. Its hero, Ralph Dinsmore, had been inspired by a Quaker household's piety and virtue just before he had enlisted in the Northern army.

49. Dreiser's *Bulwark* relied heavily on, and borrowed from, a series of religious memoirs written by a prominent Philadelphia Quaker and historian of the Friends, Rufus M. Jones, who published these volumes between 1902 and 1934. Dreiser met Jones in late 1938, and it appears that Dreiser may have read the first of Jones's books, *A Boy's Religion from Memory* (1902), as early as 1902/3, the period after the publication of *Sister Carrie* when Dreiser was living in Philadelphia (Friedrich, "A Major Influence on Theodore Dreiser's *The Bulwark*," 180–93). Friedrich also provides a list of the many books (a number of them heavily marked and annotated) related to Quakerism discovered in Dreiser's personal library, including a several of the novels discussed in this essay (182n). Finally, Friedrich provides evidence that Dreiser's crucial immersion in Woolman's *Journal* dates from his first meeting with Jones, and that a number of events in *The Bulwark* were inspired by incidents recounted in Woolman's *Journal* ("Theodore Dreiser's Debt to Woolman's *Journal*," 385–90).

50. Dreiser, *Bulwark*, 253.

51. Ibid., 185.

52. It is readily apparent that the turn to secularism that Dreiser finally resists in *The Bulwark* is a movement that Jenny Franchot has trenchantly described for religious belief in general: "Belief's transformation into pastness is, in fundamental respects, the narrative of Western culture's birth into the modern" ("Unseemly Commemoration," 39). F. O. Matthiessen, *Theodore Dreiser*, 251. Matthiessen researched his book in the years following Dreiser's death in 1945; the study was published after Matthiessen's suicide in 1951. Trilling, "Reality in America," 19, 20.

53. Qtd. in Templin, "The Quaker Influence on Walt Whitman," 168.

Chapter 6. Staging Quakerism

1. Dibdin, "The Quaker," 32.

2. Johnson and Burling, "The American Stage, 1665–1774," 77.

3. As Jason Shaffer suggests, even well after the theater was permitted to exist by order of royal decree, the colonial lawmakers themselves decided to discourage such activities. Citing the Continental Congress of 1774 from a "broad non-importation, non-consumption, and non-exportation agreement that discouraged 'every species of extravagance and dissipation, especially all horse racing, and all kinds of gaming, cock-fighting, exhibitions of shews, plays, and other expensive diversions and entertainments'" ("Making 'an Excellent Die,'" 1).

4. Boskin, *Sambo*, 72.

5. Murdock, *Triumphs of Love*, 32.

6. Ibid., 52.

7. Ibid.

8. On Longfellow's decline in popularity during the twentieth century, see Lawrence Buell's introduction to Longfellow's *Selected Poems,* vii–xxxvi. See also Irmscher, *Longfellow Redux,* for a full-scale study of Longfellow that argues for the poet's continuing importance.

9. Longfellow, *Selected Poems,* 68–69.

10. Ibid., 170–73.

11. Ibid., 212, 213.

12. Ibid., 233.

13. Ibid., 246.

14. "Dramatic Theaters," 7.

15. "Payton's Theater," 7.

16. James, *Varieties of Religious Experience,* 7.

17. This silent film was probably based on the popular Broadway play *The Quaker Girl,* starring Louise Glaum and William Desmond Taylor, which saw 240 performances at New York's Park Theater in 1911 and 1912 (Internet Broadway Database, www.ibdb.com).

18. No plot line available, but several characters are described as Quakers. Starring Dorothy Gish (http://www.friendsmedia.org/quaker-film.htm).

19. Includes a minor character named "A Quaker" and played by Malcolm Williams (http://www.friendsmedia.org/quaker-film.htm).

20. According to www.friendsmedia.org, in this film, "Marion Davies plays a Quaker girl raised by two very strict aunts. In this Pygmalion-like story Davies transforms from plain duck to lovely swan with lots of Hollywood glitz."

21. Perry, summary of *The Quack Quakers,* 5.

22. Ibid., 6–7.

23. William Ashley ("Billy") Sunday (1863–1935) had a long career as a professional baseball player before turning to temperance preaching and Christian evangelism, becoming the most famous preacher of his day. At huge revivals during the peak of his career (1914–20), he claimed to have produced tens of thousands of converts.

24. Perry, summary of *The Quack Quakers,* 7.

25. Ibid., 8.

26. Ibid.

27. This film title and date refer to the American release. In 1941, the same film had been released for British theaters under the title *Penn of Pennsylvania* (directed by Lance Comfort, original screenplay by Anatole de Grunwald; cast: William Penn [Clifford Evans], Gulielma Springelt [Deborah Kerr], Charles II [Dennis Arundell], George Fox [James Harcourt], Samuel Pepys [Henry Oscar], Admiral Penn [Charles Carson]).

28. Although this would be John Wayne's first attempt at producing a film with significant Quaker content, an earlier film Western featuring a Quaker schoolmarm, *The Lady from Cheyenne* (1941), had already appeared a few years

earlier, thus demonstrating that applying Quaker ideas to the themes of violence and lawlessness that pervade the Western genre could be both marketable and thematically useful.

29. Turner, *Frontier in American History.*

30. *High Noon*'s screenplay, written by Carl Foreman, is based on the short story "The Tin Star" by John W. Cunningham. Also prominent among the Quaker films of the period is William Wyler's popular and Oscar-winning *Friendly Persuasion* (1956), based on a sequence of short stories of the same name by the Quaker author Jessamyn West (who was, incidentally, a cousin of Richard M. Nixon, also a birthright Quaker). For a thorough discussion of the political context of *Friendly Persuasion,* whose theme is similar to that of *High Noon* in that it shows the challenges offered to Quaker belief and social values by modern culture, see Cull, "Richard Nixon and the Political Appropriation of 'Friendly Persuasion,'" 240–41.

31. Slotkin, *Gunfighter Nation,* 395.

Works Cited

Achinstein, Sharon. "Romance of the Spirit: Female Sexuality and Religious Desire in Early Modern England." *ELH* 69 (2002): 413–38.

Acts and Laws, of His Majesties Colony of Connecticut in New-England. Boston: Printed by Bartholomew Green and John Allen, 1702.

Adams, Hannah. *A Summary History of New-England, from the First Settlement at Plymouth, to the Acceptance of the Federal Constitution.* Dedham, MA: Printed for the author, by H. Mann and J. H. Adams, 1799.

Ahlstrom, Sydney. *A Religious History of the American People.* New Haven: Yale University Press, 1974.

Alcott, Louisa May. *Work.* Boston: Roberts Brothers, 1873.

Allen, Gay Wilson, and Roger Asselineau. *St. John de Crèvecoeur: The Life of an American Farmer.* New York: Viking, 1987.

Amory, Hugh, and David D. Hall, eds. *A History of the Book in America.* Vol. 1, *The Colonial Book in the Atlantic World.* Chapel Hill: University of North Carolina Press, 2000.

Anderson, Benedict. *Imagined Communities: Reflections on the Origin and Spread of Nationalism.* London: Verso, 1983.

Angel and the Badman. Directed by James Edward Grant. With John Wayne. 1947.

Anonymous. "An Ode." *New York Commercial Advertiser.* Apr. 8, 1812.

Anonymous. Review of "The Revival of Quakerism." *Edinburgh Review* 174 (July 1891): 194–220.

Anonymous. "John Greenleaf Whittier." Review of *The Complete Poetical Works of John Greenleaf Whittier* (1876). *Catholic World* 24 (Jan. 1877): 433–44.

Appelbaum, Patricia. "Quakers." *Encyclopedia of New England.* Edited by Burt Feintuch and David H. Watters. New Haven: Yale University Press, 2005.

Ashbridge, Elizabeth. *Some Account of the Early Part of the Life of Elizabeth Ashbridge: Who Died, in the Truth's service, at the House of Robert Lecky, in the County of Carlow, Ireland, the 16th of 5th month, 1755 / Written by Herself.* 1774. Philadelphia: Printed for Benjamin and Thomas Kite, 1807.

Ayoub, Raymond. "The Persecution of 'An Innocent People' in Seventeenth-Century England." *Quaker Studies* 10.1 (2005): 46–66.

Baker, Naomi. "'Men of Our Own Nation': Gender, Race, and the Other in Early Modern Quaker Writing." *Literature and History*, 3rd ser., 10 (2001): 1–25.

Baltzell, E. Digby. *Puritan Boston and Quaker Philadelphia: Two Protestant Ethics and the Spirit of Class Authority and Leadership.* New York: The Free Press, 1979.

Bancroft, George. *History of the United States of America: From the Discovery of the Continent.* 6 vols. New York: D. Appleton and Company, 1885.

Banner, Lois W. *American Beauty.* New York: Alfred A. Knopf, 1983.

Barbour, Hugh, and Arthur O. Roberts. *Early Quaker Writings, 1650–1700.* Grand Rapids, MI: William B. Eerdmans, 1973.

Barclay, A. R. "The Advices of the Elders at Balby." *Letters & c. of Early Friends.* London, 1841.

Barclay, Robert. *An Apology for the True Christian Divinity.* [1676, Latin]. 5th ed. in English. London: T. Sowle, 1703.

———. *The Anarchy of the Ranters and Other Libertines, the Hierarchy of the Romanists and Other Pretended Churches, Equally Refused and Refuted, in a Two-fold Apology for the . . . Quakers.* 1676. London: T. Sowle, 1717.

Barnard, Ella Kent. *Dorothy Payne, Quakeress: A Side-Light upon the Career of "Dolley" Madison.* Philadelphia: Ferris and Leach, 1909.

Bartram, William. *The Travels of William Bartram.* 1791. Naturalist's edition. Edited by Francis Harper. Athens: University Georgia Press, 1998.

Battey, Thomas C. *The Life and Adventures of a Quaker among the Indians.* 1875. Edited by Alice Marriott. Norman: University of Oklahoma Press, 1968.

Beach, Rebecca Gibbons. *The Puritan and the Quaker: A Story of Colonial Times.* New York: G. P. Putnam, 1879.

Beauty's Worth. Directed by Robert G. Vignola. With Marion Davies, Forrest Stanley, and June Elvidge. 1922.

Beck, Benjamin S. "'A Witness Lasting, Faithful, True': The Impact of Photography on Quaker Attitudes to Portraiture." http://web.ukonline.co.uk/benjaminbeck/dissertation/ointroduction.htm. Accessed June 6, 2005.

Beebe, Ralph K. *A Garden of the Lord: A History of Oregon Yearly Meeting of Friends Church.* Portland, OR: Barclay Press, 1968.

Beecher, Catharine E. *Letters to the People on Health and Happiness.* New York: Arno Press and the New York Times, 1855.

Benezet, Anthony. *A Short Account of the Religious Society of Friends.* 1780. Philadelphia: Merritt for Kimber and Conrad, 1814.

———. *Observations on the Inslaving, Importing, and Purchasing of Negroes: With Some Advice Thereon, Extracted from the Epistle of the Yearly-Meeting of the People Called Quakers, Held at London in the Year 1748.* Germantown, PA: Printed by C. Sower, 1760.

———. *A Short Account of that Part of Africa, Inhabited by the Negroes: With Respect to the Fertility of the Country, the Good Disposition of Many of the Natives, with the Manner by which the Slave Trade Is Carried on, etc.* Philadelphia: Printed by W. Dunlap, 1762.

———. *Some Observations on the Situation, Disposition and Character of the Indian Natives of This Continent.* Philadelphia: Joseph Crukshank, 1784.

Bercovitch, Sacvan. *The Puritan Origins of the American Self.* New Haven: Yale University Press, 1975.

———. "The Ritual of Consensus." In *The Rites of Assent: Transformations in the Symbolic Construction of America*, 29–67. New York: Routledge, 1993.

Besse, Joseph. *Collection of the Sufferings of the People Called Quakers.* 1733, 1738. 2 vols. London, 1753.

Bird, Robert Montgomery. *Nick of the Woods; or The Jibbenainosay. A Tale of Kentucky.* 1837. Edited by Mark Van Doren. New York: Macy-Masius, The Vanguard Press, 1928.

———. *Sheppard Lee.* New York: Harper and Brothers, 1836.

Bishop, George. *New England Judged, by the Spirit of the Lord.* 1661. 2 vols. London: T. Sowle, 1703.

Blessing-Eyster, Nellie. *A Chinese Quaker: An Unfictitious Novel.* New York: Fleming H. Revell Company, 1902.

Bond, Samson. *A Publick Tryal of the Quakers in Barmudas upon the First Day of May, 1678.* Boston in New England: Printed by Samuel Green, upon Assignment of Samuel Sewall, 1682.

Boorstin, Daniel J. *The Americans: The Colonial Experience.* New York: Vintage Books, 1964.

Boskin, Joseph. *Sambo: The Rise and Demise of an American Jester.* New York: Oxford University Press, 1986.

Boswell, Samuel. *Life of Johnson.* 1791. 3rd rev. ed. . Edited by Pat Rogers. Oxford: Oxford University Press.

Bradbury, Osgood. *The Fair Quakeress, or the Perjured Lawyer.* New York: R. M. De Witt, 1857.

Braithwaite, William C. *The Beginnings of Quakerism.* London: Macmillan, 1912.

———. *The Second Period of Quakerism.* London: Macmillan, 1919.

Brissot de Warville, Jacques-Pierre. *New travels in the United States of America, performed in 1788. Containing the latest and most accurate observations.* Translated by Joel Barlow. 2 vols. London: J. S. Jordan, 1794.

Brooks, Joanna. "Held Captive by the Irish: Quaker Captivity Narratives in Frontier Pennsylvania." *New Hibernia Review* 8.3 (Autumn 2004): 31–46.

Buckmaster, Henrietta. *Let My People Go: The Story of the Underground Railroad and the Growth of the Abolitionist Movement.* New York: Harper and Brothers, 1941.

Budd, Thomas. *A Testimony and caution to Such as Do make a Profession of Truth Who Are in Scorn Called Quakers: and More Especially Such as Who Profess to Be Ministers of the Gospel of Peace, That They Should Not Be Concerned in Worldly Government.* [Philadelphia: s.n., 1692].

Buell, Lawrence. *New England Literary Culture: From Revolution through Renaissance.* Cambridge: Cambridge University Press, 1986.

Bugg, Francis. *The Great Mystery of the Little Whore Unfolded, and Her Witchcrafts . . . Discovered. Whereby the Quakers Are Once More Set in Their True Light. By Way of Dialogue between First, a Church of England Man. Secondly, a Protestant Dissenter. Thirdly, a Right-Bred Quaker* London: Printed for the Author, and Sold by Tho. Bennet, R. Wilkins, Edw. Evets; and Ralph Smith, 1705.

——. *Goliath's Head Cut Off with His Own Sword, and the Quakers Routed by Their Own Weapons: by a Dialogue Tripartite. . . . Whereby the Great Mystery of the Little Whore Is Farther Unfolded.* London: Printed for the Author, and Sold by R. Wilkin, J. Knapton, W. Carter; and R. Smith, 1708.

Burroughs, Caroline M. "Quaker Character." *Ladies Repository* 3.11 (1844): 321–25.

Butler, Jon. *Awash in a Sea of Faith: Christianizing the American People.* Cambridge, MA: Harvard University Press, 1990.

Cadbury, Henry J. "Defoe, Bugg and the Quakers." *Journal of Friends Historical Society* 42: 70–72.

——. "Negro Membership in the Society of Friends." *Journal of Negro History* 21.2 (1936): 151–213.

Canby, Henry Seidel. *Classic Americans: A Study of Eminent American Writers from Irving to Whitman, with an Introductory Survey of the Colonial Background of Our National Literature.* New York: Harcourt, Brace and Company, 1931.

——. *Our House.* New York: Macmillan, 1919.

Carlson, David. "Farmer versus Lawyer: Crèvecoeur's Letters and the Liberal Subject." *Early American Literature* 38 (2003): 257–79.

Casper, Scott E. *Constructing American Lives: Biography and Culture in Nineteenth-Century America.* Chapel Hill: University of North Carolina Press, 1999.

Caulfield, Anna Breiner. *Quakers in Fiction: An Annotated Bibliography.* Northampton, MA: Pittenbruach Press, 1993.

Centlivre, Susanna. *A Bold Stroke for a Wife.* London, 1718.

Chauncy, Charles. "Enthusiasm Described and Caution'd Against." In *The Great Awakening: Documents Illustrating the Crisis and Its Consequences,* edited by Alan Heimert and Perry Miller, 228–56. Indianapolis: Bobbs-Merrill, 1967.

Child, Lydia Maria. *The Letters of Lydia Maria Child.* Introduction by John Greenleaf Whittier. Appendix by Wendell Phillips. Boston: Houghton, Mifflin, 1883.

——. *Isaac T. Hopper: A True Life.* New York: Dodd, Mead and Company, 1853.

Chu, Jonathan M. *Neighbors, Friends, or Madmen: The Puritan Adjustment to Quakerism in Seventeenth-Century Massachusetts Bay.* Westport, CT: Greenwood, 1985.

Clark, Charles Heber (Max Adeler). *The Quakeress: A Tale.* Philadelphia: John C. Winston, 1905.

Clarkson, Thomas. *A Portraiture of Quakerism. Taken from a View of the Education and Discipline, Social Manners, Civil and Political Economy, Religious Principles and Character of the Society of Friends.* 3 vols. New York: Samuel Stansbury, 1806.

———. *An Essay on the Slavery and Commerce of the Human Species, Particularly the African. Translated from a Latin Dissertation, Which Was Honoured with the First Prize in the University of Cambridge, for the Year 1785, with Additions.* Dublin: P. Byrne and W. Porter, 1786.

———. *The History of the Rise, Progress, and Accomplishment of the Abolition of the African Slave Trade by the British Parliament.* New York: John Taylor, 1836.

Cohn, Norman. *The Pursuit of the Millennium: Revolutionary Millenarians and Mystical Anarchists of the Middle Ages.* 1961. Rev. ed. Oxford: Oxford University Press, 1981.

The Courageous Mr. Penn. Directed by Lance Comfort. Screenplay by Anatole de Grunwald. With Clifford Evans and Deborah Kerr. 1942.

Crabtree, Sarah. "'A Beautiful and Practical Lesson of Jurisprudence': The Transatlantic Quaker Ministry in an Age of Revolution." *Radical History Review* 99 (Fall 2007): 51–79.

Crèvecoeur, J. Hector St. John de. *Letters from an American Farmer.* Rev. ed. 1783. Edited by Susan Manning. London: Oxford University Press, 1997.

———. *More Letters from the American Farmer: An Edition of the Essays in English Left Unpublished by Crèvecoeur.* Edited by Dennis D. Moore. Athens: University of Georgia Press, 1995.

Croese, Gerard. *General History of the Quakers, Containing The Lives, Tenents, Sufferings, Tryals, Speeches, and Letters Of All the Most Eminent Quakers, Both Men and Women; From the First Rise of That Sect, Down to This Present Time. Collected from Manuscripts, &c. A Work Never Attempted Before in English. To Which Is Added, A Letter Writ by George Keith, and Sent by Him to the Author of This Book: Containing a Vindication of Himself, and Several Remarks on This History.* London: Printed for John Dunton, 1696.

Crothers, A. Glenn. "Quaker Merchants and Slavery in Early National Alexandria, Virginia: The Ordeal of William Hartshorne." *Journal of the Early Republic* 25 (Spring 2005): 47–77.

Cull, Nicholas J. "Richard Nixon and the Political Appropriation of 'Friendly Persuasion.'" *Historical Journal of Film, Radio and Television* 19 (June 1999): 239–46.

Cummings, Glenn Nelson. "Exercising Goodness: The Antislavery Quaker in American Writing, 1774–1865." PhD diss., University of Virginia, 1996.

Damrosch, Leo. *The Sorrows of the Quaker Jesus: James Nayler and the Puritan Crackdown on the Free Spirit.* Cambridge, MA: Harvard University Press, 1996.

Dandelion, Pink, ed. *The Creation of Quaker Theory: Insider Perspectives.* Burlington, VT: Ashgate, 2004.

——. *An Introduction to Quakerism.* Cambridge: Cambridge University Press, 2007.

Darnton, Robert. "The Grub Street Style of Revolution: J.-P. Brissot, Police Spy." *Journal of Modern History* 40 (1968): 301–27.

Davis, Rebecca Harding. *Life in the Iron Mills and Other Stories.* 1861. Edited by Tillie Olson. New York: The Feminist Press at the City University of New York, 1972.

——. *Waiting for the Verdict.* 1867. Upper Saddle River, NJ: The Gregg Press, 1968.

——. *Dallas Galbraith.* Philadelphia: J. B. Lippincott, 1868.

Defoe, Daniel. *The Life, Adventures and Piracies of the Famous Captain Singleton.* 1720. Introduction by James Sutherland. London: Dent, 1963.

Dibdin, Charles. *The Quaker: A Comic Opera in Two Acts as Performed at the Theatre in Boston.* Boston: Printed by P. Edes and S. Etheridge, for William P. Blake, no. 59, Cornhill, and William T. Clap, no. 90, Newbury-Street, 1794.

Douglass, Frederick. *My Bondage and My Freedom.* 1855. In *Autobiographies,* 103–452. Edited by Henry Louis Gates. New York: Library of America, 1996.

——. *The Life and Times of Frederick Douglass.* 1893. In *Autobiographies,* 453–1048. Edited by Henry Louis Gates. New York: Library of America, 1996.

[Dove, David James]. *The Quaker Unmask'd; or, Plain Truth: Humbly address'd to the Consideration of All the Freemen of Pennsylvania.* 2nd ed. Philadelphia: Printed by Andrew Steuart [*sic*], in Second Street, 1764.

Down to the Sea in Ships. Directed by Elmer Clifton. With Raymond McKee and Clara Bow. New Bedford: The Whaling Film Corporation, 1922.

Drinker, Elizabeth Sandwith. *Extracts from the Diary of Elizabeth Drinker.* Edited by Henry D. Biddle. Philadelphia: J. B. Lippincott, 1889.

"Dramatic Theaters." *Brooklyn Eagle,* Sept. 2, 1902, 7.

Dreiser, Theodore. *The Bulwark: A Novel.* Garden City, NJ: Doubleday and Company, 1946.

Editorial. *Flake's Bulletin* (Galveston, TX). Vol. 2, no. 243, 4. Mar. 31, 1867.

Emerson, Ralph Waldo. "George Fox." *The Early Lectures of Ralph Waldo Emerson.* Vol. 1 (1833–1836), 64–82. Edited by Stephen E. Whicher and Robert E. Spiller. Cambridge, MA: Harvard University Press, 1959.

Eyster, Mrs. Nellie. "A Day among the Quakers." *Harper's New Monthly Magazine* 31 (Sept. 1870): 537–41.

Fields, James T. "The Quaker Girls." [sheet music] Composed with an accompaniment for the piano forte by J. D. Beckel. Philadelphia: T. C. Andrews, 1858.

Finke, Roger, and Rodney Starke. *The Churching of America: Winners and Losers in Our Religious Economy, 1776–1990*. New Brunswick, NJ: Rutgers University Press, 1992.

Fischer, David Hackett. *Albion's Seed: Four British Folkways in America*. New York: Oxford University Press, 1989.

Fitch, William Edwards. *Some Neglected History of North Carolina: Being an Account of the Regulators and of the Battle of Alamance, the First Battle of the American Revolution*. New York: Neale, 1905.

Fletcher, Mrs. A. "The Quaker's Daughter: Founded on Fact." *Ladies' Repository: A Monthly Periodical, Devoted to Literature, Arts, and Religion* 19.12 (1859): 712–16.

Foucault, Michel. *Discipline and Punish: The Birth of the Prison*. 1975. Translated by Alan Sheridan. New York: Vintage Books, 1977.

"The Four-Legg'd Quaker: To the Tune of the Dog and Elder's Maid, or, the Lady's Fall." [s.1.: s.n.], 1664.

Fox, George. *Some Principles of the Elect People of God Who in Scorn Are Called Quakers, For all People throughout all Christendome to Read over, and thereby their own States to Consider*. London: Printed for Robert Wilson, 1661.

———. *George Fox's Book of Miracles*. Edited by Henry J. Cadbury. Cambridge: Cambridge University Press, 1948.

———. *A Declaration from the Harmless & Innocent People of God Called Quakers Against All Sedition, Plotters & Fighters in the World, for the Removing of the Ground of Jealousie and Suspition from Both Magistrates and People in the Kingdome Concerning Wars and Fightings*. London, 1660.

Fox, Margaret Askew Fell. *A Brief Collection of Remarkable Passages and Occurrences Relating to the Birth, Education, Life, Conversion, Travels, Services, . . .* London: J. Sowle, 1710.

Franchot, Jenny. "Unseemly Commemoration: Religion, Fragments, and the Icon." In *Religion and Cultural Studies*, edited by Susan L. Mizruchi, 38–55. Princeton: Princeton University Press, 2001.

———. "Invisible Domain: Religion and American Literary Studies." *American Literature* 67 (1995): 833–42.

Franklin, Benjamin. *The Autobiography of Benjamin Franklin*. Edited by Leonard W. Labaree et al. 2nd ed. New Haven: Yale University Press, 2003.

Friedrich, Gerhard. "Theodore Dreiser's Debt to Woolman's *Journal*." *American Quarterly* 7 (Winter 1955): 385–92.

———. "A Major Influence on Theodore Dreiser's *The Bulwark*." *American Literature* 29 (May 1957): 180–93.

Frith, Francis. *The Quaker Ideal*. London: Edward Hicks, Junior, 1894.

Fuller, S. Margaret. *Woman in the Nineteenth Century*. 1845. Facsimile edition with textual apparatus by Joel Myerson. Columbia: University of South Carolina Press, 1980.

Gardner, Sarah M. H. *Quaker Idyls.* New York: Henry Holt and Company, 1884.

Garrison, William Lloyd. "Free Produce among the Quakers." *Atlantic Monthly* 22, no. 132 (Oct. 1868): 485–94.

Gaskill, Malcolm. *Witchfinders: A Seventeenth-Century English Tragedy.* London: John Murray, 2005.

Gay, Peter. *The Enlightenment: An Interpretation.* Vol. 2, *The Science of Freedom.* New York: Alfred A. Knopf, 1969.

Gerona, Carla. *Night Journeys: The Power of Dreams in Transatlantic Quaker Culture.* Charlottesville: University of Virginia Press, 2004.

Gill, Catie. *Women in the Seventeenth-Century Quaker Community: A Literary Study of Political Identities, 1650–1700.* London: Ashgate, 2005.

Goering, Wynn M. "'To Obey, Rebelling': The Quaker Dilemma in *Moby-Dick.*" *New England Quarterly* 54 (1981): 519–38.

Gough, John. *A History of the People Called Quakers. From Their First Rise to the Present Time, and From the Writings of That People.* 4 vols. Dublin: Robert Jackson, 1789.

Grabo, Norman S. "Crèvecoeur's American: Beginning the World Anew." *William and Mary Quarterly,* 3rd ser., 48 (Apr. 1991): 159–72.

Green, James N. "The Book Trade in the Middle Colonies, 1680–1720." In *The Colonial Book in the Atlantic World,* edited by Amory and Hall, 199–223. Vol. 1 of *A History of the Book in America.* Chapel Hill: University of North Carolina Press, 2000.

Green, John Richard. *A Short History of the English People.* 3 vols. London: Macmillan, 1993.

Greer, Sarah D. *Quakerism; or, the Story of My Life. By a Lady Who for Forty Years Was a Member of the Society of Friends.* Philadelphia: J. W. Moore, 1852.

Greven, Philip. *The Protestant Temperament: Patterns of Child-Rearing, Religious Experience, and the Self in Early America.* 1977. Chicago: University of Chicago Press, 1978.

Gummere, Amelia Mott. *The Quaker: A Study in Costume.* Philadelphia: Ferris and Leach, 1901.

———. *Witchcraft and Quakerism: A Study in Social History.* Philadelphia: The Biddle Press, 1908.

Gura, Philip F. *Jonathan Edwards: America's Evangelical.* New York: Hill and Wang, 2005.

———. *A Glimpse of Sion's Glory: Puritan Radicalism in New England, 1620–1660.* Middletown, CT: Wesleyan University Press, 1986.

Hales, Robert B. *Memoirs of Robert Hales: The English Quaker Giant, and His Wife, the Giantess, the Tallest and Largest Pair in the World, Written by Himself.* New York: [s.n.], 1849.

Hall, David D., ed. *Lived Religion in America.* Princeton: Princeton University Press, 1997.

———. *Worlds of Wonder, Days of Judgment*. New York: Knopf, 1989.

Hall, David J. "The Study of Eighteenth-Century English Quakerism: From Rufus Jones to Larry Ingle." *Quaker Studies* 5.2 (2001): 105–19.

Hallowell, Mrs. J. L. "A Quaker Woman." *Atlantic Monthly* 30 (Aug. 1872): 220–25.

Hallowell, Richard P. *The Quaker Invasion of Massachusetts*. 2nd ed. Boston: Houghton, Mifflin and Company, 1883.

Hamm, Thomas D. *The Transformation of American Quakerism: Orthodox Friends, 1800–1907*. Bloomington: Indiana University Press, 1988.

———. *The Quakers in America*. New York: Columbia University Press, 2003.

———. "George Fox and the Politics of Late Nineteenth Century Quaker Historiography." In *The Creation of Quaker Theory: Insider Perspectives*, edited by Pink Dandelion. Burlington, VT: Ashgate, 2004.

Hamm, Thomas D., Margaret Marconi, Gretchen Kleinhen Salinas, and Benjamin Whitman. "The Decline of Quaker Pacifism in the Twentieth Century: Indiana Yearly Meeting of Friends as a Case Study." *Indiana Magazine of History* 96.1 (2000): 44–71.

Hanaford, Mrs. Joseph H. *Lucretia, the Quakeress, or Principle Triumphant*. Boston: Buffum, 1853.

Hancock, John. *Reasons for Withdrawing from Society with the People Called Quakers*. New York: Printed and Sold by G. and R. Waite, 1801.

Harding, Brian. Introduction. Nathaniel Hawthorne, *The Scarlet Letter*. Oxford: Oxford University Press, 1990.

Harpham, Geoffrey Galt. *The Ascetic Imperative in Culture and Criticism*. Chicago: University of Chicago Press, 1987.

Hawthorne, Nathaniel. *The Gentle Boy: A Thrice-Told Tale*. Boston: Weeks, Jordan and Co., 1839.

———. *The House of Seven Gables and The Snow-Image and Other Twice-Told Tales*. 1851. Boston: Houghton Mifflin, 1883.

———. *The American Notebooks*. Edited by Randall Stewart. New Haven: Yale University Press, 1932.

Hedrick, Joan E. *Harriet Beecher Stowe: A Life*. New York: Oxford University Press, 1994.

Hentz, Caroline Lee. *The Planter's Northern Bride*. Philadelphia: T. D. Peterson, 1854.

Heyd, Michael. "The Reaction to Enthusiasm in the Seventeenth Century: Towards an Integrative Approach." *Journal of Modern History* 53.2 (June 1981): 258–80.

Heyrman, Christine Leigh. *Commerce and Culture: The Maritime Communities of Colonial Massachusetts, 1690–1750*. New York: W. W. Norton, 1984.

Higginson, Thomas Wentworth. *John Greenleaf Whittier*. New York: Macmillan, 1902.

High Noon. Directed by Fred Zinnemann. With Gary Cooper and Grace Kelley. 1952. Fiftieth Anniversary Collector's Edition DVD, 2002.

Hill, Christopher. *The World Turned Upside Down: Radical Ideas during the English Revolution*. London: Penguin, 1972,

Hintz, Howard W. *The Quaker Influence in American Literature*. 1940. Port Washington, NY: Kennikat Press, 1965.

Hochschild, Adam. *Bury the Chains: Prophets and Rebels in the Fight to Free an Empire's Slaves*. Boston: Houghton Mifflin, 2005.

Holifield, E. Brooks. *Theology in America: Christian Thought from the Age of the Puritans to the Civil War*. New Haven: Yale University Press, 2003.

Hopper, Isaac T. *Kidnappers in Philadelphia: Isaac Hopper's Tales of Oppression, 1780–1843*. Edited by Daniel E. Meaders. New York: Garland Publishing, 1994,

Hoskens, Jane. *The Life and Spiritual Sufferings of That Faithful Servant of Christ Jane Hoskens, a Public Preacher Among the People Called Quakers*. Philadelphia: William Evitt, 1771.

Husband, Hermon. "Some Remarks on Religion." In *The Great Awakening: Documents Illustrating the Crisis and Its Consequences*, edited by Alan Heimert and Perry Miller, 636–54. Indianapolis: Bobbs-Merrill, 1967.

——. *Some Remarks on Religion, With the Author's Experience in Pursuit Thereof, For the Consideration of All People, Being the Real Truth of What Happened, Simply Delivered, Without the Help of School-Words, or Dress of Learning*. Philadelphia: Printed by William Bradford, for the Author, 1761.

——. *The Second Part of the Naked Truth; or, Historical Account of the Actual Transactions of Quakers in their Meetings of Business*. [New Bern, NC?]: Printed for the author, 1768.

Ingle, H. Larry. *Quakers in Conflict: The Hicksite Reformation*. Knoxville: University of Tennessee Press, 1986.

Irmscher, Christoph. *Longfellow Redux*. Champaign: University of Illinois Press, 2006.

James, William. *The Varieties of Religious Experience*. 1902. Cambridge, MA: Harvard University Press, 1985.

Janney, Samuel M. *The Life of William Penn: With Selections from His Correspondence and Autobiography*. Philadelphia: Hogan, Perkins and Co., 1852.

——. *The Life of George Fox: With Dissertations of His Views Concerning the Doctrines, Testimonies, and Discipline of the Christian Church*. Philadelphia: Lippincott, 1853.

Johnson, Odai, and William J. Burling. *The American Stage, 1665–1774: A Documentary Calendar*. Madison, NJ: Fairleigh Dickinson University Press, 2001.

Jones, Rufus M. *The Quakers in the American Colonies*. New York: Russell and Russell, 1962.

——. *The Later Periods of Quakerism*. 2 vols. London: Macmillan, 1921.

——. *Spiritual Reformers of the Sixteenth and Seventeenth Centuries*. London: Macmillan, 1914.

Jorns, Auguste. *The Quakers as Pioneers in Social Work* [*Studien über die Sozialpolitik der Quäker*]. Trans. Thomas Kite Brown, Jr. New York: Macmillan, 1931.

Karlsen, Carol F. *The Devil in the Shape of a Woman: Witchcraft in Colonial New England*. 1987. New York: Vintage Books, 1989.

Keith, Philip. "The Idea of Quakerism in American Literature." PhD diss., University of Pennsylvania, 1971.

Kimber, Thomas. "The Treatment of Quakers as a Character in American Fiction, 1825–1925." PhD diss., University of Southern California, 1953.

Koch, Adrienne, ed. *Jefferson and Madison: The Great Collaboration*. New York: Oxford University Press, 1964.

"A Lady." *The Quaker. A Novel, in a Series of Letters, by a Lady*. 3 vols. London: Printed for William Lane, 1785.

Lamb, Charles. "A Quaker Meeting." *Mercury* (New Bedford, MA), Vol. 27, no. 35, 7 Mar. 1834. 1–4.

———. "A Quaker's Meeting." In *The Essays of Elia*. 1820–23. Edited by Homer Woodbridge. New York: Macmillan, 1941.

Lapsansky, Emma Jones, and Anne A. Verplanck, eds. *Quaker Aesthetics: Reflections on a Quaker Ethic in American Design and Consumption*. Philadelphia: University of Pennsylvania Press, 2003.

Loughran, Trish. "The Romance of Classlessness: A Response to Thomas Augst." *American Literary History* 19 (2007): 324–28.

Leach, Robert J., and Peter Gow. *Quaker Nantucket: The Religious Community behind the Whaling Empire*. Nantucket, MA: Mill Hill Press, 1996.

Lee, Marian [Anna Botsford Comstock]. *Confessions to a Heathen Idol*. New York: Doubleday, Page and Company, 1907.

Lee, Mary Catherine. *A Quaker Girl of Nantucket*. Boston: Houghton, Mifflin and Company, 1889.

Lee-Whitman, Leanna. "Silks and Simplicity: A Study of Quaker Dress as Depicted in Portraits, 1718–1855." PhD diss., University of Pennsylvania, 1987.

Leeds, Daniel. *News of a Trumpet Sounding in the Wilderness, or The Quakers Antient Testimony Revived, Examined and Compared with Itself, and also with Their New Doctrine, etc.* [New York]: Printed and Sold by William Bradford at the Bible in New York, 1697.

Lester, Elizabeth B. *The Quakers: A Tale*. New York: James Eastburn and Company, 1818.

Levenduski, Cristine. *Peculiar Power: A Woman Preacher in Eighteenth-Century America*. Washington, D.C.: Smithsonian Institution Press, 1996.

Levy, Barry. *Quakers and the American Family: British Settlement in the Delaware Valley*. New York: Oxford University Press, 1988.

———. "'Tender Plants': Quaker Farmers and Children in the Delaware Valley, 1681–1735." *Journal of Family History* 3 (1978): 116–35.

Longfellow, Henry Wadsworth. *Selected Poems*. Edited by Lawrence Buell. New York: Penguin, 1988.

Loughran, Trish. "The Romance of Classlessness: A Response to Thomas Augst." *American Literary History* 19.2 (2007): 324–28.

Louis, Jeanne Henriette. "The Nantucket Quakers' Message as an Alternative to Benjamin Franklin's Message to the French Revolution." *Quaker Studies* 5.1 (2000): 9–17.

Macaulay, T. B. *The History of England from the Accession of James II.* 5 vols. 1848. Philadelphia: Porter and Coates, n.d.

Mack, Phyllis. "Religion, Feminism, and the Problem of Agency: Reflections on Eighteenth-Century Quakerism." *Signs* 29 (2003): 149–77.

———. *Visionary Women: Ecstatic Prophecy in Seventeenth-Century England.* Berkeley: University of California Press, 1995.

Marietta, Jack. *The Reformation of American Quakerism.* Philadelphia: University of Pennsylvania Press, 1984.

Mather, Cotton. *Magnalia Christi Americana; or, The ecclesiastical history of New-England from its first planting in the year 1620 unto the year of Our Lord 1698, in seven books.* 1702. Edited by Thomas Robbins. Translation of the Hebrew, Greek, and Latin quotations by Lucius F. Robinson. New York: Russell and Russell, 1967.

———. *Little Flocks Guarded Against Grievous Wolves: An Address unto Those Parts of New-England Which are Most Exposed unto Assaults, from the Modern Teachers of the Mislead Quakers . . . with Just Reflections upon the Extreme Wickedness, of George Keith, Who Is the Seducer that Now Most Ravines upon the Churches in This Wilderness.* Boston: Printed by Benjamin Harris and John Allen, at the London-Coffee-House, 1691.

Matthiessen, F. O. *Theodore Dreiser.* American Men of Letters. New York: William Sloane Associates, 1951.

McKanan, Dan. *Identifying the Image of God.* New York: Oxford University Press, 2002.

Melville, Herman. *Moby-Dick, or, The Whale.* 1851. Edited by Harrison Hayford, Hershel Parker, and G. Thomas Tanselle. Evanston, IL: Northwestern-Newberry, 1988.

———. *White-Jacket, or, The World in a Man-of-War.* 1850. Edited by Harrison Hayford, Hershel Parker, and G. Thomas Tanselle. Evanston, IL: Northwestern-Newberry, 1970.

Miller, Perry. *The New England Mind: From Colony to Province.* Cambridge, MA: Harvard University Press, 1953.

———. *The Raven and the Whale: The War of Words and Wits in the Era of Poe and Melville.* New York: Harcourt, Brace, 1956.

Mitchell, S. Weir. *Hugh Wynne: Free Quaker.* 1896. Ridgewood, NJ: The Gregg Press, 1967.

———. *Hephzibah Guinness; Thee and You; and A Draft on the Bank of Spain.* Philadelphia: J. B. Lippincott, 1880.

Moore, R. Laurence. *Religious Outsiders and the Making of Americans.* New York: Oxford University Press, 1986.

Murdock, John. *The Triumphs of Love, or Happy Reconciliation.* Philadelphia: R. Folwell, 1795.

Myles, Anne G. "From Monster to Martyr: Re-Presenting Mary Dyer." *Early American Literature* 36 (2001): 1–30.

Nathans, Heather S. *Early American Theater from the Revolution to Thomas Jefferson: Into the Hands of the People.* Cambridge: Cambridge University Press, 2003.

Neal, John. *Rachel Dyer: A North American Story.* Portland, ME: Published by Shirley and Hyde, 1828. Facsimile edition. Edited by John D. Seelye. Gainesville, FL: Scholars' Facsimiles and Reprints, 1964.

Nelson, Jacquelyn S. *Indiana Quakers Confront the Civil War.* Indianapolis: Indiana Historical Society, 1991.

Norton, John. *The Heart of New England Rent at the Blasphemies of the Present Generation.* London, 1659.

O'Keefe, John. *The Young Quaker; or, the Fair American.* Boston, 1797. [AAS broadside]

"One of her descendants." *Edith, or, the Quaker's Daughter.* New York: Mason Brothers, 1856.

Paine, Thomas. *The Life and Major Writings of Thomas Paine.* Edited by Philip S. Foner. New York: The Citadel Press, 1945.

Parrington, Vernon Louis. *Main Currents in American Thought: An Interpretation of American Literature from the Beginnings to 1920.* 3 vols. New York: Harcourt, Brace and Company, 1927.

"Payton's Theater." *Brooklyn Eagle,* Sept. 11, 1900, 7.

Perry, Montayne. Summary of *The Quack Quakers* (B/W movie, 1916, Kalem Film, directed by Harry Millarde, scenario by Samuel J. Taylor, with H. L. Davenport [Peter Pinkham], Ethel Teare [Rosie Pinkham], Victor Rottam [Tom], Gus Leonard [Uncle Ezra]). *Moving Picture Stories,* July 28, vol. 8, no. 187, 5–9. www.silentera.com/archive/movPicStories/1916/.

Pestana, Carla Gardina. "Martyred by the Saints: Quaker Executions in Seventeenth-Century Massachusetts." In *Colonial Saints: Discovering the Holy in the Americas, 1500–1800,* edited by Allan Greer and Jodi Bilinkoff, 169–91. New York: Routledge, 2003.

———. "The City upon a Hill under Siege: The Puritan Perception of the Quaker Threat to Massachusetts Bay, 1656–1661." *New England Quarterly* 56 (1983): 323–53.

Peters, Kate. *Print Culture and the Early Quakers.* Cambridge: Cambridge University Press, 2005.

Pfaelzer, Jean. *Parlor Radical: Rebecca Harding Davis and the Origins of American Social Realism.* Pittsburgh: University of Pittsburgh Press, 1996.

"Philanthropos." *The Quakers Assisting to Preserve the Lives of the Indians in the Barracks, Vindicated and Proved to be Consistent with Reason, Agreeable to Our Law, Hath an Inseperable Connection with the Law of God, and Exactly Agreeable with the Principles of the People Called Quakers.* Philadelphia: Printed by Anthony Armbruster, 1764.

Philbrick, Nathaniel. "The Nantucket Sequence in Crèvecoeur's *Letters from an American Farmer.*" *New England Quarterly* 64 (1991): 414–32.

———. *Abram's Eyes: The Native American Legacy of Nantucket Island.* Nantucket Island: Mill Hill Press, 1998.

Philips, Edith. *The Good Quaker in French Legend.* Philadelphia: University of Pennsylvania Press, 1932.

"Philopatrius." *The Quaker Unmask'd; or, Plain Truth: Humbly Addres'd to the Consideration of all the Freemen of Pennsylvania.* 2nd ed. Philadelphia: Printed by Andrew Stuart, in Second Street, 1764.

Plumley, Benjamin Rush [Ruth Plumley, pseud.]. *The Lays of Quakerdom.* Reprinted from *The Knickerbocker of 1853–54–55.* Philadelphia: The Biddle Press, 1911.

Pratt, Charles E. "The Dancing Quakers: Sung by Miss Lydia Thompson and Mr. Harry Taylor. In the Burlesque of Sinbad the Sailor." New York: Ditson and Co., 1873.

Pyle, Howard. "Old-Time Life in a Quaker Town." *Harper's New Monthly Magazine* 62 (Dec. 1880–Mar. 1881): 178–90.

"Quakerism; or, the Story of My Life." [review, copied from the *Athenaeum*]. *Living Age,* vol. 30, no. 376 (Aug. 2, 1851): 233–36.

"Quakerism; or, the Story of My Life." [review, copied from the *Christian Remembrancer*]. *Living Age,* vol. 30, no. 392 (Nov. 22, 1851): 337–55.

"The Quaker of the Olden Time." *Living Age,* vol. 9, no. 133 (May 2, 1846): 225.

"The Quaker Poet's Anniversary Kept in Brooklyn." *Brooklyn Eagle,* Dec. 19, 1887, 2.

"The Quaker's Wife." *Harper's New Monthly Magazine,* vol. 9, no. 54 (Nov. 1854): 771–76.

Rath, Richard Cullen. *How Early America Sounded.* Ithaca: Cornell University Press, 2003.

"Recent Novels." *Nation* 737 (Aug. 14, 1879): 114–15.

Reisler, Marsha. "Voltaire's Quaker Letters as Strategical Truth: Altering the Reader's Structure of Perception in the Service of a Higher Vision." *Studies in Eighteenth-Century Culture* 9 (1979): 429–54.

Reynolds, David. *Walt Whitman: A Cultural Biography.* New York: Alfred A. Knopf, 1995.

———. *Beneath the American Renaissance: The Subversive Imagination in the Age of Emerson and Melville.* Cambridge, MA: Harvard University Press, 1988.

Richmond, Jerry. "Quaker Beliefs and Customs." http://www.rootsweb.com/quakers/quakerinfo.htm.

Ritner, William D. *The Rival's Revenge! or, The Lovely Quakeress, Catherine Middleton, the Skilful Gamester in Disguise.* Philadelphia: M. L. Barclay, 1854.

Rorty, Richard. *Philosophy and Social Hope.* New York: Penguin, 1999.

Rose, Jane Attridge. *Rebecca Harding Davis.* Twayne's United States Authors Series. New York: Twayne Publishers, 1993.

Rourke, Constance. *American Humor: A Study of the National Character.* 1931. New York: New York Review Books, 2004.

Runyan, David. "Types of Quaker Writings by Year: 1650–1699." In *Early Quaker Writings, 1650–1700,* edited by Hugh Barbour and Arthur O. Roberts, 567–76. Grand Rapids, MI: William B. Eerdmans, 1973.

Runyon, N. P. *The Quaker Scout.* New York: The Abbey Press, 1900.

Russell, Elbert. *The History of Quakerism.* 1942. Richmond, IN: Friends United Press, 1979.

Schmidgall, Gary. *Intimate with Walt: Selections from Whitman's Conversations with Horace Traubel, 1882–1892.* Iowa City: University of Iowa Press, 2001.

Several Laws and Orders Made at Several General Courts in the Years 1661. 1662. 1663. Printed and published by order of the General Court held at Boston the 20th of October, 1663. [Cambridge, MA: Printed by Samuel Green, 1663].

Sewel, William. *The History of the Rise, Increase, and Progress, of the Christian People Called Quakers. Intermixed with Several Remarkable Occurrences. Written Originally in Low Dutch and also Translated by Himself into English. A New Edition, to which Is Appended, An Interesting Narrative of the Sufferings of William Moore, John Philly, and Richard Seller.* First published 1717, first English edition 1722. 2 vols. Philadelphia: B. and T. Kite, 1811.

Shadwell, Charles. *The Fair Quaker of Deal; or, the Humours of the Navy. A Comedy, As It Is Acted at the Theatre-Royal in Drury Lane.* London: James Knapton, 1715.

Shaffer, Jason. "Making 'an Excellent Die': Death, Mourning, and Patriotism in the Propaganda Plays of the American Revolution." *Early American Literature* 41 (2006): 1–27.

Sievers, Julie. "Awakening the Inner Light: Elizabeth Ashbridge and the Transformation of Quaker Community." *Early American Literature* 36 (2001): 235–62.

Slotkin, Richard. *Regeneration Through Violence: The Mythology of the American Frontier, 1600–1850.* Middletown, CT: Wesleyan University Press, 1973.

Smith, Joseph. *Biblioteca Anti-Quakeriana; or, A Catalogue of Books Adverse to the Society of Friends.* London: Joseph Smith, 1873. New York: Kraus Reprint Co., 1968.

———. *A Descriptive Catalogue of Friends' Books. or Books Written by Members of the Society of Friends, Commonly Called Quakers, from Their First Rise to the Present Time, Interspersed with Critical Remarks, and Occasional Biographical Notices.* 2 vols. 1867. New York: Kraus Reprint Co., 1970.

Sobel, Mechal. *Teach Me Dreams: The Search for Self in the Revolutionary Era.* Princeton: Princeton University Press, 2000.

[Spofford, Harriet Prescott]. "The Quaker Poet." *Harper's New Monthly Magazine* 68 (1884): 171–88.

Steele, Betty Jean. "Quaker Characters in Selected American Novels, 1823–1899." PhD diss., Duke University, 1974.

Stowe, Harriet Beecher. "Immediate Emancipation: A Sketch." *New-York Evangelist*, Jan. 2, 1845.

———. *Uncle Tom's Cabin, or, Life Among the Lowly*. 1852. Edited by Ann Douglas. New York: Penguin, 1981.

Tarter, Michelle Lise. "'Go North!': The Journey towards First-Generation Friends and Their Prophecy of Celestial Flesh." In *The Creation of Quaker Theory: Insider Perspectives*, edited by Pink Dandelion, 83–98. Burlington, VT: Ashgate, 2004.

Taylor, Bayard. "The Quaker Widow." *The Poems of Bayard Taylor*. Boston: Ticknor and Fields, 1865. [Originally published in *Harper's New Monthly Magazine*, vol. 21, no. 125 (Oct. 1860): 577–80.]

———. *Hannah Thurston: A Story of American Life*. 1863. New York: G. P. Putnam's Sons, 1879.

———. *The Story of Kennett*. New York: G. P. Putnam, 1866.

Taylor, John. *An Account of Some of the Labours, Exercises, Travels and Perils, by Sea and Land, of John Taylor, of York: And Also His Deliverances by Way of Journal. . . .* London: J. Sowle, 1710.

Templin, Lawrence. "The Quaker Influence on Walt Whitman." *American Literature* 42 (May 1970): 165–80.

Thomas, Keith. *Religion and the Decline of Magic: Studies in Popular Beliefs in Sixteenth and Seventeenth Century England*. New York: Oxford University Press, 1971.

Tiro, Karim M. "'We Wish to Do You Good': The Quaker Mission to the Oneida Nation, 1790–1840." *Journal of the Early Republic* 26 (2006): 353–76.

Tocqueville, Alexis de. *Democracy in America*. 1835, 1840. Edited by J. P. Mayer. Translated by George Lawrence. Garden City, NY: Anchor Books, 1969.

Tolles, F. B. "Emerson and Quakerism." *American Literature* 10 (1938): 142–65.

Trilling, Lionel. "Reality in America." In *The Liberal Imagination*, 3–22. New York: Viking Press, 1950.

Trowbridge, John Townsend. *Cudjo's Cave*. Boston: J. E. Tilton Company, 1864. Facsimile edition. Edited by Dean Rehberger. Tuscaloosa: University of Alabama Press, 2001.

Turpie, M. C. "A Quaker Source for Emerson's Sermon on the Lord's Supper." *New England Quarterly* 17 (1944): 95–101.

Turner, Frederick Jackson. *The Frontier in American History*. 1893. New York: Henry Holt and Company, 1920. http://xroads.virginia.edu/~HYPER/TURNER/home.html.

Twain, Mark, and Charles D. Warner. *The Gilded Age*. 1873. New York: Oxford University Press, 1996.

Tweed, Thomas A. *Crossing and Dwelling: A Theory of Religion*. Cambridge, MA: Harvard University Press, 2006.

Vaux, Roberts. *Memoirs of the Life of Anthony Benezet.* Philadelphia: James P. Parke, 1817.

Voltaire. *Philosophical Dictionary.* 1764.

Weddle, Meredith Baldwin. *Walking in the Way of Peace: Quaker Pacifism in the Seventeenth Century.* New York: Oxford University Press, 2001.

White, Andrew. "A 'Consuming' Oppression: Sugar, Cannibalism and John Woolman's 1770 Slave Dream." *Quaker History* 96.2 (Fall 2007): 1–27.

Weems, M. L. *The Life of William Penn.* Philadelphia: Uriah Hunt, 1829.

Wermuth, Paul. *Bayard Taylor.* New York: Twayne, 1973.

Whiting, John. *A Catalogue of Friends Books; Written by Many of the People, Called Quakers, From the Beginning or First Appearance of the Said People.* London: J. Sowle, 1708.

Whittier, John Greenleaf. *The Poetical Works of John Greenleaf Whittier.* Boston: Houghton, Mifflin and Company, 1892.

———. *Leaves from Margaret Smith's Journal in the Province of Massachussetts Bay, 1678–9.* Boston: Ticknor, Reed and Fields, 1849.

Widmer, Edward. *Young America: The Flowering of Democracy in New York City.* New York: Oxford University Press, 1999.

Wilkinson, Richard. *The Quaker's Wedding. A Comedy. As It Is Acted at the Theatre-Royal by His Majesty's Servants.* London: Bernard Lintot, 1723.

Wilson, Ellen Gibson. *Thomas Clarkson: A Biography.* New York: St. Martin's Press, 1990.

Wilson, John. "On Reading Mr. Clarkson's History of the Abolition of the Slave Trade." In *The Isle of Palms and Other Poems,* 357–61. Edinburgh: Printed by James Ballantyne for Longman, Hurst, Rees, Orme, and Brown, 1812.

Woodson, C[arter]. G. "Anthony Benezet." *Journal of Negro History* 2 (1917): 37–50.

Woolman, John. *The Journal of John Woolman.* Edited by J[ohn] G[reenleaf] Whittier. Boston: Osgood, 1872.

———. *The Journal and Major Essays of John Woolman.* Edited by Phillips P. Moulton. New York: Oxford University Press, 1971.

Wright, Luella M. *The Literary Life of the Early Friends.* 1932. New York: AMS Press, 1966.

Zboray, Ronald J. *A Fictive People: Antebellum Economic Development and the American Reading Public.* New York: Oxford University Press, 1993.

Ziff, Larzer. *Puritanism in America: New Culture in a New World.* New York: Viking, 1973.

Index

abolitionism: American debates, 6, 51,
133, 161–62; English, 19, 93, 107–
16, 243n38; influence of Woolman,
66, 68, 130, 238n10; oratory and
dramatic aspects, 24, 188, 192–97,
250n26; of Quakers, 18, 21, 59, 66–
77, 108, 137–38, 152, 165–73, 180,
225. *See also* Clarkson, Thomas;
Quakers; Underground Railroad;
Woolman, John
*Account of Some of the Labours, Exercises,
Travels and Perils, by Sea and Land,
of John Taylor, of York, An* (Taylor),
35, 233n41
*Account of that Part of Africa Inhabited by
Negroes, An* (Benezet), 73
Adamites, 9, 45
Adams, Hannah, 45; *A Summary History
of New-England*, 45
Adrianople, 105
African Americans, 64, 67, 71–77, 82, 126,
197, 238n5; portrayed in colonial
theater, 193–96; prohibited from at-
tending Quaker meetings, 243n25.
See also abolitionism; slavery
AFSC. *See* American Friends Service
Committee
Ahlstrom, Sydney, 31
Alamance (North Carolina), Battle of,
80. *See also* Husband, Herman
alcohol consumption, 7, 12; by Quakers,
12, 23, 32, 225. *See also* plain style;
Quakers; temperance
Alcott, Amos Bronson, 72, 178

Alcott, Louisa May, 180–81
Allard, Carel
Allen, Ethan, 131
All Souls Universalist Church (Brooklyn,
New York), 157
"All the Quakers Are Shoulder Shakers
(Down in Quaker Town)," 209
American Friends Service Committee
(AFSC), 215, 231n12; awarded
Nobel Peace Prize, 215
American Note-Books, The (Hawthorne),
158
American Renaissance (Matthiessen), 131
American Revolution. *See* Revolutionary
War
American Tragedy, An (Dreiser), 182
Amish, 25, 231n12
Anabaptists, 9
Andarko, Oklahoma, 146
Angel and the Badman (film), 25, 215–20
Anglicanism. *See* Church of England
Annapolis, Maryland, 190
Anne (queen), 106–7
Anthony, Susan B., 66
antimodernism, 7, 13, 23, 184, 203, 204,
226
antinomianism, 11, 29, 30, 36, 37, 111,
235n51. *See also* Quakers
Apology for the True Christian Divinity, An
(Barclay), 17, 55, 56, 109, 113
Apponagansett, Massachusetts, 210
Arapahoe (Native American tribe), 147
Arnold, Benedict, 46, 131
Ashbridge, Elizabeth, 15, 64, 130

Athenaeum, 143
Atlantic Monthly, 123–24, 130, 152, 178, 196
Austin, Ann, 42, 44
autobiography, 15, 53, 76, 130–45, 236n38. *See also* biography

Baltimore, Maryland, 78, 190
Bancroft, George, 59, 124, 125; admiration of Quakers, 124–25
Baptists, 9, 11, 18, 54, 163, 197
Barbados, 42, 43, 104; Quakers banished to, 232n29
Barclay, Robert, 17, 56, 57, 108; influences Quaker discipline, 112–13
Barclay, Robert (of Reigate), 241n6
Barnum's Museum, 153
Barringer, Charles, 203
Bartram, John, 82
Bartram, William, 145
Battey, Thomas, 22, 130–33, 152; *The Life and Adventures of a Quaker among the Indians,* 134, 145–51
Beach, Rebecca Gibbons, 172
Beauty's Worth (film), 25, 206
Beebe, Ralph K., 55
Bellingham, Richard, 44
Benezet, Anthony, 18, 67, 68, 71, 78, 84, 122, 123; abolitionist views of, 72–75, 114; as Quaker educator, 70–73, 76, 238n14
Bercovitch, Sacvan, 4, 10, 29, 228n14
Berg, David, 209
biography, 20–22, 76, 91, 128–58, 224; Emerson on, 166. *See also* Ashbridge, Elizabeth; autobiography; Battey, Thomas; Douglass, Frederick; Greer, Sarah; Hopper, Isaac T.; Penn, William; Whittier, John Greenleaf
Bird, Robert Montgomery, 23; *Nick of the Woods,* 23, 175, 176, 251n36
Bishop, George, 39, 60, 94
Bold Stroke for a Wife, A, 24, 189
Book of Martyrs (Foxe), 97, 242n10
Boorstin, Daniel J., 65

Boston, Massachusetts: arrival of Quaker missionaries, 42, 61; early Quaker activities, 34, 38; early theater, 189–90; literary scene, 152, 166, 178, 196; lyceum culture, 166; persecution of Quakers, 29, 36–46, 102, 105, 106, 199, 233n36; religious periodicals, 137
Boswell, James, 64. *See also* Johnson, Samuel
Bow, Clara, 211
Bradford, William, 19. *See also* New England; Puritans
Bradford, William (Quaker printer), 229n24
Bred in the Bone (film), 25, 206
Brend, W., 106
Brissot de Warville, Jacques-Pierre, 84–85
Bristol, England, 93
Bristow, Frank L., 205
British Friends Service Council, 215
Bronner, Edwin B., 51
Brooklyn, 157
Brooklyn Eagle, The (newspaper), 157, 188, 203
Brown, Charles Brockden, 189
Brownson, Orestes A., 69, 178
Bryant, William Cullen, 157
Bucks County, Pennsylvania, 161
Budd, Thomas, 48–49
Buell, Lawrence, 172
Bugg, Francis, 102, 244n22
Bulwark, The (Dreiser), 182, 185
Burke, Edmund, 167
Burns, Robert, 156
Burroughs, George, 164–65
Byron, George Gordon (lord), 157

Cadbury, Henry J., 82
Caddoes (Native American tribe), 147
Calvinism, 9, 109
Cambridgeshire, England, 109
Camden, New Jersey, 170
Canby, Henry Seidel, 169, 249n22
Cape Cod, Massachusetts, 46, 49

capital punishment, 120

Captain Black Beaver, 148–51

Carey, Matthew, 134

Carlson, David, 81–82

Carolinas (colonial). *See* Husband, Herman; North Carolina; Regulators

Cart and Whip Act, 27, 52, 101

Catholic and the Quaker, The (Child), 168

Catholics. *See* Roman Catholicism

Caution and Warning to Great Britain and Her Colonies, on the Calamitous State of the Enslaved Negroes, A (Benezet), 73

Centlivre, Susanna, 24

Channing, William Ellery, 168

Charles I (king), 97

Charles II (king), 12, 39–41, 47, 50, 101, 106, 201, 202; debt to William Penn, 50, 136, 212, 228n19, 223n33

Charleston, South Carolina, 81–82

Chauncy, Charles, 75

Cherokee (Native American tribe), 147

Child, Lydia Maria, 76, 167–68

Choctaw (Native American tribe), 147

Christianity, 3–18, 27, 29, 31–32, 47–61, 70, 107, 109, 111–26, 134–36, 139, 141, 145, 148–49, 160–61, 163, 167–68, 173, 178, 181, 184, 185, 188, 193, 213, 224. *See also* Protestantism; Roman Catholicism

Christian Remembrancer, The, 137

Christians. *See* Christianity

Christianson, Wenlock, 100–101

Christus (Longfellow), 199

Chu, Jonathan, 44

Church of England, 6, 10, 17, 27, 28, 29, 33, 35, 54, 61, 97, 102–5, 136, 144, 163; Clarkson's membership in, 109

civil law, 9, 31, 35, 36, 43, 46, 48, 49, 106; in New England, 49, 201

civil rights, 14, 231n12; for Native Americans, 74; for women, 3, 14, 15, 43, 66, 165, 180, 181; for workers, 171. *See also under* women

Civil War (American), 7, 71, 125, 129, 130, 131, 133, 137, 138, 145, 152, 154, 161,

173, 178–81; Quaker participation in, 227n8, 231n12, 251n48

Civil War (English), 230n2

Clarissa: or the History of a Young Lady (Richardson), 162

Clark, Mary, 105

Clarkson, Catherine, 243n34

Clarkson, Thomas, 19–21, 61, 94, 107–27, 243n38; church membership of, 109; documentation of slave trade, 110; education, 109–10; *Essay on the Slavery and Commerce of the Human Species,* 109; friendship with Wordsworth and Coleridge, 110; influence by Benezet and Woolman, 114; influence on Emerson, 249n17; *A Portraiture of Quakerism,* 108–27; support of French Revolution, 110

clergy, 28, 30, 57, 86, 87, 97, 98; Anglican, 98, 103, 132; Puritan, 44; recorded (Quaker), 6, 11, 12, 14; Roman Catholic, 143; unpaid, 11, 12, 29, 73. *See also* ministers

Clifton, Elmer, 210

Coleridge, Samuel Taylor, 110–11

Comanche (Native American tribe), 147, 150

Comfort, Lance, 212

Congregationalism, 9, 29, 30, 54, 57. *See also* Protestantism

Connecticut, 43; banishment of Quakers, 45

conscientious objection, 13, 74, 215

consumerism, 7, 62, 119; opposed by Quakers, 23

Cooper, Gary, 25, 220

Cooper, James Fenimore, 16, 35, 249n22; Leatherstocking Tales, 23, 168, 169, 217

Copeland, John, 41

Courageous Mr. Penn, The (film), 25, 212–14, 220

Courtship of Miles Standish, The (Longfellow), 198

Crabtree, Sarah, 64

Creeks (Native American tribe), 147

Crèvecoeur, J. Hector St. John de, 18, 58, 68, 115; influence by Woolman, 88; *Letters from an American Farmer,* 80–91, 239n28
Crew, Caroline, 60
Crockett, Davy, 4
Cromwell, Oliver, 29, 47, 104, 201; religious toleration of, 51, 103
Cudjoe's Cave (Trowbridge), 78
Curtis, George William, 133

Daily Crescent (New Orleans), 185
Dakota (Native American tribe), 147
Damrosch, Leo, 32, 41
Dancing Girl, The (film), 25, 206
Dancing Girl, The (play), 203
"Dancing Quakers, The" (Pratt), 188
Daniel Boone, 141
Davis, Rebecca Harding, 16, 169–77
Dedham, Massachusetts, 41
de Grunwald, Anatole, 212
Delaware (Native American tribe), 48, 150, 241n46
Delaware River Valley, 29, 49, 53, 76, 84, 86, 93, 115, 124, 173, 193, 199
Democracy in America (Tocqueville), 4
Dibdin, Charles, 189–90
Dickinson, Anna E., 21
Dickinson, Emily, 131, 152, 156
Don Juan; or, the Libertine Destroyed, 190
Douglass, Frederick, 250n26
Down to the Sea in Ships (film), 25, 210–12
drama, 23; closet drama, 198–202; popularity compared with cinema, 24, 188, 204; Quaker attitudes toward, 124; Quakers represented in, 24, 169, 188–96
Dreiser, Theodore, 16, 26, 196, 203, 204; *An American Tragedy,* 182; *The Bulwark,* 23, 182–85, 252n49; influence of Quakers on, 184, 252n49; *Jennie Gerhardt,* 182; *Sister Carrie,* 26, 182, 204
Drinker, Elizabeth, 65
Drinker, Henry, 65

Duxbury, Massachusetts, 45
Duyckinck, Evert, 134
Dyer, Mary, 35, 38, 55, 100, 105, 200, 224, 225; described by Quaker historians, 104; as literary subject, 161, 164–66; persecution and execution of, 38, 94, 100; travels in Barbados, 233n41. *See also* Quakers; women

Edinburgh Review, 52, 116
Ellwood, Thomas, 33
Emerson, Ralph Waldo, 96, 131, 157, 166, 178; affinity for Quaker beliefs, 167–68, 242n7; lecture on George Fox, 166–67; study of Quaker writers, 97, 166, 249n17
Endicott, John, 39, 113; fictional treatment by Longfellow, 198–202; prosecution of Mary Dyer, 39, 100
England, 104, 108; attitudes toward Quakers, 49–50, 112, 133, 136, 144, 189, 193; immigration to America, 155; Quaker origins in, 3, 6, 14, 17–19, 27–43, 101–4, 120–21, 204, 213, 225; religious debates, 9, 23, 24, 46, 54, 92–97, 100, 107, 115, 163; role in American Revolution, 79; war with France, 110. *See also* abolitionism; Church of England; print culture; Protestantism; Quakers
Enlightenment, 63
Episcopal Church, 146. *See also* Church of England
Essay on the Slavery and Commerce of the Human Species (Clarkson), 109, 114
Evangeline (Longfellow), 197–99
Evans, Clifford, 212
Evelyn, John, 34

Fair Quaker of Deal; or, the Humours of the Navy, The, 24, 190
Falmouth, Massachusetts, 46
familists, 9
Fell, Margaret. *See* Fox, Margaret Askew Fell

Fell, Thomas, 14, 32

fiction, 20, 224; best sellers, 23, 51, 152; compared to film, 188; local color, 59, 124, 152, 162, 182, 185; Quaker avoidance of, 117, 119, 140; Quakers described in, 21–25, 60, 130, 132, 142, 157–86; and Quaker worship, 12. *See also* print culture; theater

Fields, James T., 152, 196, 197

film: silent, 204–12

Fischer, David Hackett, 173

Fisher, Mary, 42, 44, 104, 105, 161. *See also* Quakers

Fisher, Sarah Logan, 65

Fitch, William Edwards, 79

Five Civilized Tribes (Native American), 147

Flake's Bulletin (Texas), 128

"Four-Legg'd Quaker, The" (anon.), 129

Fox, George, 11–14, 32, 33, 35, 40, 41, 49–53, 95, 96–99, 103, 120, 122, 125, 128, 130, 166, 167, 185, 213, 214, 224, 225, 227n13, 228n19, 230n6, 243n35; *Book of Miracles*, 29; on dreams, 99; literacy of, 32, 231n16; meditations in a hollow tree, 28; physically attacked, 213; on Quaker prosperity, 49; travels in America, 46

Fox, Margaret Askew Fell, 14, 32, 96; marriage to George Fox, 32, 236n69; political activities, 96; *Womens Speaking Justified*, 55, 228n19, 231n15

Foxe, John, 97, 242n10

France, 71, 84, 107; and Quaker community, 89, 90–91; war with England, 107, 110. *See also* French Revolution

Franklin, Benjamin, 70, 73, 80, 91, 135; life in France, 84; as Poor Richard, 136; Quaker family members, 239n20

French Revolution, 29, 58, 83, 87, 91, 110, 243n32

Fry, Elizabeth, 142

Fuller, Sarah Margaret, 166, 249n15, 249n16. *See also* transcendentalism

Gentle Boy, The (Hawthorne), 162, 172

George I (king), 107

George II (king), 82

George Fox's Book of Miracles (Cadbury), 29

Gilded Age, 62, 203–4

Giles Corey of the Salem Farms (Longfellow), 199

Girondins, 84

Germantown, Pennsylvania, 71

God's Revenge Against Murder (Weems), 134

Goering, Wynn M., 174

Goliath's Head Cut Off with His Own Sword (Bugg), 102

Gow, Peter, 83

Gracechurch Street Meeting (London), 50

Grant, James Edward, 215

Great Migration, 99

Great Mystery of the Little Whore Unfolded, The (Bugg), 102

Greer, Sarah, 22, 131, 133, 151, 152

Grimké, Angelina, 165

Grounds of Holy Life, The (Turford), 55

Grub Street, 58

Gunnison, Alman, 157

Gura, Philip F., 9, 10

Gurney, Joseph John, 7, 50, 142, 246n17

Gurneyites. *See* Gurney, Joseph John

Hales, Robert, 151, 153, 246n31

Halloran, John, 215

Hallowell, Mrs. J. L., 124

Hallowell, Richard P., 58, 59, 126

Hamm, Thomas D., 50

Hancock, John, 61

Hannah Thurston: A Story of American Life (Taylor), 177

Harper's New Monthly Magazine, 123, 133, 152, 156

Harrington, John F., 205

Harvard College, 95, 131, 172, 198

Hathorne, William, 159

hats: George Fox on, 49; Quaker refusal to doff, 11, 30, 80, 122, 213

Haverhill, Massachusetts, 155

Hawthorne, Nathaniel, 92, 131, 158–59, 162, 172, 200; description of Elizabeth Lloyd, 158–59
Haymarket Theatre (Boston), 190
Heart of New England Rent, The (Norton), 35, 200
Heyrmann, Christine, 57
Hicks, Elias, 7, 51, 235n61, 245n10, 248n7
Hicksites. *See* Hicks, Elias
Higginson, Thomas Wentworth, 154–56
High Noon (film), 25, 220–22, 225
Hinduism, 26
Histoire philosophique et politique des établissements et du commerce des Européens dans les deux Indes (Raynal), 88
History of England from the Accession of James II, The (Macaulay), 83
History of the Rise, Increase, and Progress, of the Christian People Called Quakers, The (Sewel), 19, 93–94
History of the United States of America (Bancroft), 124–25
Holder, Christopher, 41
Holland, 71, 104
Holmes, Oliver Wendell, 152
Hopper, Isaac T., 67, 68, 76–79
Hoskens, Jane, 53, 236n68
Huckleberry Finn, 141
Hugh Wynne: Free Quaker (Mitchell), 181
Husband, Herman, 67, 78, 79, 94
Hymen's Recruiting Sergeant (Weems), 134

"I Like Your Apron and Your Bonnet and Your Little Quaker Gown" (song), 205
"Immediate Emancipation" (Stowe), 165–66
Indians. *See* Native Americans
Industrial Revolution, 64, 170, 171
inner light, 3–4, 6, 8, 10–12, 26, 28–33, 73, 78, 88, 99, 106, 112–13, 126, 160, 163, 172, 175, 177, 186, 202, 214, 219, 225; described by Benezet, 123. *See also* Fox, George; Quakers
inward light. *See* inner light
Iowa, 146

Ipswich, Massachusetts, 34, 60
Isaac T. Hopper: A True Life (Child), 76
Islam, 26, 105–6
Ivanhoe (Scott), 139

Jamaica, 104, 232n29
James II (king), 40
James, Henry, 4
James, William, 204
Jefferson, Thomas, 63, 74
Jennie Gerhardt (Dreiser), 182
John Endicott (verse drama), 198
Johnson, Samuel, 21; attitude toward Quakers, 237n3; on preaching by Quaker women, 54
Jones, Rufus, 108
Journal of John Woolman, The (Woolman), 66–71, 130, 184, 238n10; edited by Whittier, 130; influence on Clarkson, 114; influence on Crèvecoeur, 88; influence on Dreiser, 252n49; influence on Murdock, 194
Judaism, 102, 163

Kalmar, Bert, 209
Karlesen, Carol F., 43
Keith, George, 55, 126
Kelly, Grace, 25, 220, 225
Kiowa (Native American tribe), 147–48
Knickerbocker (magazine), 161
Kundera, Milan, 11, 12

"Laboring Classes, The" (Brownson), 69
Lamb, Charles, 63, 97, 158
Lancashire, England, 32
Lancaster, Pennsylvania, 74
Later Periods of Quakerism, The (Jones), 108
Lawrence, Alfred F., 205
Lays of Quakerism, The (Plumley), 161
Leach, Robert J., 83
Leatherstocking Tales. *See* Cooper, James Fenimore
Leaves from Margaret Smith's Journal in the Province of Massachusetts Bay, 1678–9 (Whittier), 245n1

Leaves of Grass (Whitman), 152, 156
Ledyard, Charles, 131
Lee, Charles, 131
Lee, Eliza Buckminster, 172
Lee Avenue Theatre (New York City),
 203
Leslie, Edgar, 209
Lester, Elizabeth B., 162–64
Letters from an American Farmer
 (Crèvecoeur), 80–91
Lettres philosophiques (Voltaire), 87
Levy, Barry, 58, 87, 90, 114, 115
Liberal Imagination, The (Trilling), 185
Library of American Biography (Sparks), 131
Life and Adventures of a Quaker among the In-
 dians, The (Battey), 133–51
Life and Memorable Actions of George Wash-
 ington, The (Weems), 133
Life and Spiritual Sufferings of the Faithful
 Servant of Christ Jane Hoskens, The
 (Hoskens), 53
Life in the Iron Mills (Davis), 169–76
Life of Elizabeth Ashbridge, The (Ash-
 bridge), 15
Life of William Penn, The (Weems), 110,
 132–35
Littell's Living Age, 137, 142
Little Flocks Guarded Against Grievous Wolves
 (Mather), 126
"Little Shaking Quakers, The" (song),
 205
London, 80; Benezet early life in, 71; in-
 crease in Quaker population, 104;
 Quaker meeting, 50; Quaker per-
 secutions, 98; theater, 189; woman
 Quaker preaching, 104; World War
 II German attacks, 212
London Fire, 33
Longfellow, Henry Wadsworth, 152, 157,
 197–201, 253n8
Loughran, Trish, 16
Louis, Jeanne Henriette, 90
Lowell, James Russell, 152, 157–58
Luther, Martin, 167
Lyrical Ballads (Wordworth and Cole-
 ridge), 110

Macaulay, Thomas Babington, 83
Mack, Phyllis, 52, 63–64, 117
Magnalia Christi Americana (Mather), 20,
 95–96, 126, 234n47
Mahomet (prophet), 105
Mahomet (sultan), 105
Main-Street (Hawthorne), 92
Manifest Destiny, 131
Marietta, Jack, 114
Marquette, Père Jacques, 131
Marriott, Alice, 147
Marshfield, Massachusetts, 45
Martha's Vineyard, Massachusetts, 82,
 87–88
Marxism, 69, 185–86
Massachusetts, 5, 10, 18–19, 26, 30, 32,
 34, 38–39, 53, 57, 61, 68, 101, 126,
 159, 164, 172, 200–202, 210, 230n9;
 General Court, 27, 35, 36, 38, 40;
 laws regarding Quakers, 27, 36–44
Massachusetts Bay Colony. *See*
 Massachusetts
Mather, Cotton, 19, 44, 132; *Magnalia*
 Christi Americana, 20, 95–96, 126,
 234n47
Matthiessen, F. O., 131, 184, 252n52
McCarthyism, 222
Melville, Herman, 16, 131, 152, 174–76,
 198; *Moby-Dick*, 23, 138–40, 174,
 210; *White-Jacket*, 174
Memoirs of Robert Hales (Hales), 151
Memoirs of the Life of Fox (Tuke), 166
Memoirs of the Private and Public Life of
 William Penn (Clarkson), 110
Mennonites, 13, 231n12
Mercury (New Bedford newspaper), 97
Methodism, 18, 54, 97, 240n37. *See also*
 Wesley, John
Michelangelo, 167
Middle Passage, 110. *See also* African
 Americans; slavery
Mifflin, Warner, 84
Millar, John, 69
Miller, Joaquin, 157
Miller, Perry, 39, 58
Millersburg, Pennsylvania, 48

Milton, John, 157, 167

ministers, 7, 29, 49, 86, 141; Anglican, 103; authority of, 31, 33; preaching style, 14, 55; "Public Friends" as, 64; Puritan, 35, 75, 106, 202; Quaker missionaries, 7, 19, 35, 42–43, 57, 64, 93, 122, 133, 140, 146, 149, 233n41, 235n61, 240n39, 251n41; recorded (Quaker), 11, 55, 64, 66, 235n61, 238n11, 245n10; "transatlantic," 64; Unitarian, 96, 131, 168; women as, 6, 12, 14, 104, 229n22, 246n17, 249n15

missionaries. *See* ministers

Mitchell, Silas Weir, 181–82

Moby-Dick (Melville), 23, 138–40, 210; description of Quaker crew, 174–75

Moore, R. Laurence, 5, 6

Moravian Indians (Native American), 57

Mormonism, 132

Mott, Lucretia, 21; admired by Walt Whitman, 170; influence on Frederick Douglass, 250n26

Mount Vernon, New York, 135

Murdock, John, 189; literary influences on, 189; *The Triumphs of Love*, 189–96

music: popular song and Quakers, 197, 205–10; prohibitions against, 7, 13, 55, 117–19, 124; and Quaker women, 117–18; in Whittier's poetry, 156

mysticism. *See* Quakers

Nantucket Island, Massachusetts: cosmopolitanism of, 18, 68, 81–91, 174, 210, 239n20, 239n29, 240n39; in *Moby-Dick*, 174–75

Naomi (Lee), 172

Nation, The, 172

Native Americans, 7, 21, 36, 64, 66, 145, 176; relationships with Quakers, 46–47, 66, 67, 81, 87, 126, 133, 146–51, 165, 240n29, 241n46; and U.S. government policy, 145–51

Nature (Emerson), 96, 166

Nayler, James, 33, 40, 236n73; persecution and punishment of, 231n17

Neal, John, 164–65, 249n12

New Bedford, Massachusetts, 97, 128, 175, 210

Newbury, Massachusetts, 57

New England, 6–12, 17, 84, 125; histories of, 19, 95–97, 101, 126, 156–57, 164, 172, 199; New England Yearly Meeting, 229n28; Quakers in, 6–12, 23, 27–62, 84, 94, 101–2, 106, 125–26, 130, 161, 164, 212, 233n36, 233n41, 234n47, 235n50; and transcendentalism, 166

New England Judged (Bishop), 60, 94

New England Tragedies, The (Longfellow), 199

New Jersey, 53, 76, 85, 170, 172, 183; Quaker settlements, 169

New Testament, 8

New Travels in the United States of America, Performed in 1788 (Brissot de Warville), 84

New York, 53; in Cooper's fiction, 169; publishing circles, 134, 138, 178; and Quaker missionaries, 146; theater culture, 203, 207, 254n17

Nick of the Woods (Bird), 23, 175–76, 251n36

North Carolina, 46, 54, 79–80; Orange County, 79; Quaker meetings, 78, 125; Regulators movement, 79

Norton, Humphrey, 45

Norton, John, 35, 39, 44, 106, 200, 202; *The Heart of New England Rent*, 35, 37, 200; opposition to antinomians, 37, 236n72; on punishment of Quakers, 106

Nottinghamshire, England, 33

oaths, 13; Quaker refusal to swear, 28–29, 42, 48, 104, 231n15, 232n28, 235n55. *See also* Quakers

O'Keefe, John, 190

Oklahoma, 146–50

"Old Time Life in a Quaker Town" (Pyle), 124

"On Reading Mr. Clarkson's *History of the*

Abolition of the Slave Trade" (Wilson), 111. *See also* Clarkson, Thomas
Owen, John, 121
Oxford University, 121

pacifism, 6, 25–26, 47, 60, 73, 88, 175–76, 178, 185, 197, 214, 216–17, 219, 221–22, 227n8; and military service, 48, 214–15; and Quaker political activity, 65; of William Penn, 132. *See also* American Friends Service Committee; Peace Testimony; Quakers
Paine, Thomas, 67
Parker, Theodore, 178
Parrington, Vernon Louis, 8, 31
Paxton Boys, 47, 57
Payton, Etta Reed, 203
Peabody, Elizabeth, 72
Peace Testimony (Quaker), 6, 12, 26, 62, 86, 107, 127, 147, 176, 226, 228n19, 231n12, 235n56. *See also* American Friends Service Committee; pacifism
Penn, Margaret Jasper, 135
Penn, William, 33, 50, 91, 132, 169, 199; biographies of, 91, 110, 130, 135–37, 245n10; compared to Churchill, 214; film depictions of, 212–15, 220, 253n27. *See also* Pennsylvania
Pennsylvania, 15, 17, 33, 48, 53, 65, 67, 71, 76, 82, 93, 115, 212; colonial laws, 120, 191; influence of William Penn, 134–37, 21–13; legislature, 48, 90, 191; Native American tribes, 57, 74; and Quaker missionaries, 66; Quaker settlements, 46, 49–50, 69, 84, 86, 132, 134, 161, 169, 177; Whiskey Rebellion, 78–80. *See also* Penn, William; Philadelphia, Pennsylvania
Penrith, England, 110
Pestana, Carla Gardina, 30, 34
Peters, Kate, 51
Philadelphia, Pennsylvania: founding of AFSC in, 215, 231n12; Free Quakers, 251n46; health of Quakers in, 247n3;

opposition to Quakers in, 46, 48; penitentiary, 120, 148, 244n54; prohibitions against drama, 24, 191; Quaker population, 50 53, 65; Quaker schools, 71–72, 76, 146; as Quaker stronghold, 78, 83–84, 95, 135, 137, 140, 192–93, 198
Philadelphia Yearly Meeting, 8, 50, 181, 229n28
Philanthropos, 47
Philbrick, Nathaniel, 88–89
Philips, James, 109
Phillips, Edith, 84, 87
Philopatrius, 46, 47; *The Quaker Unmask'd,* 47
Pioneers, The (Cooper), 168–69
Pittsburgh, Pennsylvania, 80
Plains Indians (Native American), 22, 66, 130–34, 145–51
plain style: clothing, 7, 13, 31, 61, 116, 120–28, 137, 143, 145, 188–89, 202–4, 206, 210, 216, 224, 226, 229n21, 247n4, 250n26; domestic design and architecture, 13, 26–29, 121; language, 23, 61, 78, 121–28, 155, 178, 185, 187, 228n20. *See also* Quakers
Plea for the Poor, A (Woolman), 69–71
Plumley, Benjamin Rush, 161–62
Plumley, Ruth. *See* Plumley, Benjamin Rush
Plymouth, Massachusetts, 45, 46
poetry, 110, 131, 152, 196, 224; by Whittier, 154–56
Portraiture of Quakerism, A (Clarkson), 19, 94, 109–23
Pratt, Charles E., 188
Presbyterians, 78, 240n37
Priestly, Joseph, 168
print culture, 3; and attacks on Quakers, 129; commercial aspects, 17, 20–21, 24, 51, 168; dangers of, 119; emergence in America, 24, 123, 130, 134; nationalist themes, 131, 229n29; religious aspects, 32, 44, 51, 54, 103, 132–34, 142, 229n24; Revolutionary

print culture (*continued*)
era, 67, 83; study of, 16; transatlantic, 93

prisons, 120, 148

Protestantism, 11, 27–29, 30, 57, 86, 97, 136, 143, 168; compared to Roman Catholicism, 86, 143; Episcopal Church, 147; mainstream churches, 86, 95, 165; martyrology, 242n10; and Quaker individualism, 168; radical dissenting groups, 5, 9, 27, 32, 42, 52, 54, 61, 106, 168; Reformation, 97, 143. *See also* Puritans

Pulaski, Kazimierz, 131

Puritan and the Quaker: A Story of Colonial Times, The (Beach), 172

Puritanism. *See* Puritans

Puritans: and American identity, 4–9, 23, 58, 95, 172, 228n14; in American fiction, 162, 164, 200, 245n1, 248n10; in American poetry, 200; in colonial New England, 5, 8–9, 17, 19, 20, 26, 34–38, 44, 54, 58, 94–97, 104, 106, 124, 132, 164, 177, 200–201, 230n1; compared with Quakers, 8–10, 23, 28–30, 34–35, 38, 59, 65, 93, 102, 124, 126, 154, 172, 230n9, 240n39; English, 5, 8–9, 33–34, 61, 96, 97, 102, 104, 172; as midwives, 42; persecution of Quakers, 23, 32, 36, 37, 42, 44, 58, 59, 60, 97, 100, 102, 105–7, 125, 164, 165, 173, 234n47. *See also* Protestantism

Pyle, Howard, 124

Quack Quakers, The (film), 25, 206–10

Quaker: A Comic Opera, The (Dibdin), 189

Quakeress, The (film), 25, 206

"Quaker Girls, The" (Fields), 196–97

Quaker Invasion of Massachusetts, The (R. Hallowell), 126

Quakerism; or, the Story of My Life (Greer), 128, 137–45

Quaker Mother, A (film), 206

"Quaker of the Olden Time, The" (anon.), 92

"Quaker Poet, The" (Spofford), 152

Quakers: assaults on, 98; avoidance of music and dance, 7, 113, 117–24, 197; Conservative, 7–8; decrease in numbers, 173; described as "housecreepers," 98; discipline, 61, 112–19; evangelical, 7; family life, 85, 115–17; "fighting Quakers," 175–81; financial success of, 64, 87, 125; Hicksite, 51, 235n61, 245n10, 248n7; Irish, 61; legal views, 120; marriage practices, 58, 192; mysticism, 9, 32, 63, 67, 106, 107, 173, 201, 202–14, 220, 243n33, 243n34; opium use by, 88; opposition to slavery, 21–23, 26, 54, 64–78, 90, 129, 194, 225, 229n28, 238n10, 238n11, 239n29, 244n57; oratory, 100, 188; pacifism, 113; persecution and punishment of, 64, 98, 101, 103, 105–6, 121; programmed, 7; quietism of, 21, 57, 59, 61, 114–15, 124–25; refusal to swear oaths, 28–29, 42, 48, 100, 104, 231n15, 232n28, 235n55; religious enthusiasm, 75; role of dreams for, 33, 99, 238n10; silent meetings, 7, 11, 52–55, 73, 85, 155; "singing," 53; Swedish American tolerance of, 102; unprogrammed, 7; withdrawal from electoral politics, 65. *See also* plain style

Quakers: A Novel, in a Series of Letters (anon.), 163

Quakers: A Tale, The (Lester), 162–65

Quaker's Art of Courtship, The, 58

Quaker's Dream, The, 58

Quaker's Wanton Wife, The, 58

Quaker's Wedding, The (Wilkinson), 24, 189

Quaker Unmask'd, The (Philopatrius), 46, 47

Quaker Wedding, The, 58

"Quaker Woman, A" (Mrs. J. L. Hallowell), 124

quietism. *See* Quakers

Rachel Dyer: A North American Tale (Neal), 164–65

Ranters, 9, 45, 65, 227n13
Raynal, Abbé Guillaume Thomas
    François, 73, 88
Regulators (North Carolina), 78–80
Religious Society of Friends. *See* Quakers
Representative Men (Emerson), 131, 167
Revenge Against Adultery (Weems), 134
Revolutionary War (American), 5, 7, 18,
    19, 24, 29, 58, 66–72, 78–79, 84,
    132, 134, 154, 173, 189, 192; Quaker
    involvement in, 65, 78–80, 115, 178–
    82, 238n7, 239n21, 251n46
Rhode Island, 35, 49, 53, 146; Quakers
    banished to, 38, 39; toleration of
    Quakers in, 45–46, 235n51
Ribault, Jean, 131
Rich, Irene, 218
Richardson, Samuel, 139, 162
Richter, Daniel, 64
Robinson, William, 38; execution of, 38
Roman Catholicism, 26, 28, 54, 86, 87,
    107, 132, 136, 142–43, 163, 197–
    99; in American literature, 168, 199;
    compared to Quakerism, 17, 37, 100,
    145, 168, 240n37, 242n16; of Dreiser,
    184; persecution of Quakers, 71
Rourke, Constance, 4
Rouse, John, 41
Rousseau, Jean-Jacques, 83, 84
Russell, Elbert, 51
Russell, Gail, 215

Salem, Massachusetts, 93, 159, 164, 199
Sandwich, Massachusetts, 45, 46
Scarlet Letter, The (Hawthorne), 158, 162,
    172
Scituate, Massachusetts, 45
Scotland, 104
Scott, Walter, 139
Second Part of the Naked Truth, The (Hus-
    band), 78
Secret Sinners, The, 58
Seekers, 9, 10
Seminole (Native American tribe), 147
Sewall, Samuel, 93–94
Sewel, William, 19, 20, 38, 40, 61, 111,

    122–23, 127; criticism of Puritans,
    97–102; historical method of, 19; *The
    History of the Rise, Increase, and Progress,
    of the Christian People Called Quakers*,
    19–21, 93–108, 166, 231n17, 233n33,
    242n16, 243n31
sexuality: and antebellum print culture,
    134; incest, 58; pornography, 58;
    Quakers accused of promiscuity,
    46, 57–59, 74, 89, 190, 208; Quaker
    moral views of, 15, 25, 183–84, 197,
    208, 216, 226; of Quaker women
    ministers, 166. *See also* women
Shadwell, Charles, 24, 189
Shakers, 180
Shakespeare, William, 157
Shawnee (Native American tribe), 48
*Short Account of the Religious Society of Friends,
    A* (Benezet), 73, 122–23
Sievers, Julie, 29, 52
Sir Charles Grandison (Richardson), 139
Sister Carrie (Dreiser), 25, 182, 196, 203–4
slavery: American abolitionist movement,
    21, 25; Christian responses to, 5; de-
    picted in early American theater,
    193–96; as described in *Letters to an
    American Farmer*, 81–84; as described
    in *Uncle Tom's Cabin*, 140, 159–62; En-
    glish abolitionist movement, 19, 20,
    108–27; Quaker opposition to, 21,
    22, 23, 26, 54, 64–78, 129, 194, 225,
    229n28, 238n10, 238n11, 239n29,
    244n57; wage-slavery, 170. *See also*
    abolitionism; African Americans
Slotkin, Richard, 82, 84, 222
Smith, Adam, 69
Smith, Hannah Whitall, 170
Smith, Joseph, 132
Smyrna, 105
Society for the Diffusion of Useful
    Knowledge, 166
Solman, Alfred, 209
Some Considerations on the Keeping of Negroes
    (Woolman), 69, 194
Some Historical Account of Guinea (Benezet),
    114

Some Observations on the Situation, Disposition and Character of the Indian Natives of This Continent (Benezet), 74
Some Remarks on Religion (Husband), 78
Sparks, Jared, 131
Spofford, Harriet Precott, 131–34
Stephenson, Marmaduke, 38, 100
Story of Kennett, The (Taylor), 177
Stowe, Harriet Beecher, 16, 23, 77–78, 131, 162, 166, 174–82, 224, 247n2; contact with Quakers, 165, 248n5, 249n16; *Uncle Tom's Cabin,* 152–72, 196
Summary History of New-England, A (Adams), 45
Summary View of the Slave Trade and of the Probable Consequences of Its Abolition, A (Clarkson), 109
sumptuary laws, 42. *See also* plain style
Susquehannock (Native American tribe), 48
Swarthmore Hall, 32, 236n69

Tales of a Wayside Inn (Longfellow), 198
Taylor, Bayard, 177–78
Taylor, John, 35, 233n41
teachers, 66; Quakers as, 133, 145–51
temperance, 122, 207, 243. *See also* alcohol consumption
Temple School, 72
Templin, Lawrence, 8
theater, 12, 24, 182, 187–222; Quaker manners as, 25; Quaker piety as, 11, 34, 44; Quaker prohibitions against, 118–19
"There's a Quaker Down in Quaker Town" (song), 209
Thomas, Keith, 28
Thoreau, Henry David, 70, 131
Ticknor and Fields, 152
Tiro, Karim M., 146
Tocqueville, Alexis de, 4
Toleration Act (1689), 42
transcendentalism, 97, 166–68. *See also* Emerson, Ralph Waldo
Traubel, Horace, 170

Trilling, Lionel, 184–85
Triumphs of Love, The (Murdock), 189–96
Trowbridge, John Townsend, 178
Tryon, William, 78–80
Tuke, Henry, 166
Turford, Hugh, 55
Turner, Frederick Jackson, 217–18
Tweed, Thomas, 10
Twice-Told Tales (Hawthorne), 200

Uncle Tom's Cabin (Stowe), 152–72, 196
Underground Railroad, 14, 66, 76, 140, 154, 159, 197, 224, 248n5. *See also* *Uncle Tom's Cabin*
Unitarianism, 96, 131, 166–68

Varieties of Religious Experience, The (W. James), 204
Vaux, Roberts, 71, 73–74
Virginia, 46; legal status of Quakers in, 45; Quaker settlers, 84; Quakers exiled to, 65
Vitagraph Company of America, 25, 206
Voltaire, 58; praise for Quakers, 87, 90, 240n38

Wales, 104
Walnut Street Jail, 148
Wardwell, Eliakim, 60
Wardwell, Lydia, 60
War of Spanish Succession, 107
Washington, George, 74, 132–35, 146, 245n6
Wayne, John, 25, 215–20
Weems, Mason Locke, 130–37, 245n6
Wendlindg, Pete, 209
Wermuth, Paul, 177
Wesley, John, 97. *See also* Methodism
West Indies, 42, 126, 233n41. *See also* Barbados
Westmorland, England, 51
Whaling Film Corporation, 210
White-Jacket (Melville), 174
Whitfield, George, 78

Whiting, John, 93
Whitman, Walt, 16, 152, 156, 178, 198; attitudes toward Quakers, 154, 170, 185; compared to Whittier, 152; *Leaves of Grass*, 152, 156; opinion of Whittier, 154; Quaker family members, 235n61
Whittier, John Greenleaf, 34, 71, 133–34, 158, 167; edits Woolman's *Journal*, 130; *Leaves from Margaret Smith's Journal in the Province of Massachusetts Bay, 1678–9*, 245n1; as novelist, 245n1; on persecution of Quakers, 41; physical description, 154; as representative Quaker poet, 151–57
Wholesome Film Service, 210
Wichita Indian Agency, 146–47
Wilberforce, William, 19, 109–10, 244n38
Wilbur, John, 7, 8
Wilburites. *See* Wilbur, John
Wilkinson, Richard, 24; *The Quaker's Wedding: A Comedy*, 24, 189
Wilkinson, Thomas, 110
William III (king), 40
Willis, Nathaniel Parker, 134
Wilson, John, 111
Winthrop, John, 9, 132, 200
Wisbech, England, 109
witchcraft, 93, 199, 233n42; Quaker attitudes toward, 232n23, 234n44; Quakers accused of, 33, 42–44, 102, 104, 164–65, 234n47. *See also* women
Wolcott, William, 211
Woolman, John, 18, 62, 67–78, 84, 87, 130, 194; abolitionist views, 66, 194, 229n28, 238n11; influence on

Theodore Dreiser, 185, 252n49; *Journal*, 66, 88, 114, 130, 184, 238n10. *See also The Journal of John Woolman*
Woman in the Nineteenth Century (Fuller), 166
woman suffrage, 6, 157
women: as abolitionists, 22, 23, 69; domesticity and education of, 59, 85–89, 117–21, 160, 180; gender identity of, 25, 57; punished for Quaker beliefs, 44, 58, 60, 159; in Quaker communities, 23, 57, 59. Quaker ministry of, 6, 15, 31, 34, 43–44, 52, 54–57, 60, 64, 99, 101–5, 143, 155, 164, 170, 200, 225, 236n72; as Quaker missionaries, 83; and religious authority, 59, 200, 210–11; rights of, 3, 12, 14, 15, 25, 43, 55, 66, 102–5, 117, 155, 161, 165–66, 180, 181. *See also* civil rights
Womens Speaking Justified (M. Fox), 55
Woodbury, New Jersey, 76
Word of Remembrance and Caution to the Rich, A (Woolman), 69
Wordsworth, William, 110–11
Work (Louisa M. Alcott), 180–81
World War I, 182
World War II, 123, 212–20

Yorkshire, England, 51
Young America movement, 131. *See also* print culture
Young Quaker: A Comedy, The (O'Keefe), 190
Young Quaker; or, the Fair American, The (O'Keefe), 190

Ziff, Larzer, 50